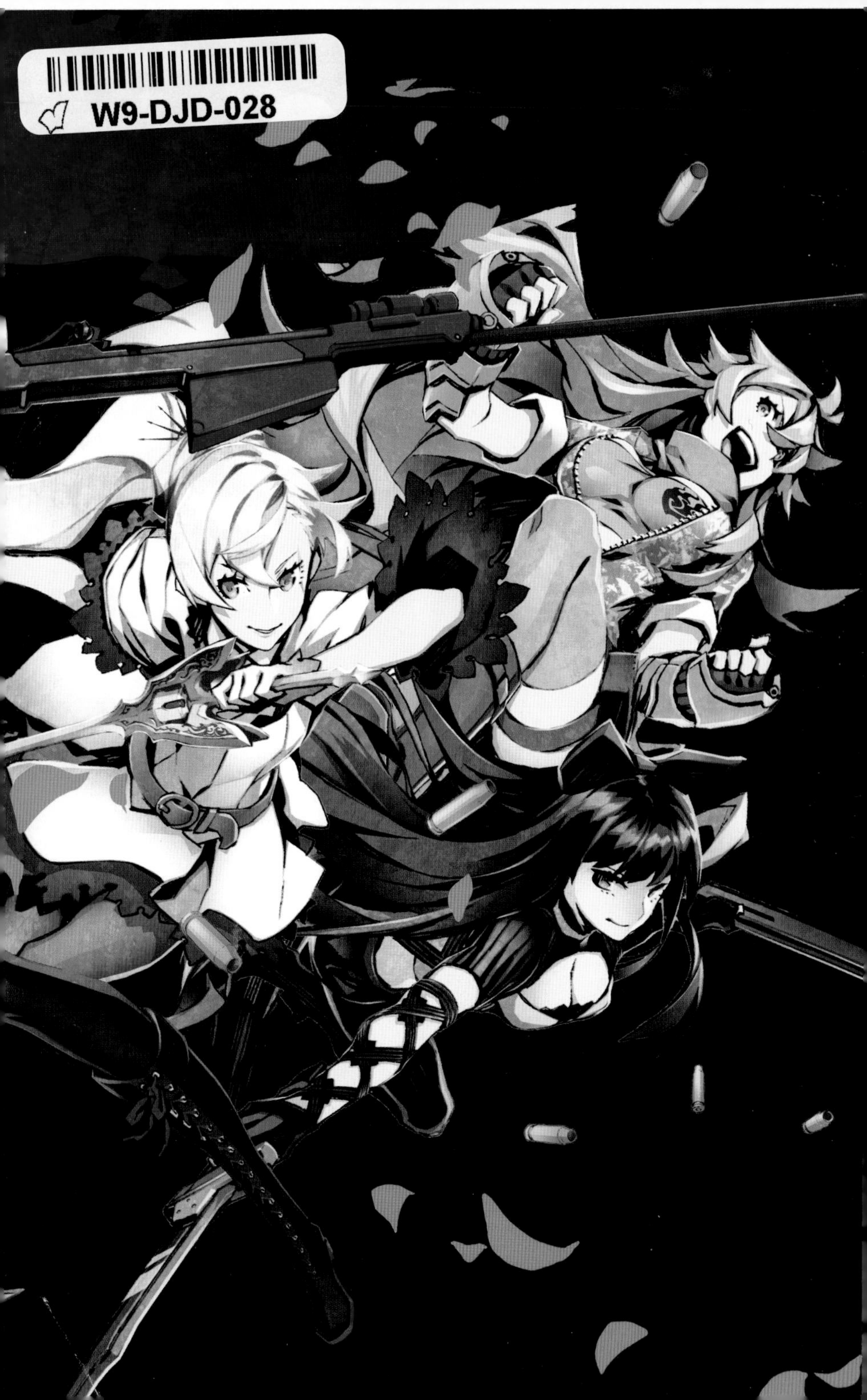

Team RWBY

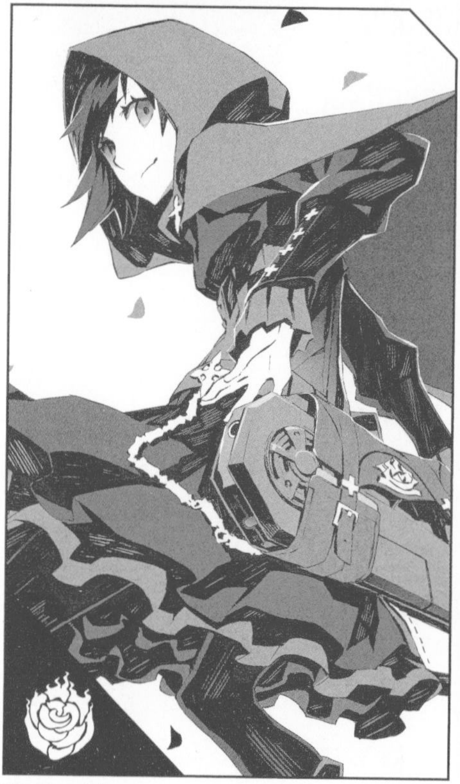

Ruby Rose

A 15-year-old girl whose natural combat skills allowed her to skip a grade and enroll at Beacon Academy.

◉**Weapon:** High-caliber sniper scythe [Crescent Rose]

◉**Semblance:** Speed

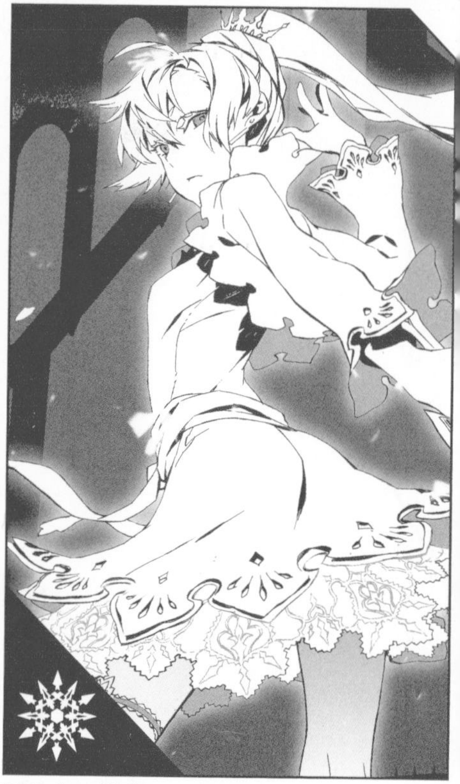

Weiss Schnee

The prideful daughter of the president of the multi-national corporation Schnee Dust Company.

◉**Weapon:** Multi-action dust rapier [Myrtenaster]

◉**Semblance:** Glyphs

Team JNPR

A group of trainees composed of Pyrrha Nikos, Nora Valkyrie and Lie Ren, and led by Jaune Arc.

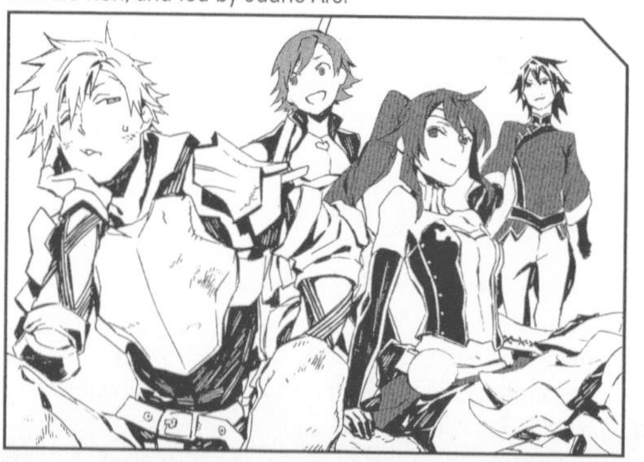

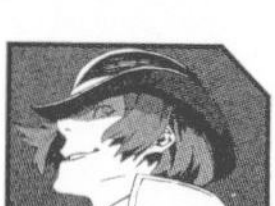

Roman Torchwick

A small-time outlaw operating within Veil, where Beacon Academy is located.

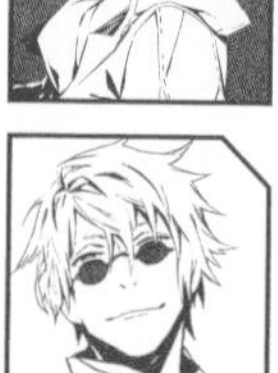

Professor Ozpin

Beacon Academy Headmaster.

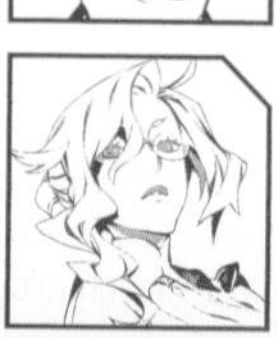

Glynda Goodwitch

Beacon Academy professor.

CHARACTERS

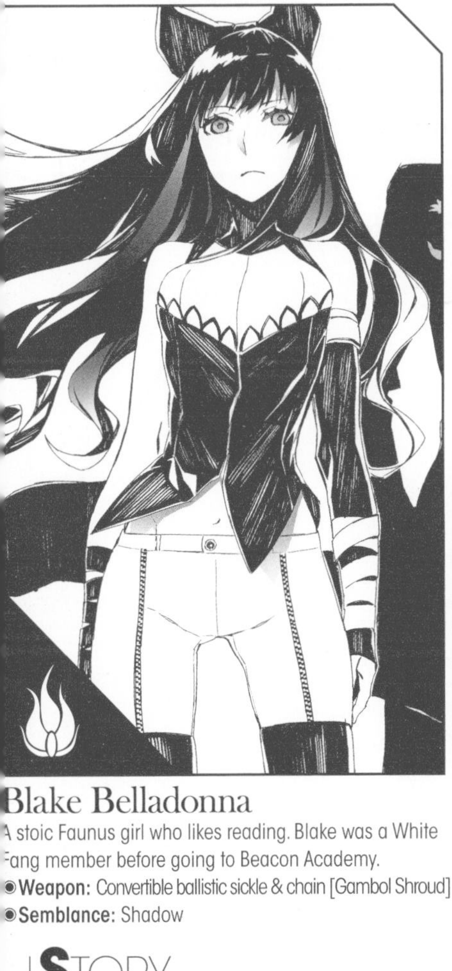

Blake Belladonna

A stoic Faunus girl who likes reading. Blake was a White Fang member before going to Beacon Academy.

◉**Weapon:** Convertible ballistic sickle & chain [Gambol Shroud]

◉**Semblance:** Shadow

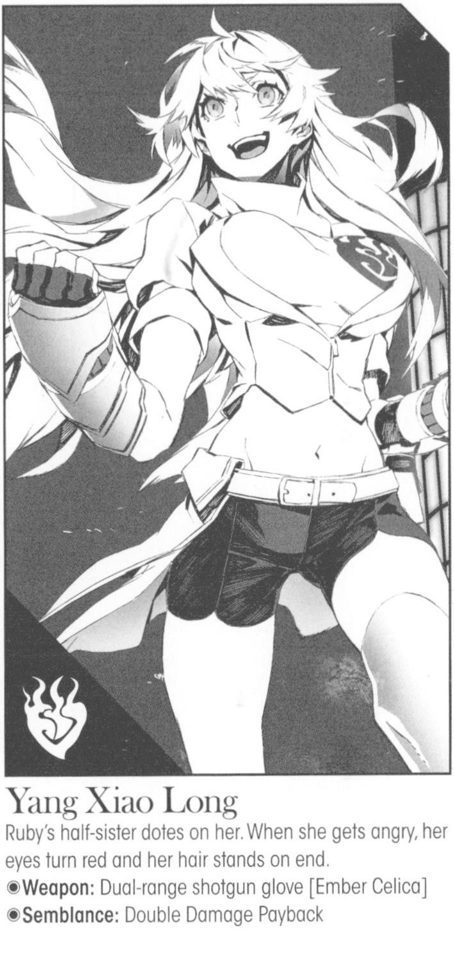

Yang Xiao Long

Ruby's half-sister dotes on her. When she gets angry, her eyes turn red and her hair stands on end.

◉**Weapon:** Dual-range shotgun glove [Ember Celica]

◉**Semblance:** Double Damage Payback

STORY

Welcome to Remnant, a world where science and magic coexist. Since ancient times, humanity has been threatened by soulless monsters called Grimm. Hunters have been tasked to subdue them and maintain peace. Aspiring to become Huntresses, four girls are enrolled at Beacon Academy, a training school for Hunters. Their growing talents are the last shred of hope for the survival of humanity.

GLOSSARY

Aura: Huntsmen and Huntresses display extraordinary combat abilities by controlling their Auras, a power that all life-forms possess. Each individual has their own unique Aura called a Semblance, which, with training, can be used in infinite ways.

Dust: Crystallized concentration of the power of nature. Dust generates various energies when it reacts to Aura. In Remnant, almost all technologies run on the power of Dust.

Faunus: A therianthrope race in Remnant that was once despised by humans, but now the two societies coexist.

White Fang: An extremist Faunus organization working to end the ongoing discrimination against them from humans and other races. White Fang began as a peaceful organization, but has lately been resorting to violence.

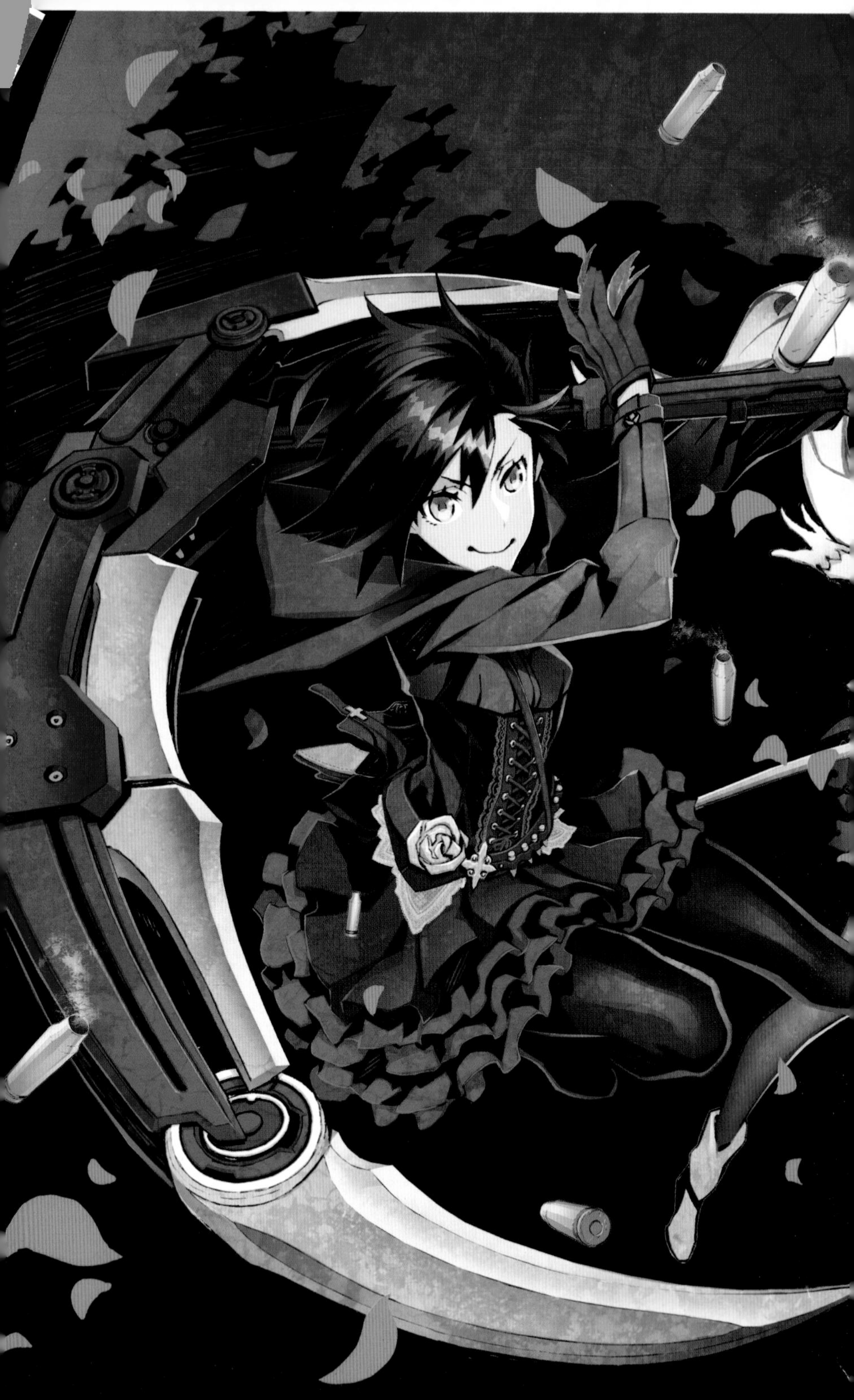

RWBY

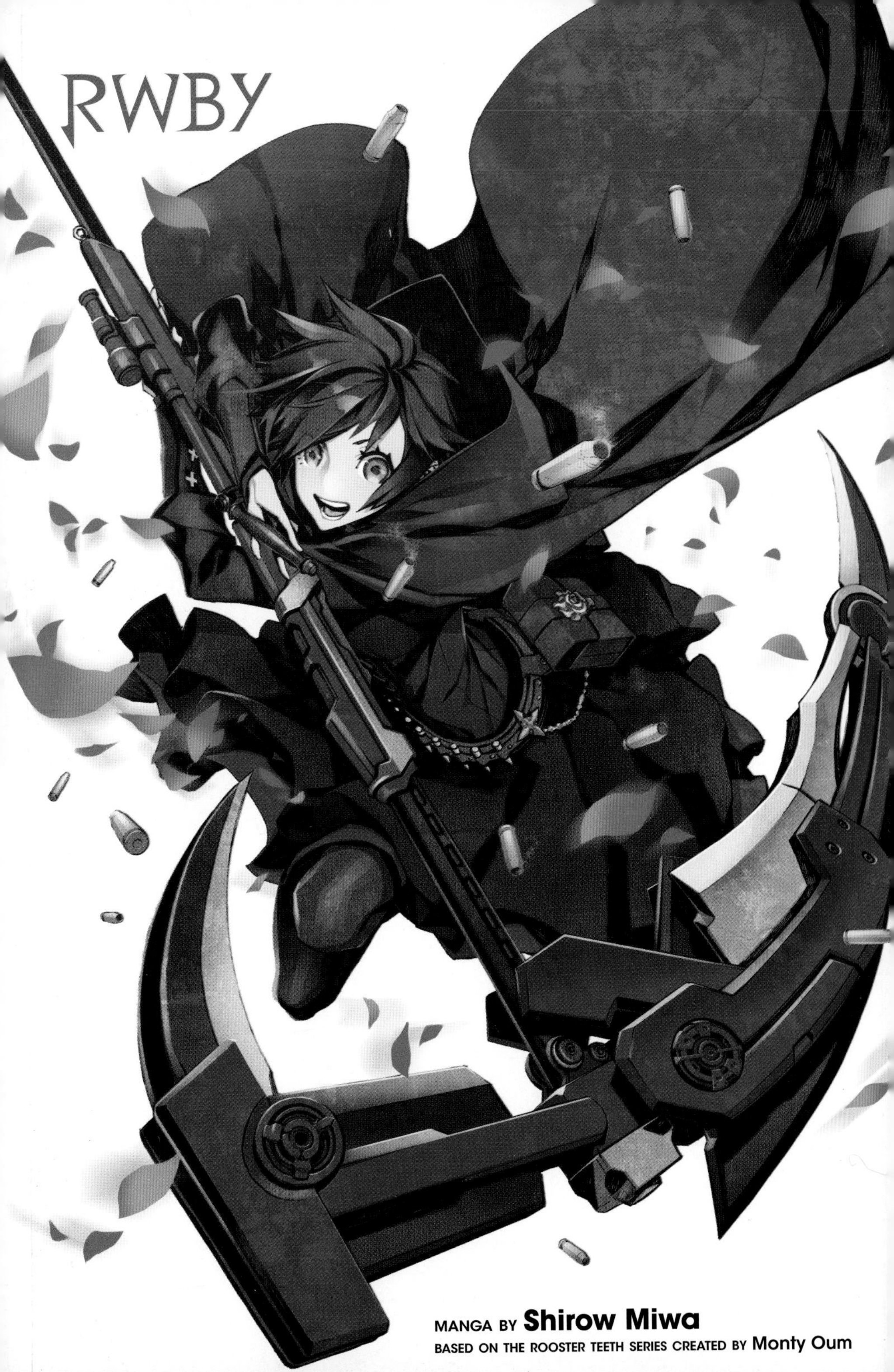

MANGA BY **Shirow Miwa**

BASED ON THE ROOSTER TEETH SERIES CREATED BY **Monty Oum**

RWBY

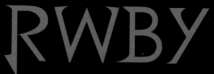

CONTENTS

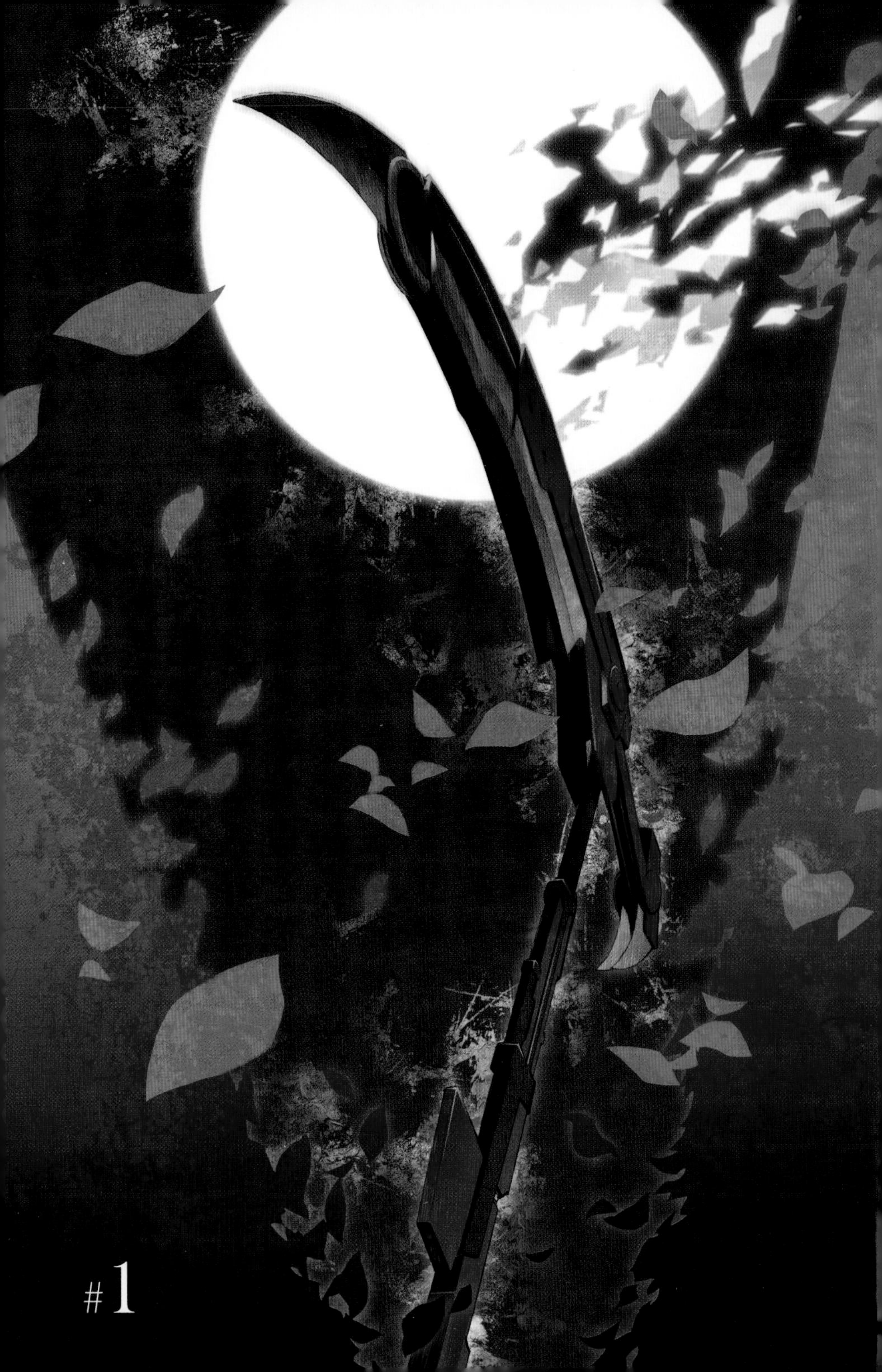
#1

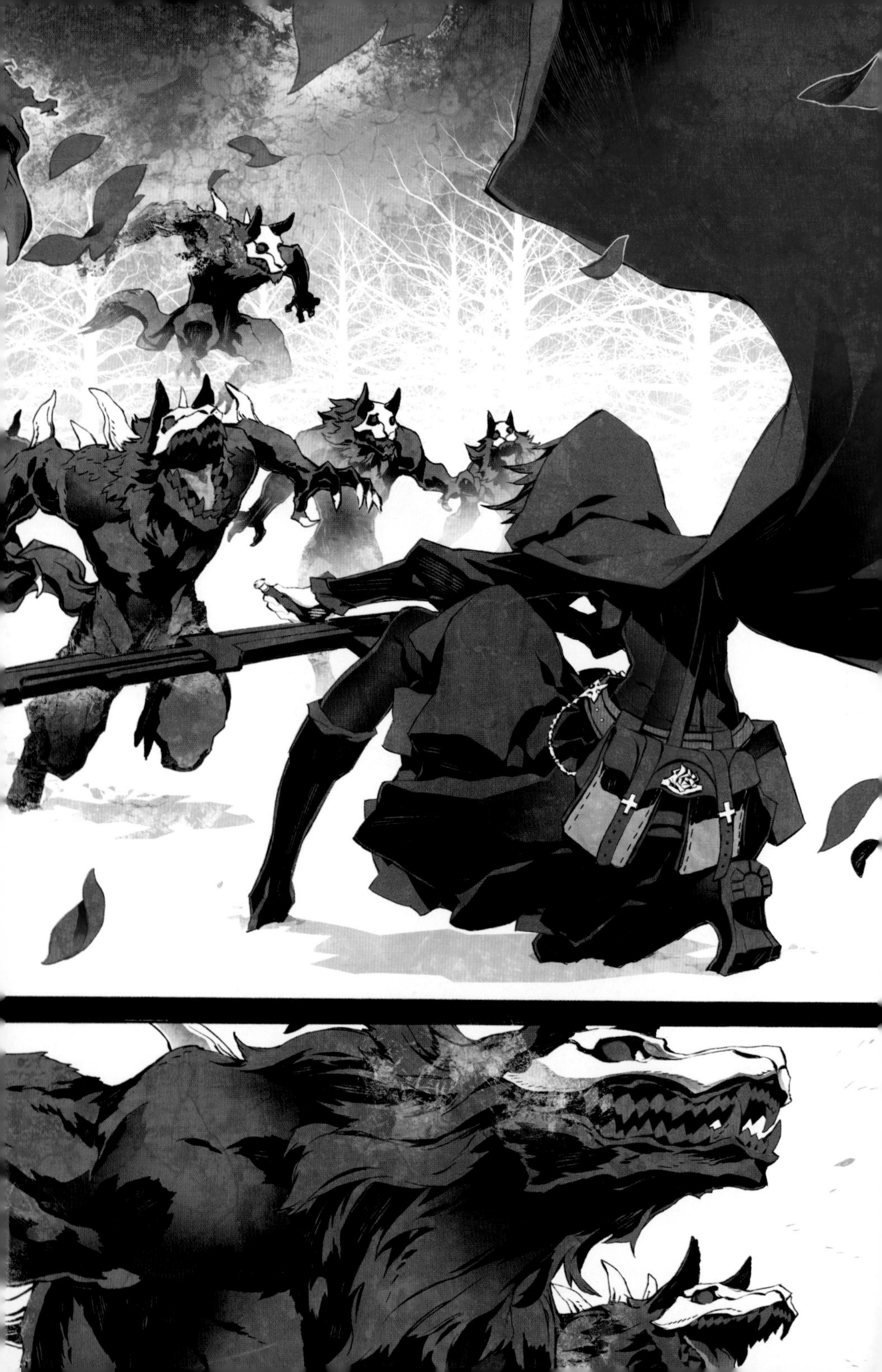

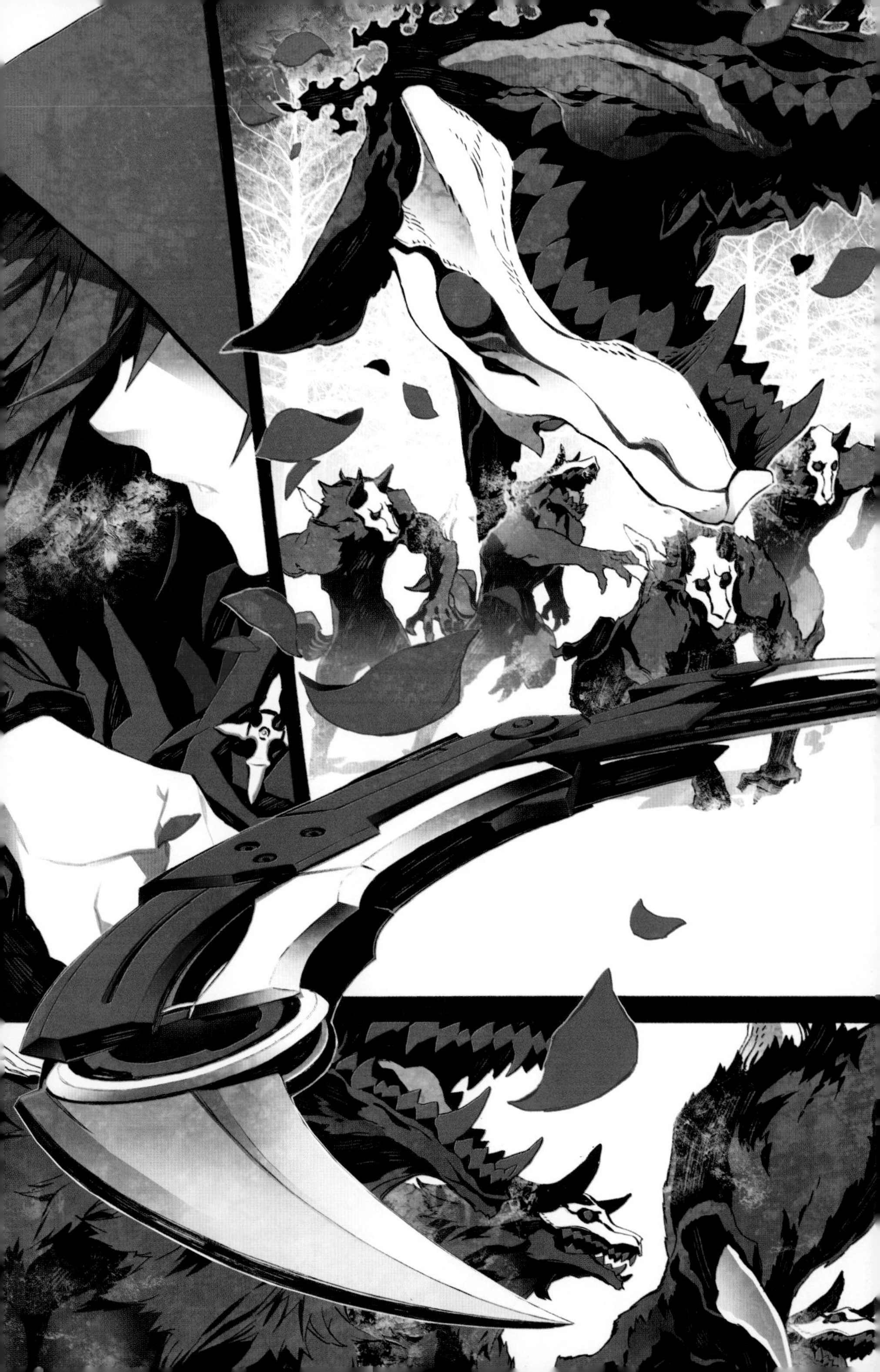

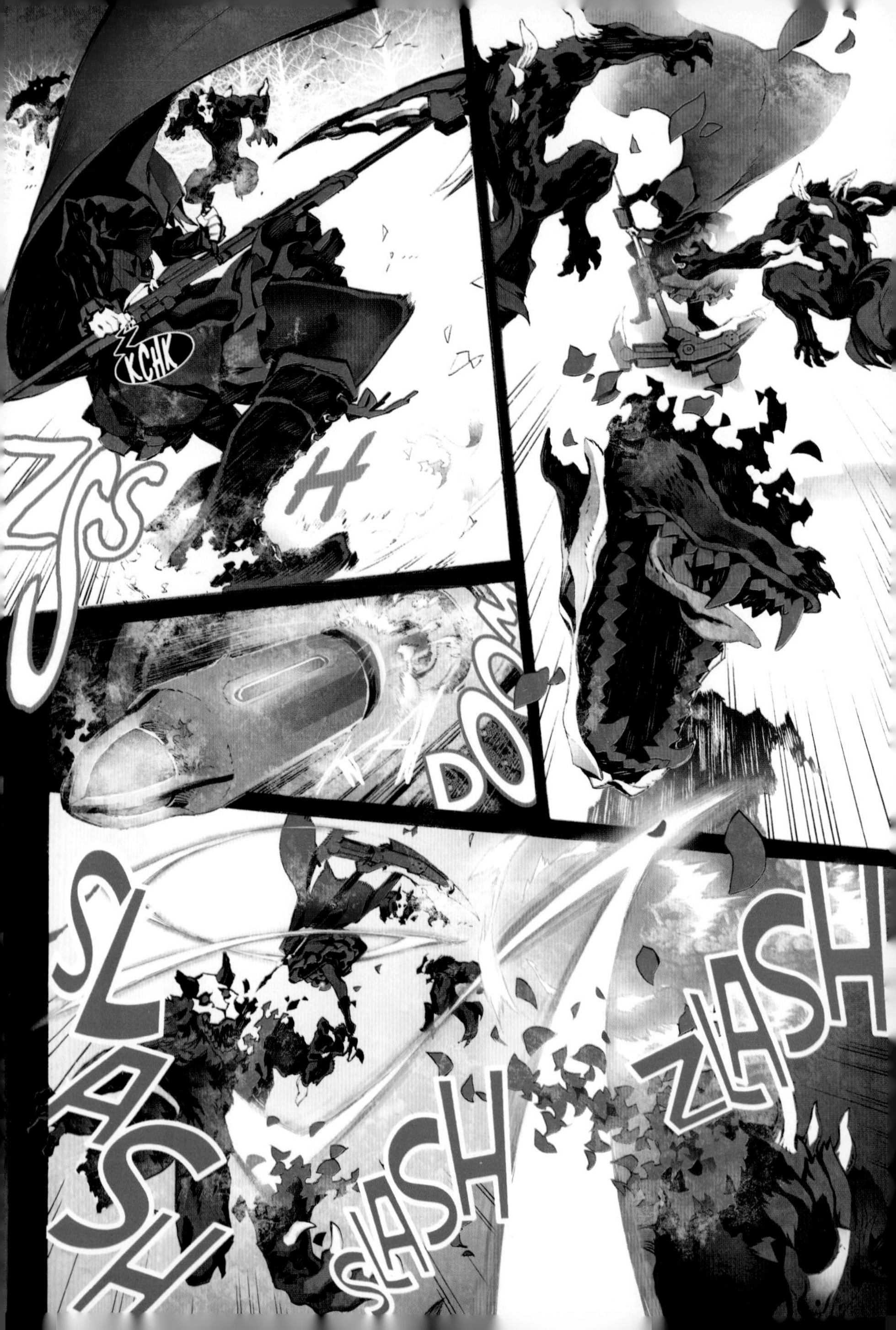
KCHK
ZSH
DOOM
ZLASH
SLASH
SLASH

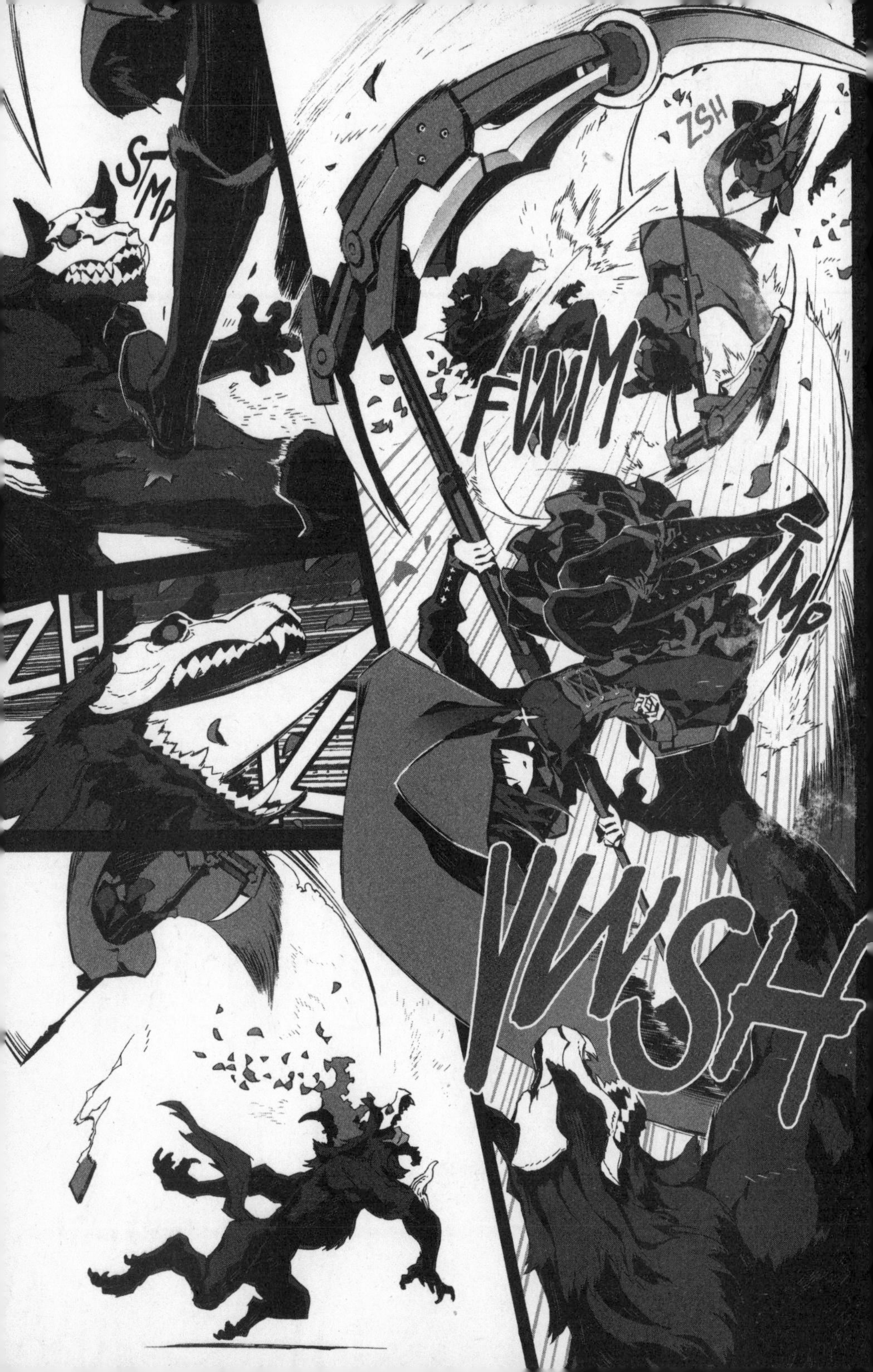
ZSH
FWIM
STMP
TMP
ZH
VWSH

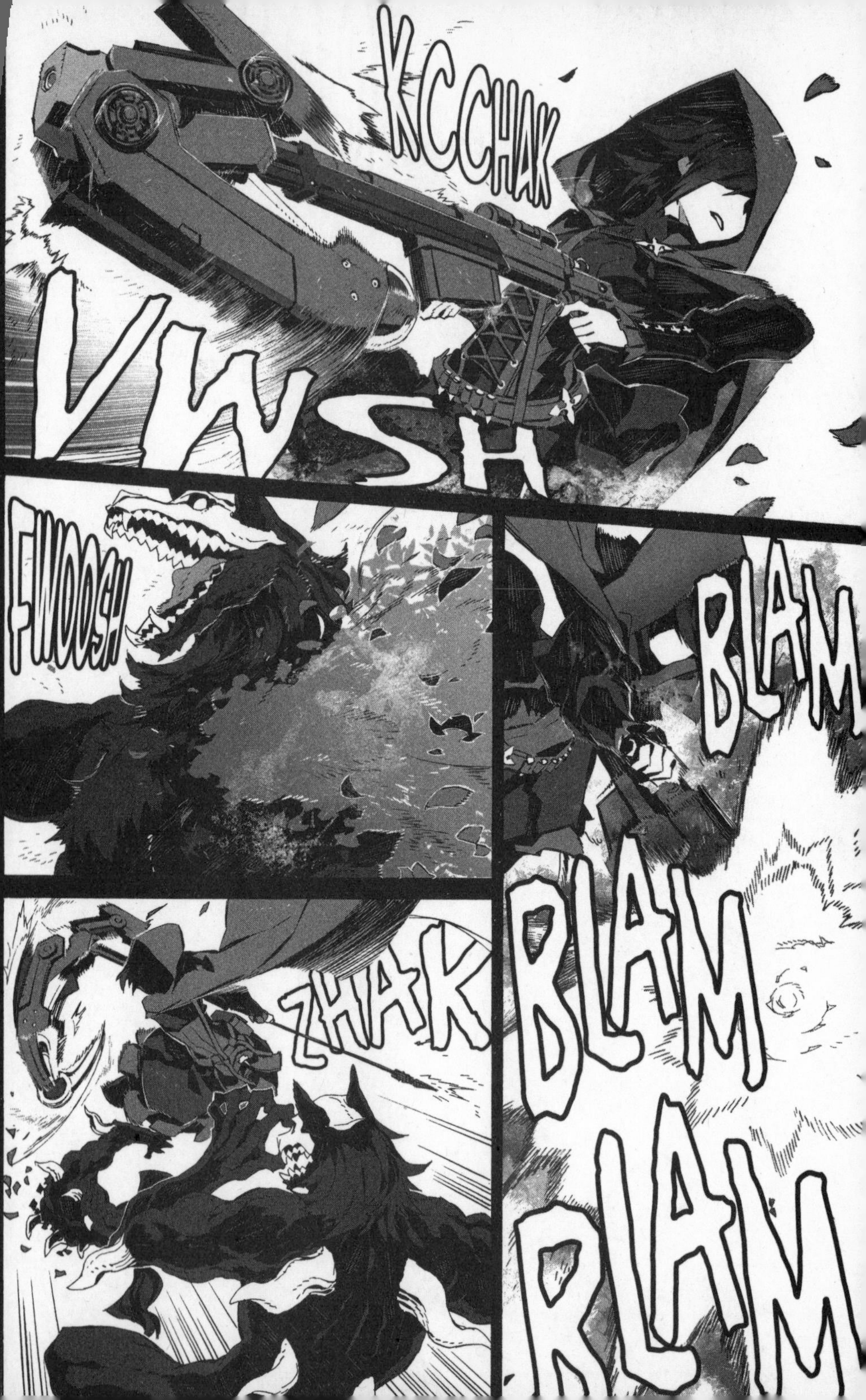
KCCHAK
VWSH
BLAM
BLAM
BLAM
FWOOSH
ZHAK

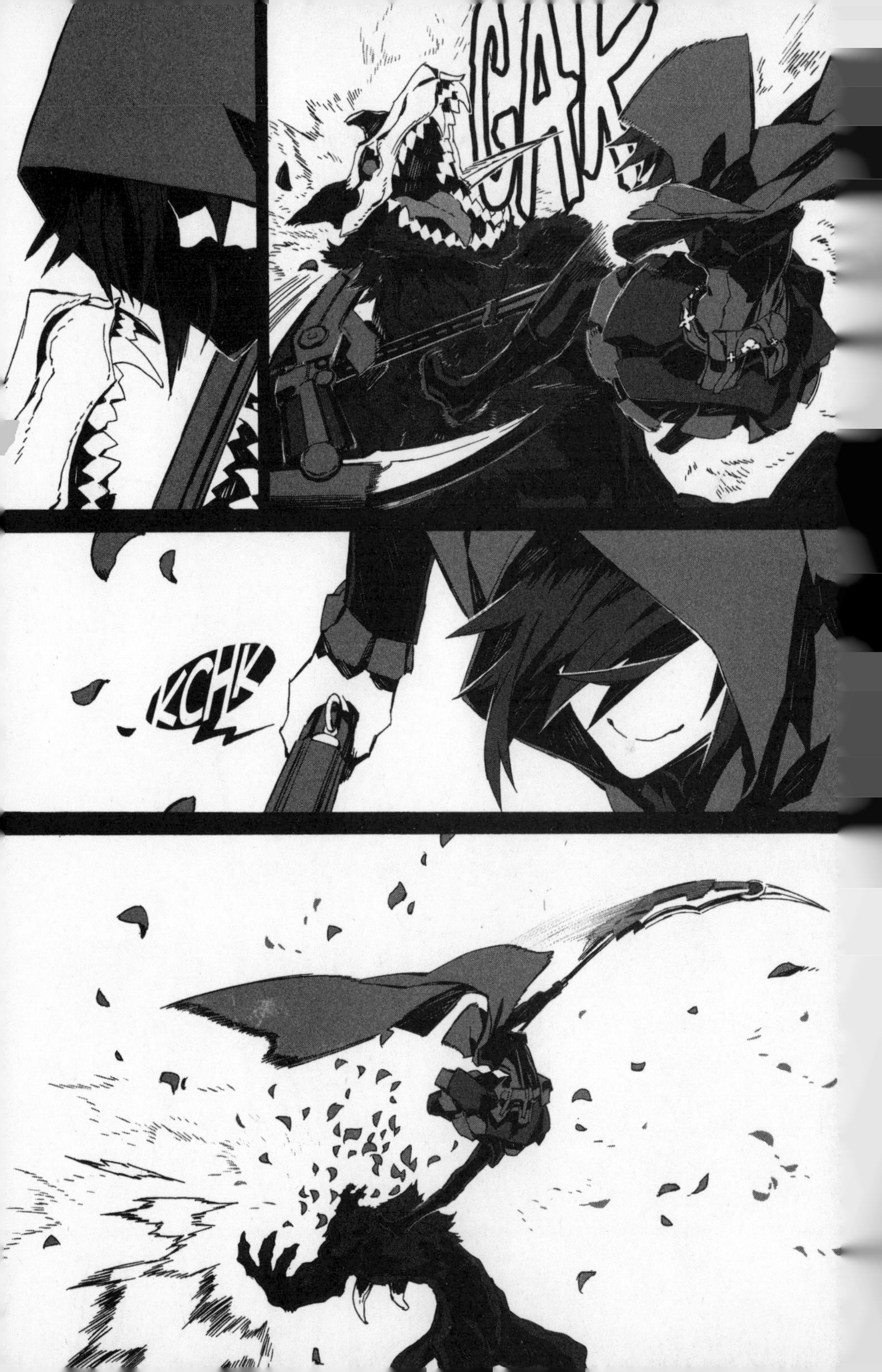
GAK
KCHK

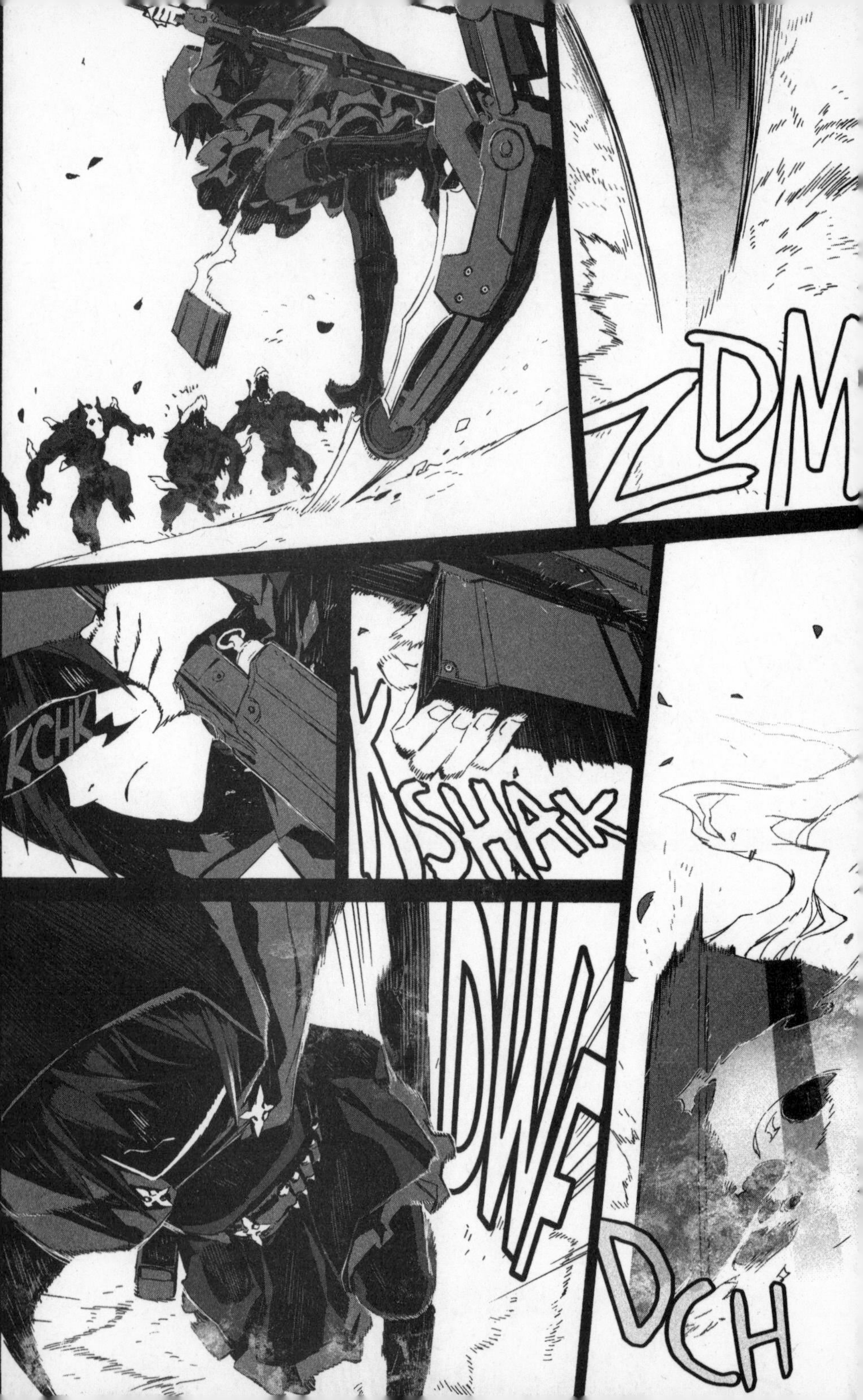
ZDM
DCH
SHAK
KCHK
DWE

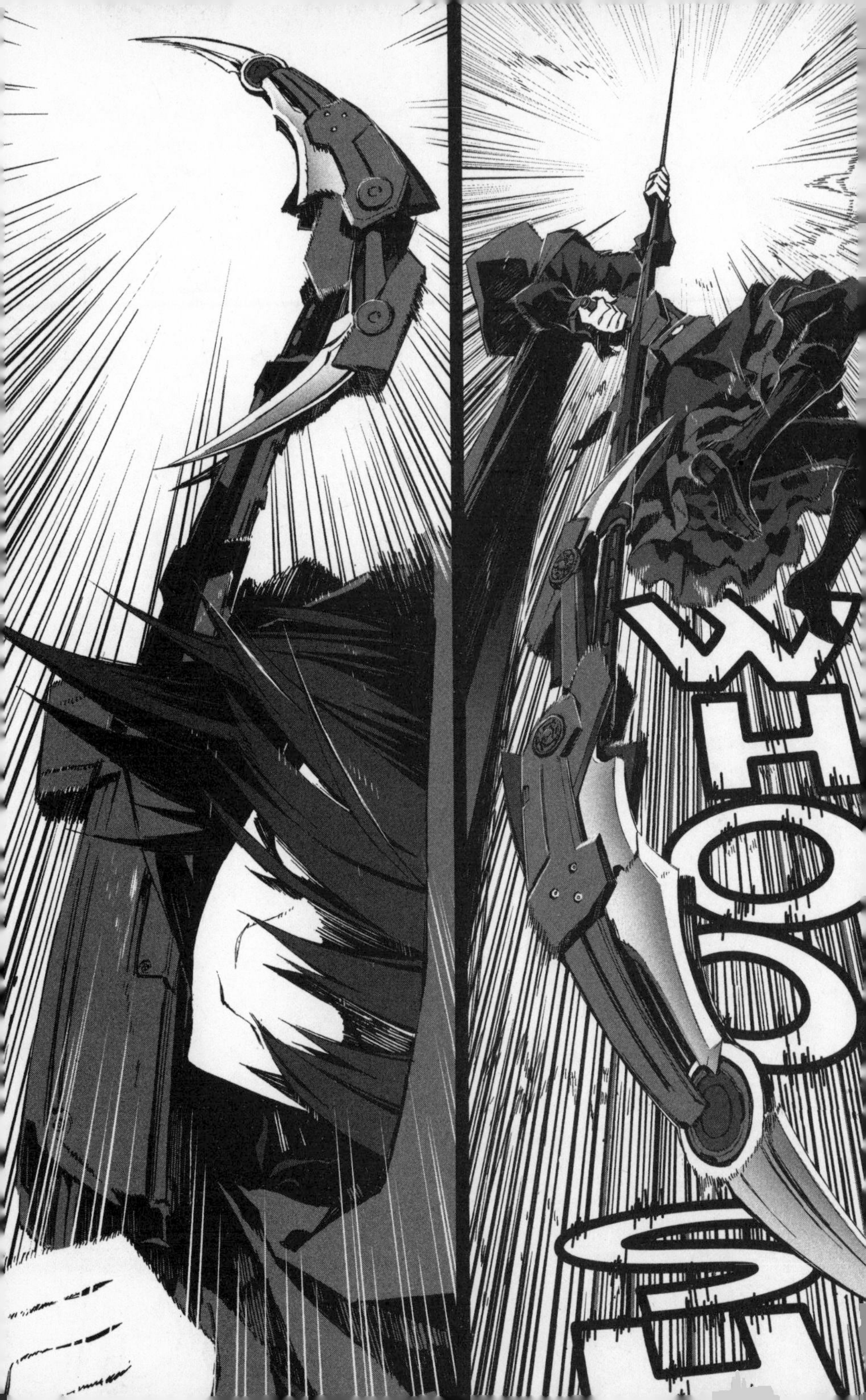
WHOOSH

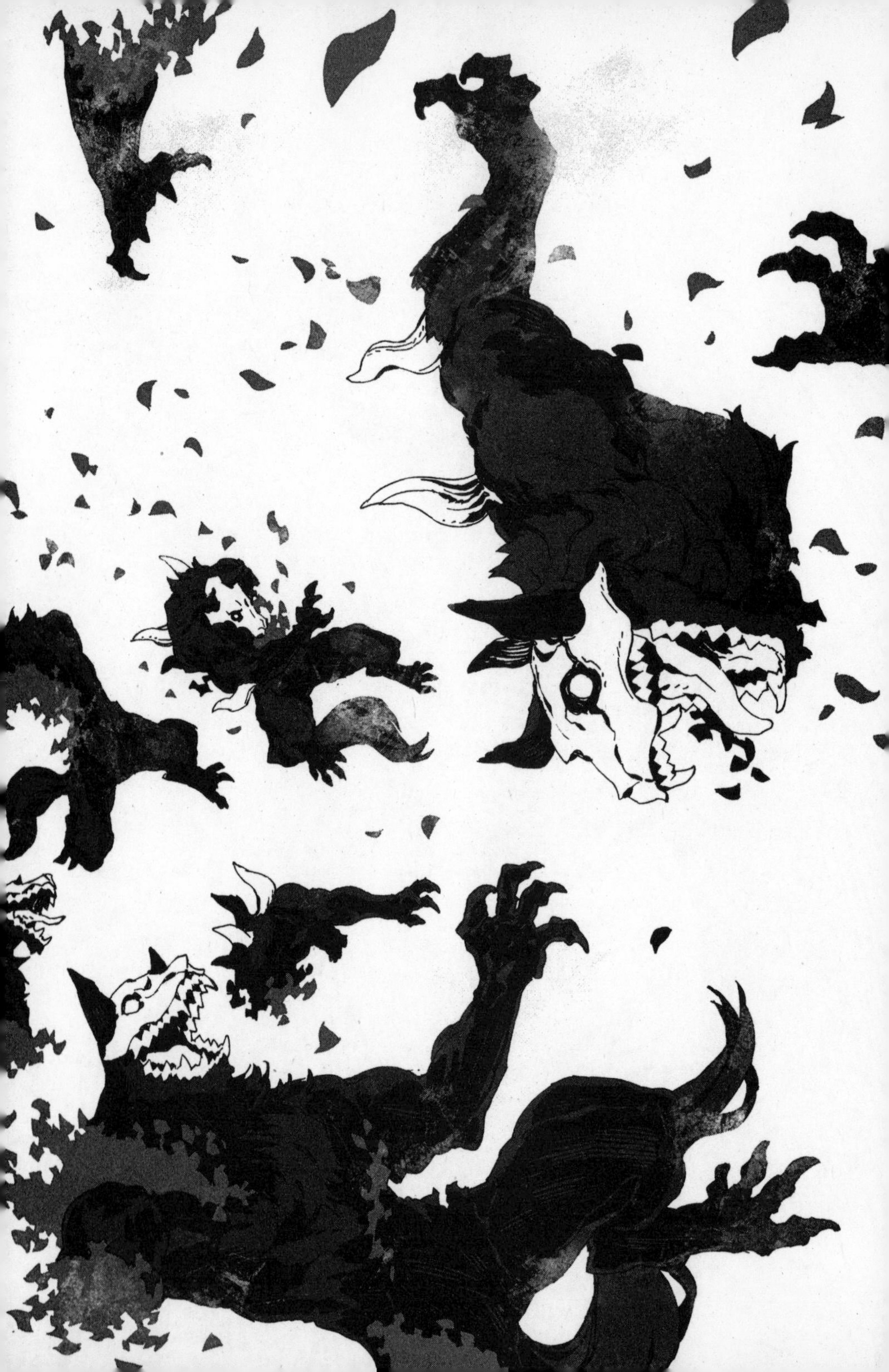

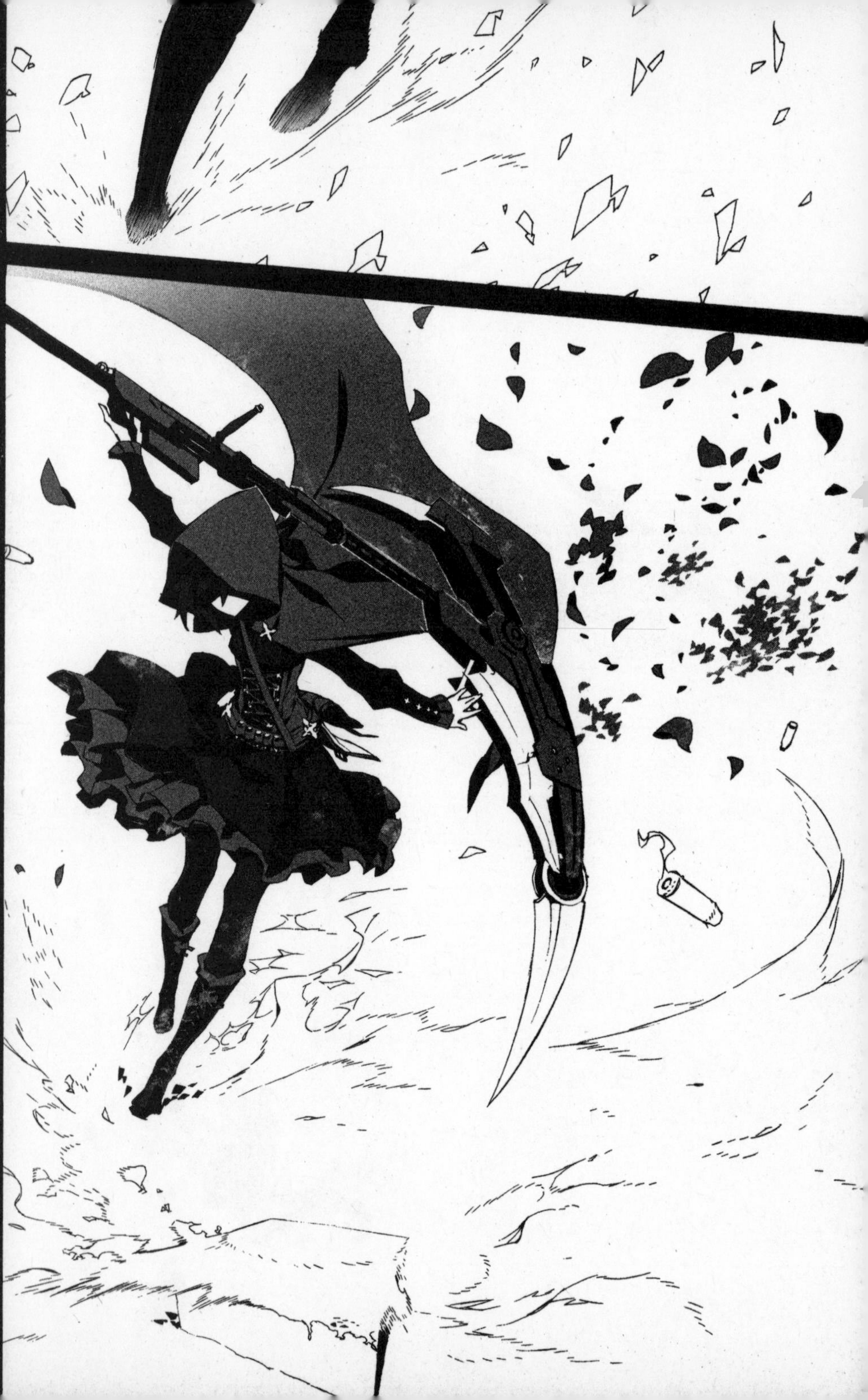

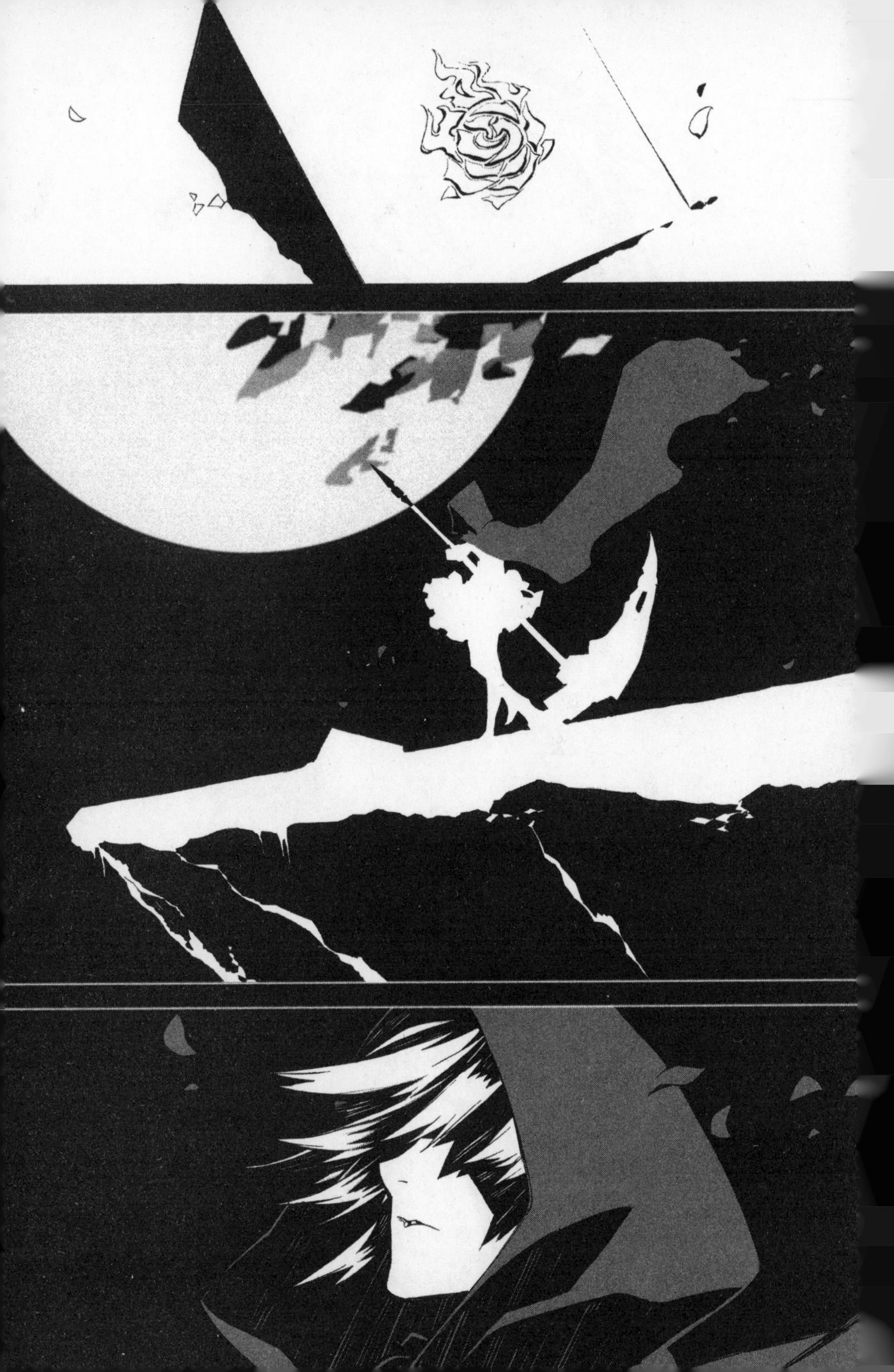

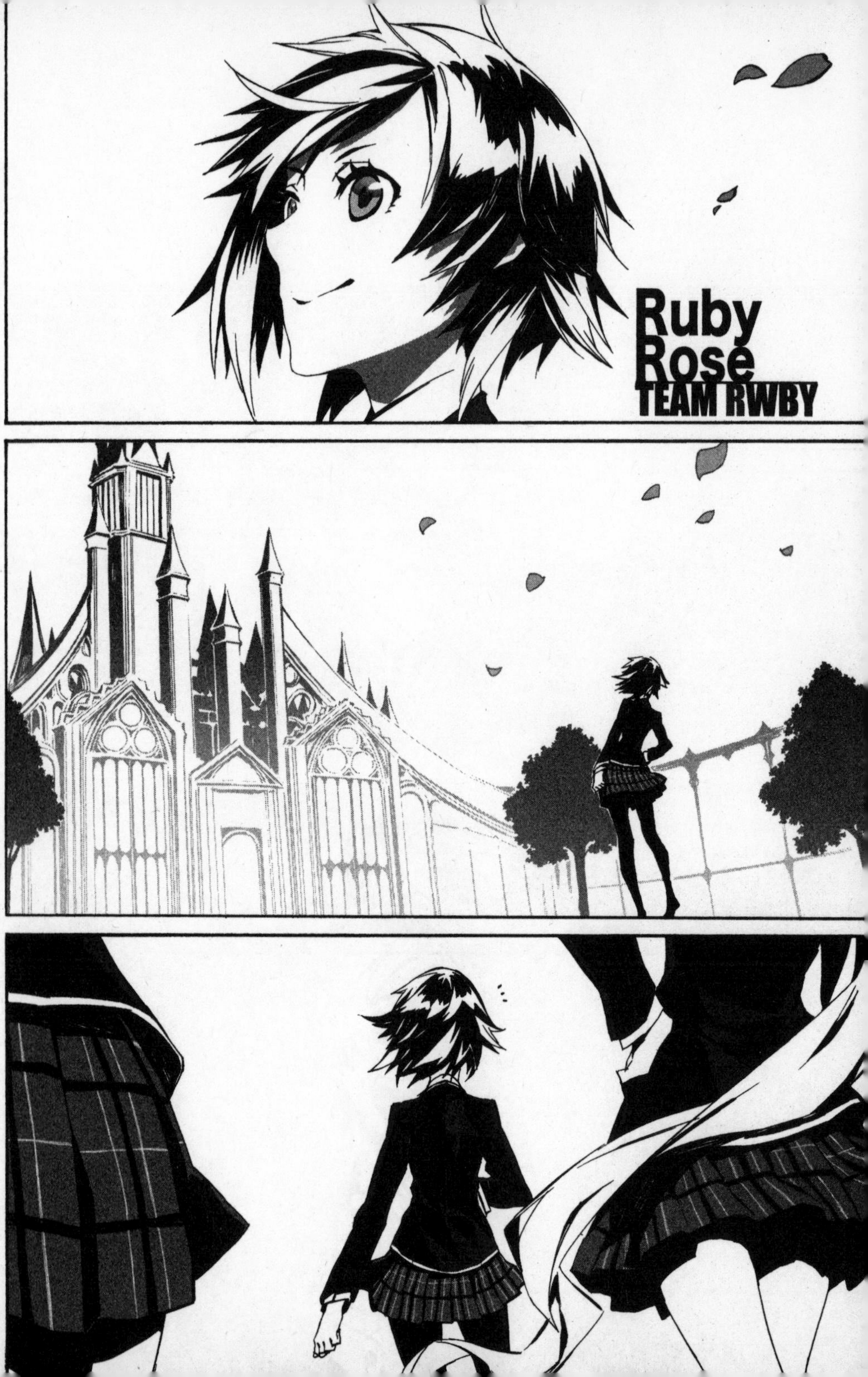
Ruby
Rose
TEAM RWBY

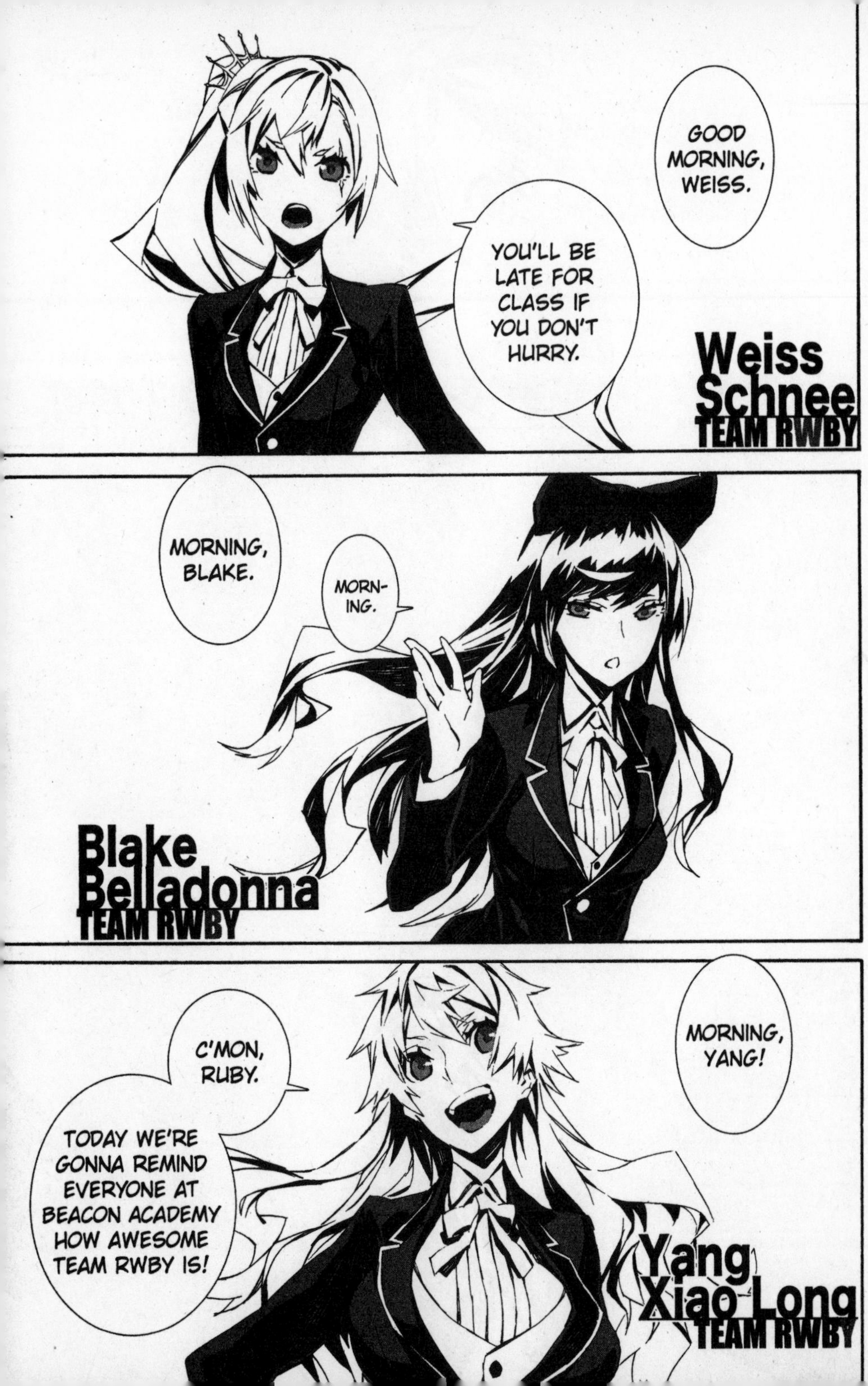
GOOD MORNING, WEISS.
YOU'LL BE LATE FOR CLASS IF YOU DON'T HURRY.
Weiss Schnee
TEAM RWBY
MORNING, BLAKE.
MORN-ING.
Blake Belladonna
TEAM RWBY
MORNING, YANG!
C'MON, RUBY.
TODAY WE'RE GONNA REMIND EVERYONE AT BEACON ACADEMY HOW AWESOME TEAM RWBY IS!
Yang Xiao Long
TEAM RWBY

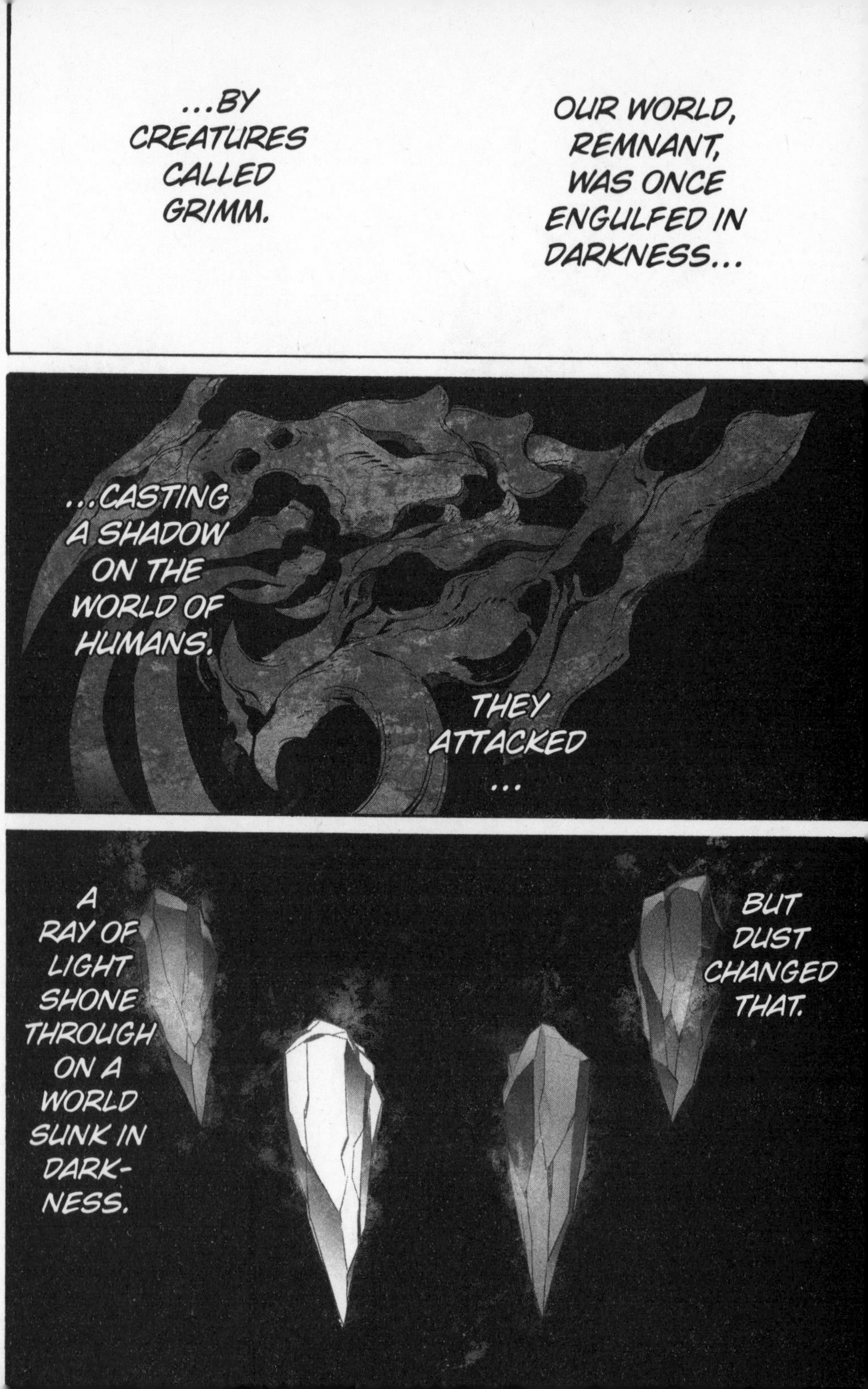
OUR WORLD, REMNANT, WAS ONCE ENGULFED IN DARKNESS...
...BY CREATURES CALLED GRIMM.
THEY ATTACKED ...
...CASTING A SHADOW ON THE WORLD OF HUMANS.
BUT DUST CHANGED THAT.
A RAY OF LIGHT SHONE THROUGH ON A WORLD SUNK IN DARK-NESS.

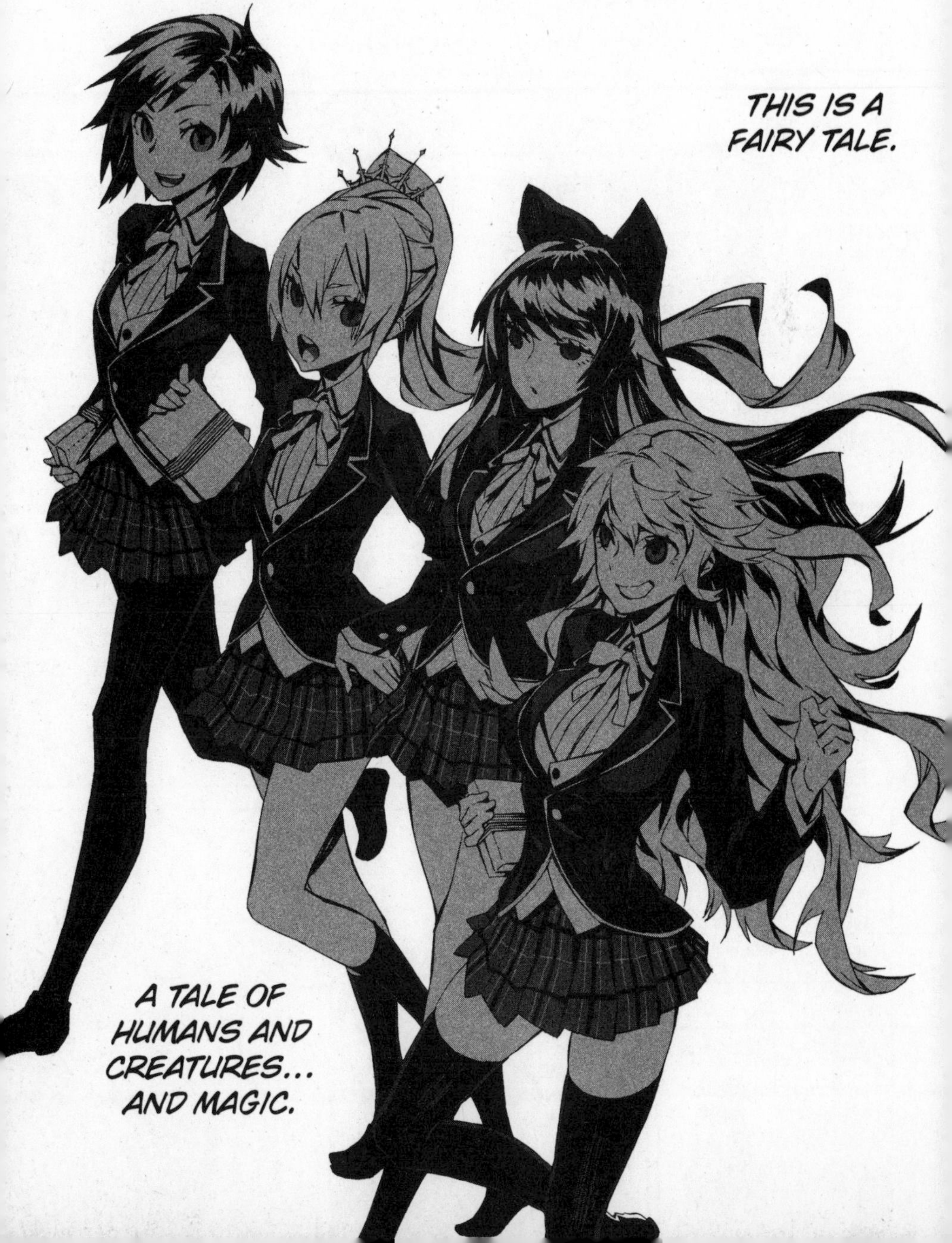
THIS IS A FAIRY TALE.
A TALE OF HUMANS AND CREATURES... AND MAGIC.

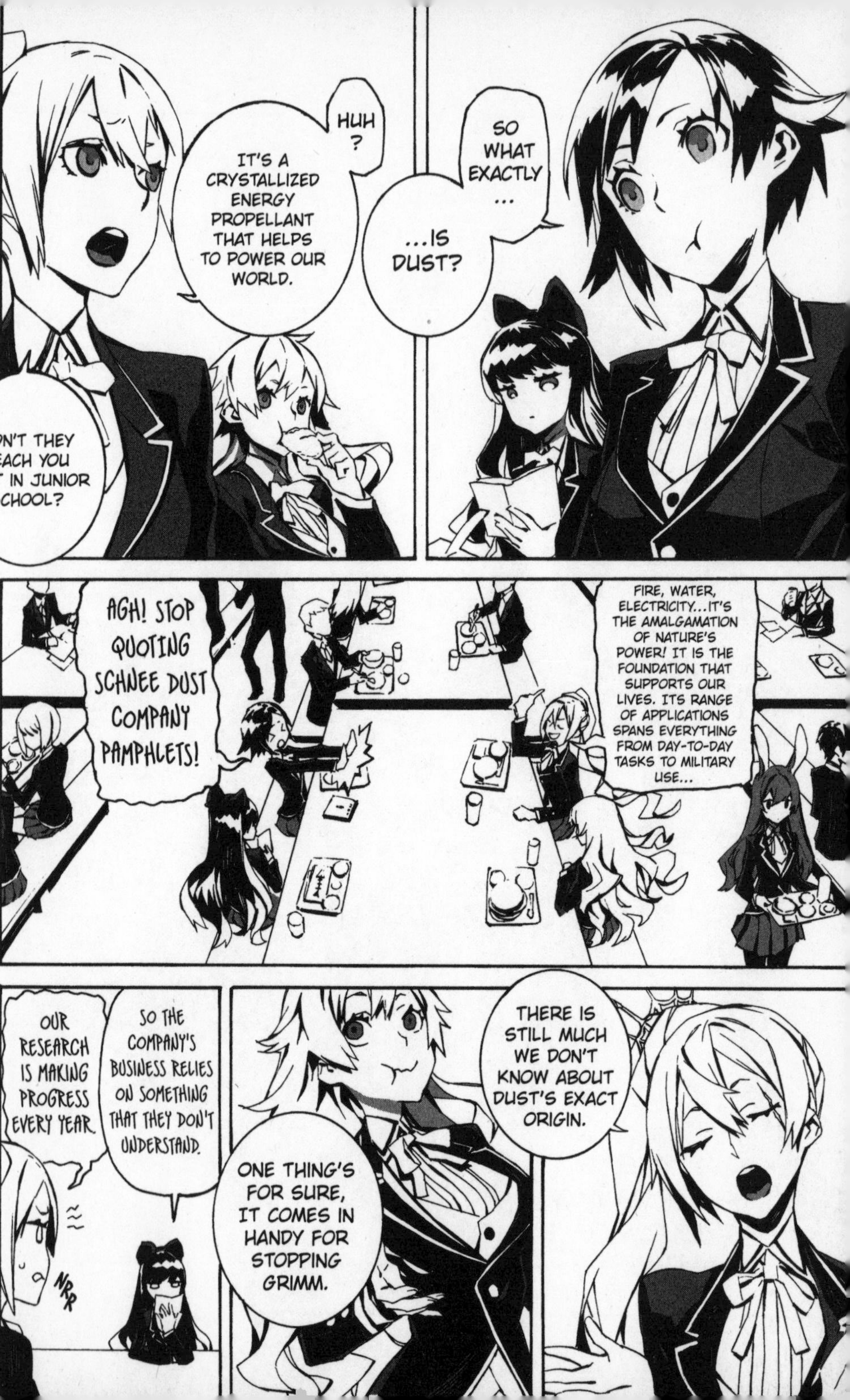
SO WHAT EXACTLY ...
...IS DUST?
HUH ?
IT'S A CRYSTALLIZED ENERGY PROPELLANT THAT HELPS TO POWER OUR WORLD.
DIDN'T THEY TEACH YOU THAT IN JUNIOR SCHOOL?
FIRE, WATER, ELECTRICITY...IT'S THE AMALGAMATION OF NATURE'S POWER! IT IS THE FOUNDATION THAT SUPPORTS OUR LIVES. ITS RANGE OF APPLICATIONS SPANS EVERYTHING FROM DAY-TO-DAY TASKS TO MILITARY USE...
AGH! STOP QUOTING SCHNEE DUST COMPANY PAMPHLETS!
THERE IS STILL MUCH WE DON'T KNOW ABOUT DUST'S EXACT ORIGIN.
ONE THING'S FOR SURE, IT COMES IN HANDY FOR STOPPING GRIMM.
SO THE COMPANY'S BUSINESS RELIES ON SOMETHING THAT THEY DON'T UNDERSTAND.
OUR RESEARCH IS MAKING PROGRESS EVERY YEAR.
NRR

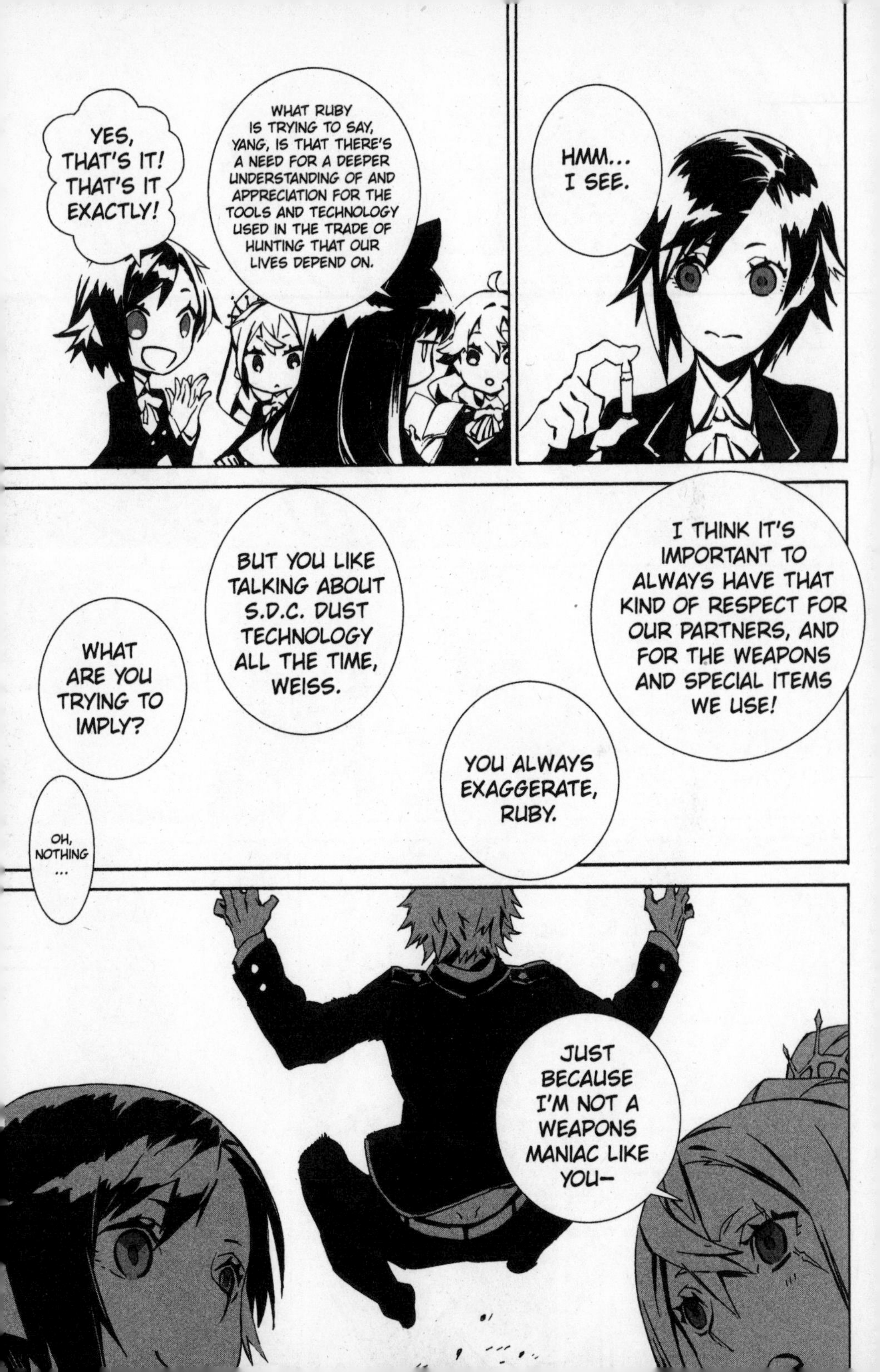
HMM... I SEE.
WHAT RUBY IS TRYING TO SAY, YANG, IS THAT THERE'S A NEED FOR A DEEPER UNDERSTANDING OF AND APPRECIATION FOR THE TOOLS AND TECHNOLOGY USED IN THE TRADE OF HUNTING THAT OUR LIVES DEPEND ON.
YES, THAT'S IT! THAT'S IT EXACTLY!
I THINK IT'S IMPORTANT TO ALWAYS HAVE THAT KIND OF RESPECT FOR OUR PARTNERS, AND FOR THE WEAPONS AND SPECIAL ITEMS WE USE!
YOU ALWAYS EXAGGERATE, RUBY.
BUT YOU LIKE TALKING ABOUT S.D.C. DUST TECHNOLOGY ALL THE TIME, WEISS.
WHAT ARE YOU TRYING TO IMPLY?
OH, NOTHING...
JUST BECAUSE I'M NOT A WEAPONS MANIAC LIKE YOU—

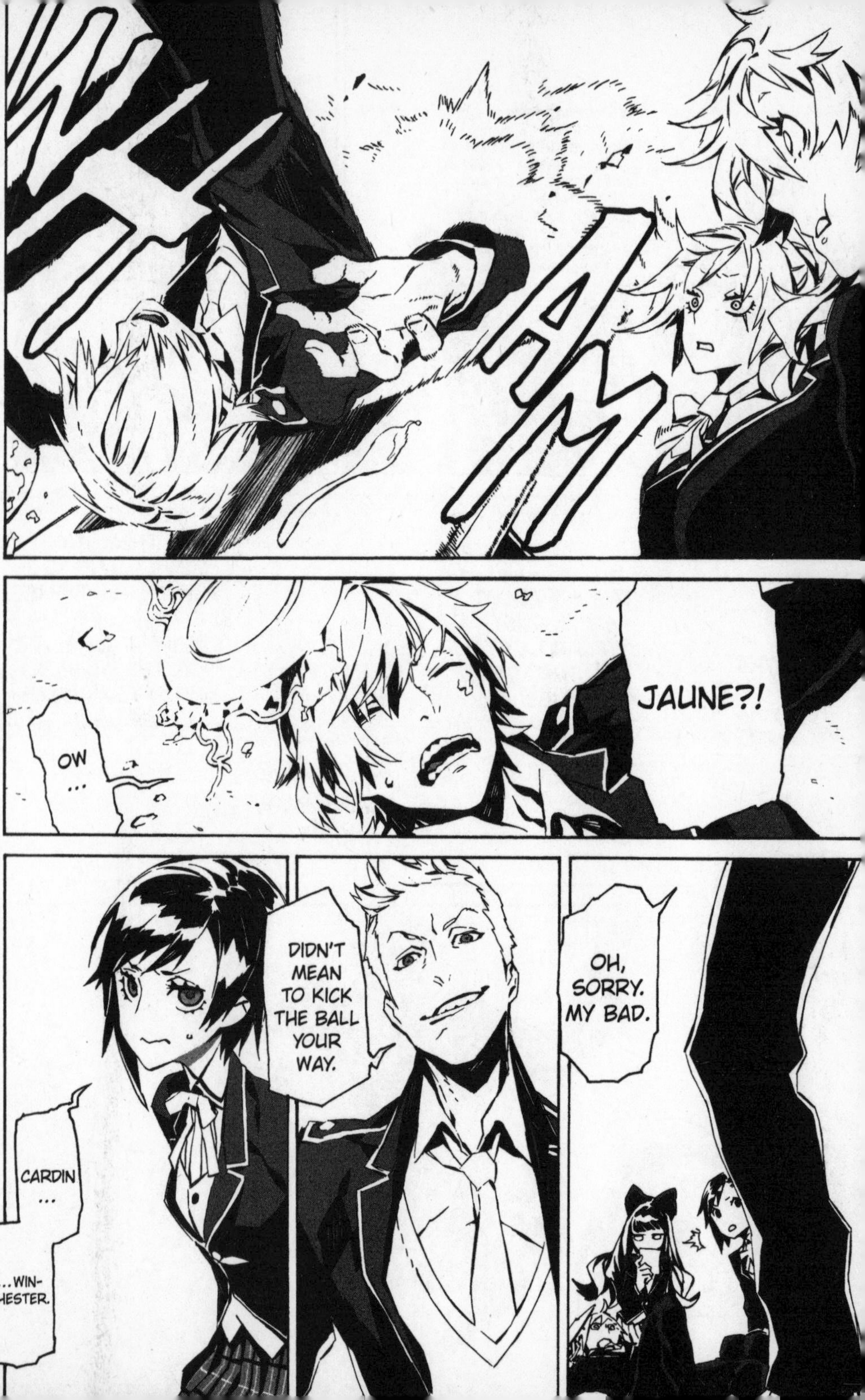
WHAM
JAUNE?!
OW ...
OH, SORRY. MY BAD.
DIDN'T MEAN TO KICK THE BALL YOUR WAY.
CARDIN ...
...WIN-CHESTER.

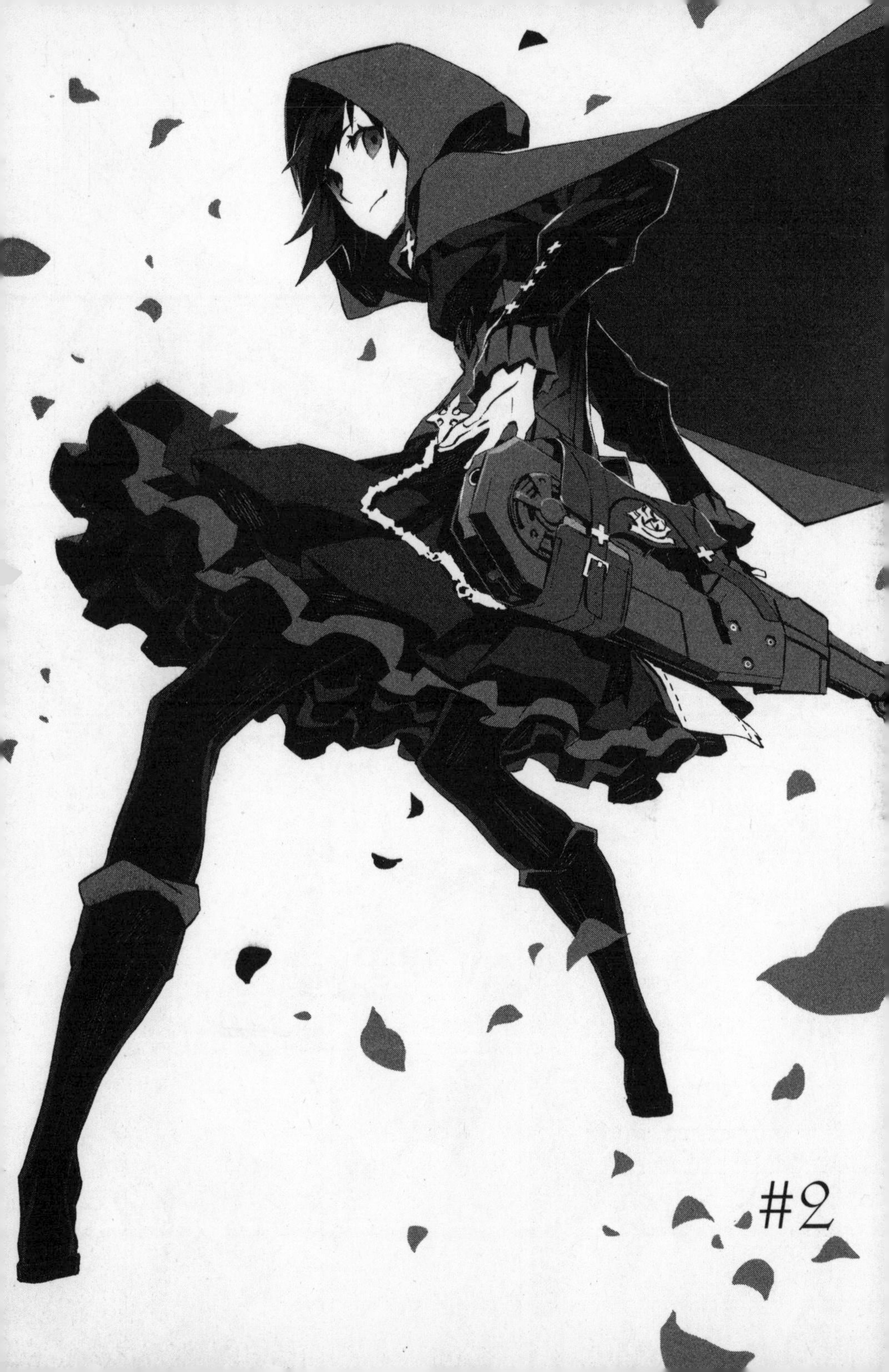

#2

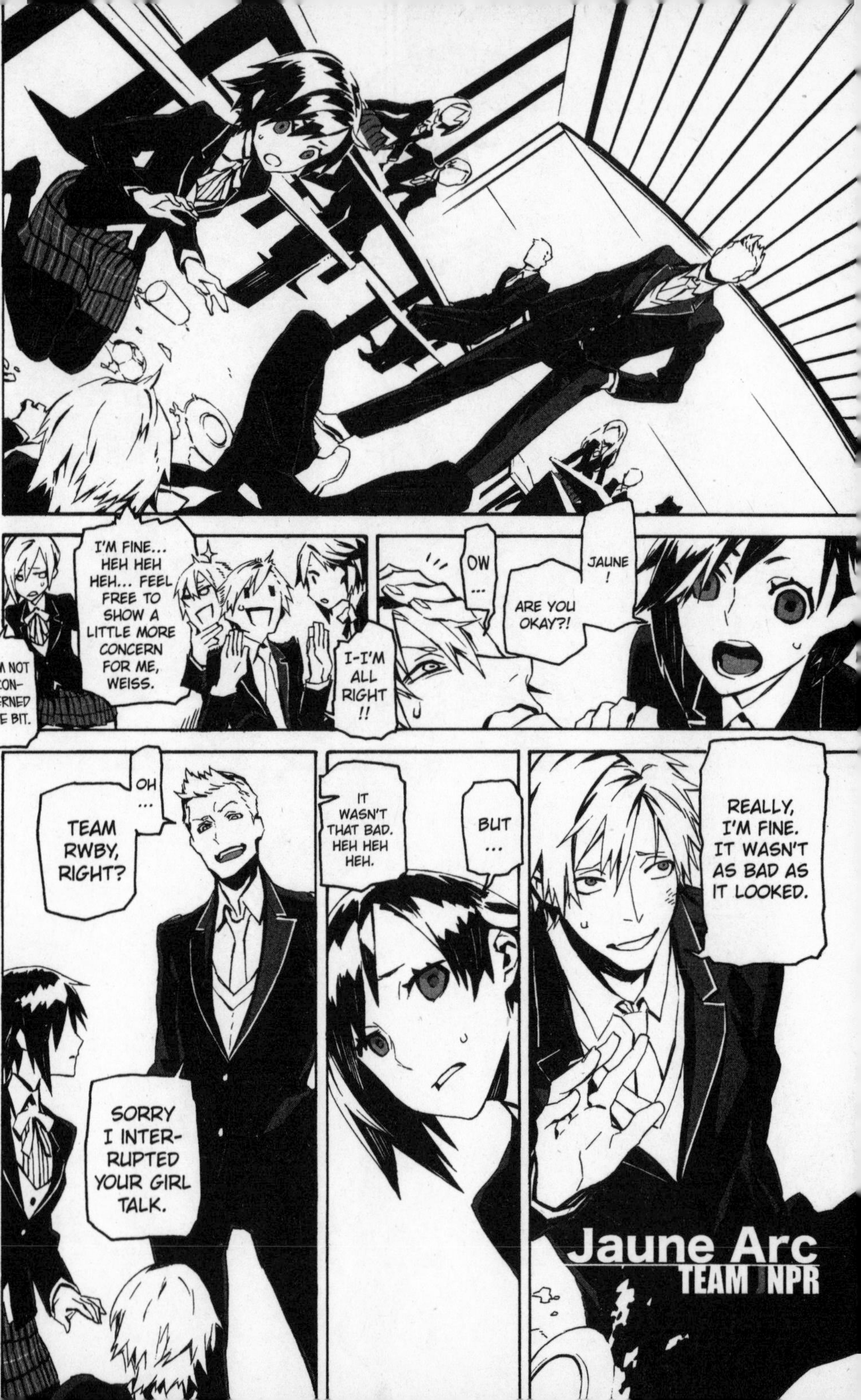
JAUNE!
ARE YOU OKAY?!
OW...
I-I'M ALL RIGHT!!
I'M FINE... HEH HEH HEH... FEEL FREE TO SHOW A LITTLE MORE CONCERN FOR ME, WEISS.
I'M NOT CONCERNED ONE BIT.
REALLY, I'M FINE. IT WASN'T AS BAD AS IT LOOKED.
BUT...
IT WASN'T THAT BAD. HEH HEH HEH.
OH...
TEAM RWBY, RIGHT?
SORRY I INTERRUPTED YOUR GIRL TALK.
Jaune Arc
TEAM JNPR

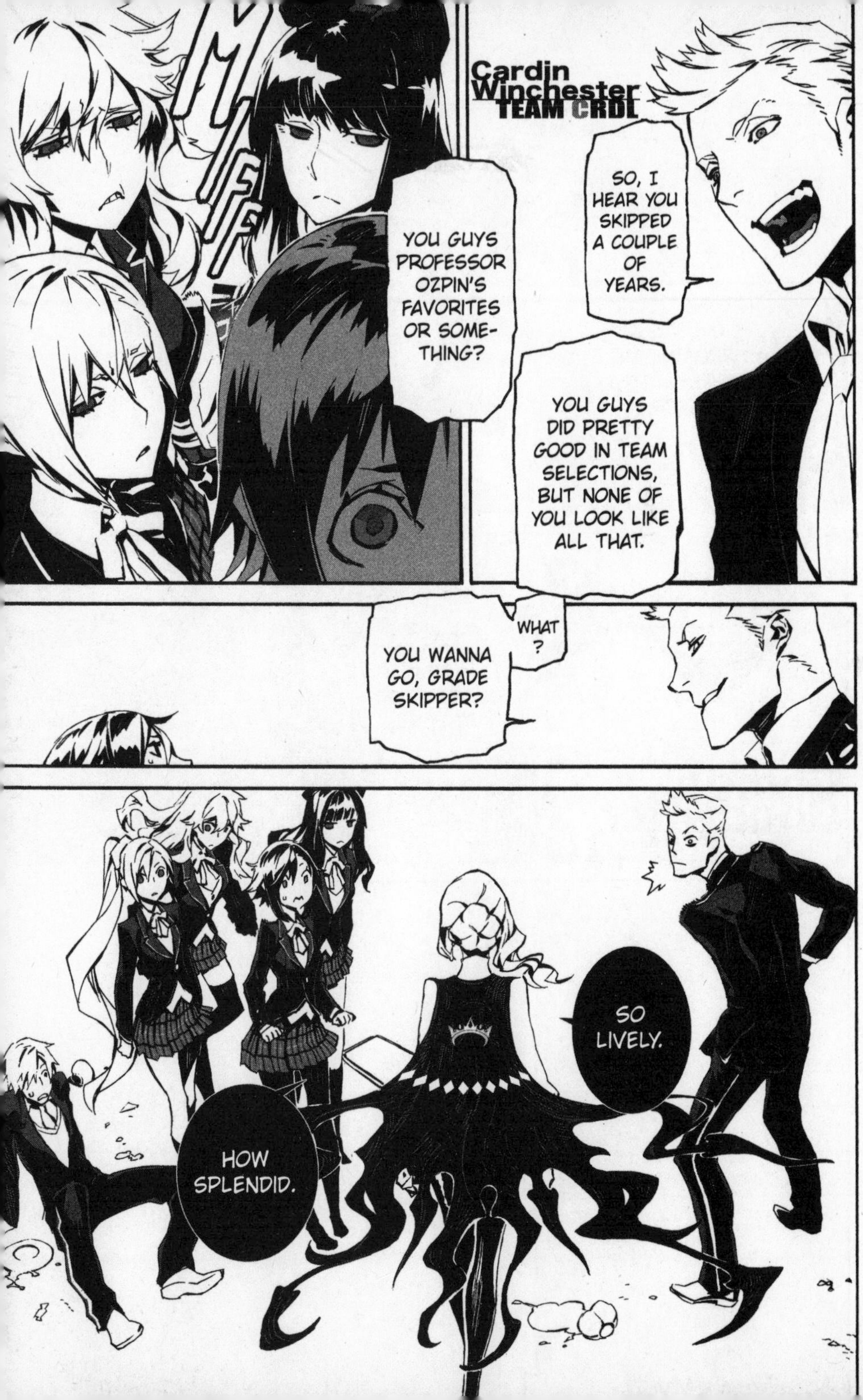
Cardin Winchester
TEAM CRDL
SO, I HEAR YOU SKIPPED A COUPLE OF YEARS.
MMFF
YOU GUYS PROFESSOR OZPIN'S FAVORITES OR SOMETHING?
YOU GUYS DID PRETTY GOOD IN TEAM SELECTIONS, BUT NONE OF YOU LOOK LIKE ALL THAT.
WHAT?
YOU WANNA GO, GRADE SKIPPER?
SO LIVELY.
HOW SPLENDID.

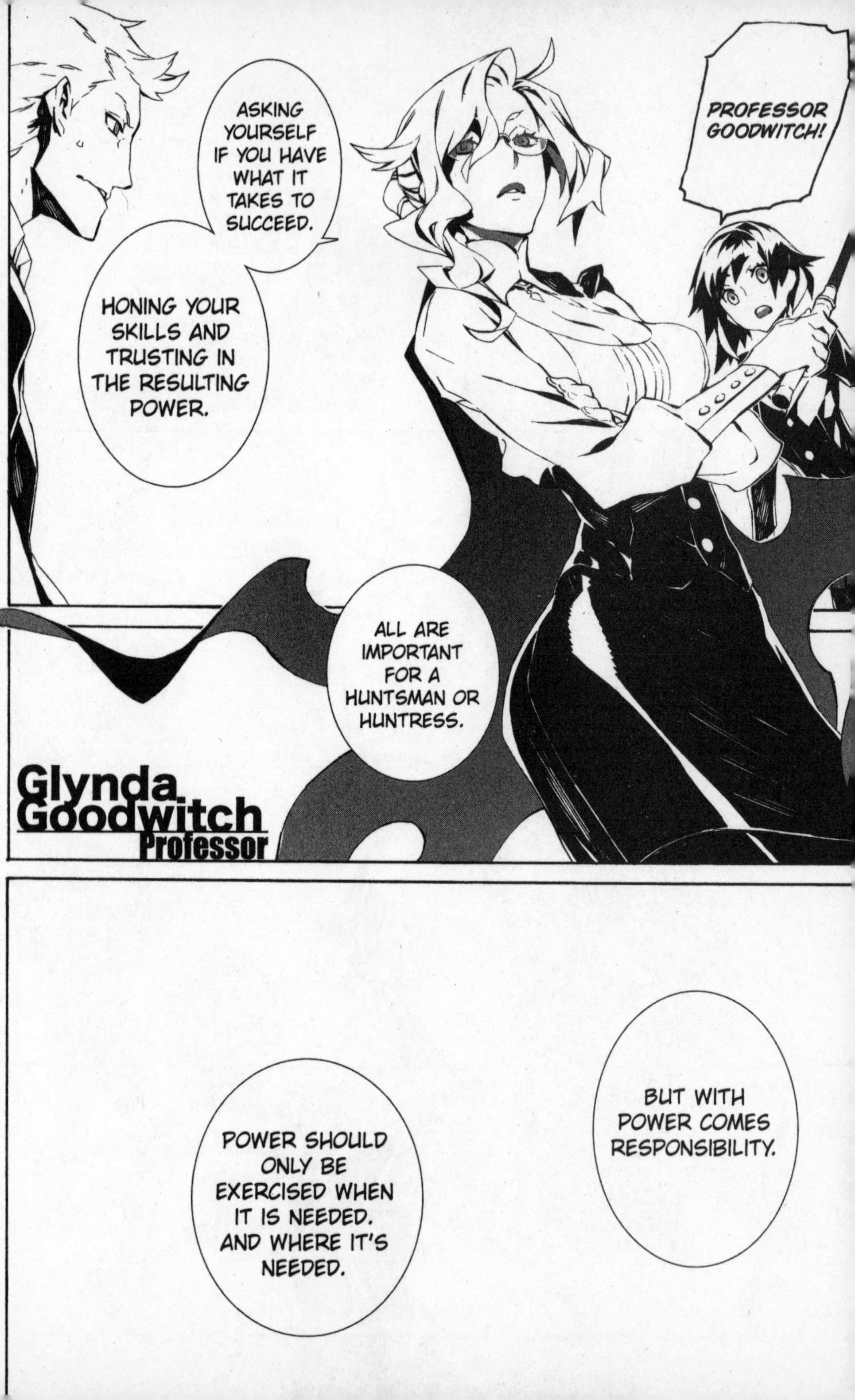
PROFESSOR GOODWITCH!
ASKING YOURSELF IF YOU HAVE WHAT IT TAKES TO SUCCEED.
HONING YOUR SKILLS AND TRUSTING IN THE RESULTING POWER.
ALL ARE IMPORTANT FOR A HUNTSMAN OR HUNTRESS.
Glynda Goodwitch
Professor
BUT WITH POWER COMES RESPONSIBILITY.
POWER SHOULD ONLY BE EXERCISED WHEN IT IS NEEDED. AND WHERE IT'S NEEDED.

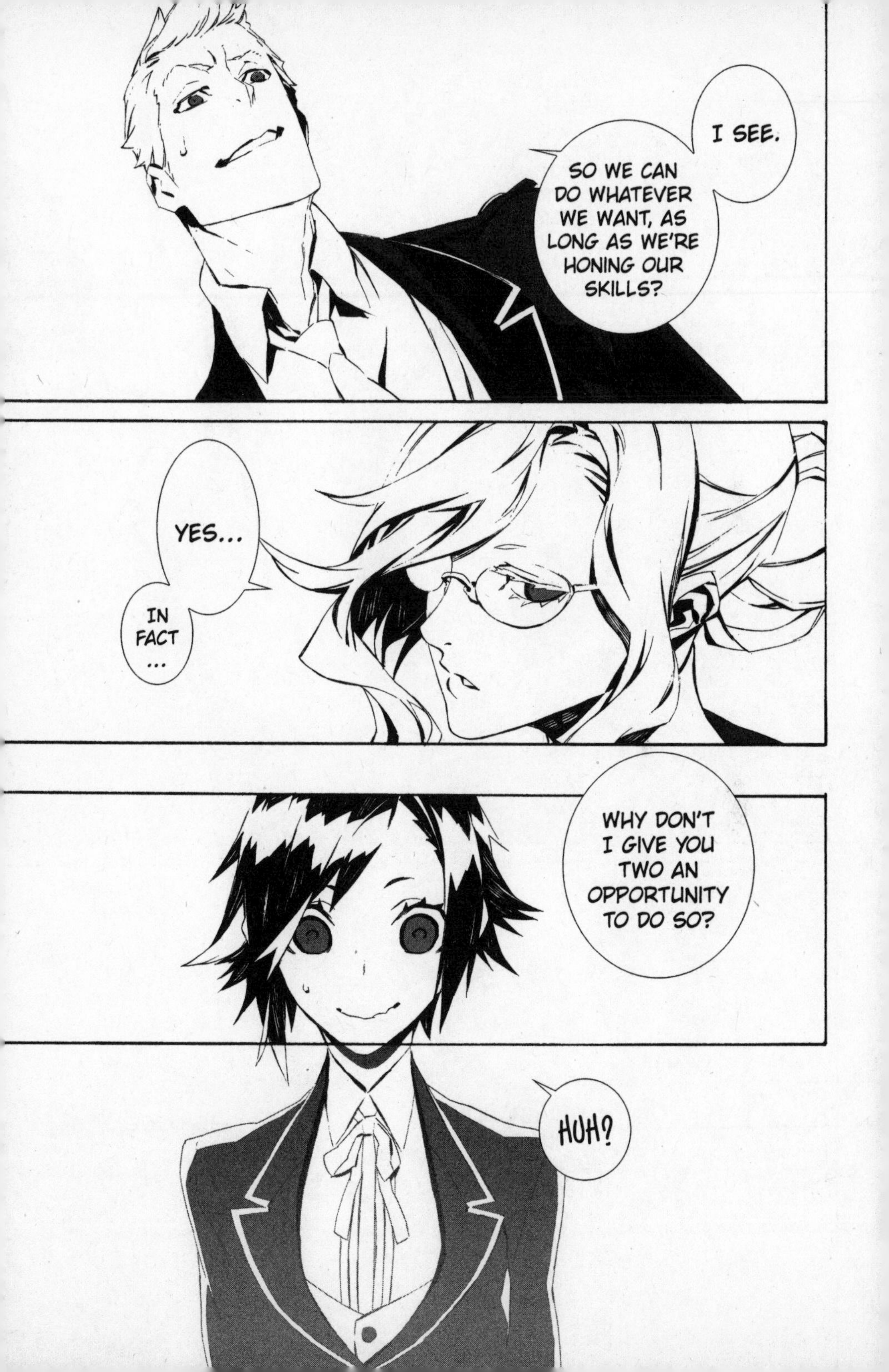
I SEE.
SO WE CAN DO WHATEVER WE WANT, AS LONG AS WE'RE HONING OUR SKILLS?
YES...
IN FACT ...
WHY DON'T I GIVE YOU TWO AN OPPORTUNITY TO DO SO?
HUH?

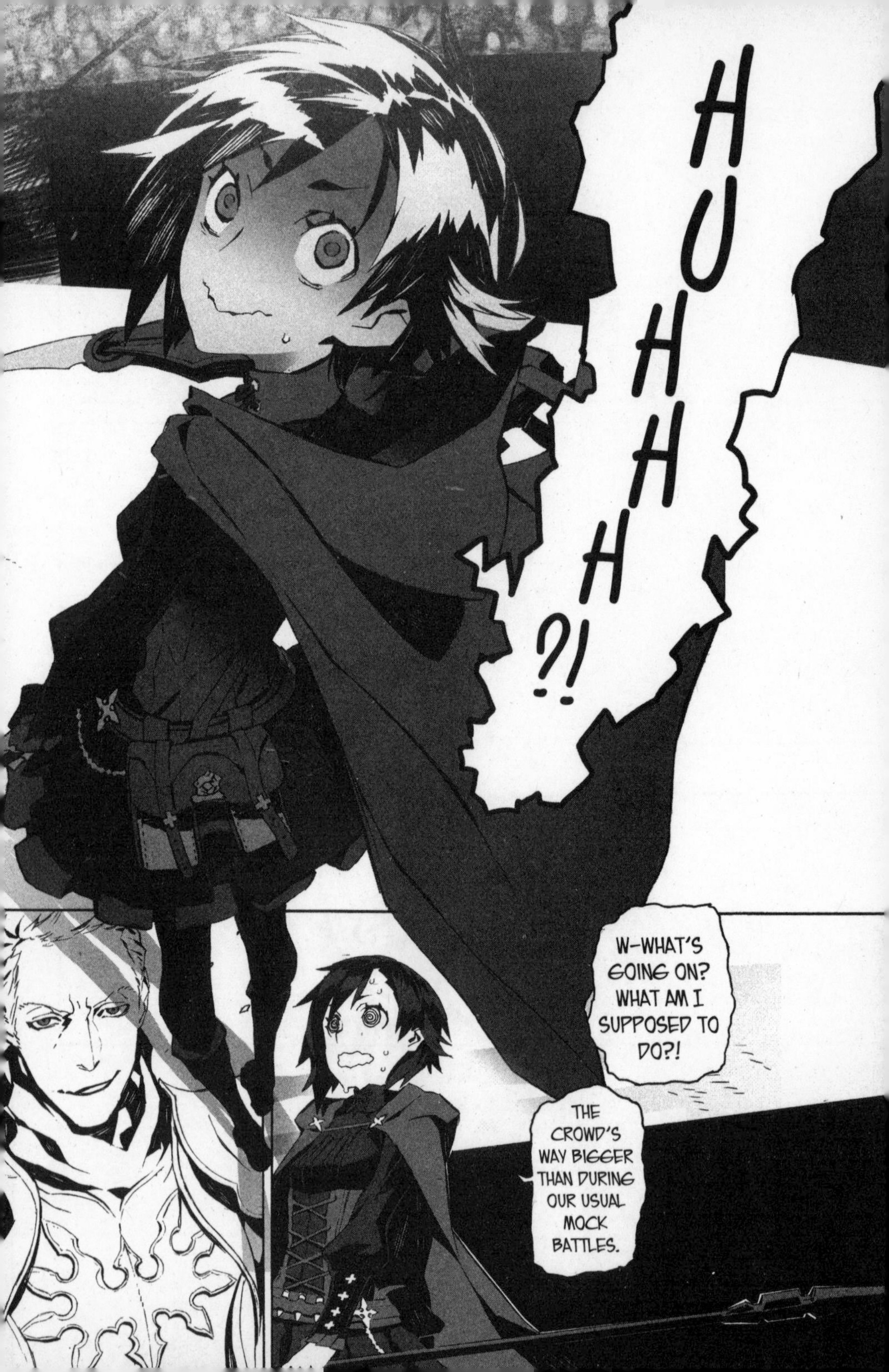
HUHHHH?!
W-WHAT'S GOING ON? WHAT AM I SUPPOSED TO DO?!
THE CROWD'S WAY BIGGER THAN DURING OUR USUAL MOCK BATTLES.

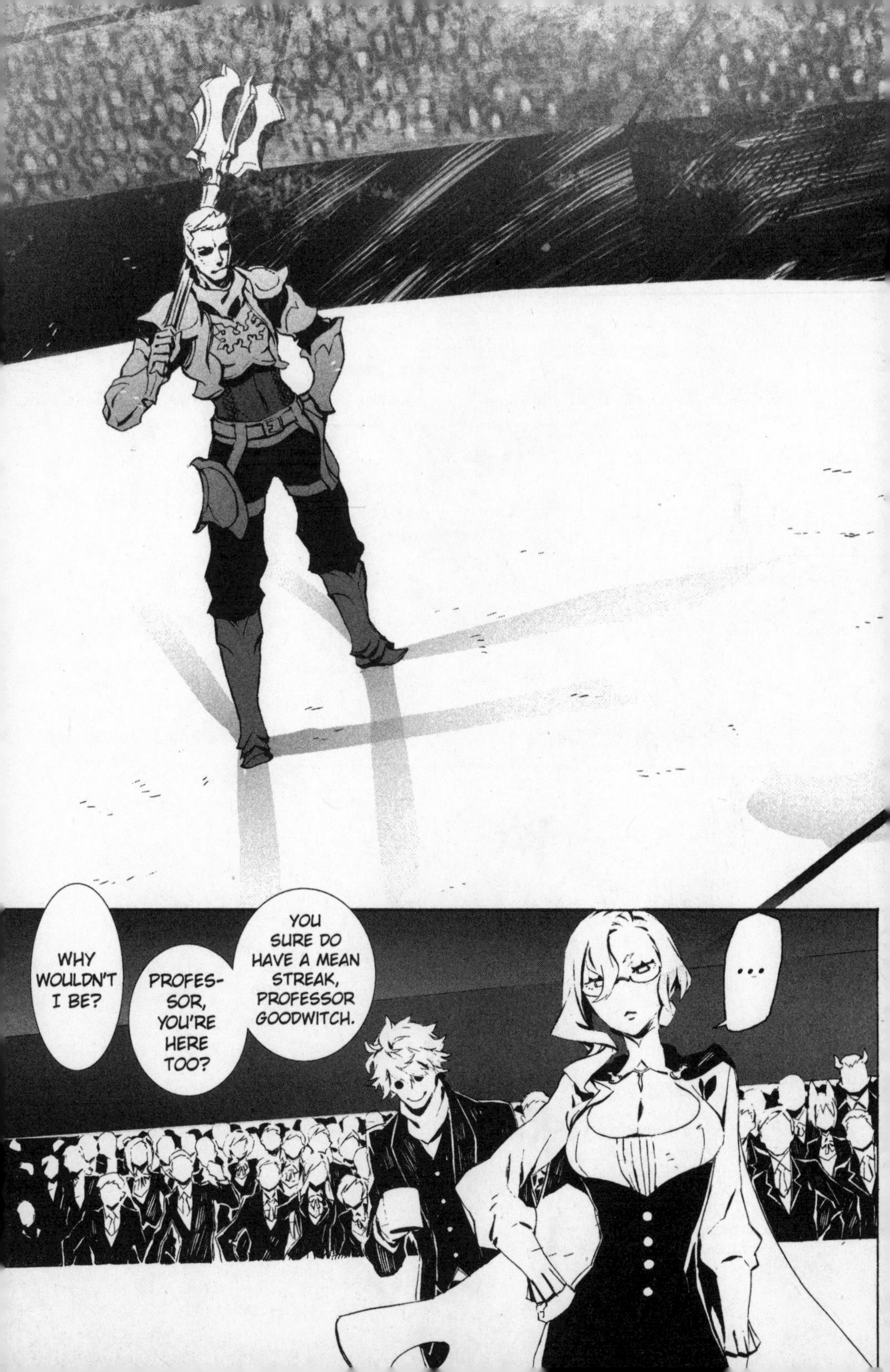
...
YOU SURE DO HAVE A MEAN STREAK, PROFESSOR GOODWITCH.
PROFES-SOR, YOU'RE HERE TOO?
WHY WOULDN'T I BE?

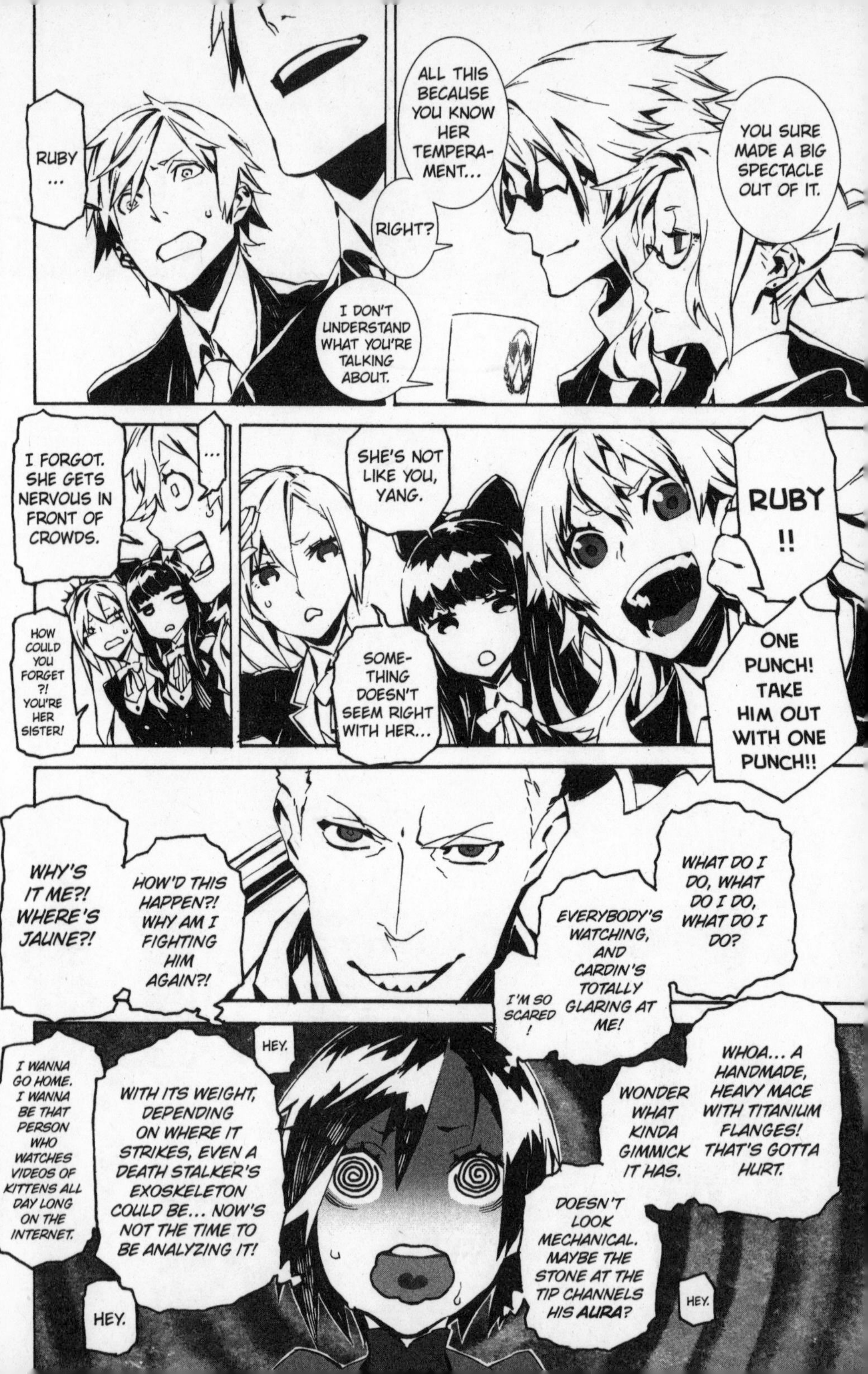
YOU SURE MADE A BIG SPECTACLE OUT OF IT.
ALL THIS BECAUSE YOU KNOW HER TEMPERA-MENT...
RIGHT?
I DON'T UNDERSTAND WHAT YOU'RE TALKING ABOUT.
RUBY ...
RUBY !!
ONE PUNCH! TAKE HIM OUT WITH ONE PUNCH!!
SHE'S NOT LIKE YOU, YANG.
SOME-THING DOESN'T SEEM RIGHT WITH HER...
...
I FORGOT. SHE GETS NERVOUS IN FRONT OF CROWDS.
HOW COULD YOU FORGET?! YOU'RE HER SISTER!
WHAT DO I DO, WHAT DO I DO, WHAT DO I DO?
EVERYBODY'S WATCHING, AND CARDIN'S TOTALLY GLARING AT ME!
I'M SO SCARED!
HOW'D THIS HAPPEN?! WHY AM I FIGHTING HIM AGAIN?!
WHY'S IT ME?! WHERE'S JAUNE?!
WHOA... A HANDMADE, HEAVY MACE WITH TITANIUM FLANGES! THAT'S GOTTA HURT.
WONDER WHAT KINDA GIMMICK IT HAS.
DOESN'T LOOK MECHANICAL. MAYBE THE STONE AT THE TIP CHANNELS HIS AURA?
HEY.
HEY.
WITH ITS WEIGHT, DEPENDING ON WHERE IT STRIKES, EVEN A DEATH STALKER'S EXOSKELETON COULD BE... NOW'S NOT THE TIME TO BE ANALYZING IT!
I WANNA GO HOME. I WANNA BE THAT PERSON WHO WATCHES VIDEOS OF KITTENS ALL DAY LONG ON THE INTERNET.
HEY.

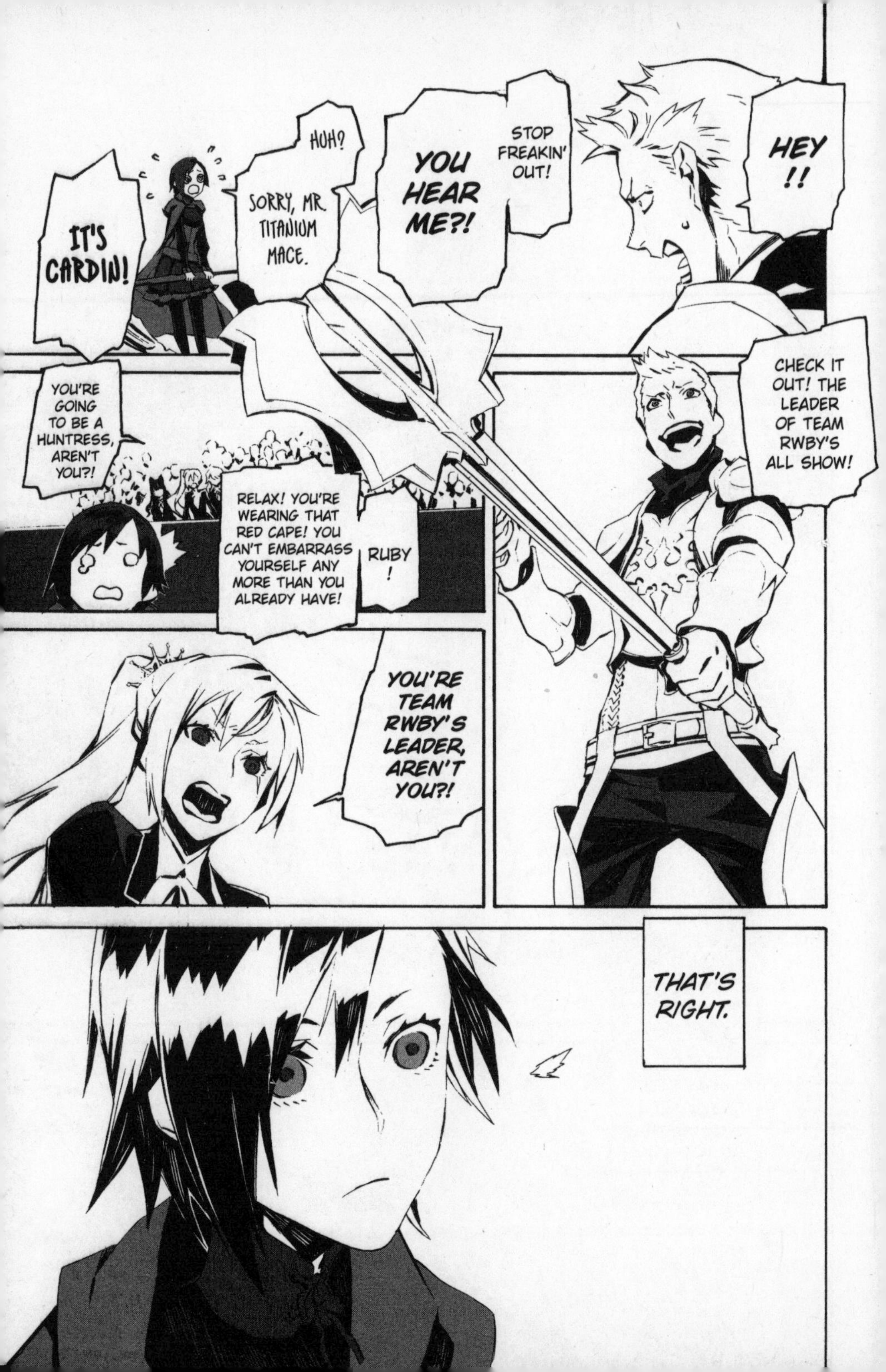
HEY !!
STOP FREAKIN' OUT!
YOU HEAR ME?!
HUH?
SORRY, MR. TITANIUM MACE.
IT'S CARDIN!
CHECK IT OUT! THE LEADER OF TEAM RWBY'S ALL SHOW!
RUBY !
RELAX! YOU'RE WEARING THAT RED CAPE! YOU CAN'T EMBARRASS YOURSELF ANY MORE THAN YOU ALREADY HAVE!
YOU'RE GOING TO BE A HUNTRESS, AREN'T YOU?!
YOU'RE TEAM RWBY'S LEADER, AREN'T YOU?!
THAT'S RIGHT.

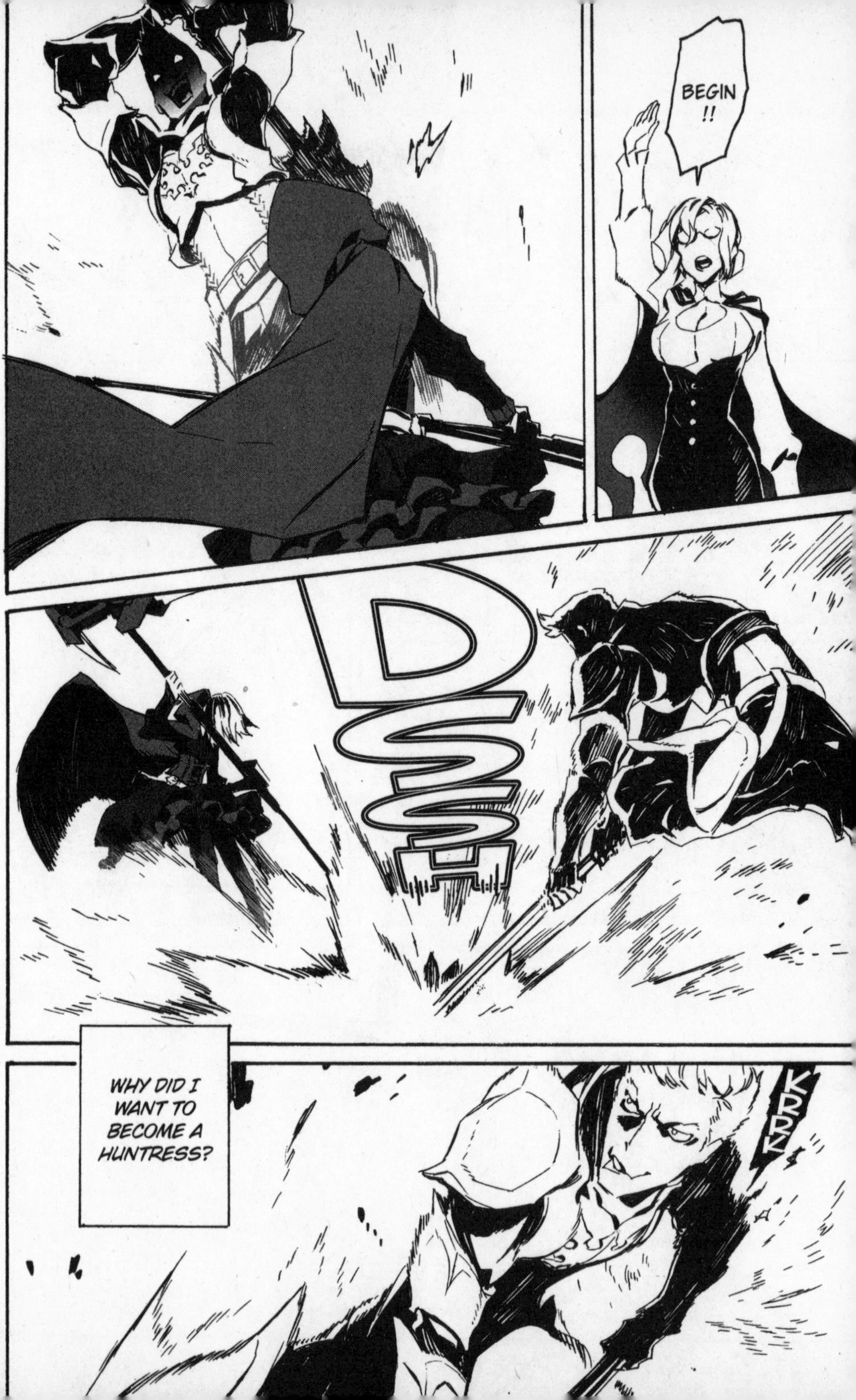
BEGIN!!
DSSH
WHY DID I WANT TO BECOME A HUNTRESS?
KRRK

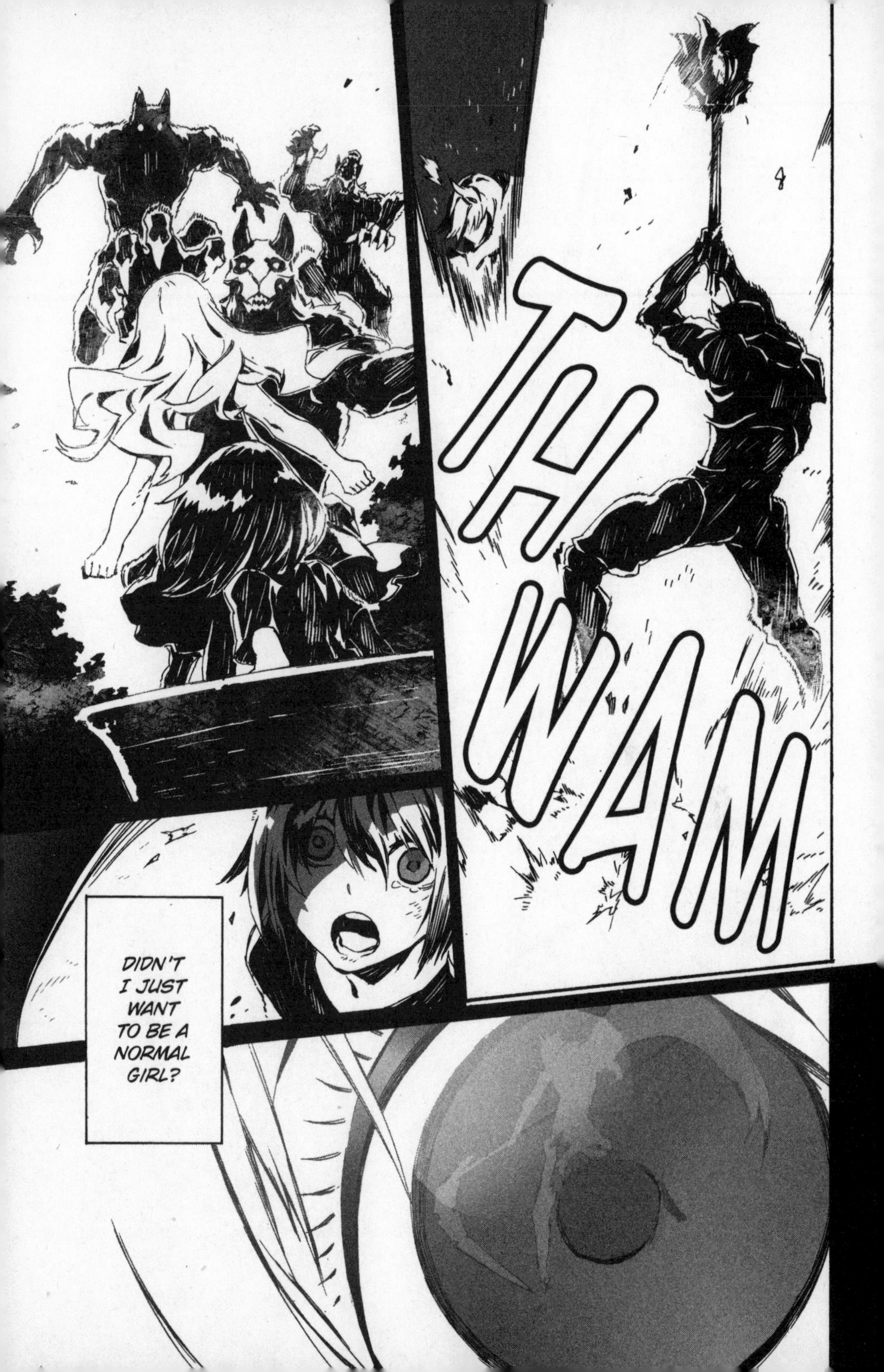
THWAM
DIDN'T I JUST WANT TO BE A NORMAL GIRL?

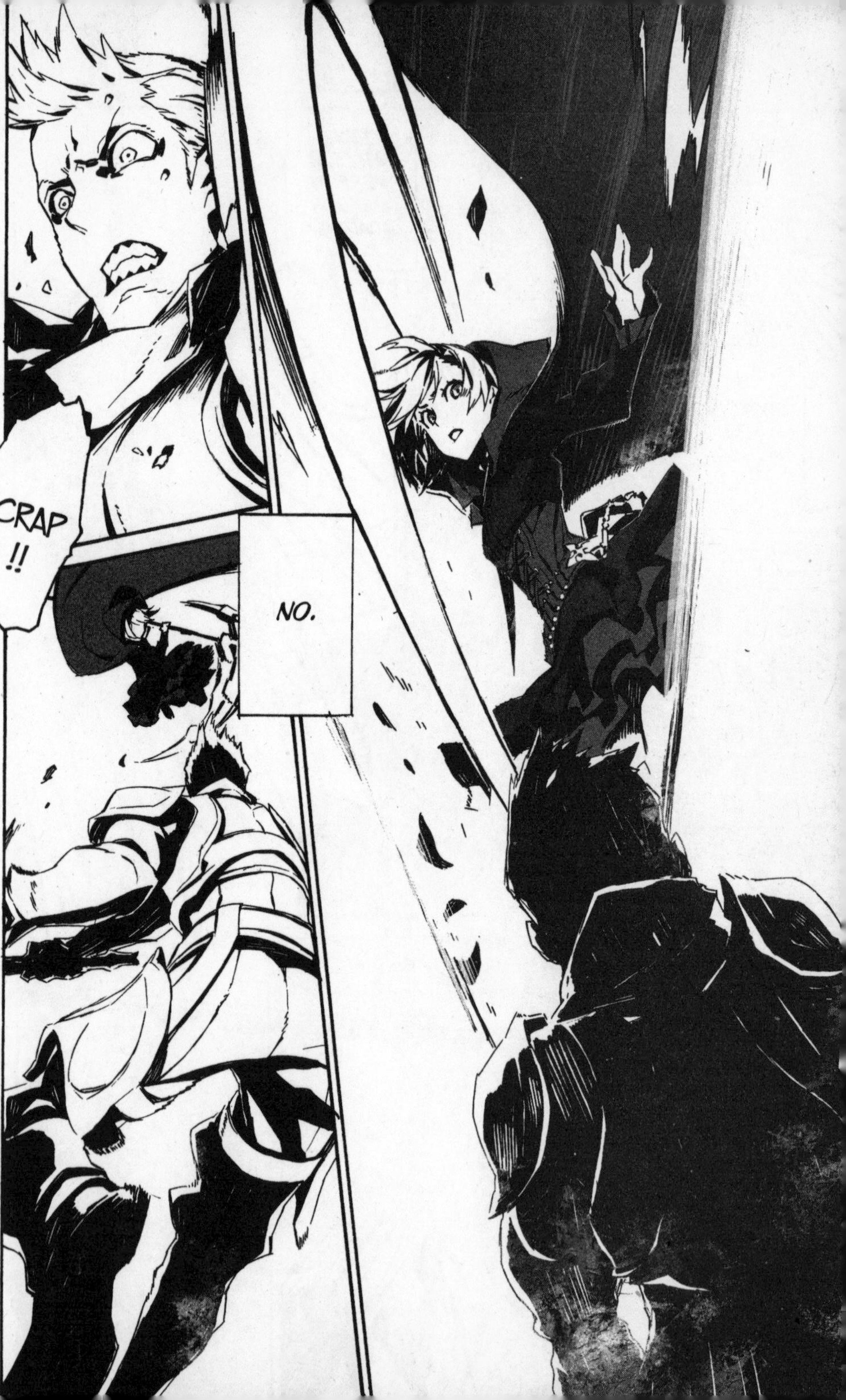
NO.
CRAP !!

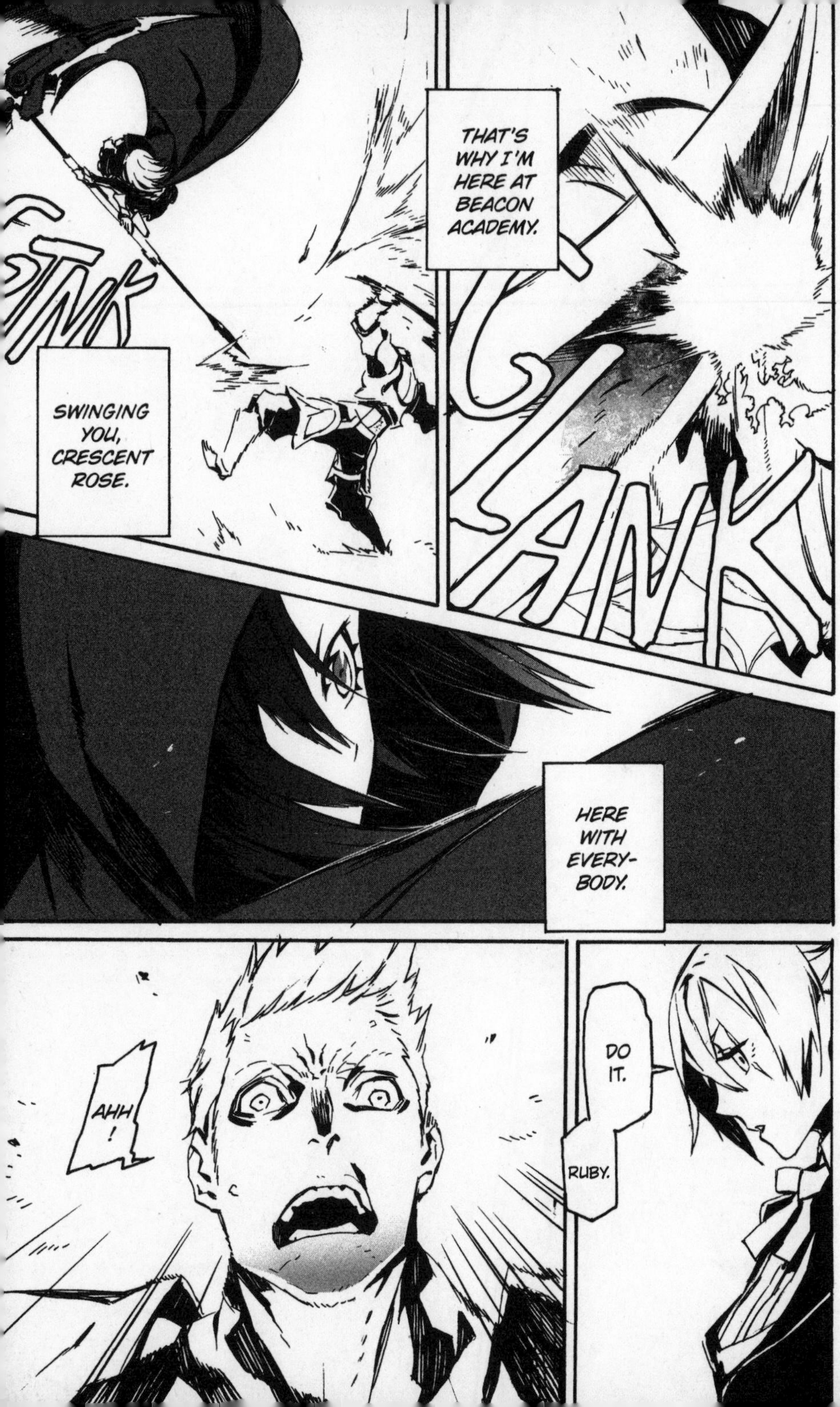
THAT'S WHY I'M HERE AT BEACON ACADEMY.
CLANK
SWINGING YOU, CRESCENT ROSE.
HERE WITH EVERY-BODY.
DO IT.
RUBY.
AHH!

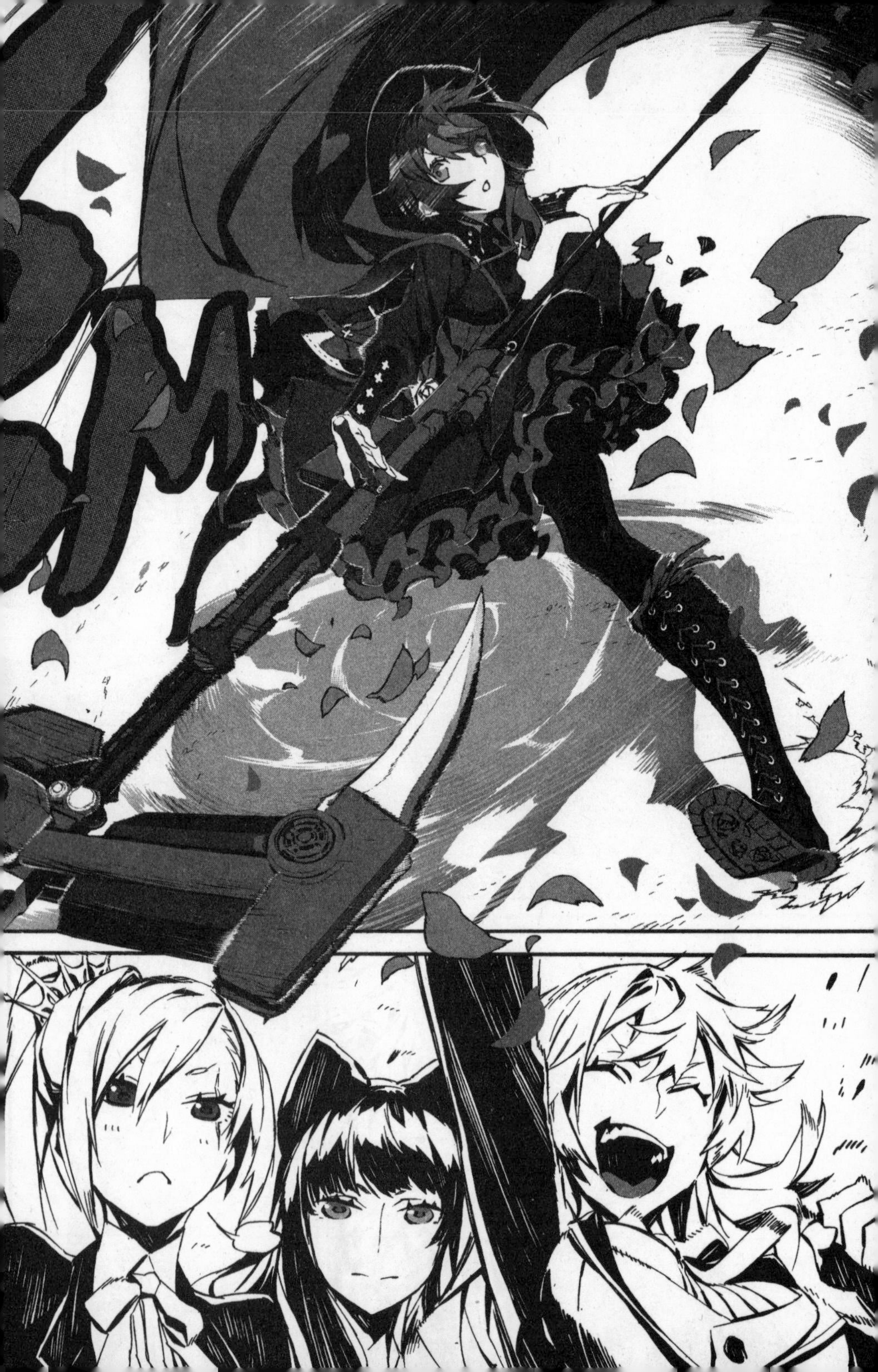

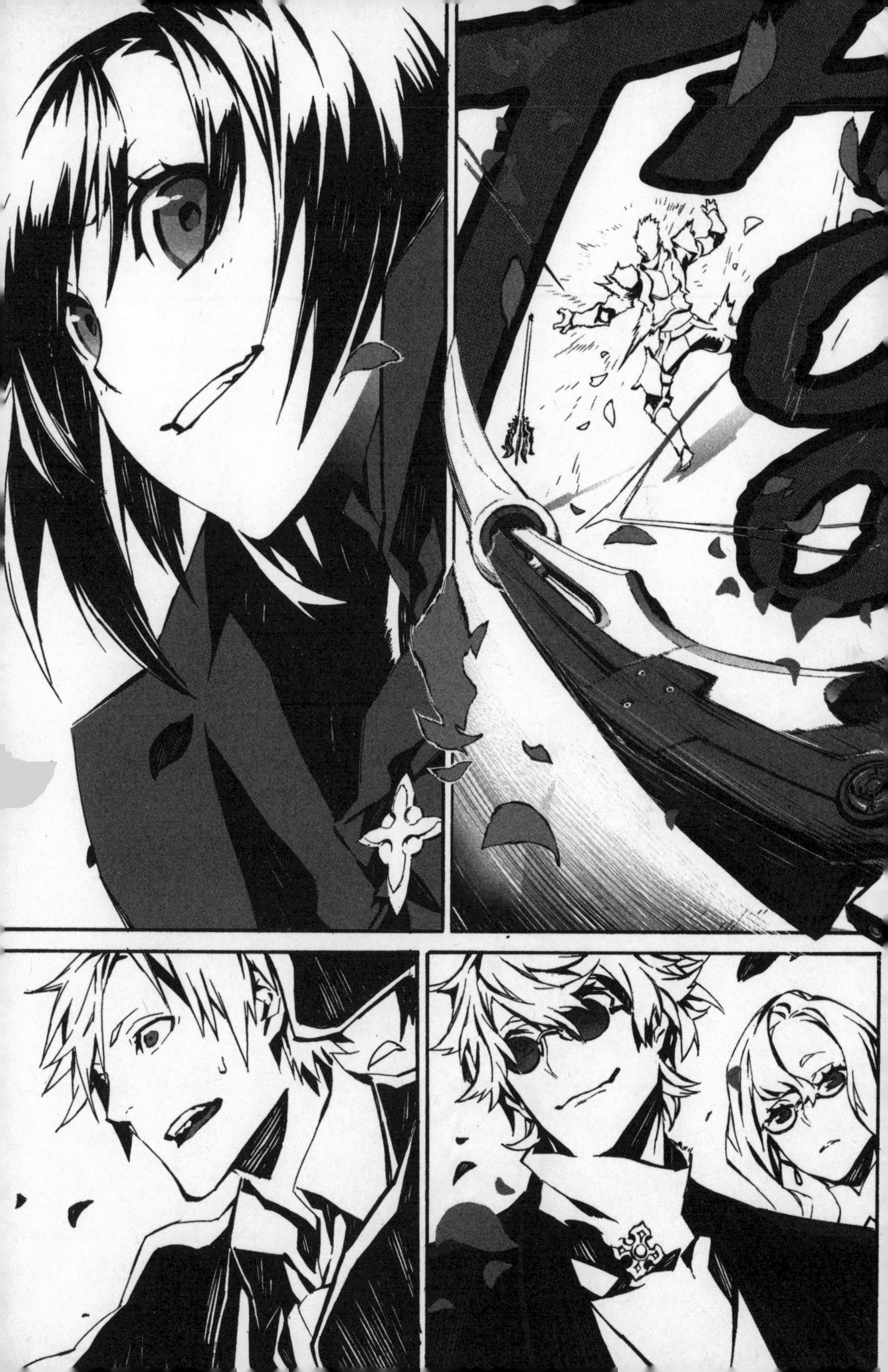

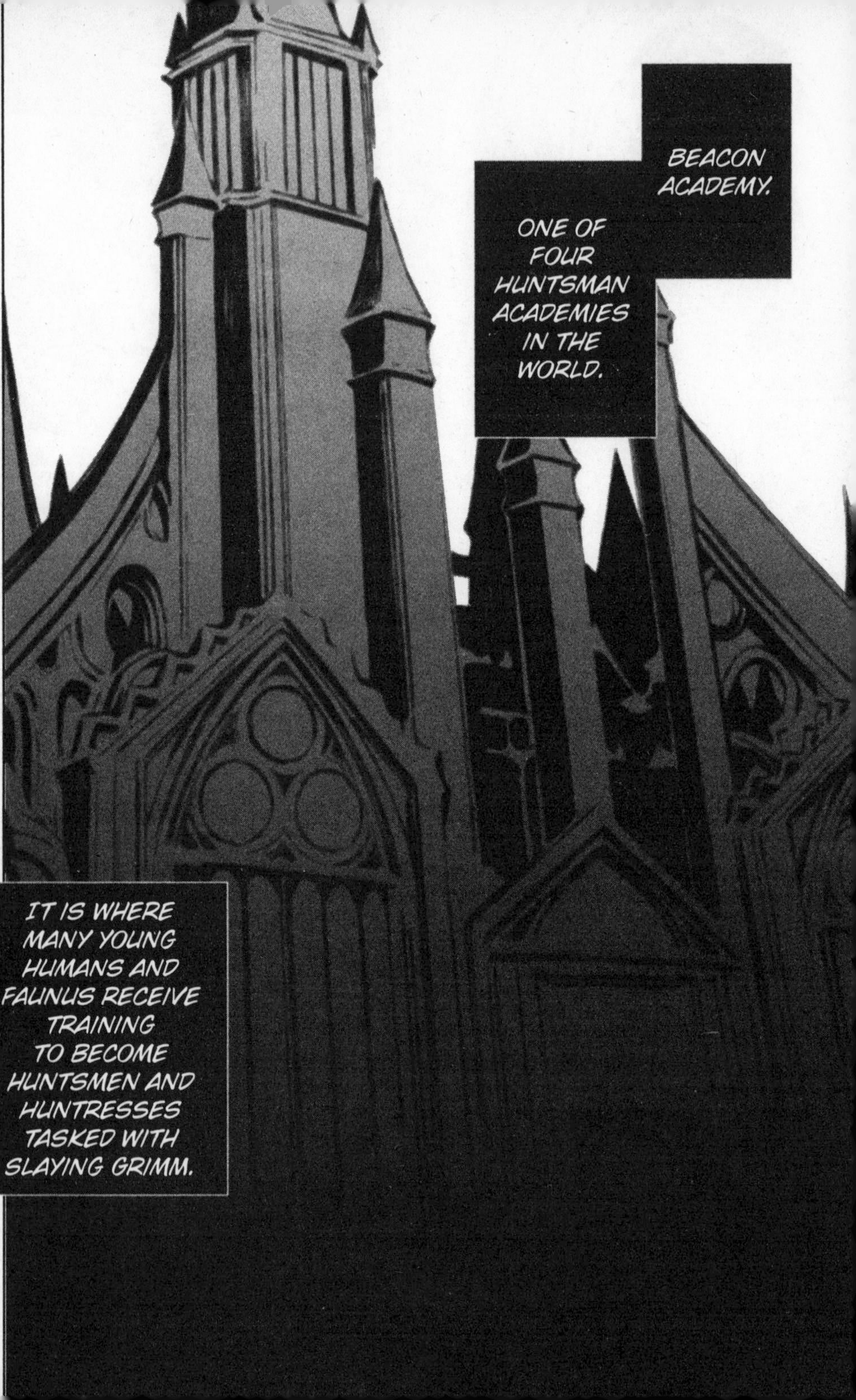
BEACON ACADEMY.
ONE OF FOUR HUNTSMAN ACADEMIES IN THE WORLD.
IT IS WHERE MANY YOUNG HUMANS AND FAUNUS RECEIVE TRAINING TO BECOME HUNTSMEN AND HUNTRESSES TASKED WITH SLAYING GRIMM.

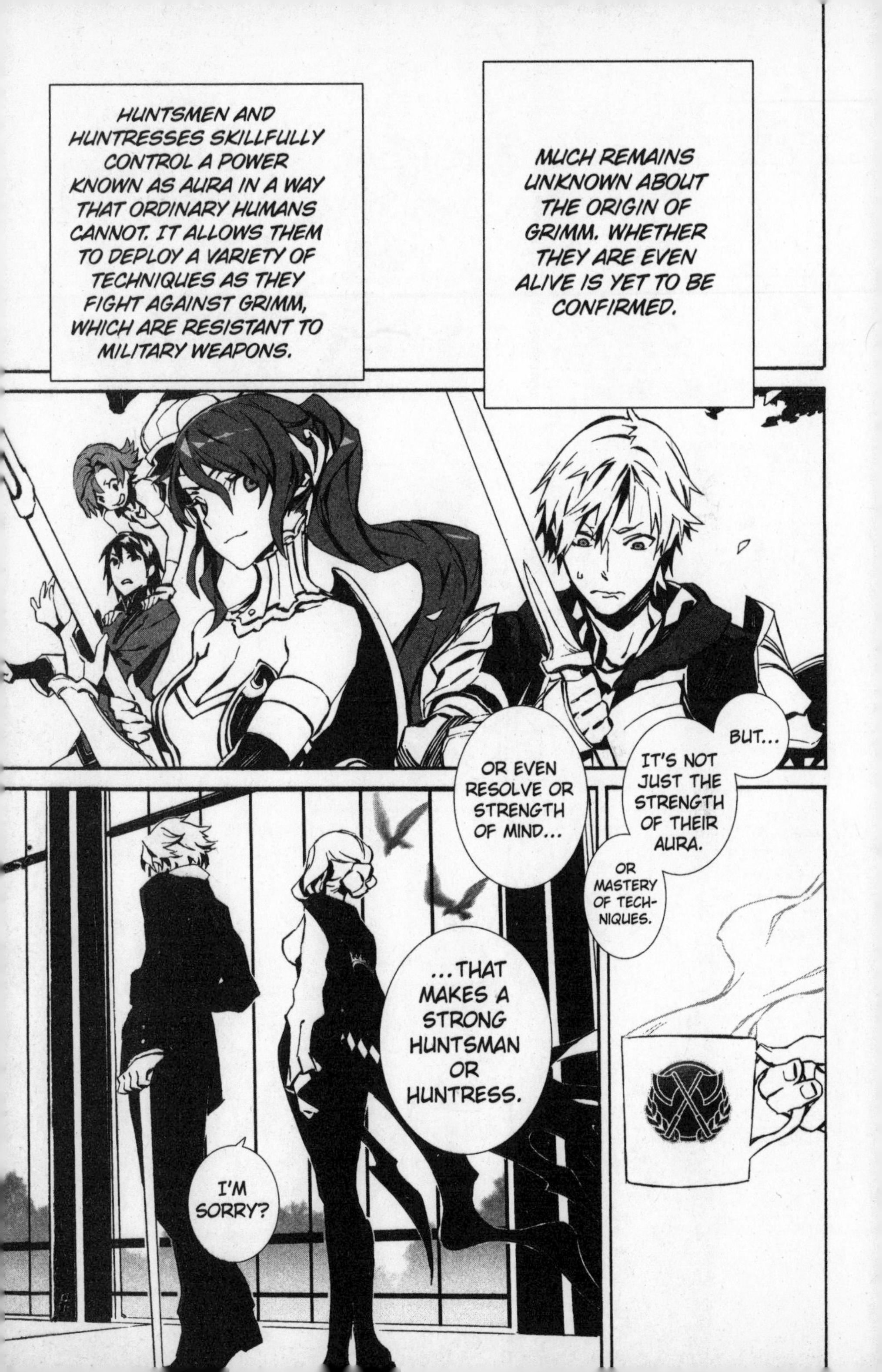
MUCH REMAINS UNKNOWN ABOUT THE ORIGIN OF GRIMM. WHETHER THEY ARE EVEN ALIVE IS YET TO BE CONFIRMED.
HUNTSMEN AND HUNTRESSES SKILLFULLY CONTROL A POWER KNOWN AS AURA IN A WAY THAT ORDINARY HUMANS CANNOT. IT ALLOWS THEM TO DEPLOY A VARIETY OF TECHNIQUES AS THEY FIGHT AGAINST GRIMM, WHICH ARE RESISTANT TO MILITARY WEAPONS.
BUT...
IT'S NOT JUST THE STRENGTH OF THEIR AURA.
OR MASTERY OF TECH-NIQUES.
OR EVEN RESOLVE OR STRENGTH OF MIND...
...THAT MAKES A STRONG HUNTSMAN OR HUNTRESS.
I'M SORRY?

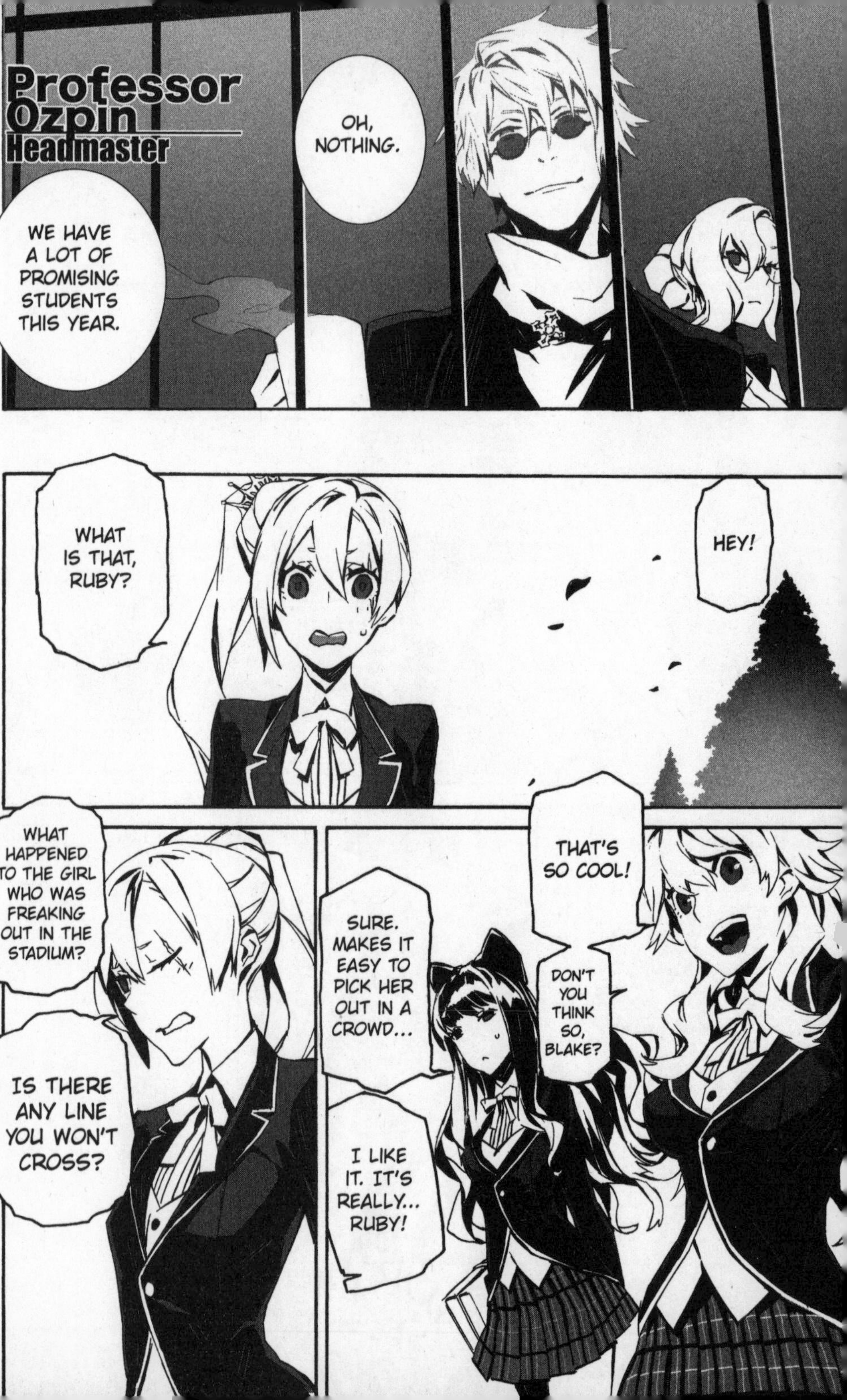
OH, NOTHING.
Professor Ozpin
Headmaster
WE HAVE A LOT OF PROMISING STUDENTS THIS YEAR.
HEY!
WHAT IS THAT, RUBY?
THAT'S SO COOL!
DON'T YOU THINK SO, BLAKE?
SURE. MAKES IT EASY TO PICK HER OUT IN A CROWD...
I LIKE IT. IT'S REALLY... RUBY!
WHAT HAPPENED TO THE GIRL WHO WAS FREAKING OUT IN THE STADIUM?
IS THERE ANY LINE YOU WON'T CROSS?

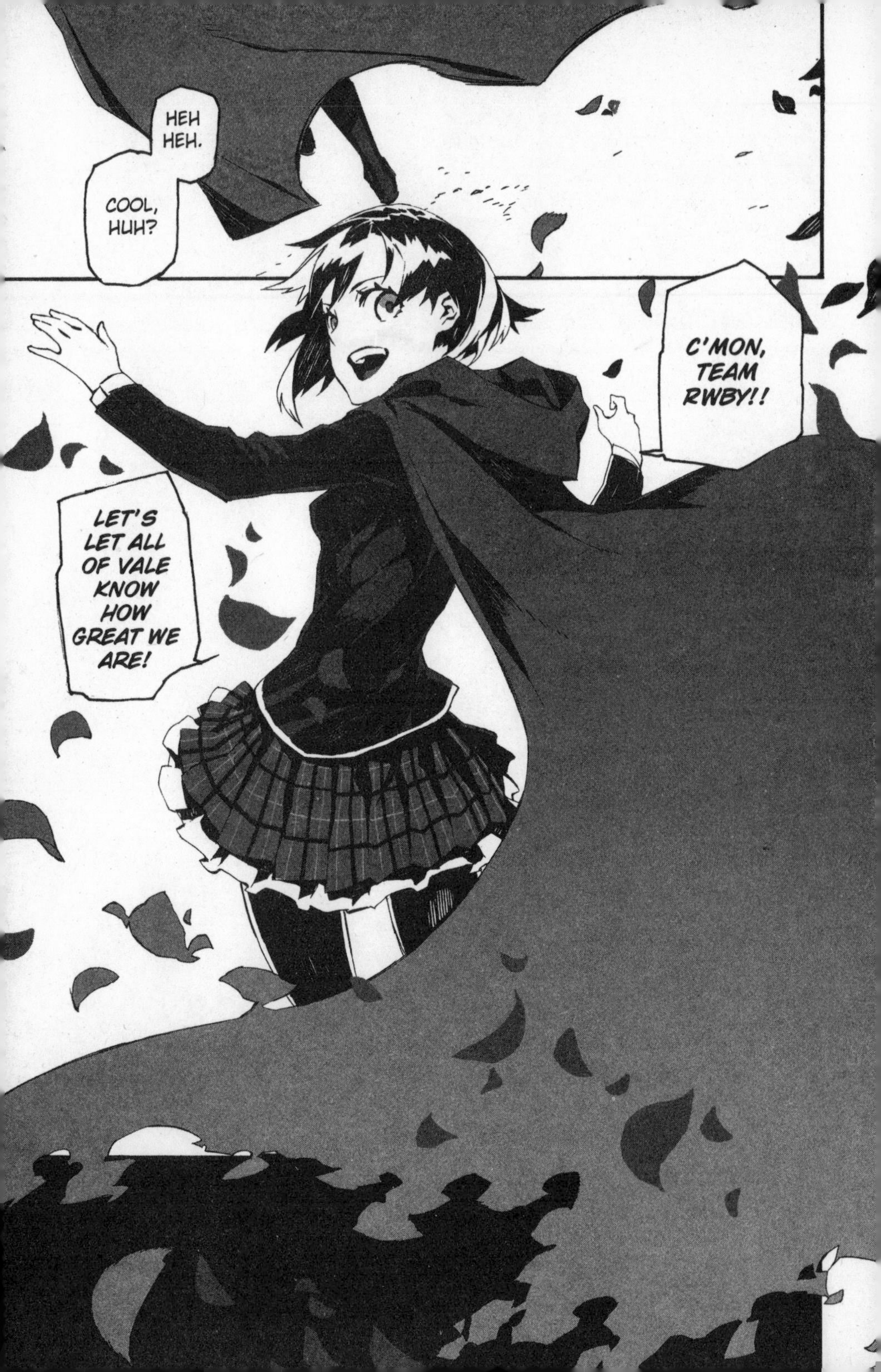
HEH HEH.
COOL, HUH?
C'MON, TEAM RWBY!!
LET'S LET ALL OF VALE KNOW HOW GREAT WE ARE!

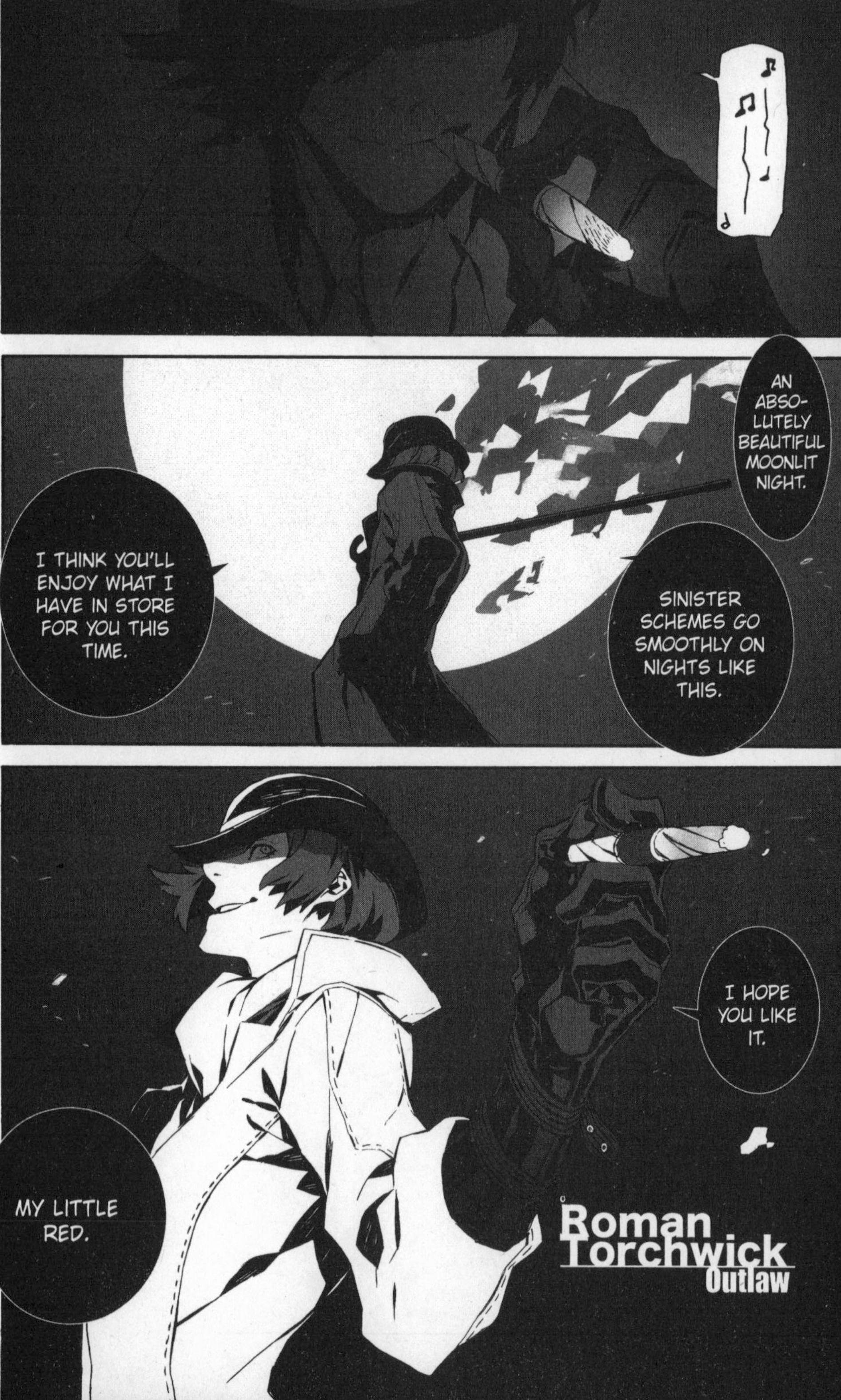
♫~♫~♪
AN ABSO-LUTELY BEAUTIFUL MOONLIT NIGHT.
SINISTER SCHEMES GO SMOOTHLY ON NIGHTS LIKE THIS.
I THINK YOU'LL ENJOY WHAT I HAVE IN STORE FOR YOU THIS TIME.
I HOPE YOU LIKE IT.
MY LITTLE RED.
Roman Torchwick
Outlaw

Ruby Rose

R

RWBY

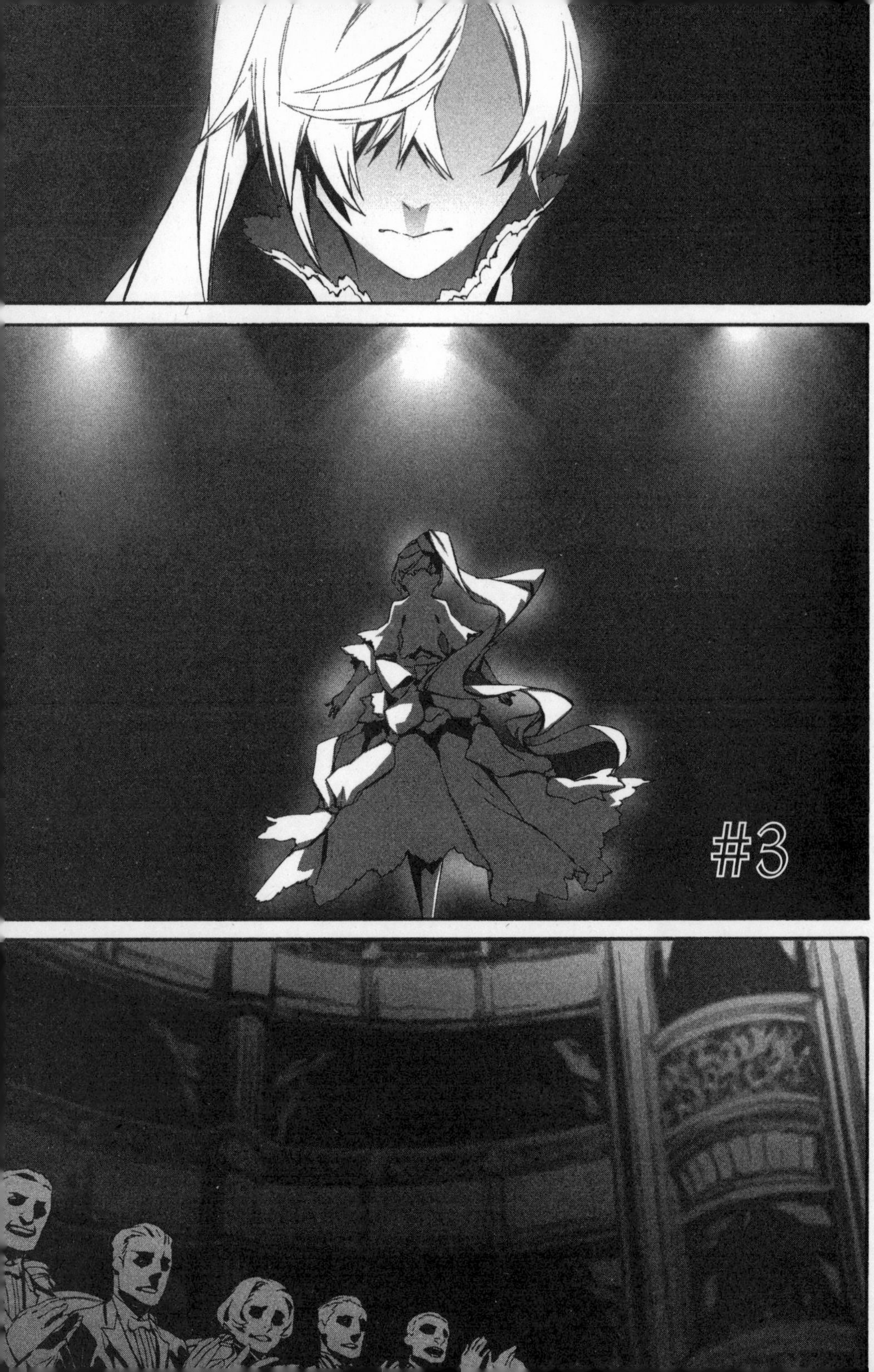
#3

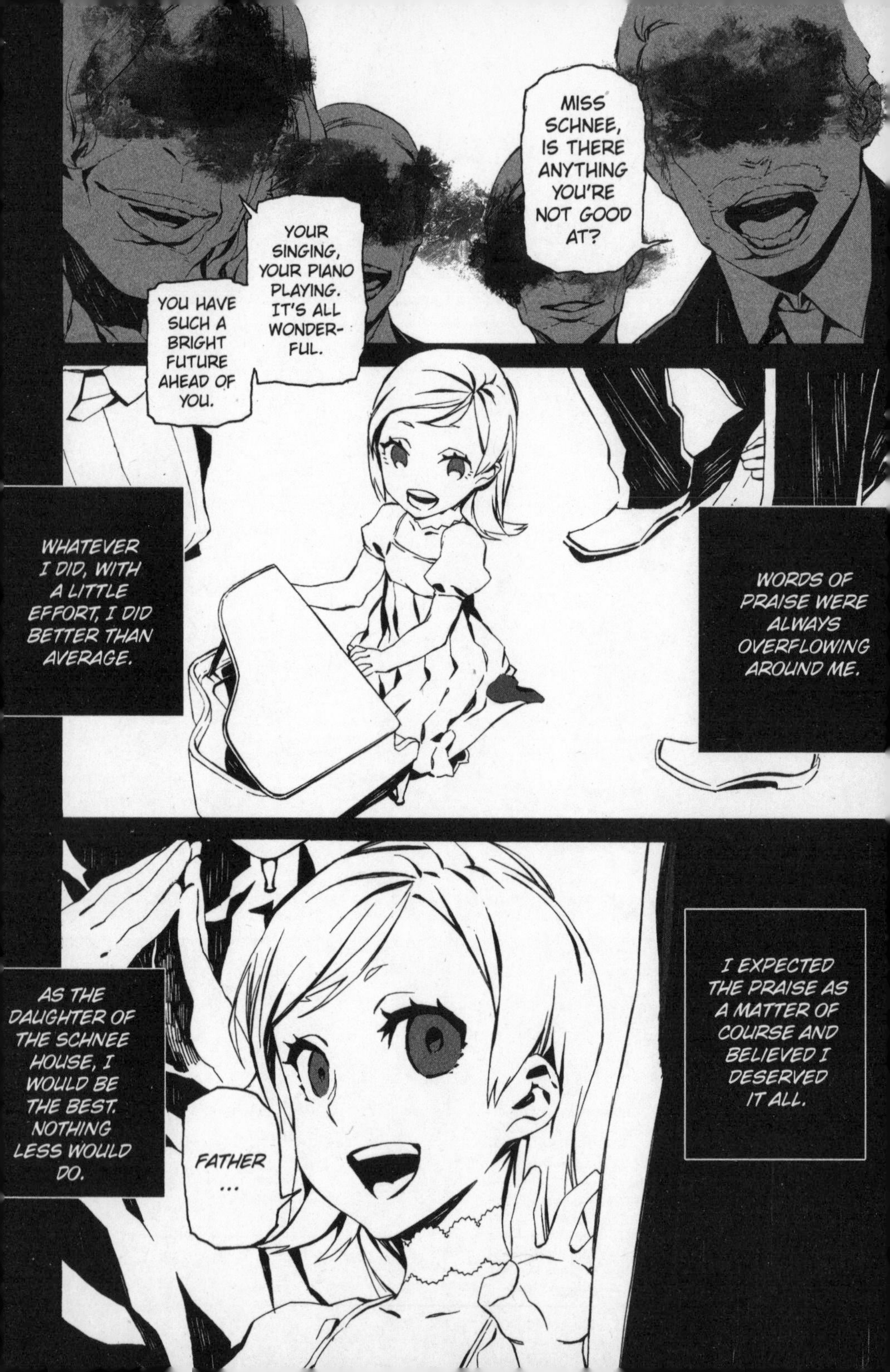
MISS SCHNEE, IS THERE ANYTHING YOU'RE NOT GOOD AT?
YOUR SINGING, YOUR PIANO PLAYING. IT'S ALL WONDERFUL.
YOU HAVE SUCH A BRIGHT FUTURE AHEAD OF YOU.
WORDS OF PRAISE WERE ALWAYS OVERFLOWING AROUND ME.
WHATEVER I DID, WITH A LITTLE EFFORT, I DID BETTER THAN AVERAGE.
I EXPECTED THE PRAISE AS A MATTER OF COURSE AND BELIEVED I DESERVED IT ALL.
AS THE DAUGHTER OF THE SCHNEE HOUSE, I WOULD BE THE BEST. NOTHING LESS WOULD DO.
FATHER ...

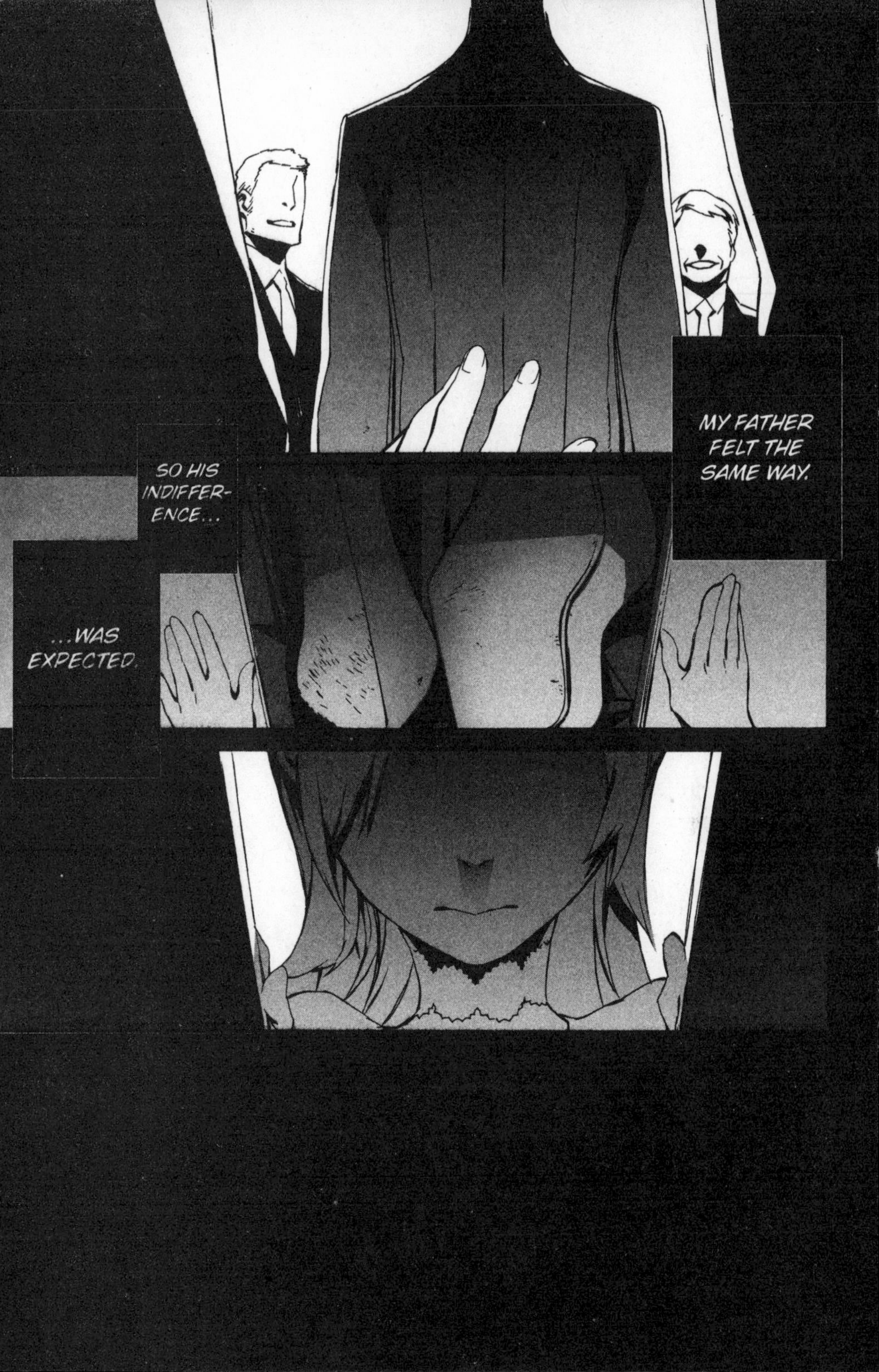
MY FATHER FELT THE SAME WAY.
SO HIS INDIFFERENCE...
...WAS EXPECTED.

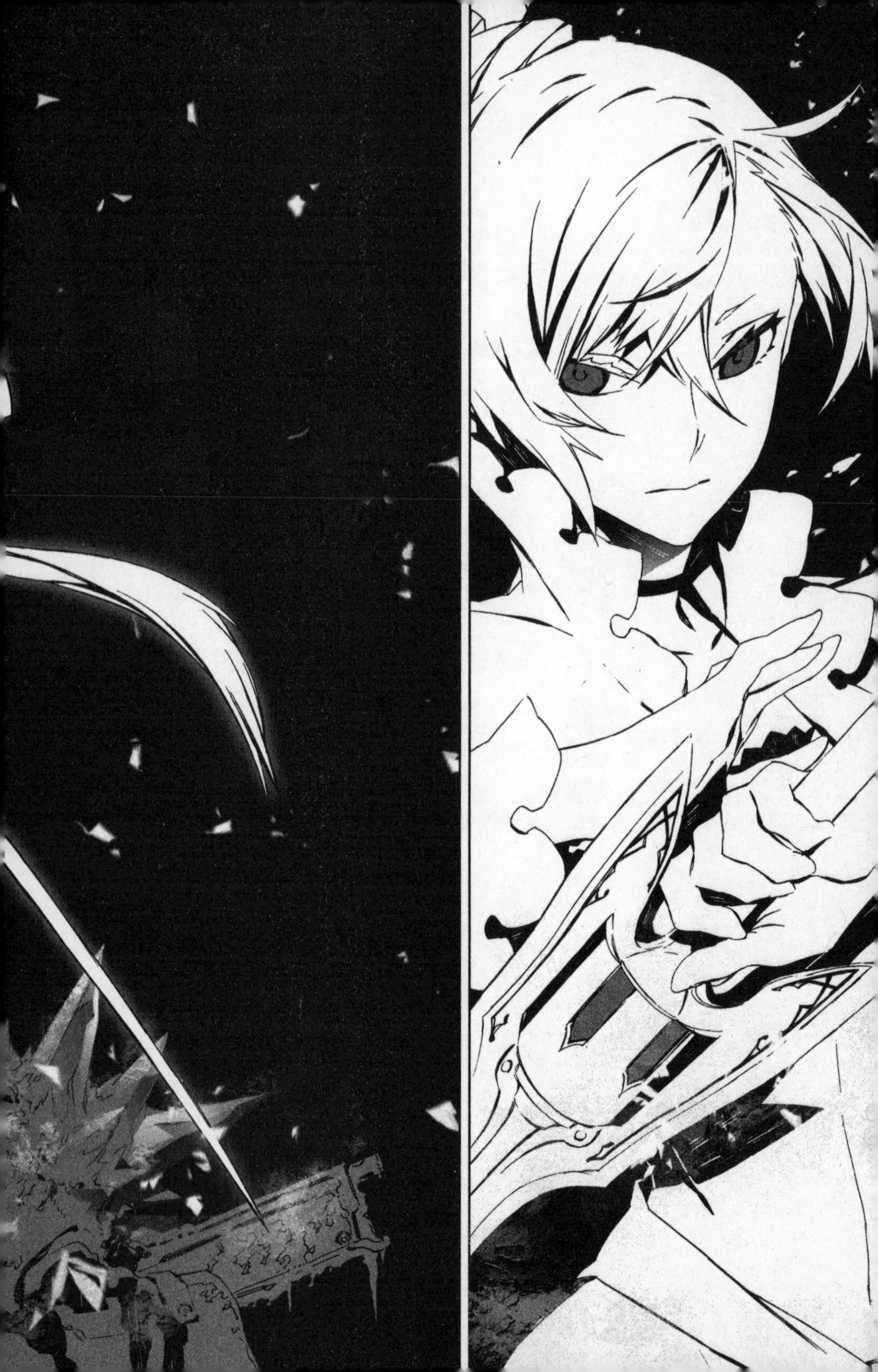

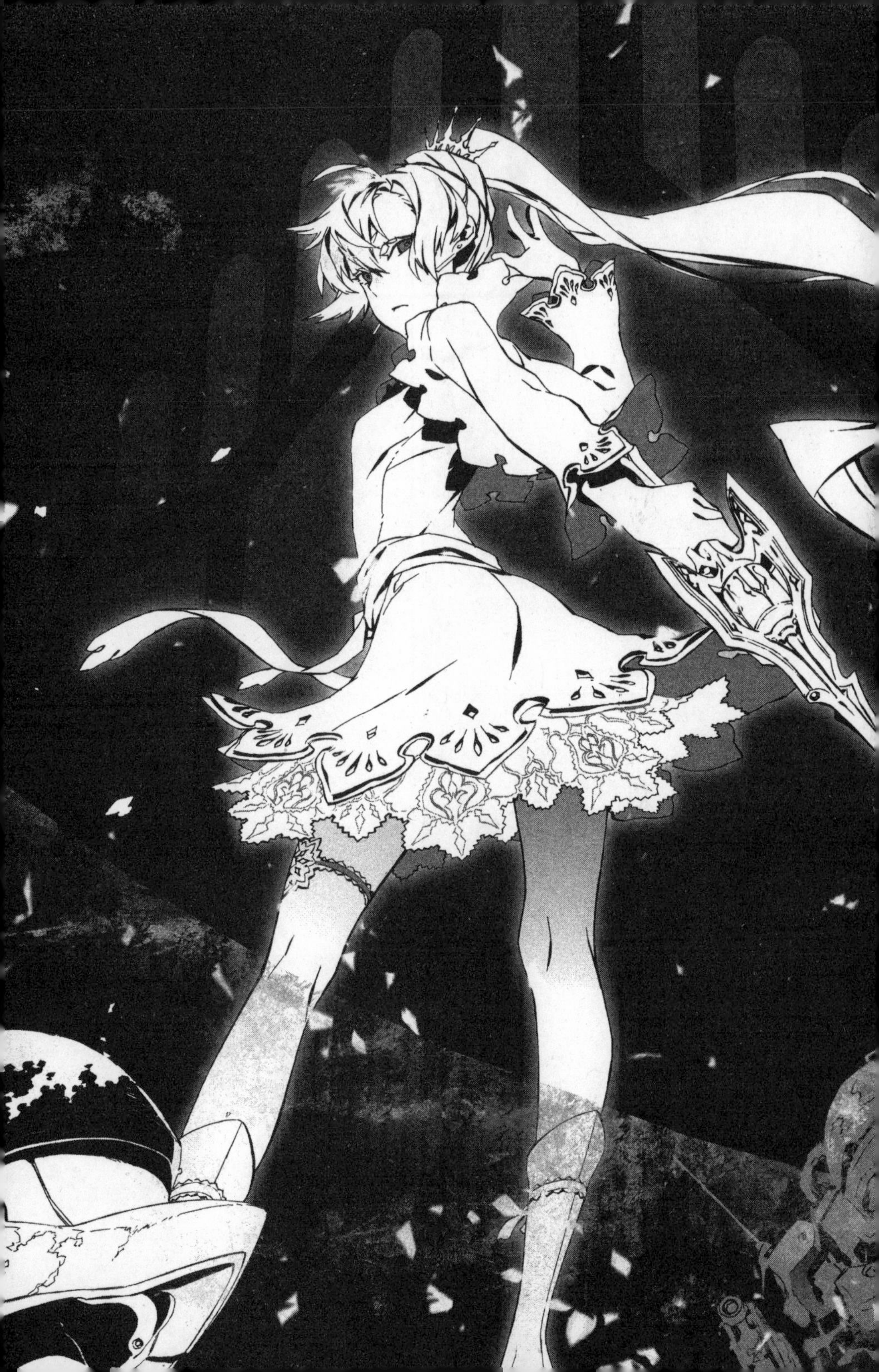

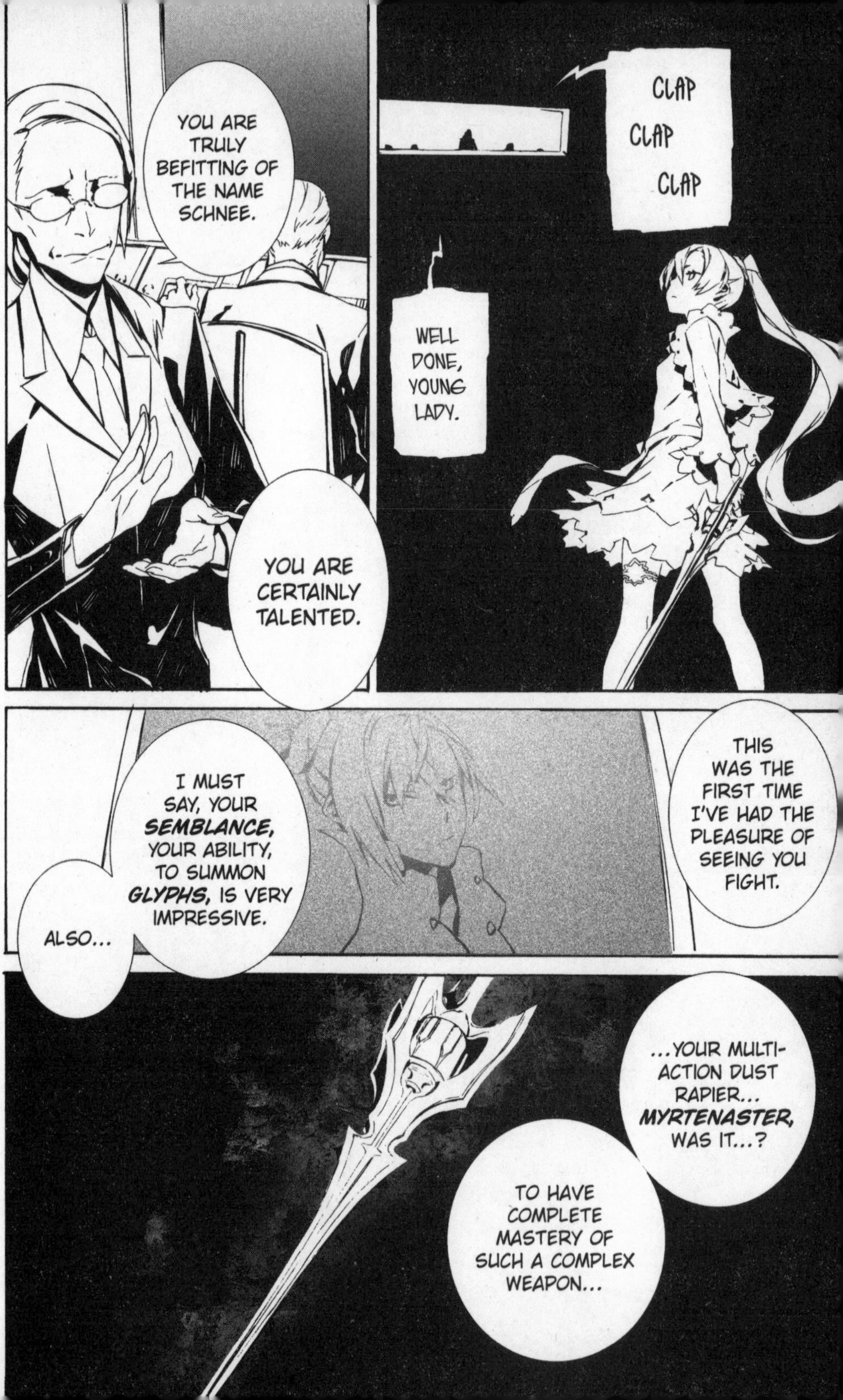
CLAP CLAP CLAP
WELL DONE, YOUNG LADY.
YOU ARE TRULY BEFITTING OF THE NAME SCHNEE.
YOU ARE CERTAINLY TALENTED.
THIS WAS THE FIRST TIME I'VE HAD THE PLEASURE OF SEEING YOU FIGHT.
I MUST SAY, YOUR **SEMBLANCE,** YOUR ABILITY, TO SUMMON **GLYPHS,** IS VERY IMPRESSIVE.
ALSO...
...YOUR MULTI-ACTION DUST RAPIER... ***MYRTENASTER,*** WAS IT...?
TO HAVE COMPLETE MASTERY OF SUCH A COMPLEX WEAPON...

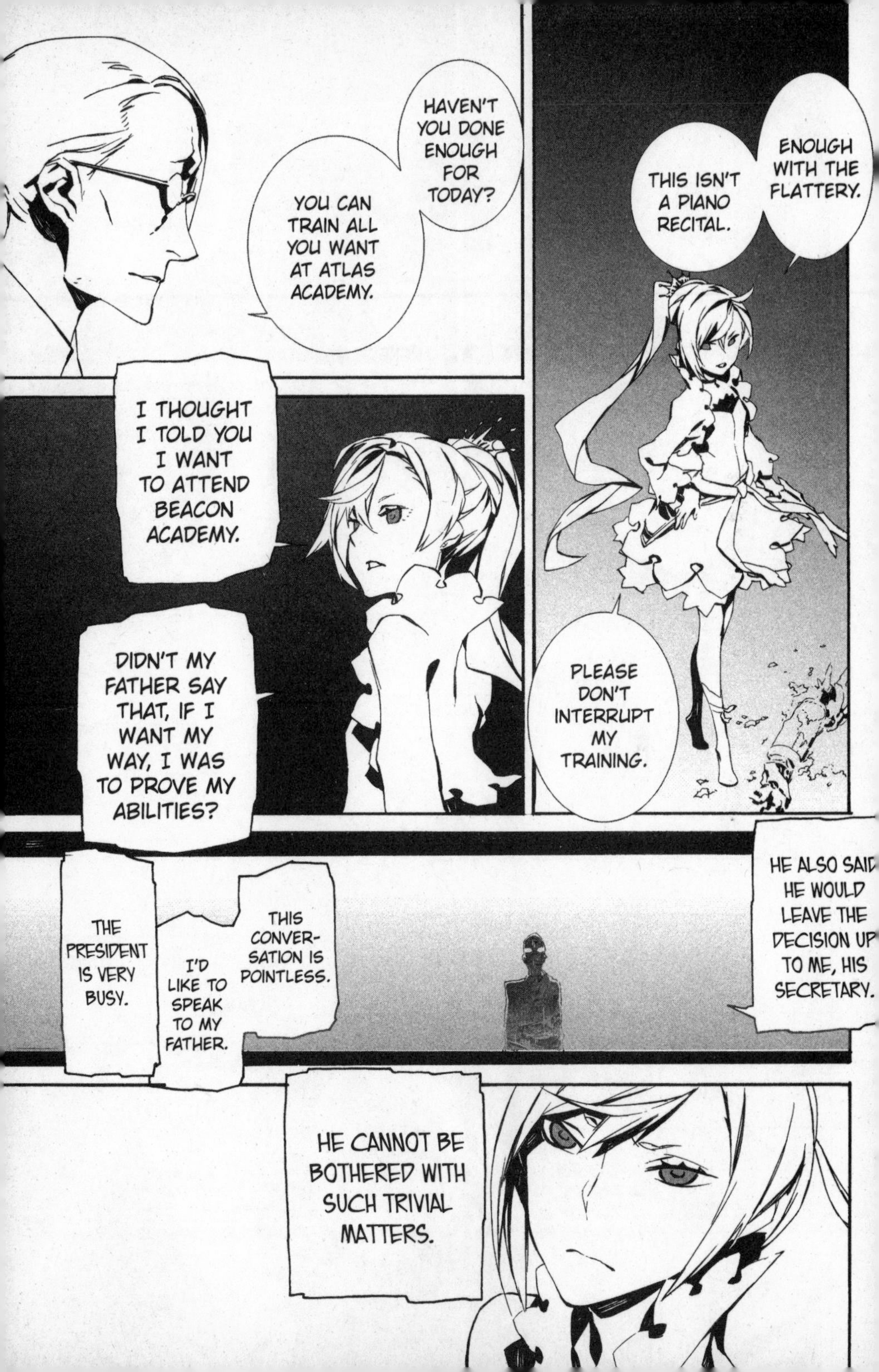
ENOUGH WITH THE FLATTERY.
THIS ISN'T A PIANO RECITAL.
PLEASE DON'T INTERRUPT MY TRAINING.
HAVEN'T YOU DONE ENOUGH FOR TODAY?
YOU CAN TRAIN ALL YOU WANT AT ATLAS ACADEMY.
I THOUGHT I TOLD YOU I WANT TO ATTEND BEACON ACADEMY.
DIDN'T MY FATHER SAY THAT, IF I WANT MY WAY, I WAS TO PROVE MY ABILITIES?
HE ALSO SAID HE WOULD LEAVE THE DECISION UP TO ME, HIS SECRETARY.
THIS CONVERSATION IS POINTLESS.
I'D LIKE TO SPEAK TO MY FATHER.
THE PRESIDENT IS VERY BUSY.
HE CANNOT BE BOTHERED WITH SUCH TRIVIAL MATTERS.

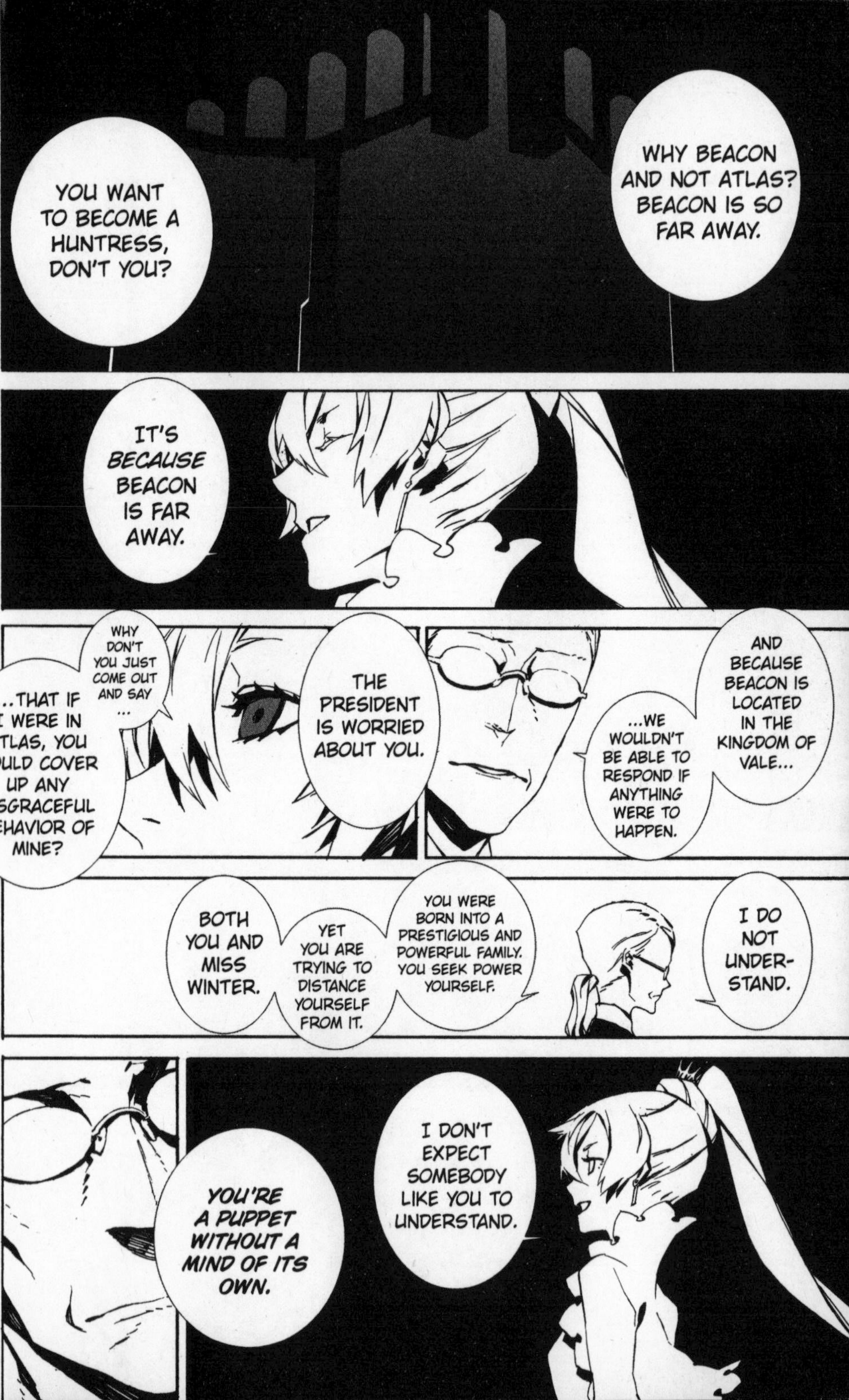
WHY BEACON AND NOT ATLAS? BEACON IS SO FAR AWAY.
YOU WANT TO BECOME A HUNTRESS, DON'T YOU?
IT'S *BECAUSE* BEACON IS FAR AWAY.
AND BECAUSE BEACON IS LOCATED IN THE KINGDOM OF VALE...
...WE WOULDN'T BE ABLE TO RESPOND IF ANYTHING WERE TO HAPPEN.
THE PRESIDENT IS WORRIED ABOUT YOU.
WHY DON'T YOU JUST COME OUT AND SAY ...
...THAT IF I WERE IN ATLAS, YOU COULD COVER UP ANY DISGRACEFUL BEHAVIOR OF MINE?
I DO NOT UNDERSTAND.
YOU WERE BORN INTO A PRESTIGIOUS AND POWERFUL FAMILY. YOU SEEK POWER YOURSELF.
YET YOU ARE TRYING TO DISTANCE YOURSELF FROM IT.
BOTH YOU AND MISS WINTER.
I DON'T EXPECT SOMEBODY LIKE YOU TO UNDERSTAND.
YOU'RE A PUPPET WITHOUT A MIND OF ITS OWN.

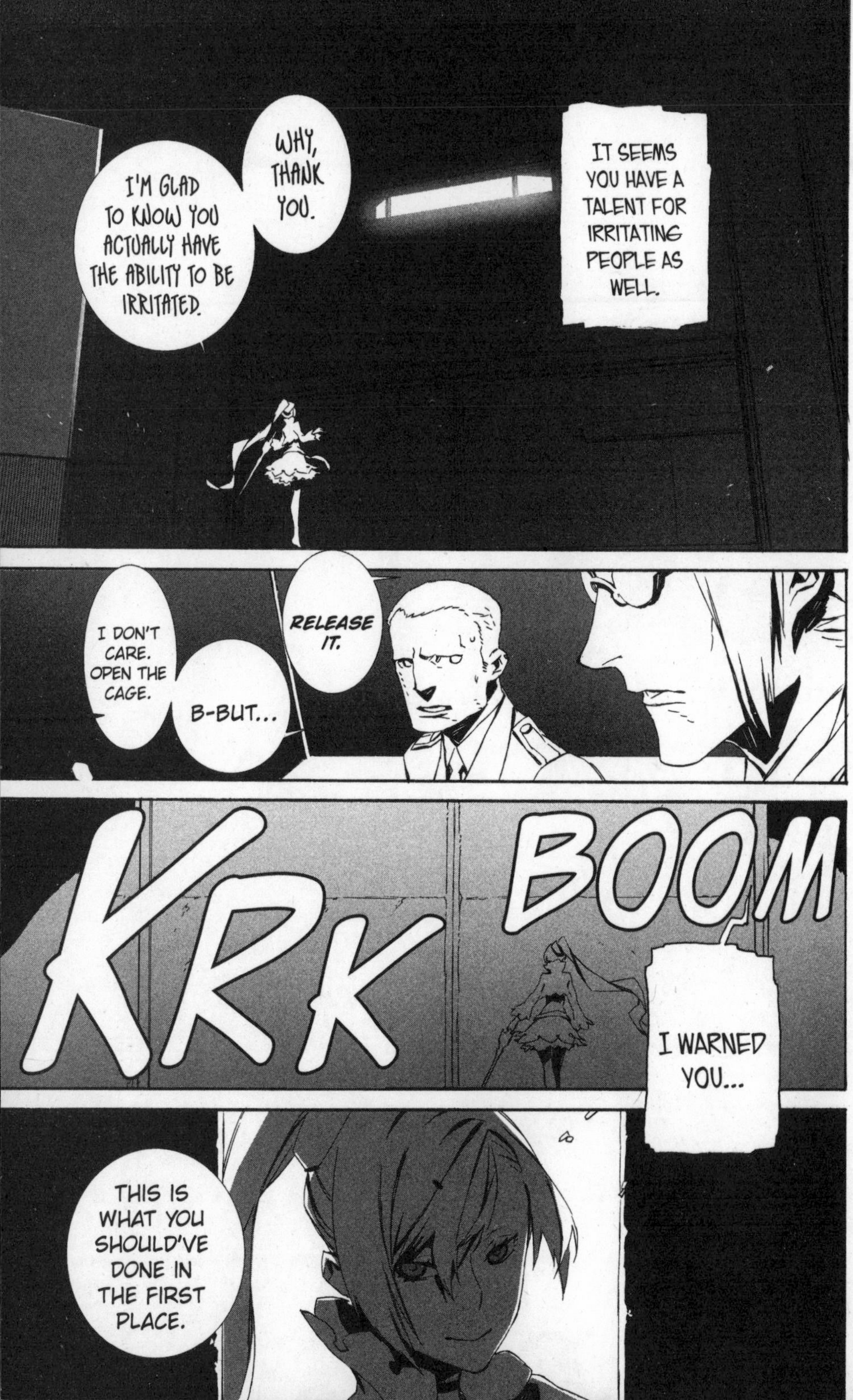
IT SEEMS YOU HAVE A TALENT FOR IRRITATING PEOPLE AS WELL.
WHY, THANK YOU.
I'M GLAD TO KNOW YOU ACTUALLY HAVE THE ABILITY TO BE IRRITATED.
RELEASE IT.
B-BUT...
I DON'T CARE. OPEN THE CAGE.
BOOM
KRK
I WARNED YOU...
THIS IS WHAT YOU SHOULD'VE DONE IN THE FIRST PLACE.

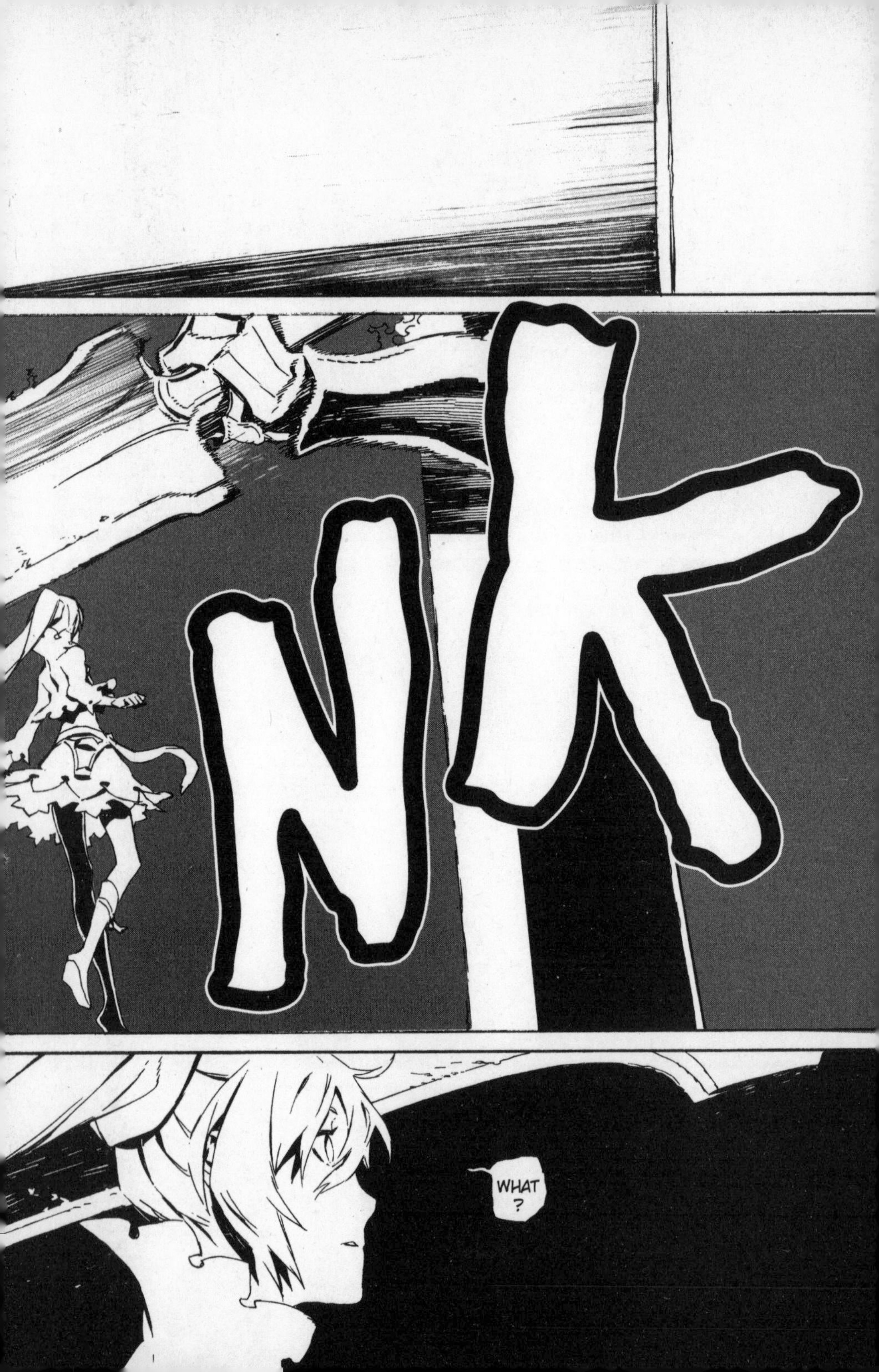
NK
WHAT
?

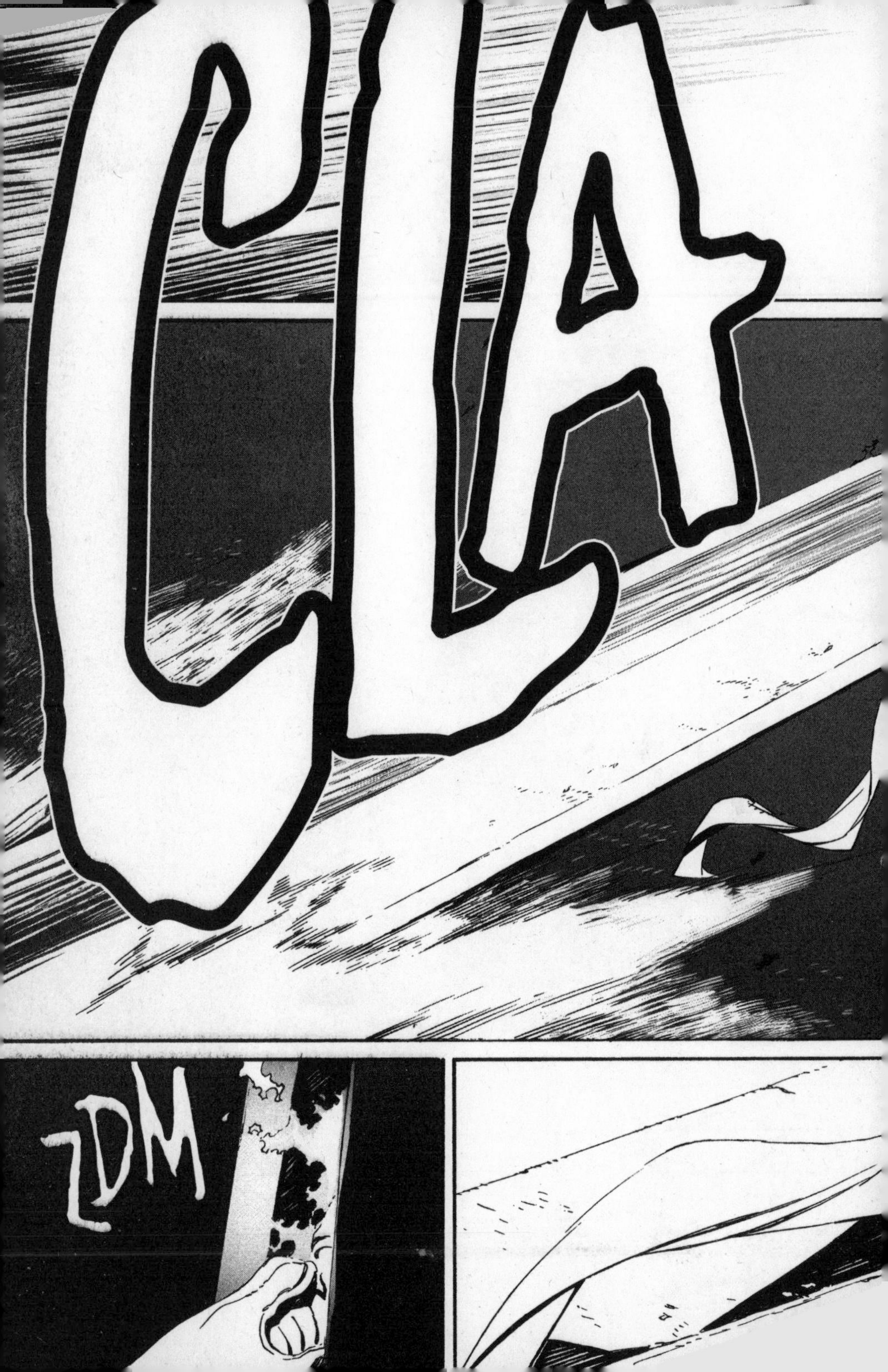
CLA
ZDM

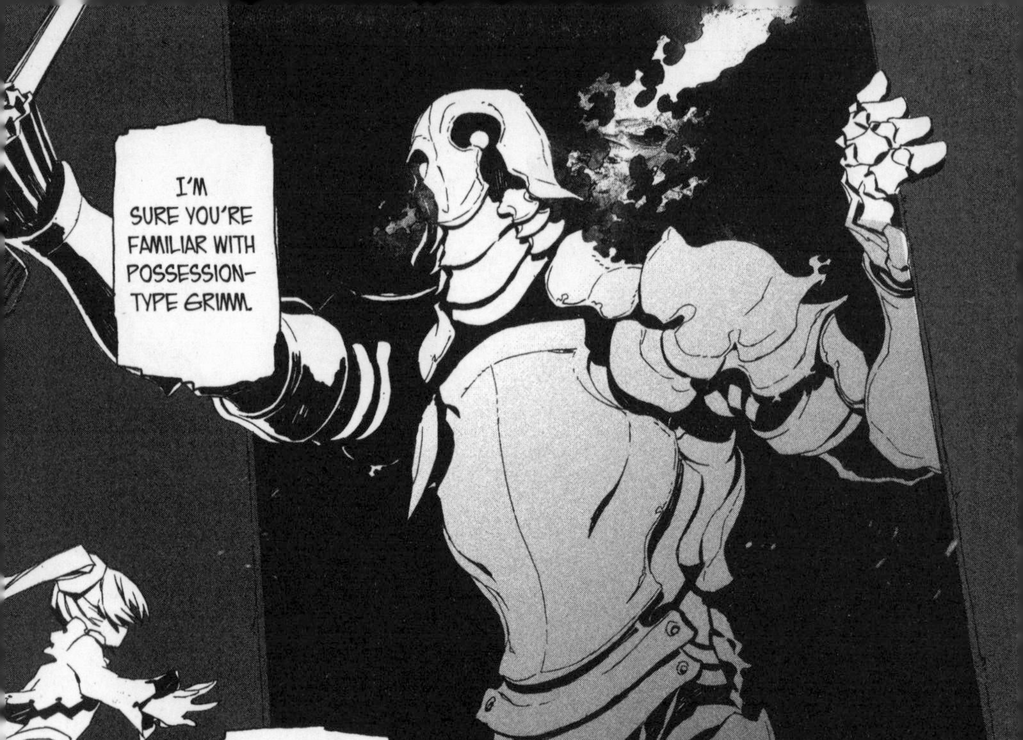
I'M SURE YOU'RE FAMILIAR WITH POSSESSION-TYPE GRIMM.
THEY ARE HUMANITY'S NEMESIS, DEPRAVED MONSTERS.

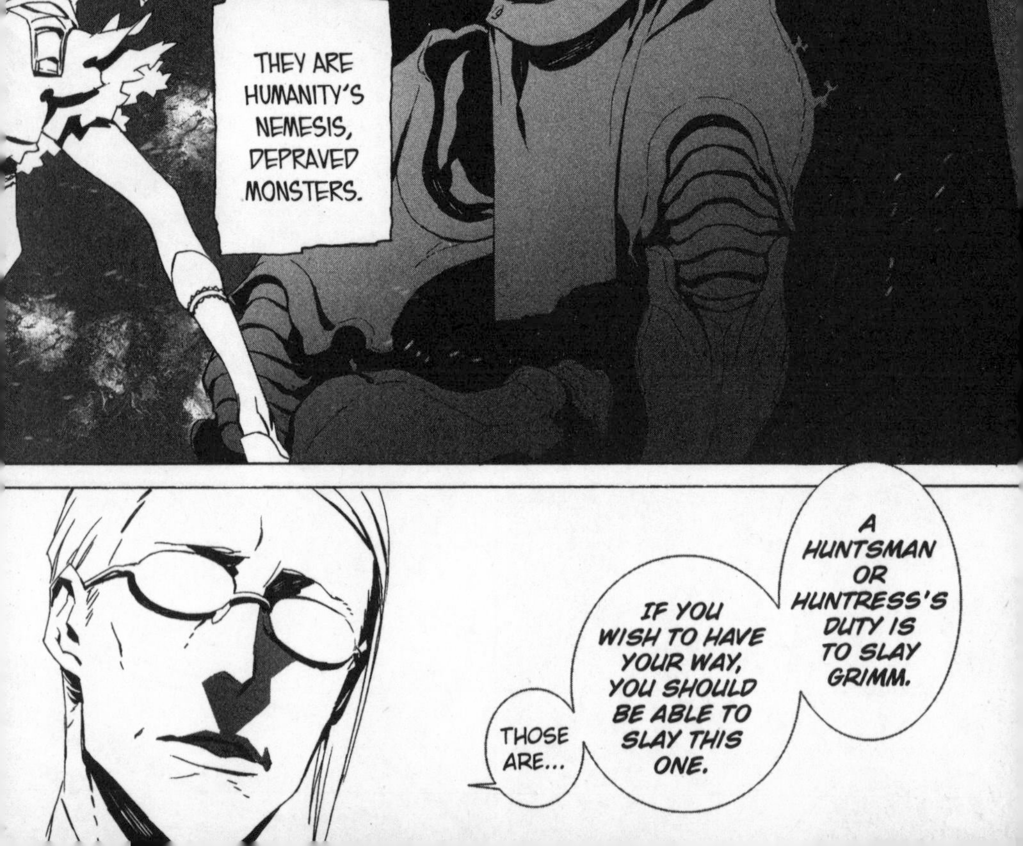
A HUNTSMAN OR HUNTRESS'S DUTY IS TO SLAY GRIMM.
IF YOU WISH TO HAVE YOUR WAY, YOU SHOULD BE ABLE TO SLAY THIS ONE.
THOSE ARE...

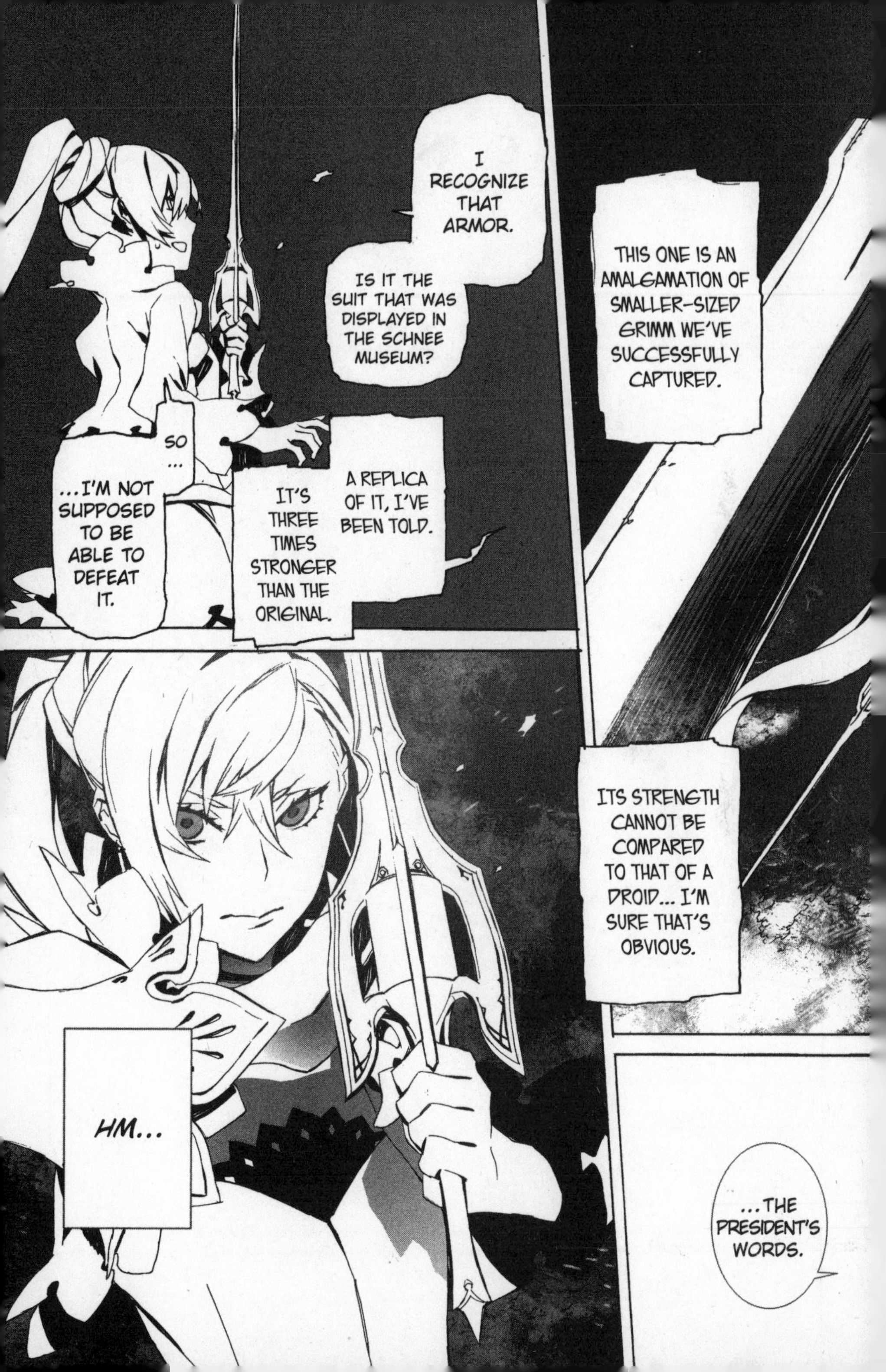
THIS ONE IS AN AMALGAMATION OF SMALLER-SIZED GRIMM WE'VE SUCCESSFULLY CAPTURED.
ITS STRENGTH CANNOT BE COMPARED TO THAT OF A DROID... I'M SURE THAT'S OBVIOUS.
I RECOGNIZE THAT ARMOR.
IS IT THE SUIT THAT WAS DISPLAYED IN THE SCHNEE MUSEUM?
A REPLICA OF IT, I'VE BEEN TOLD.
IT'S THREE TIMES STRONGER THAN THE ORIGINAL.
SO...
...I'M NOT SUPPOSED TO BE ABLE TO DEFEAT IT.
...THE PRESIDENT'S WORDS.
HM...

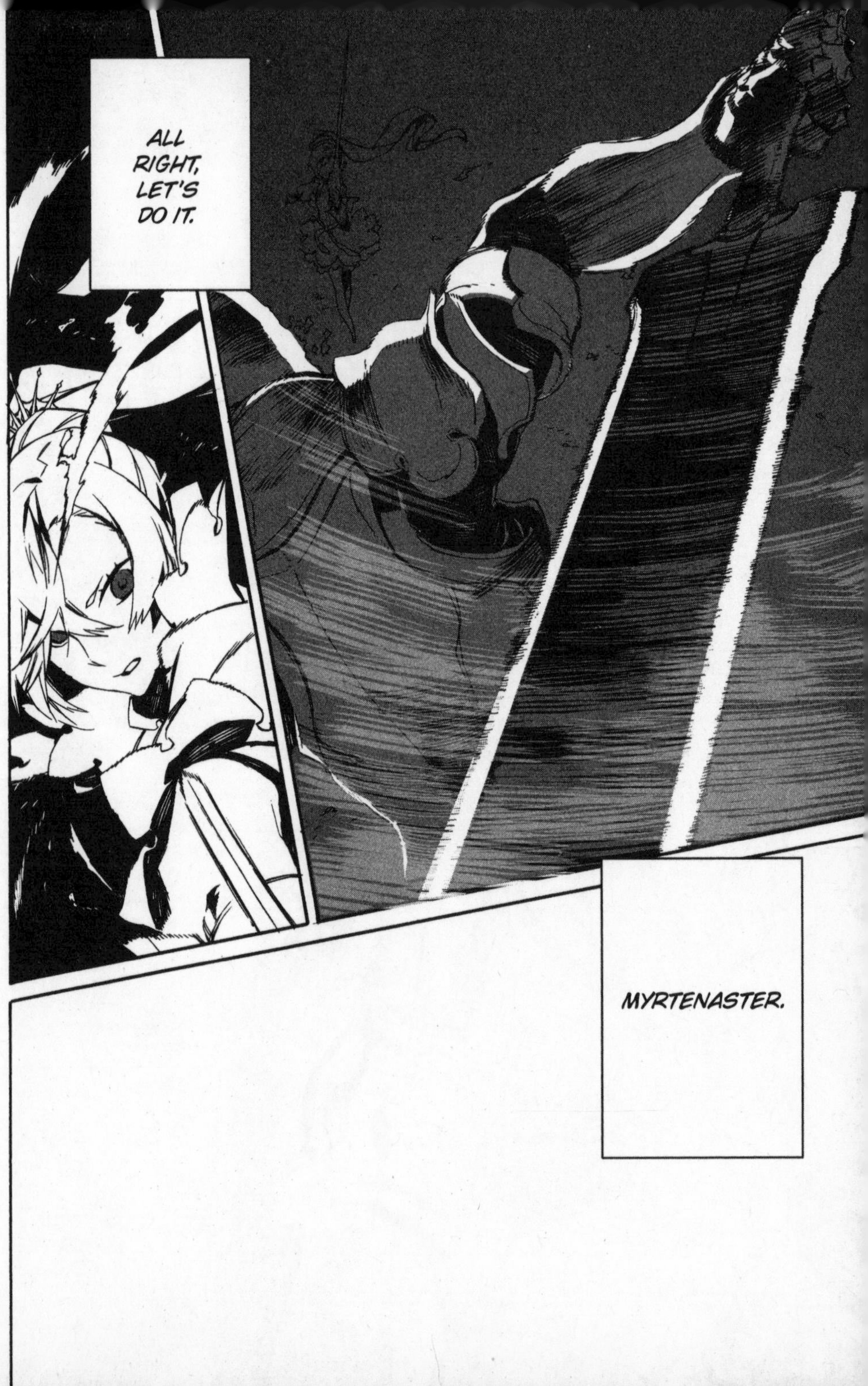
ALL RIGHT, LET'S DO IT.
MYRTENASTER.

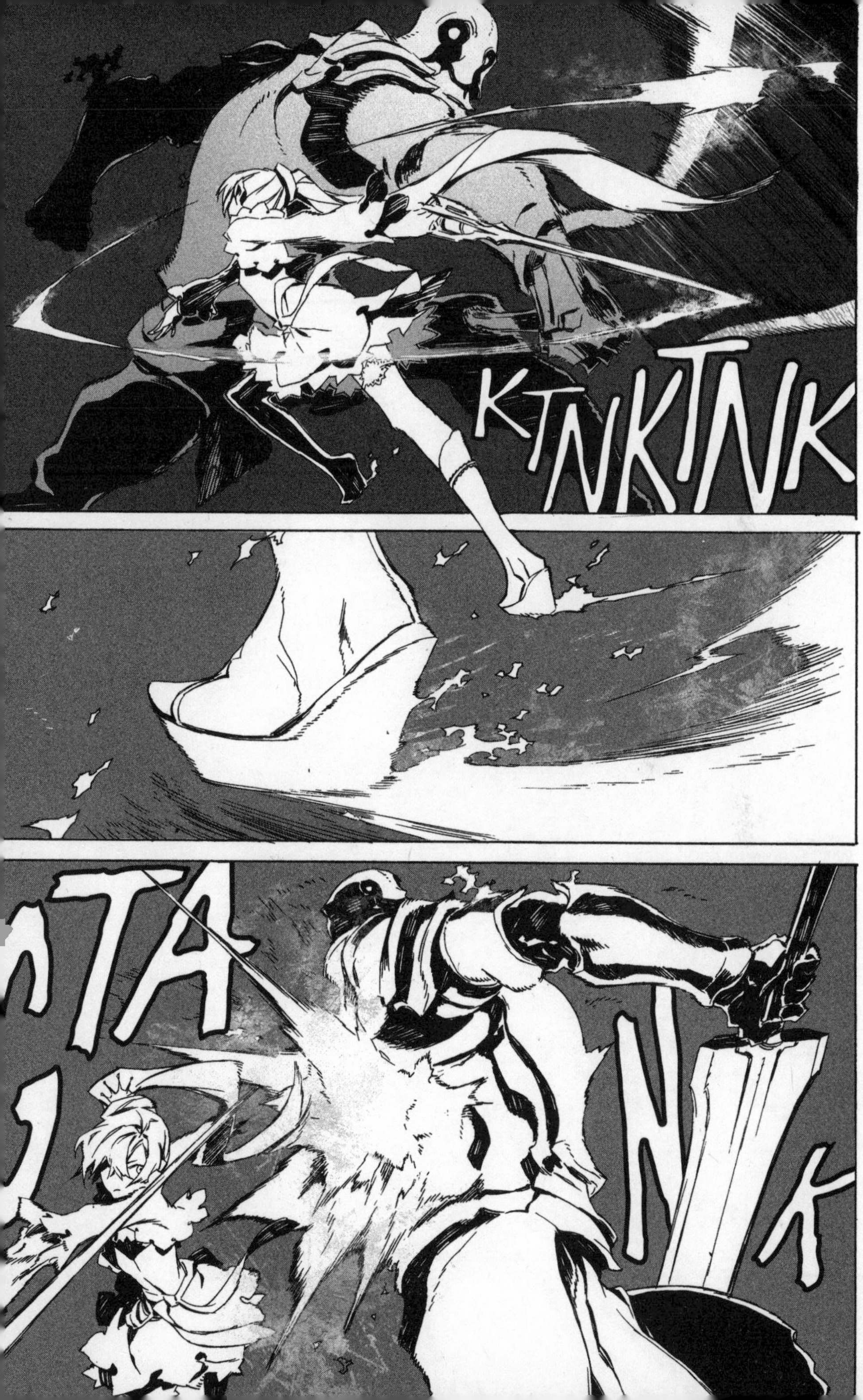
KTNKTNK
NK
TA

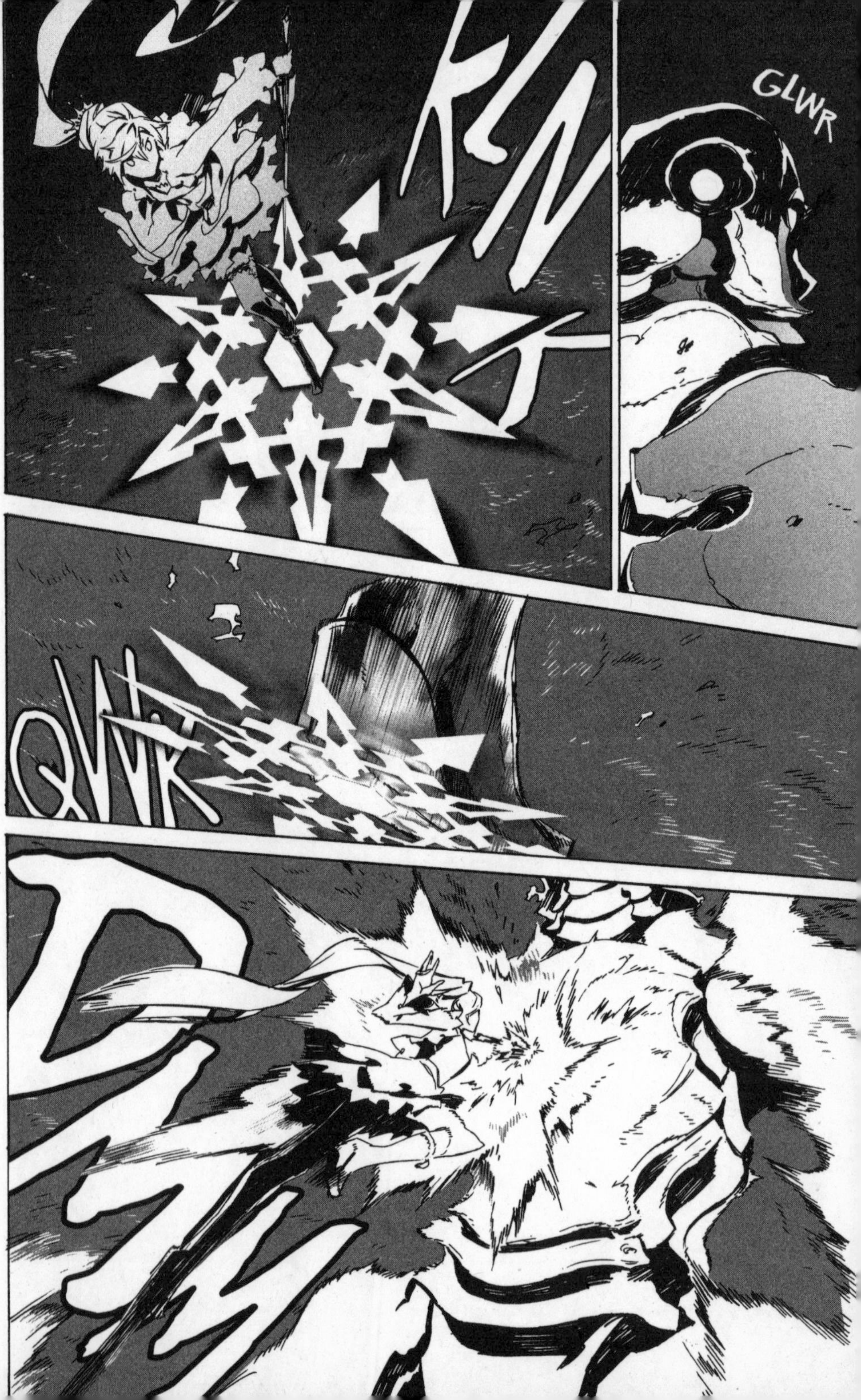
GLWR

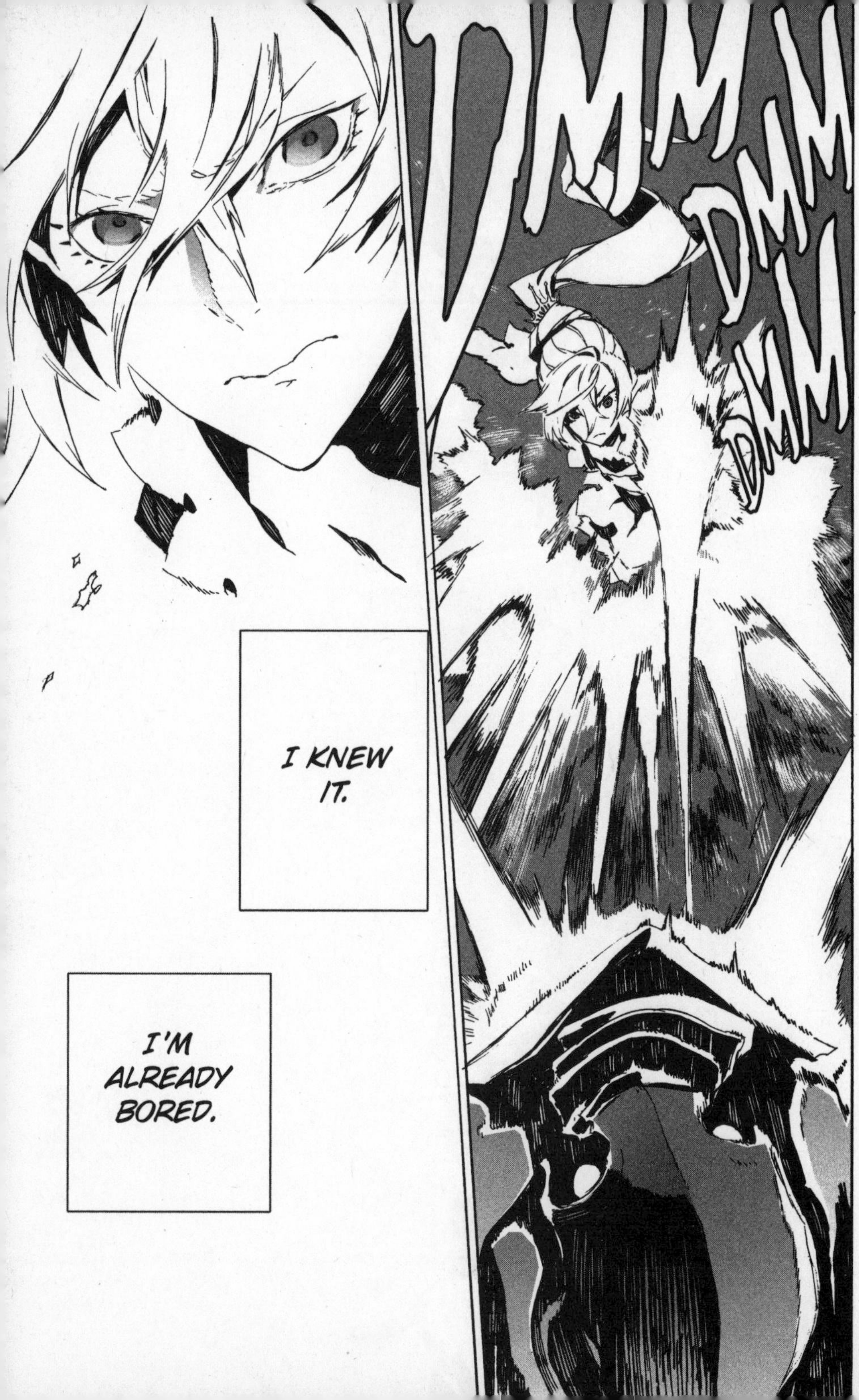
DMM
DMM
DMM
I KNEW IT.
I'M ALREADY BORED.

RWBY

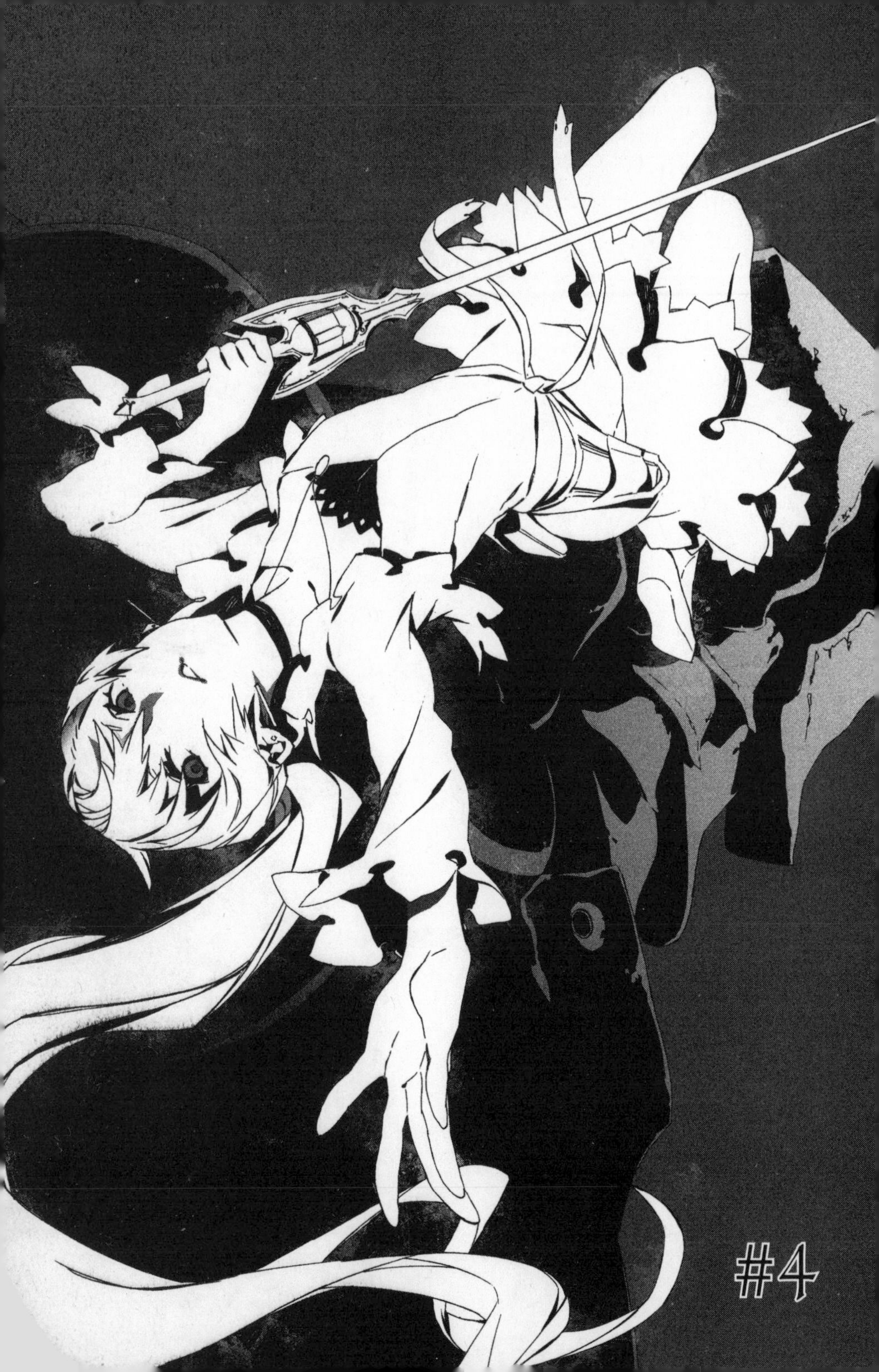
#4

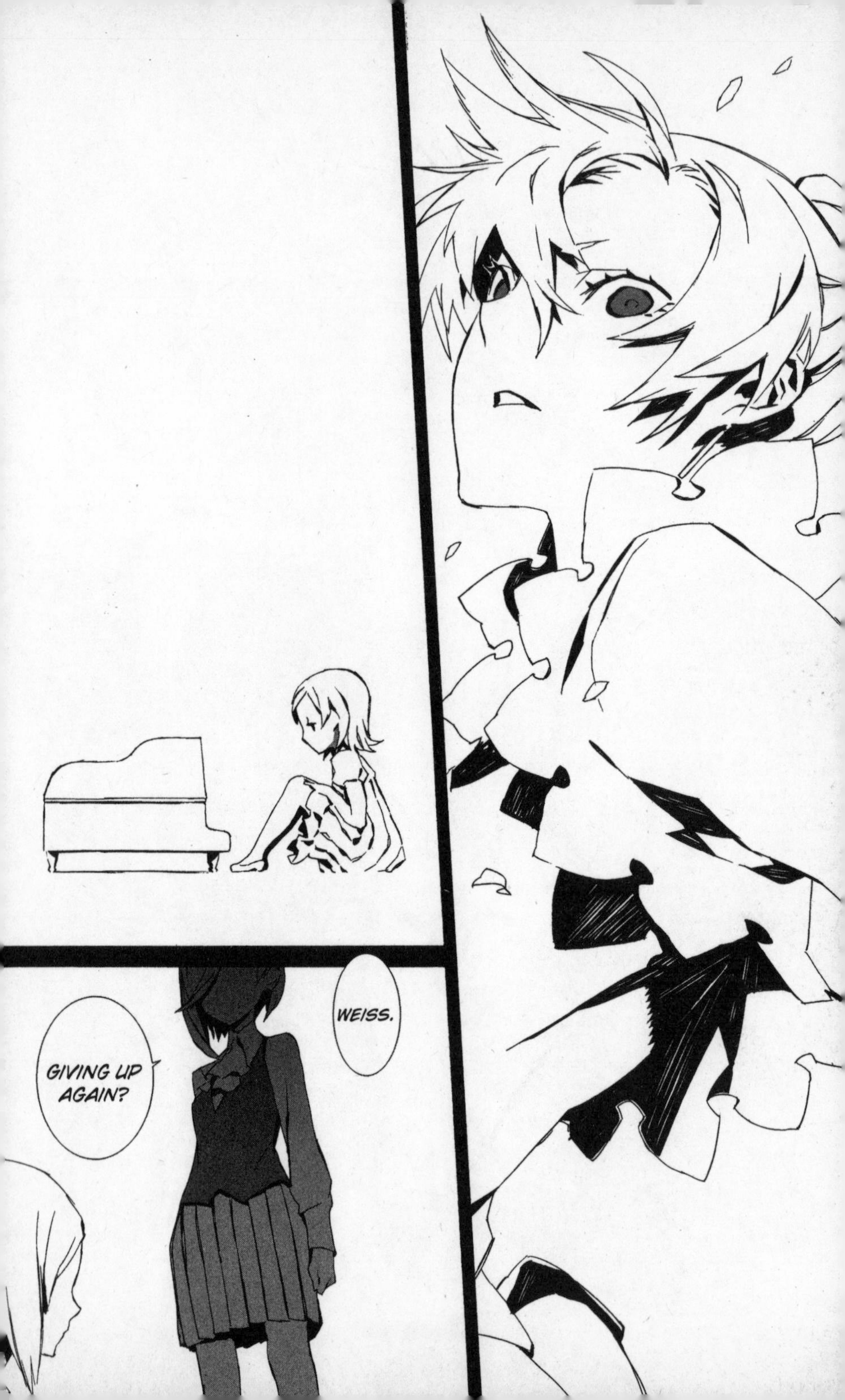
WEISS.
GIVING UP AGAIN?

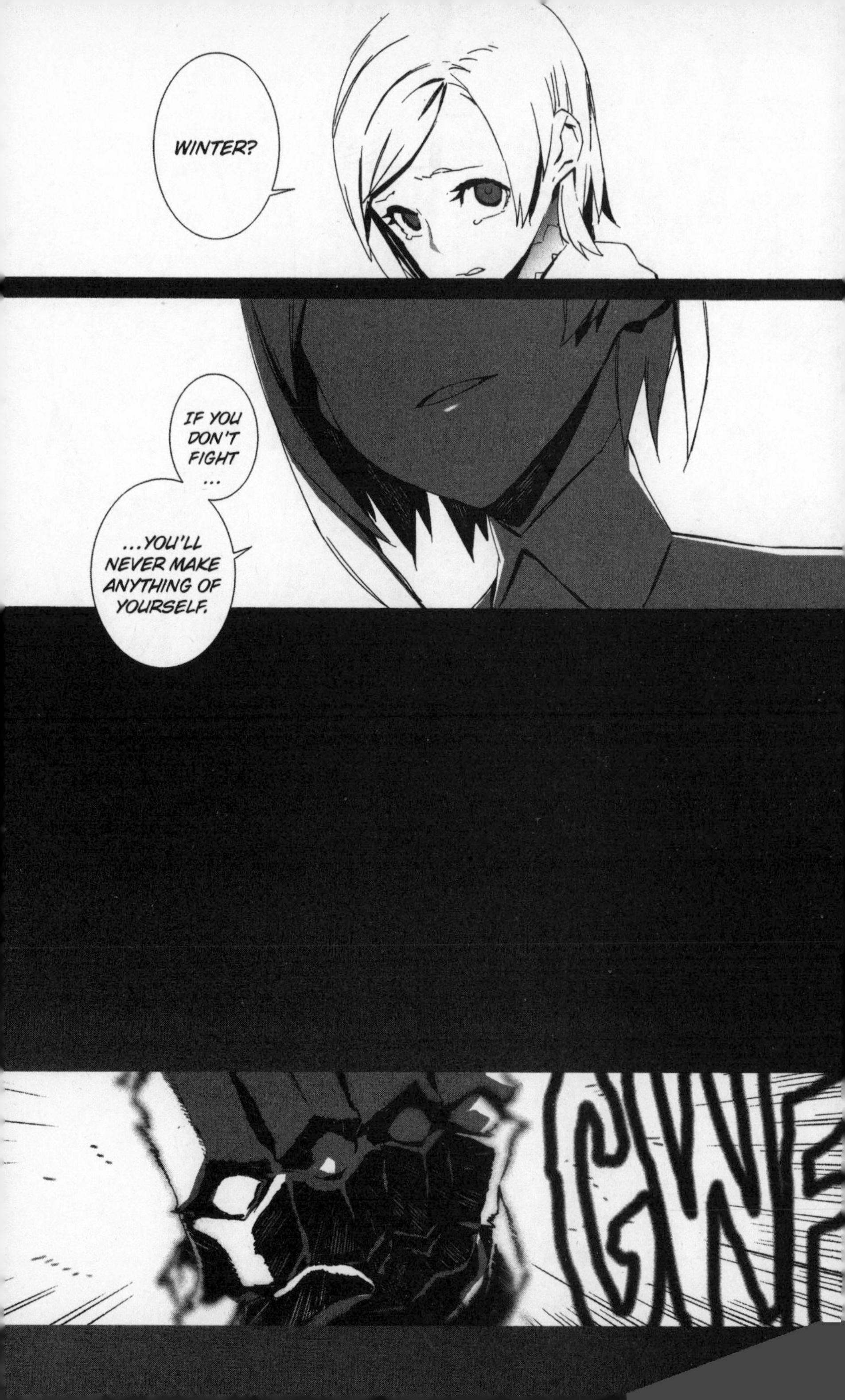
WINTER?
IF YOU DON'T FIGHT ...
...YOU'LL NEVER MAKE ANYTHING OF YOURSELF.

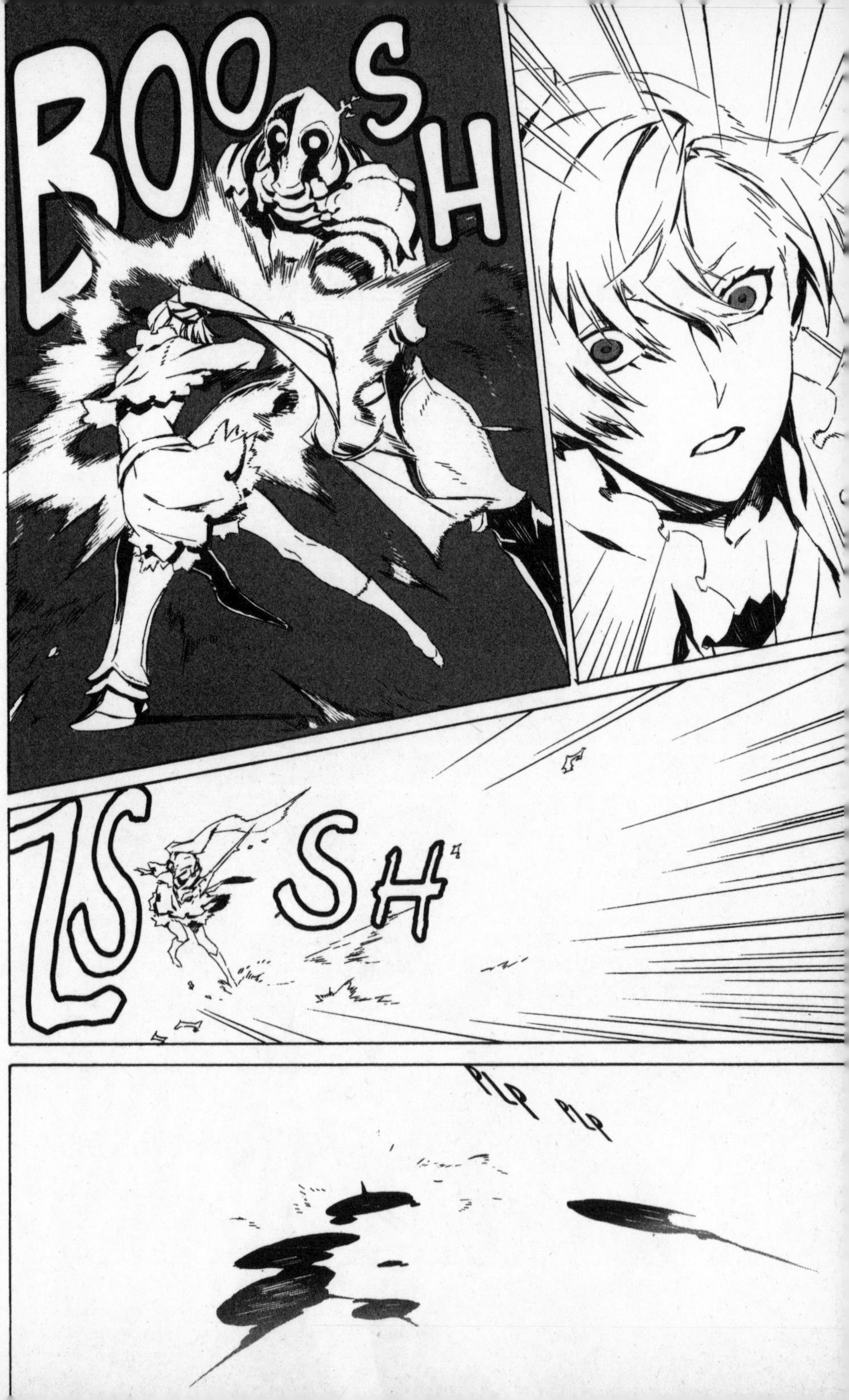
BOOOSH
ZSSH
PLIP PLIP

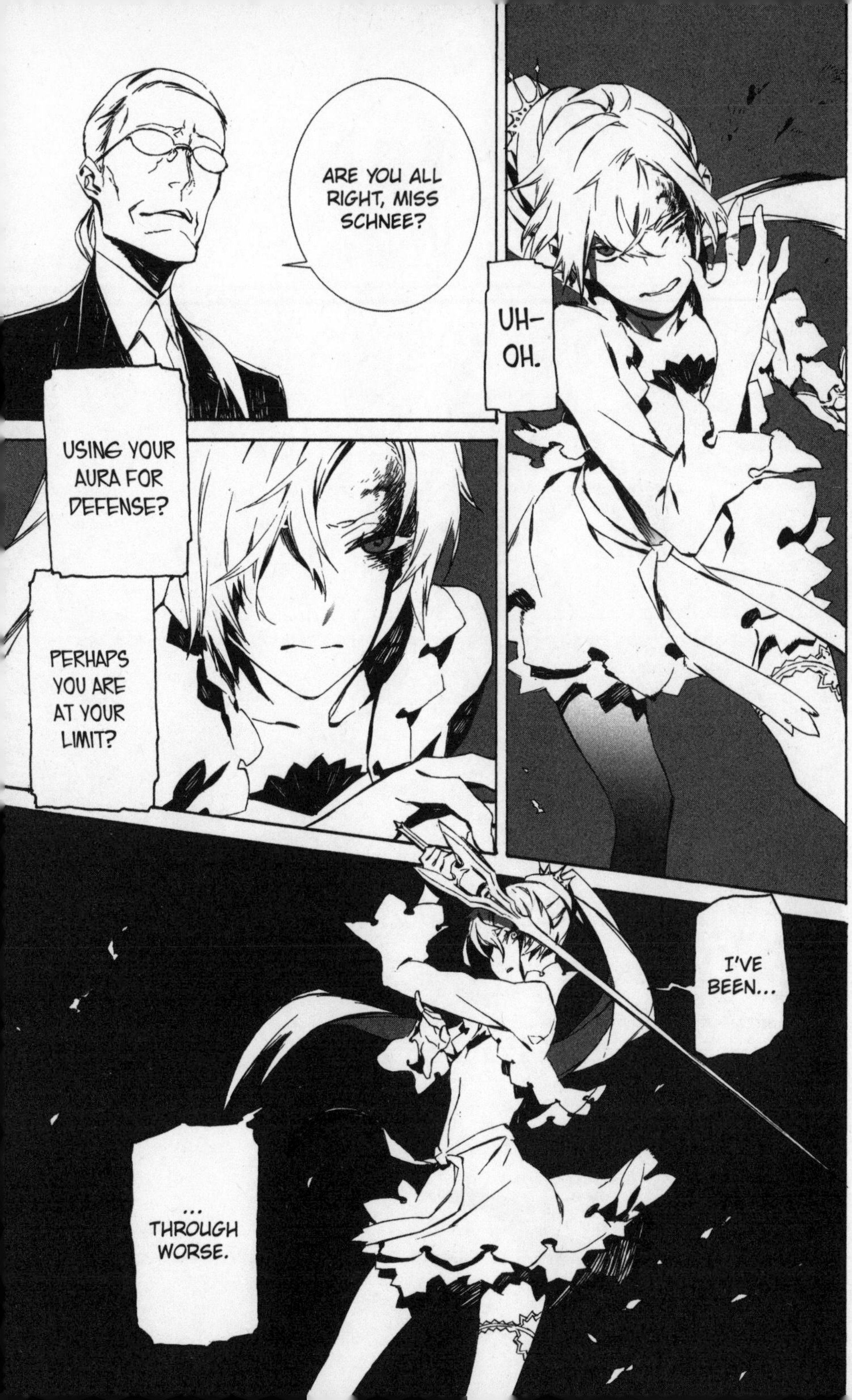
UH-OH.
ARE YOU ALL RIGHT, MISS SCHNEE?
USING YOUR AURA FOR DEFENSE?
PERHAPS YOU ARE AT YOUR LIMIT?
I'VE BEEN...
...THROUGH WORSE.

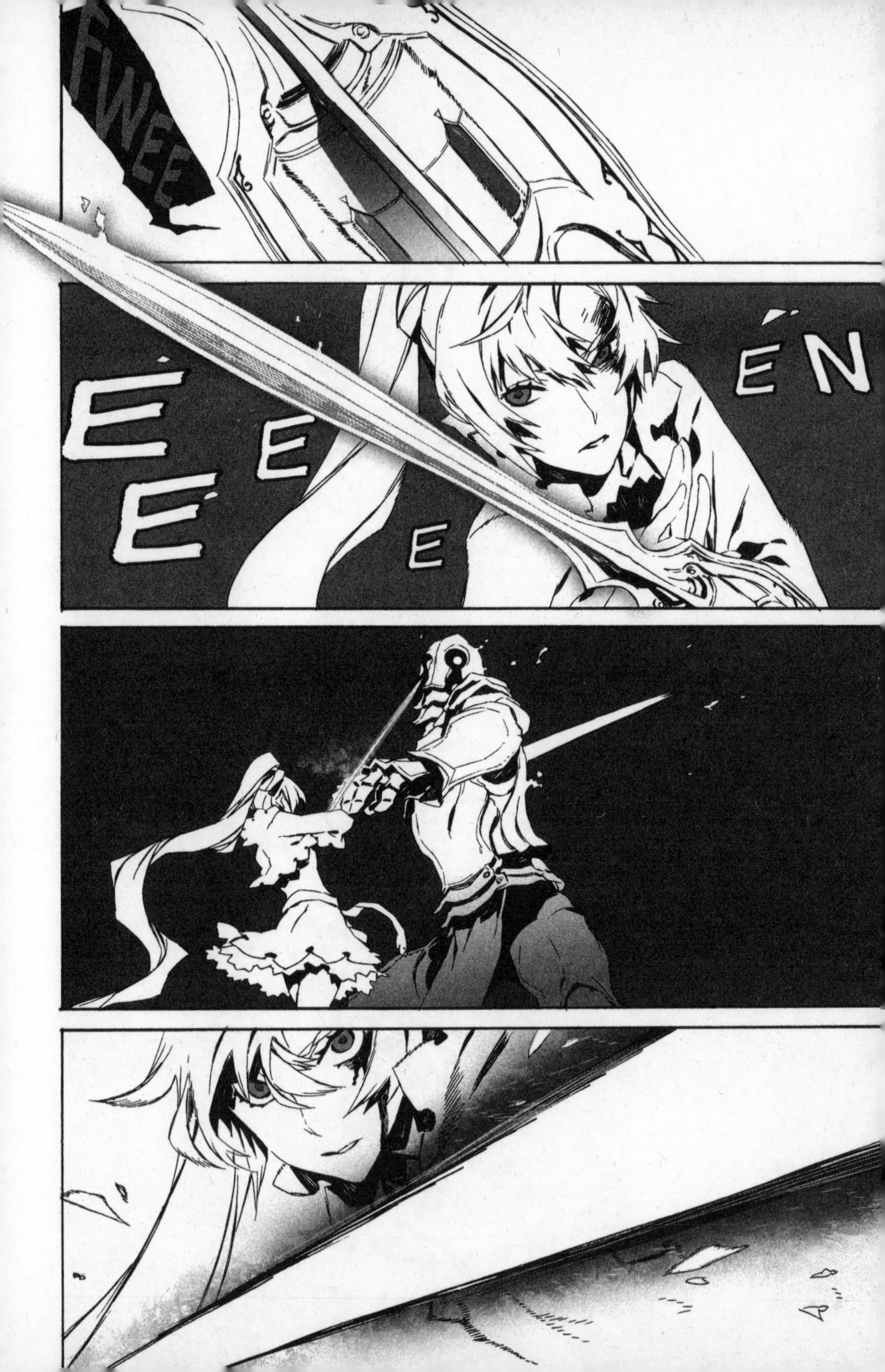
FWEE
EEEEEN

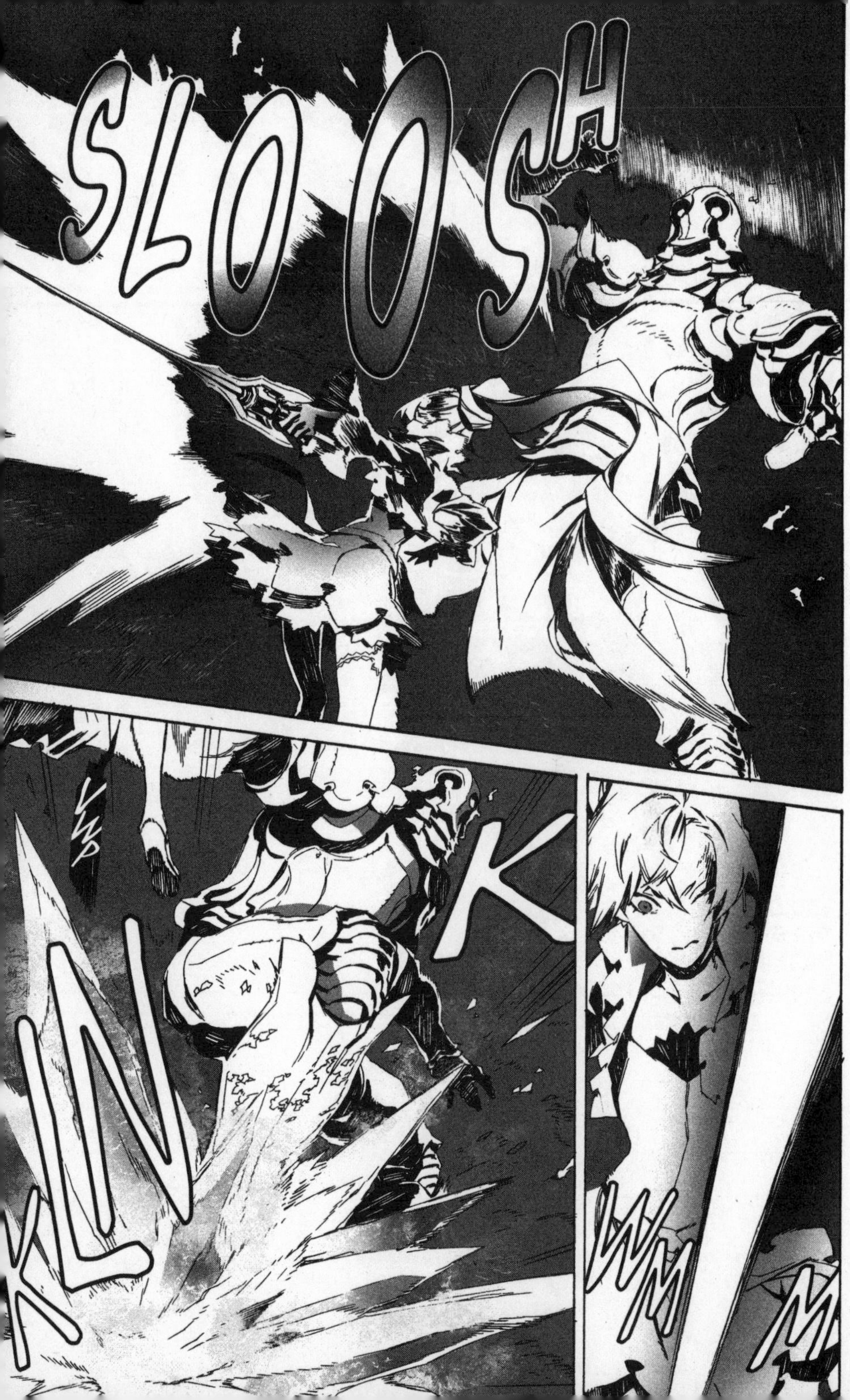
SLOOSH
WM
M
VWP
KLINK

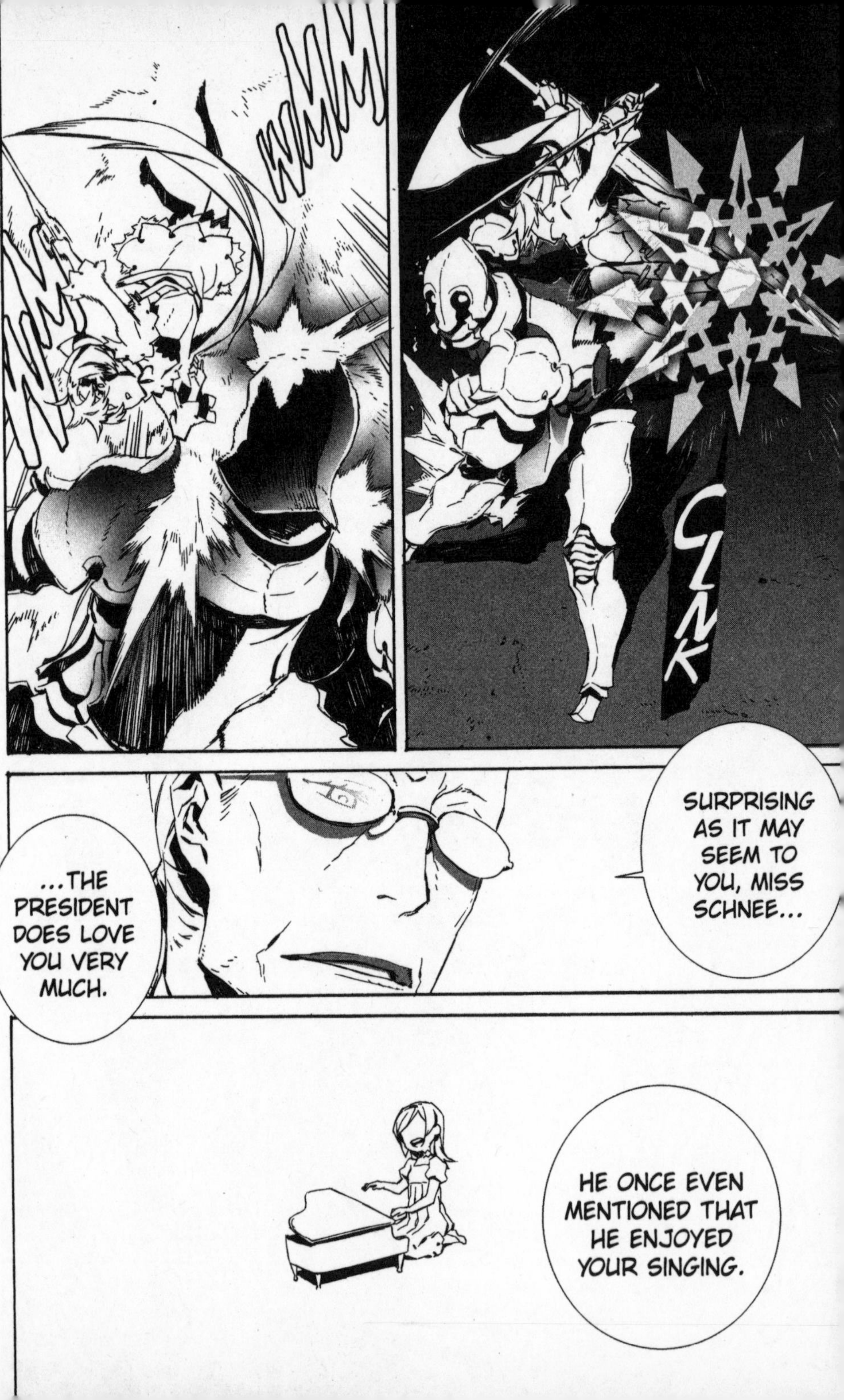
CLINK
SURPRISING AS IT MAY SEEM TO YOU, MISS SCHNEE...
...THE PRESIDENT DOES LOVE YOU VERY MUCH.
HE ONCE EVEN MENTIONED THAT HE ENJOYED YOUR SINGING.

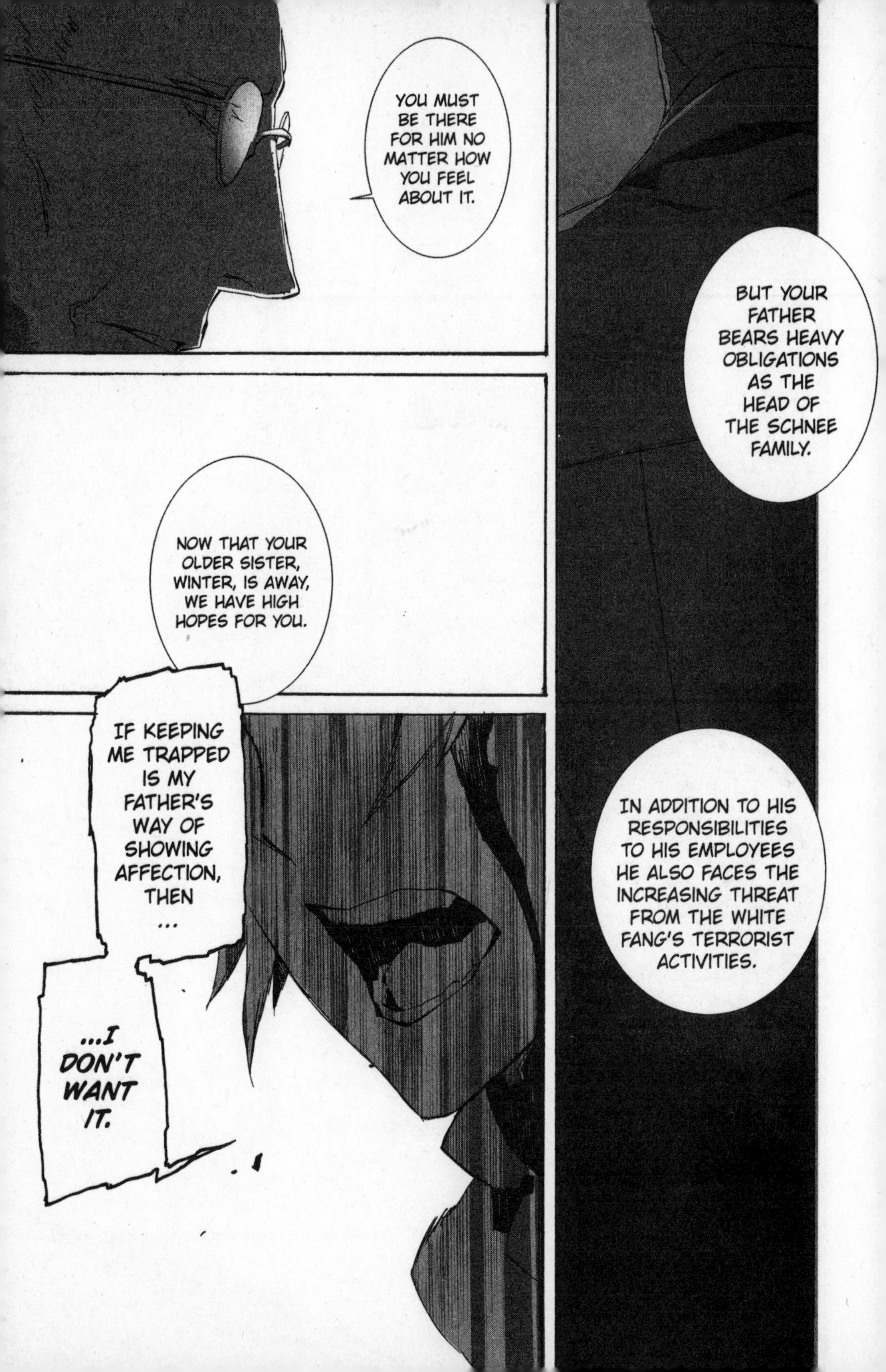
BUT YOUR FATHER BEARS HEAVY OBLIGATIONS AS THE HEAD OF THE SCHNEE FAMILY.
IN ADDITION TO HIS RESPONSIBILITIES TO HIS EMPLOYEES HE ALSO FACES THE INCREASING THREAT FROM THE WHITE FANG'S TERRORIST ACTIVITIES.
YOU MUST BE THERE FOR HIM NO MATTER HOW YOU FEEL ABOUT IT.
NOW THAT YOUR OLDER SISTER, WINTER, IS AWAY, WE HAVE HIGH HOPES FOR YOU.
IF KEEPING ME TRAPPED IS MY FATHER'S WAY OF SHOWING AFFECTION, THEN ...
...I DON'T WANT IT.

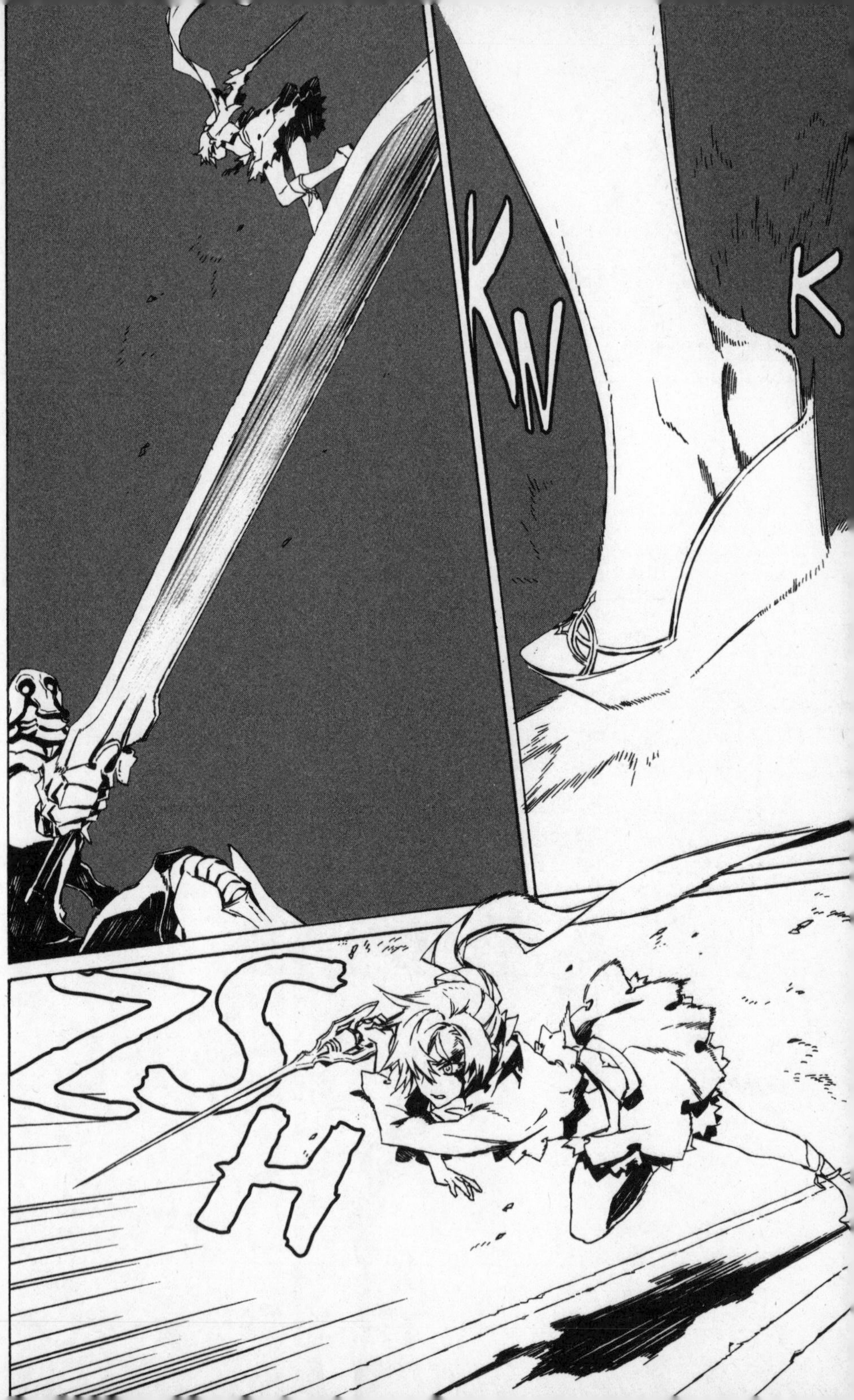
KW
K
ZSH

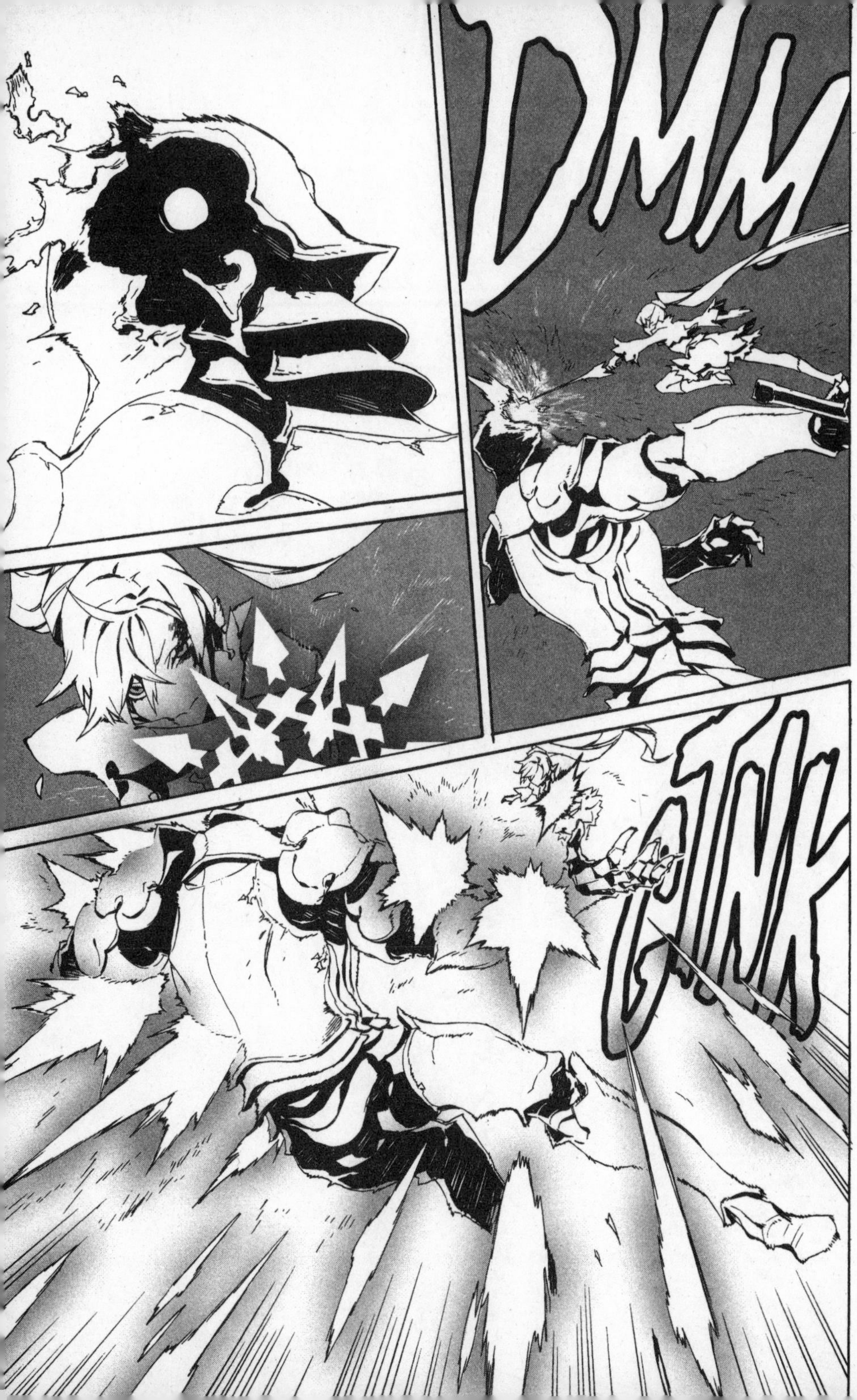
DMM
CLINK

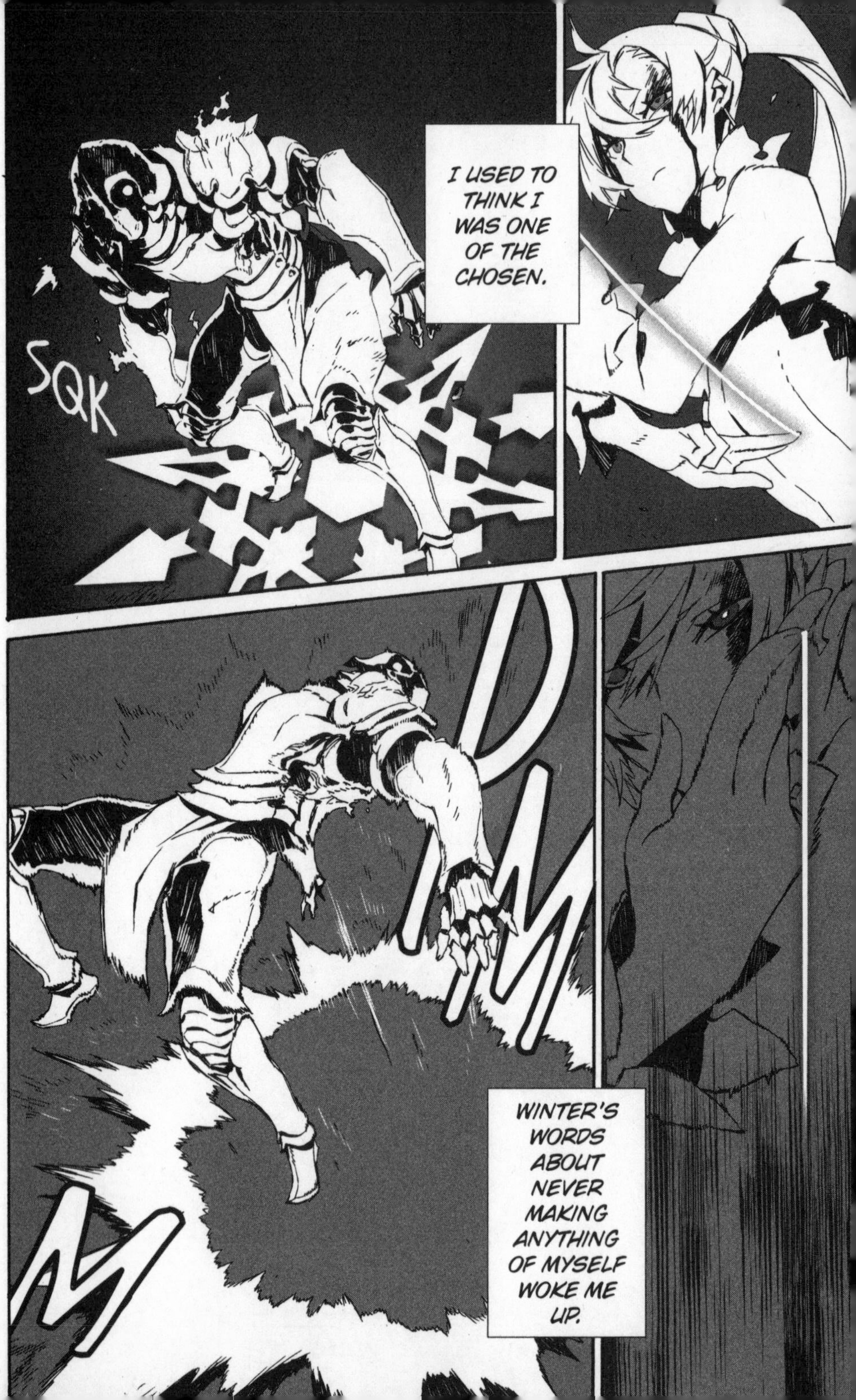
I USED TO THINK I WAS ONE OF THE CHOSEN.
SQK
WINTER'S WORDS ABOUT NEVER MAKING ANYTHING OF MYSELF WOKE ME UP.

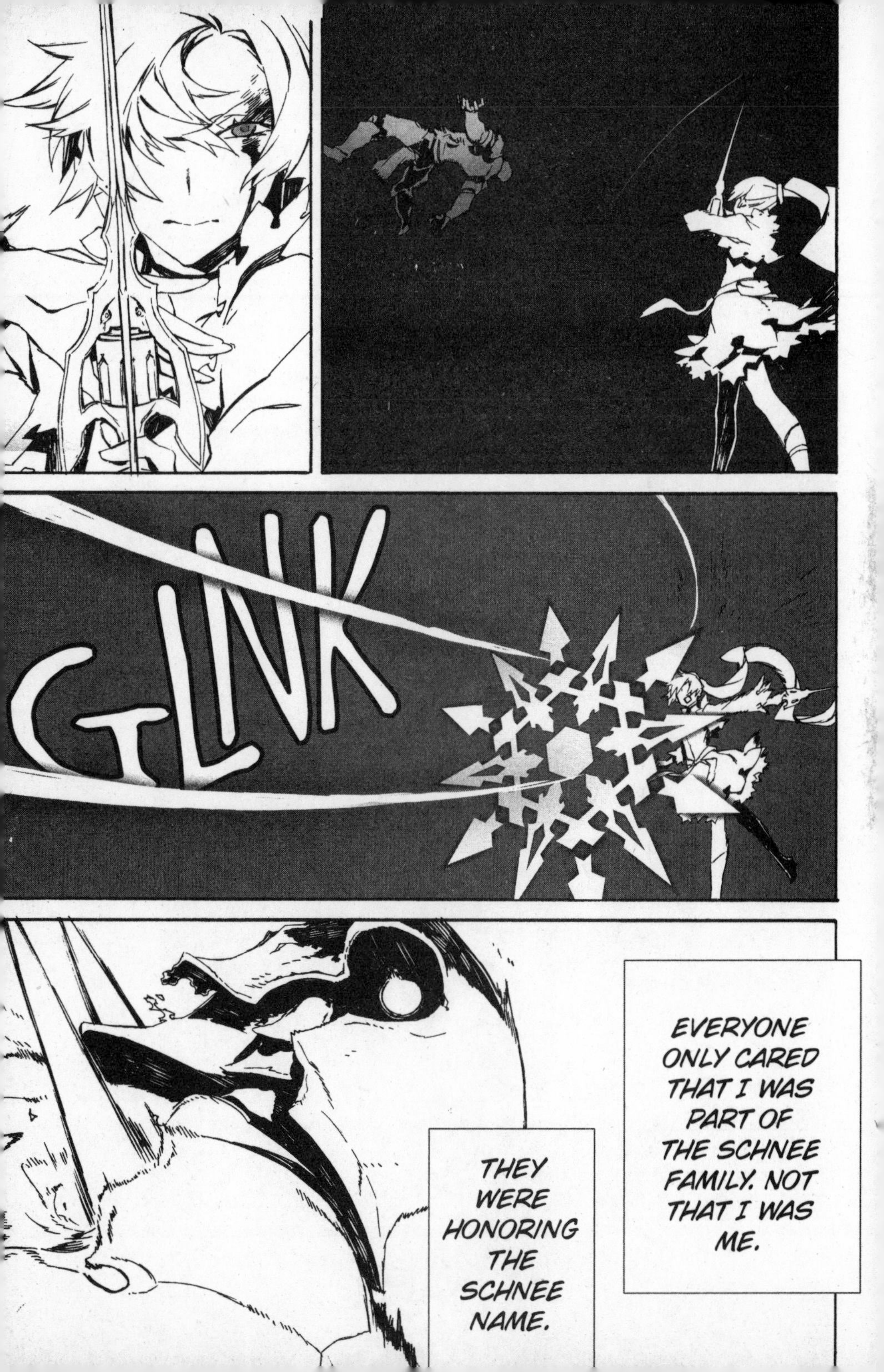
CLINK
EVERYONE ONLY CARED THAT I WAS PART OF THE SCHNEE FAMILY. NOT THAT I WAS ME.
THEY WERE HONORING THE SCHNEE NAME.

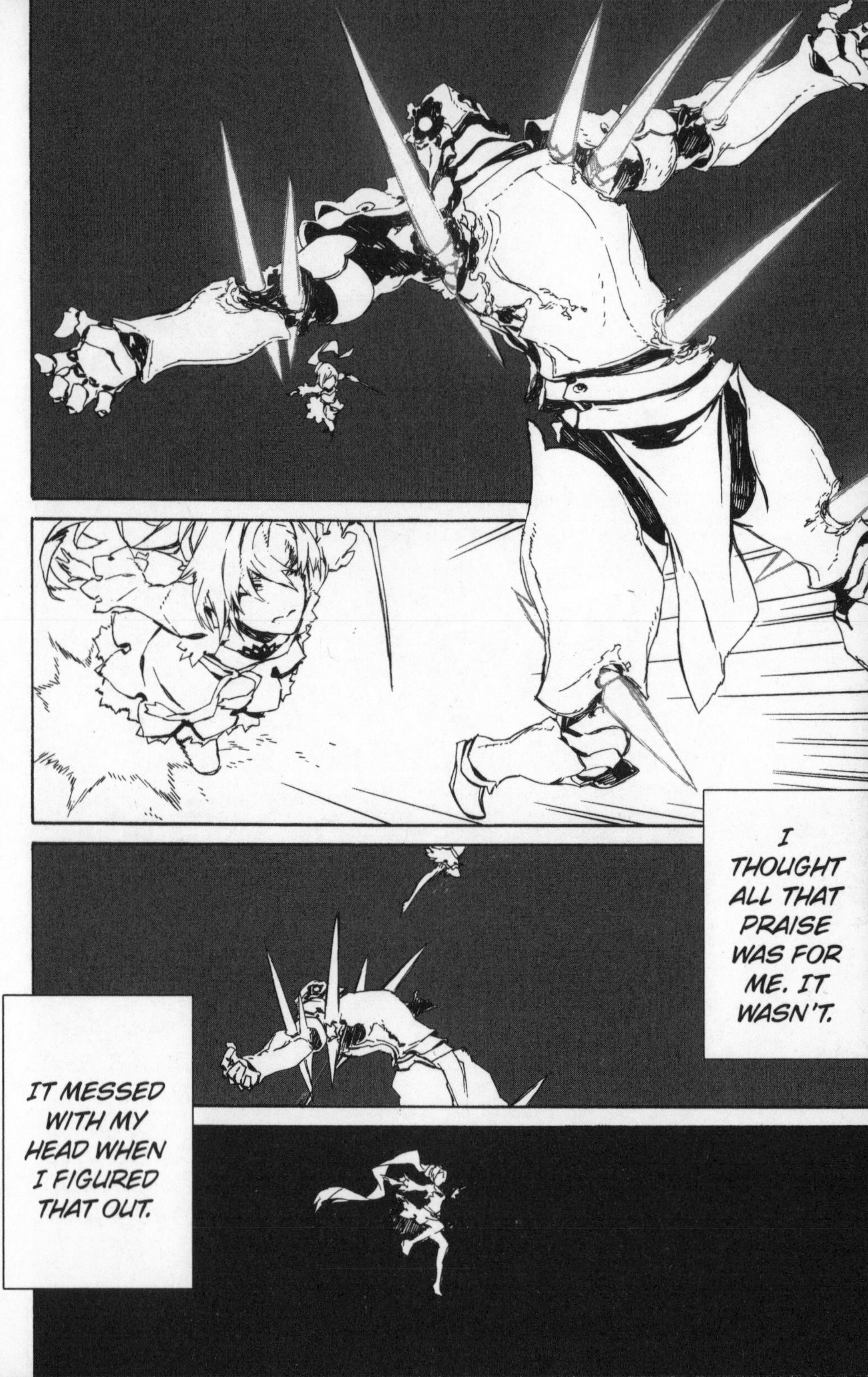
I THOUGHT ALL THAT PRAISE WAS FOR ME. IT WASN'T.
IT MESSED WITH MY HEAD WHEN I FIGURED THAT OUT.

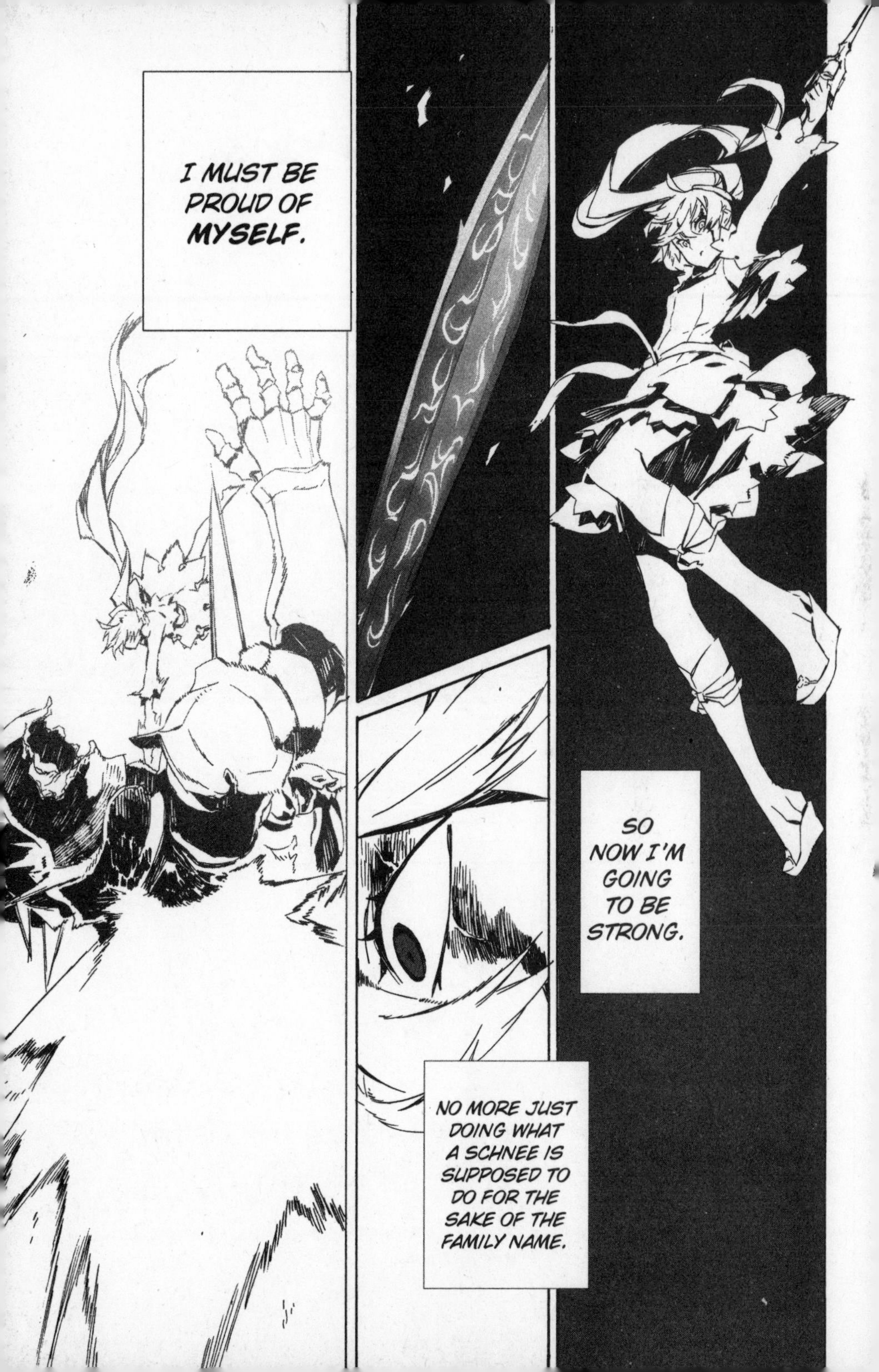
SO NOW I'M GOING TO BE STRONG.
NO MORE JUST DOING WHAT A SCHNEE IS SUPPOSED TO DO FOR THE SAKE OF THE FAMILY NAME.
I MUST BE PROUD OF MYSELF.

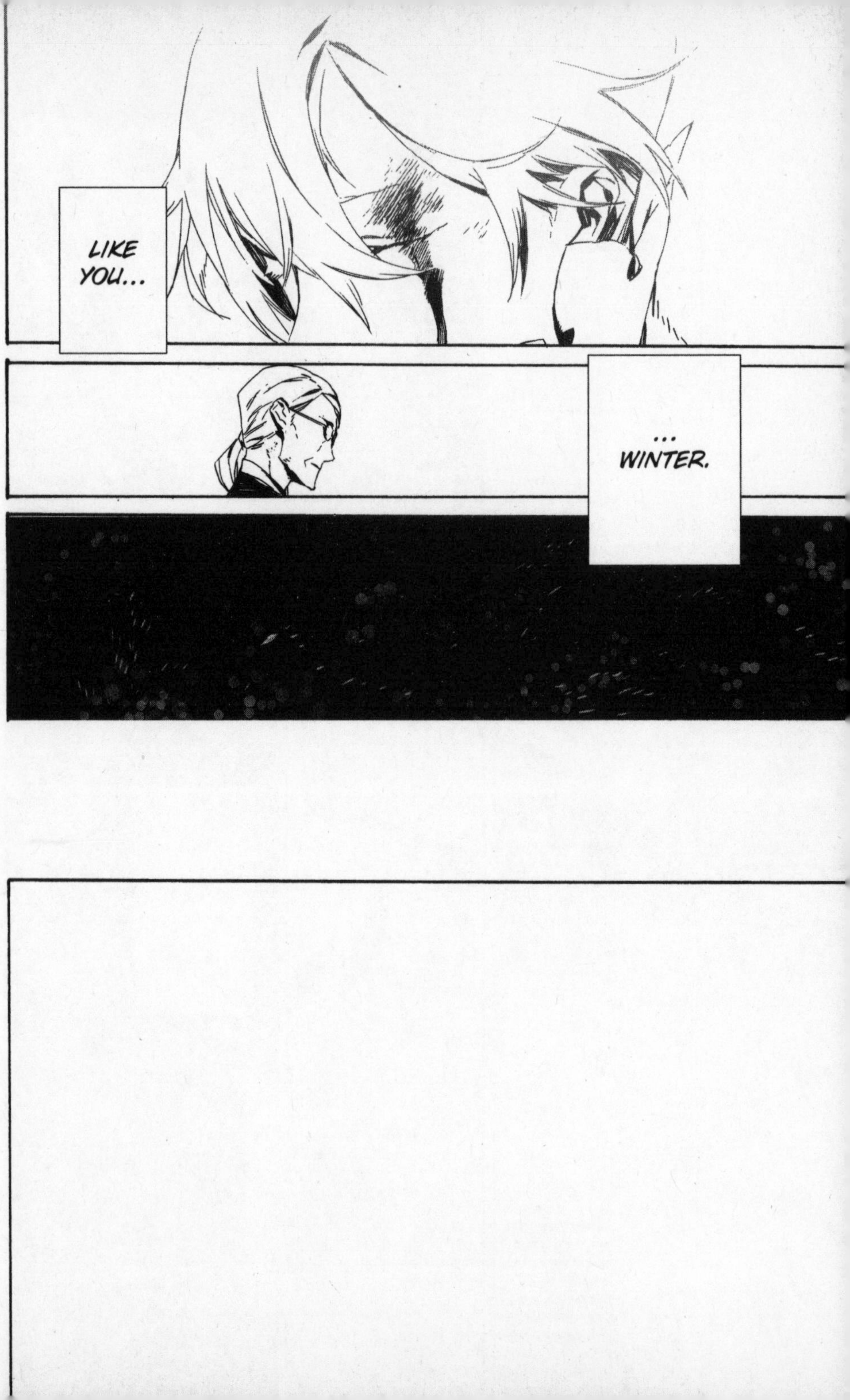
LIKE YOU...
... WINTER.

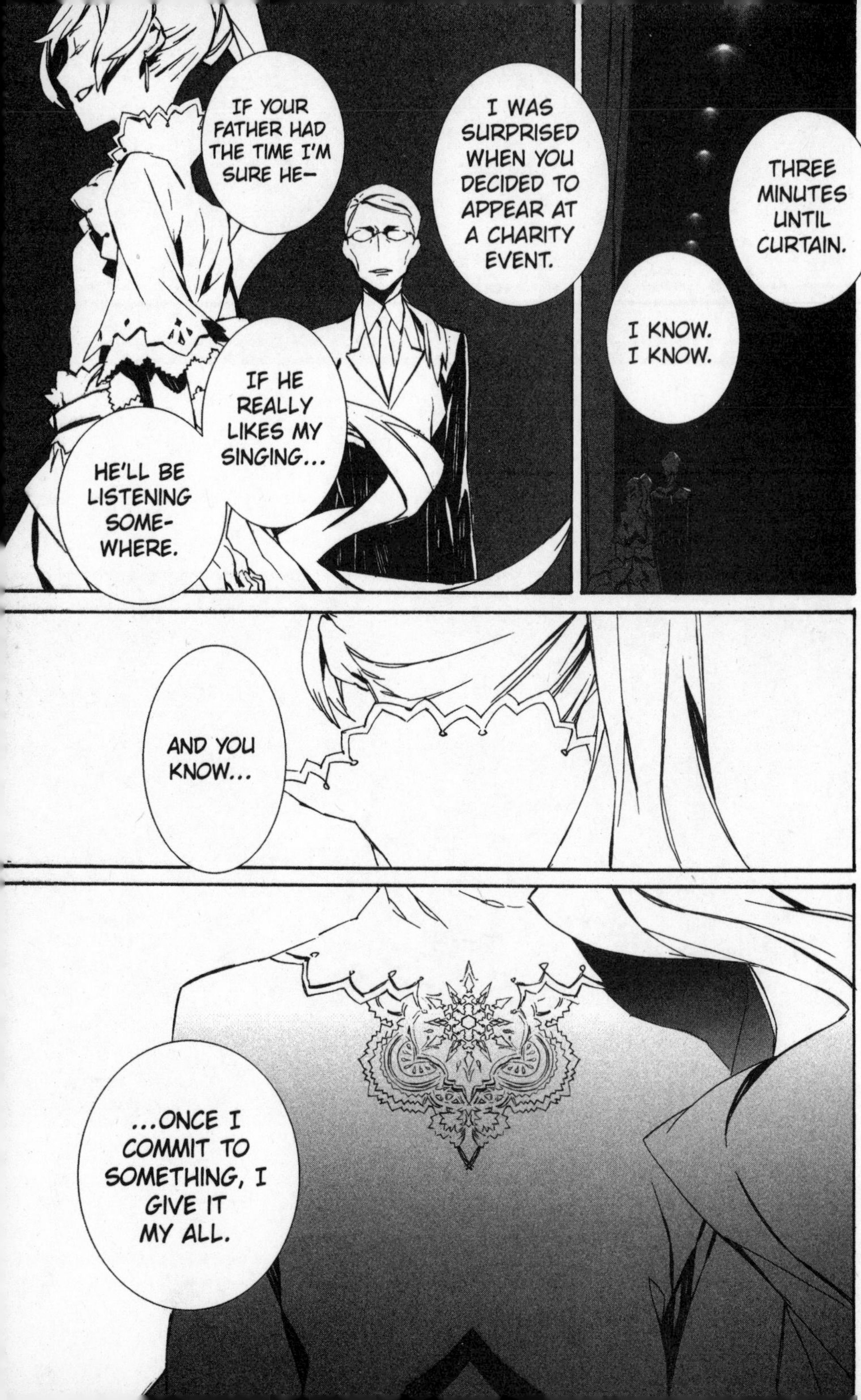
THREE MINUTES UNTIL CURTAIN.
I KNOW. I KNOW.
I WAS SURPRISED WHEN YOU DECIDED TO APPEAR AT A CHARITY EVENT.
IF YOUR FATHER HAD THE TIME I'M SURE HE—
IF HE REALLY LIKES MY SINGING...
HE'LL BE LISTENING SOME-WHERE.
AND YOU KNOW...
...ONCE I COMMIT TO SOMETHING, I GIVE IT MY ALL.

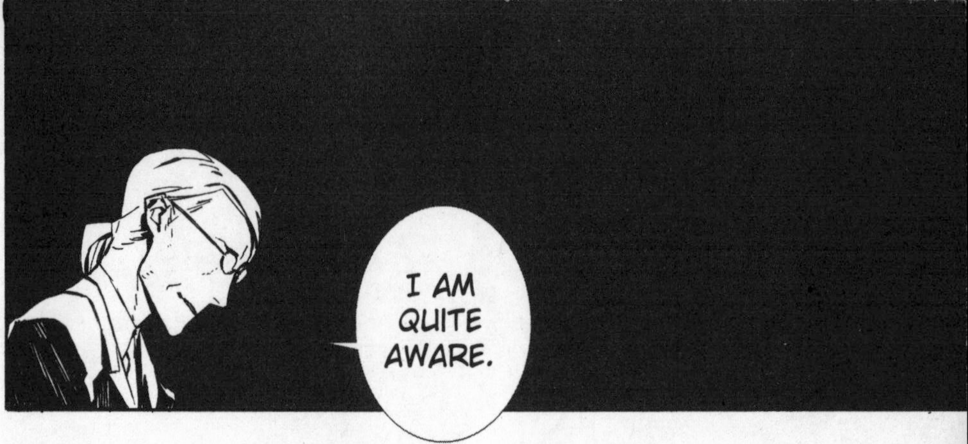
I AM QUITE AWARE.

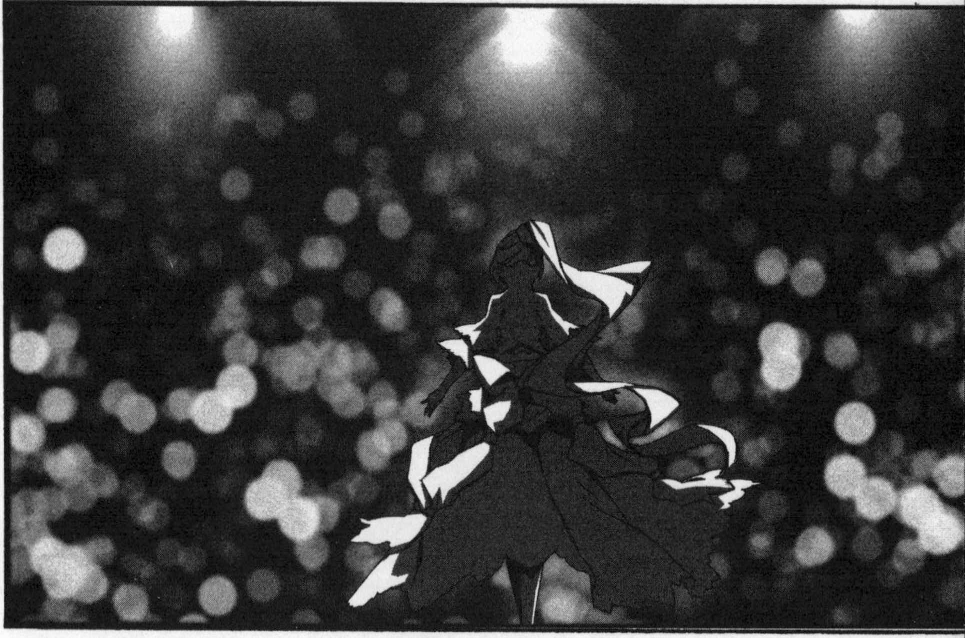

Weiss Schnee

W

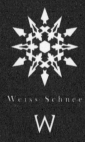

RWBY

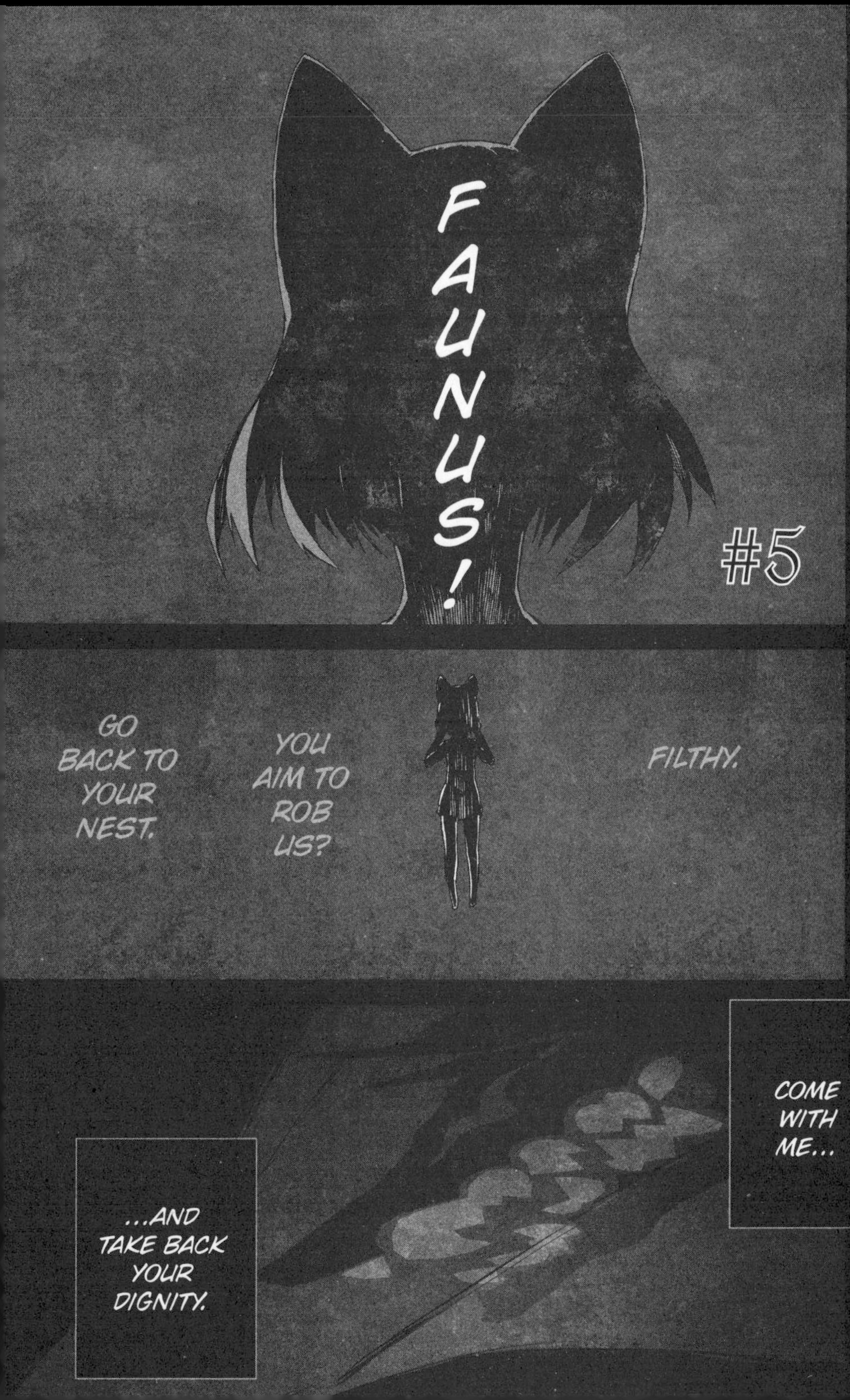
FAUNUS!
#5
FILTHY.
YOU AIM TO ROB US?
GO BACK TO YOUR NEST.
COME WITH ME...
...AND TAKE BACK YOUR DIGNITY.

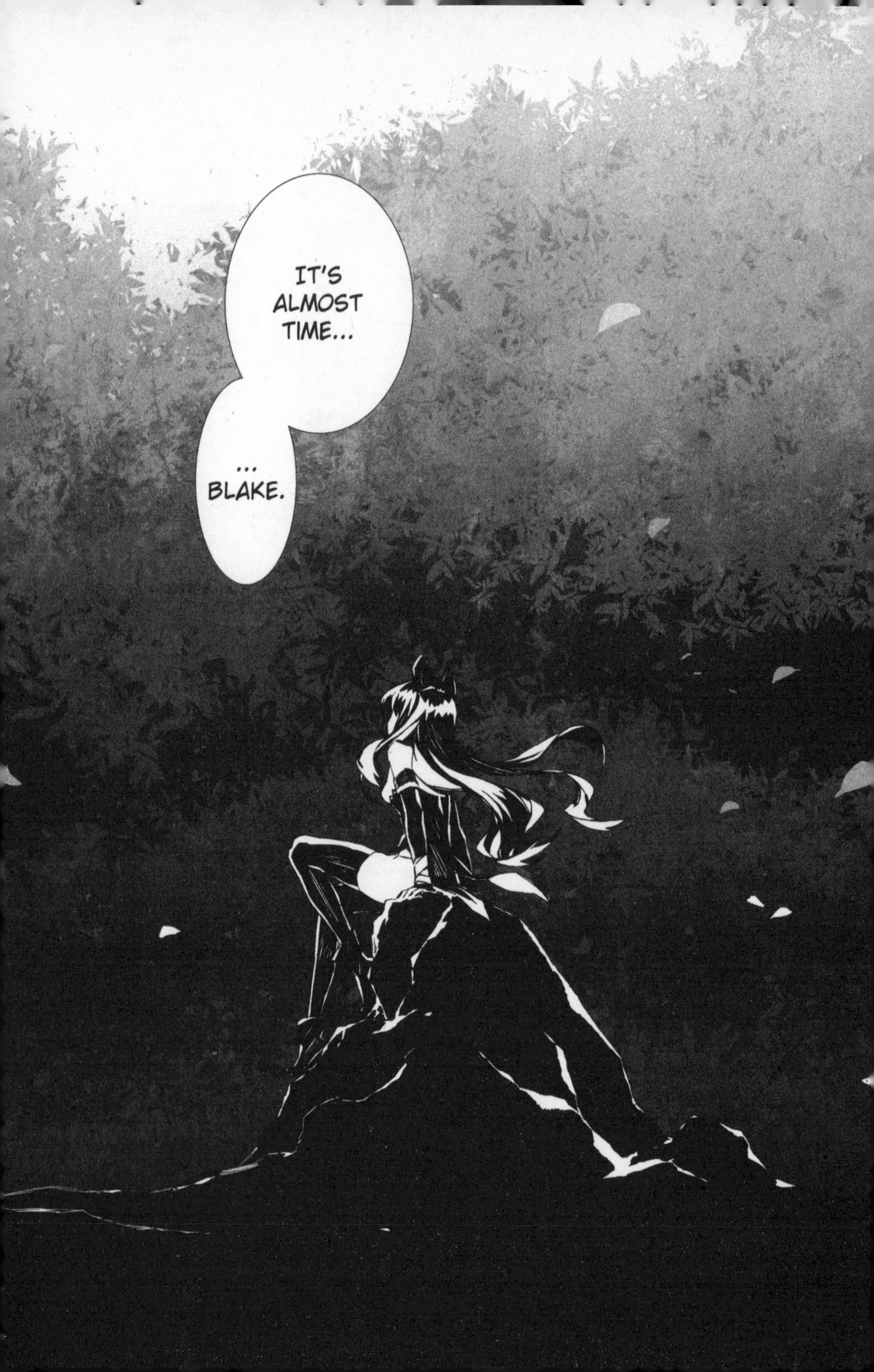
IT'S ALMOST TIME...
... BLAKE.

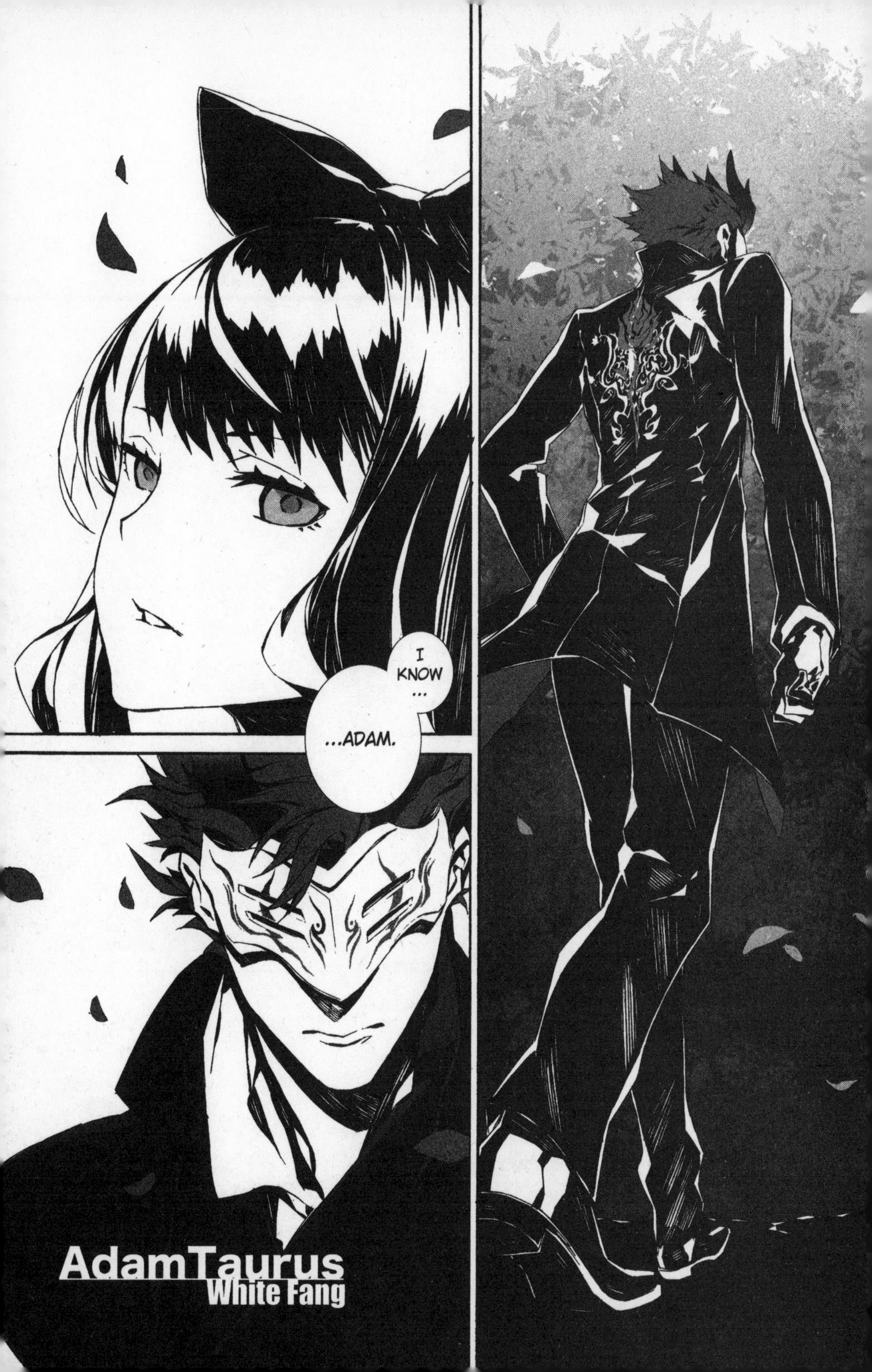
I KNOW ...
...ADAM.
AdamTaurus
White Fang

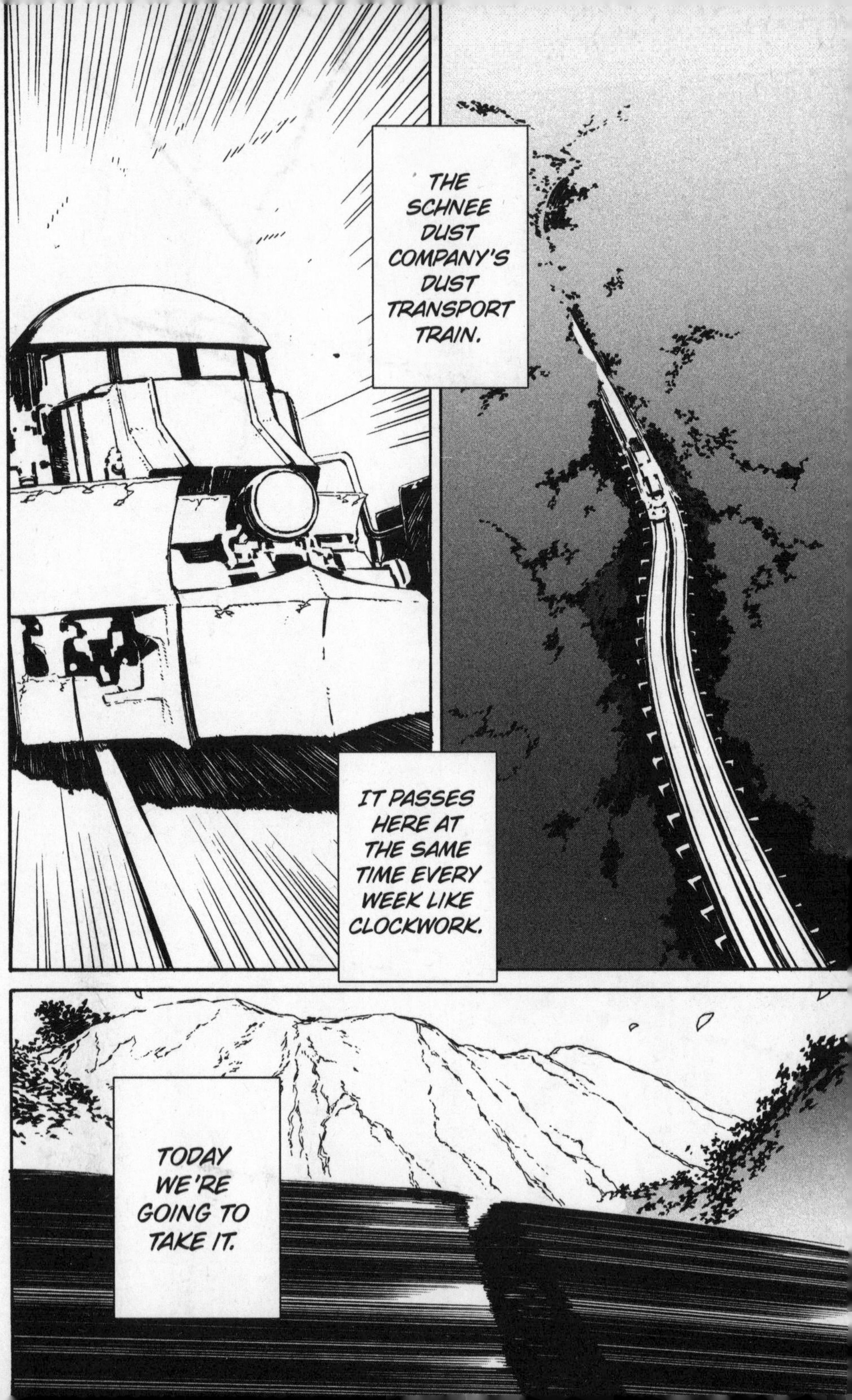
THE SCHNEE DUST COMPANY'S DUST TRANSPORT TRAIN.
IT PASSES HERE AT THE SAME TIME EVERY WEEK LIKE CLOCKWORK.
TODAY WE'RE GOING TO TAKE IT.

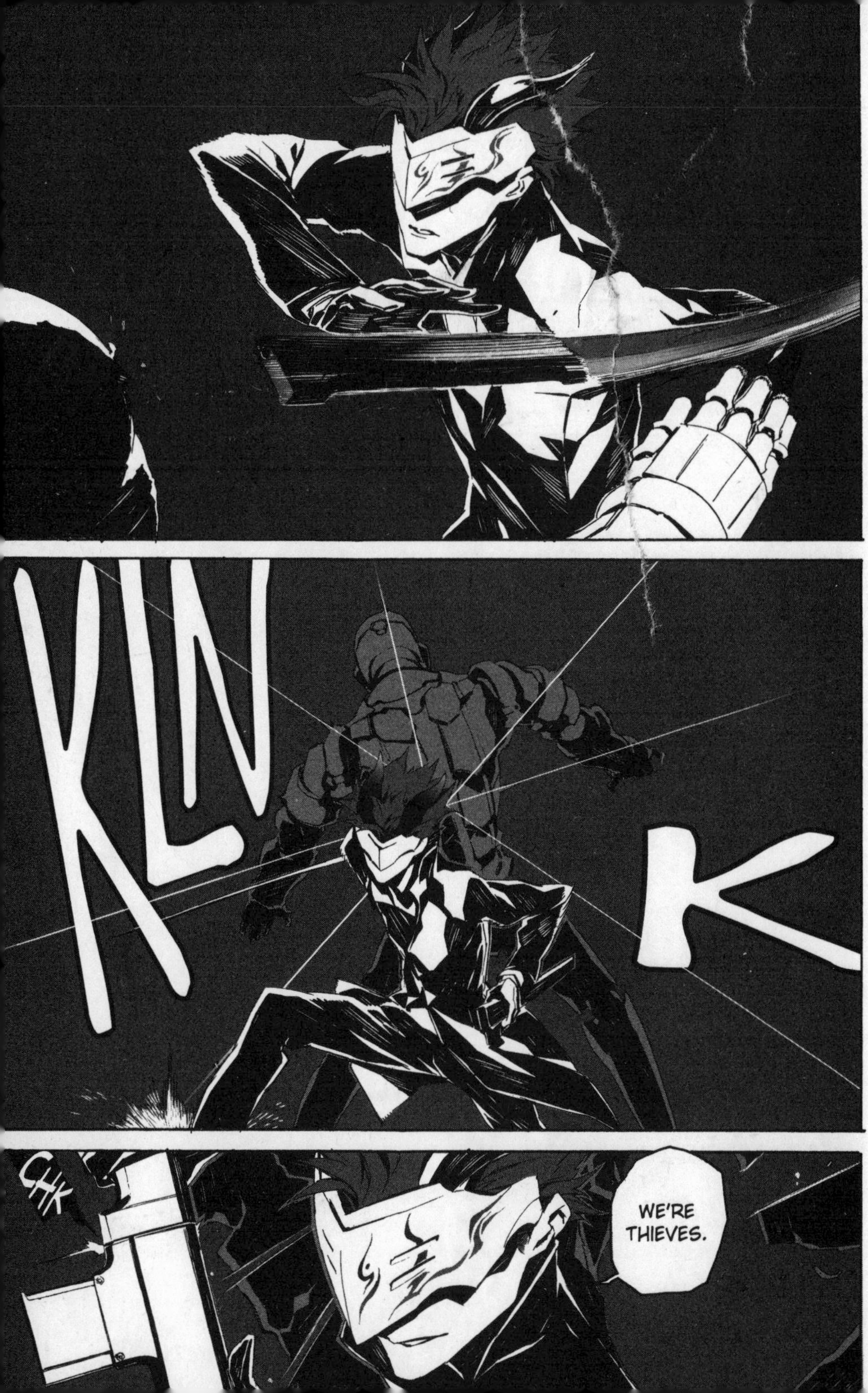
KLIN
K
WE'RE THIEVES.
CHK

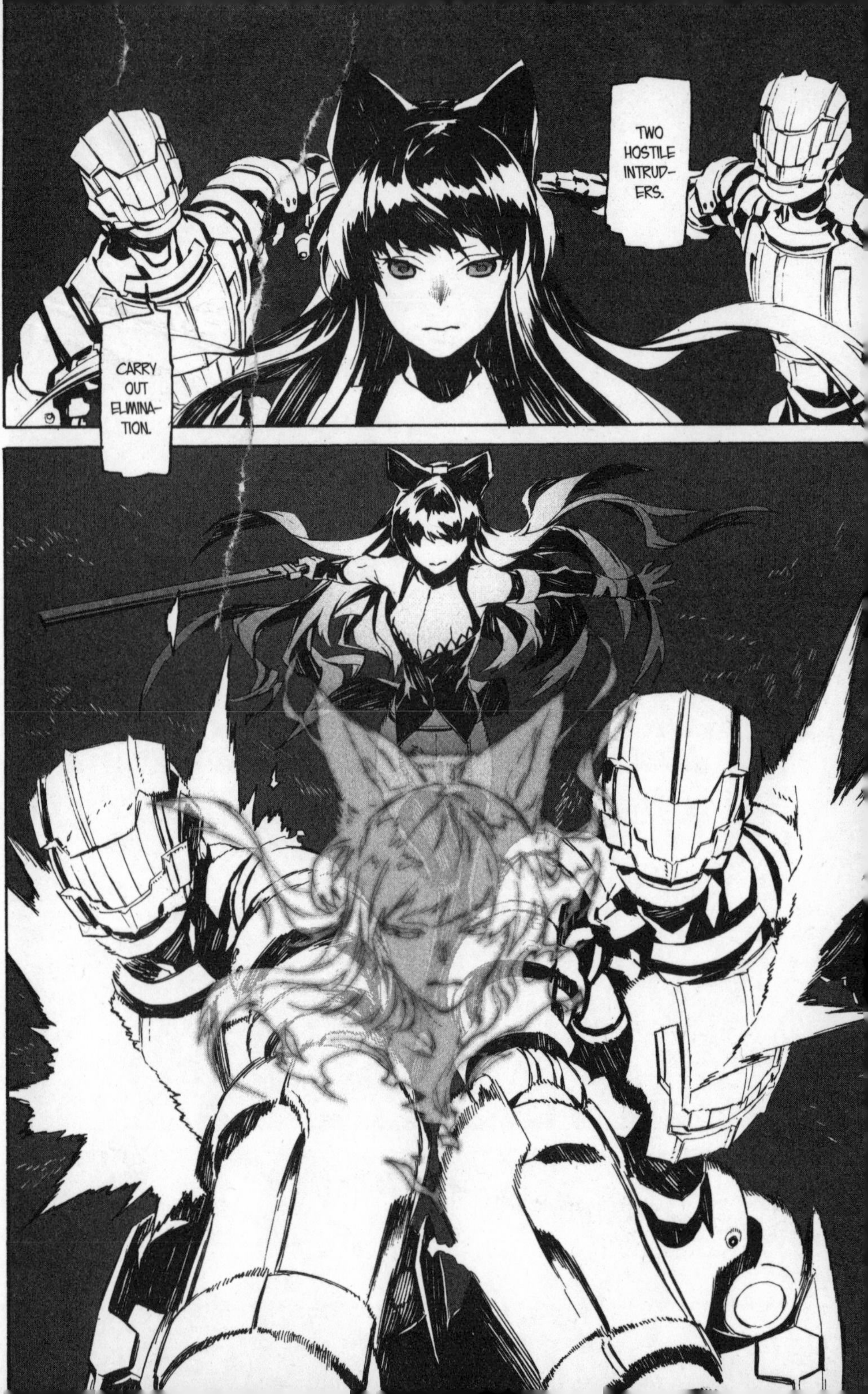
TWO HOSTILE INTRUD-ERS.
CARRY OUT ELIMINA-TION.

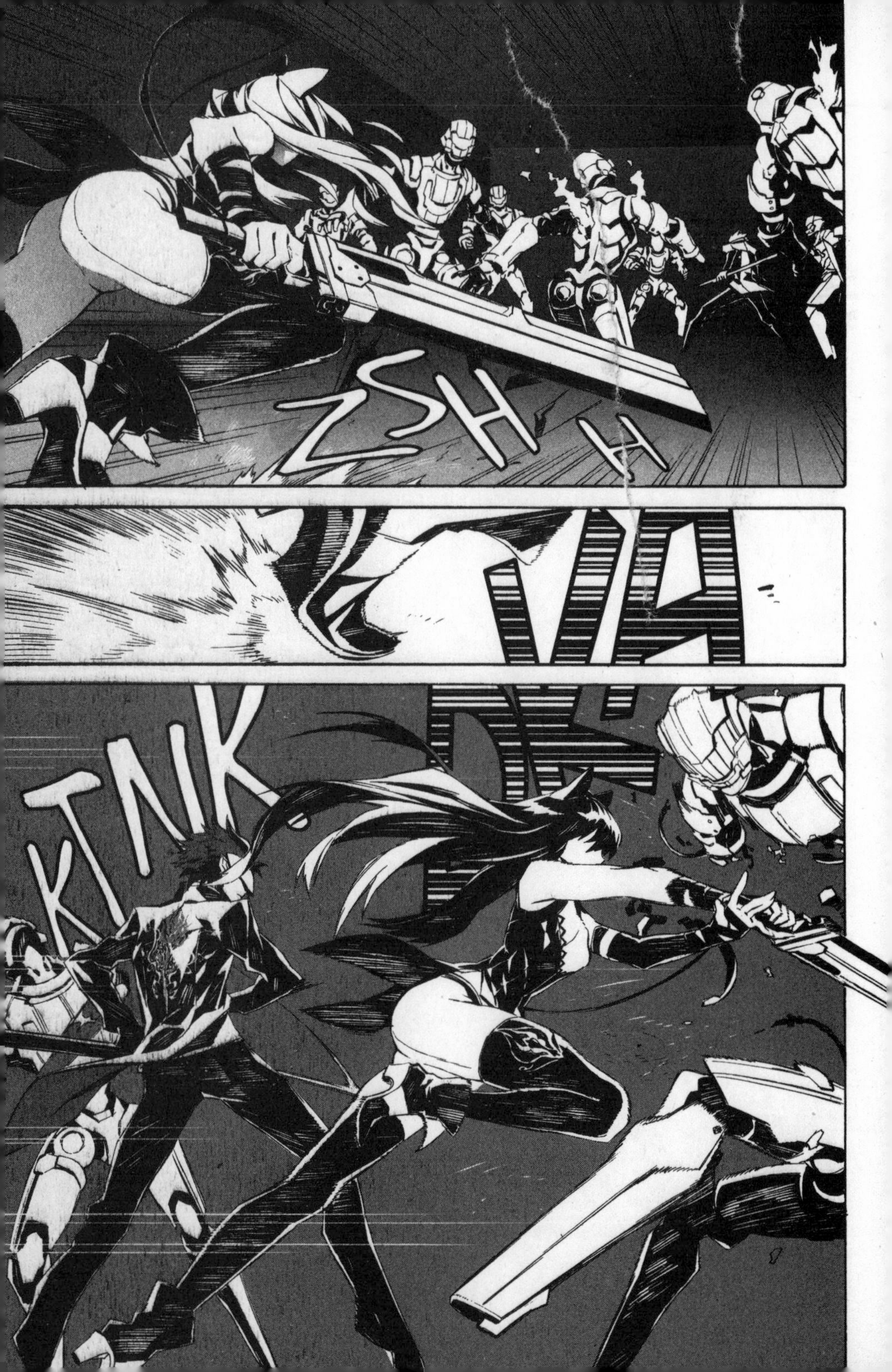
ZSHH

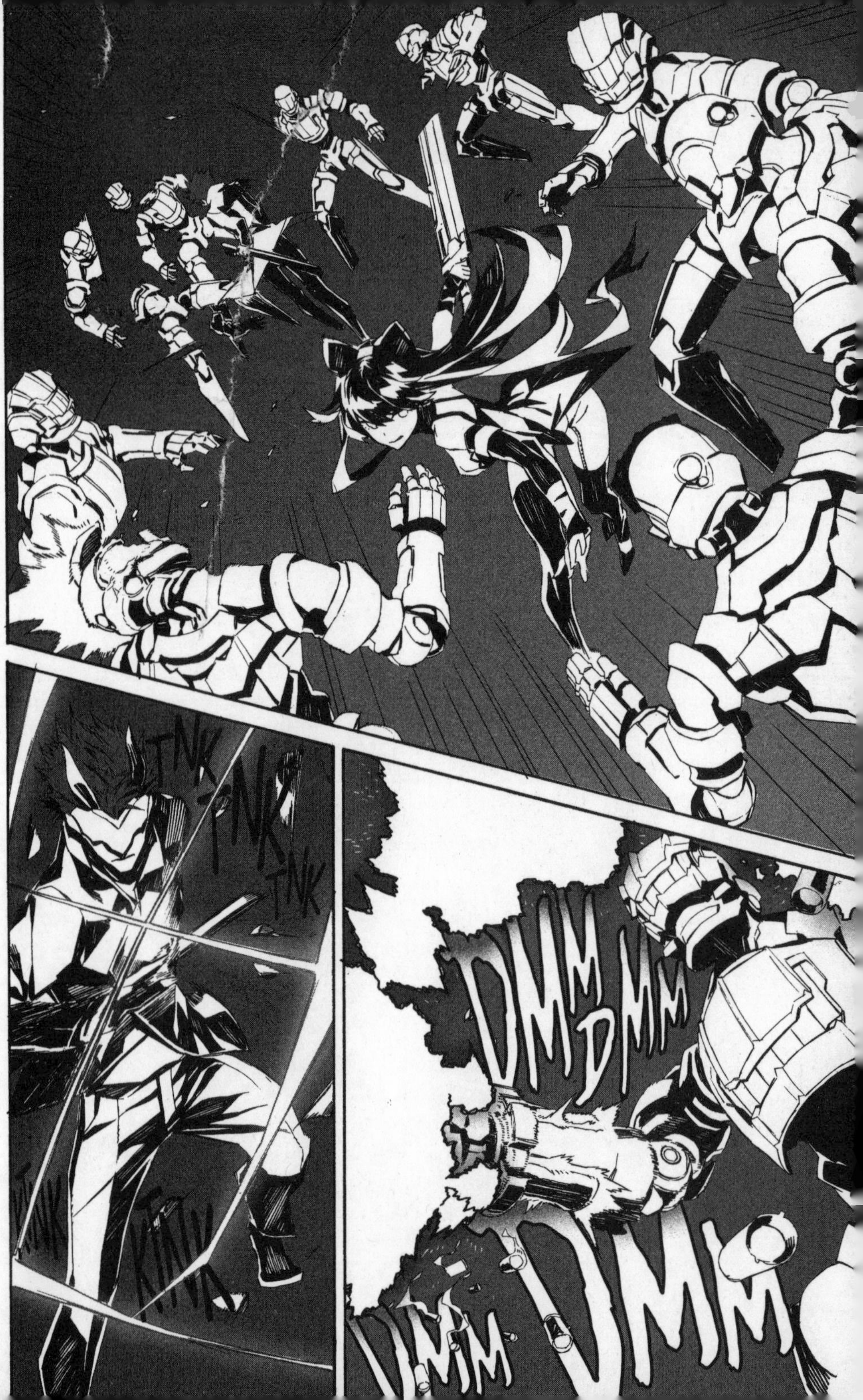
TNK
PNK
TNK
KTINK
DMM
DMM
DMM
DMM
DMM

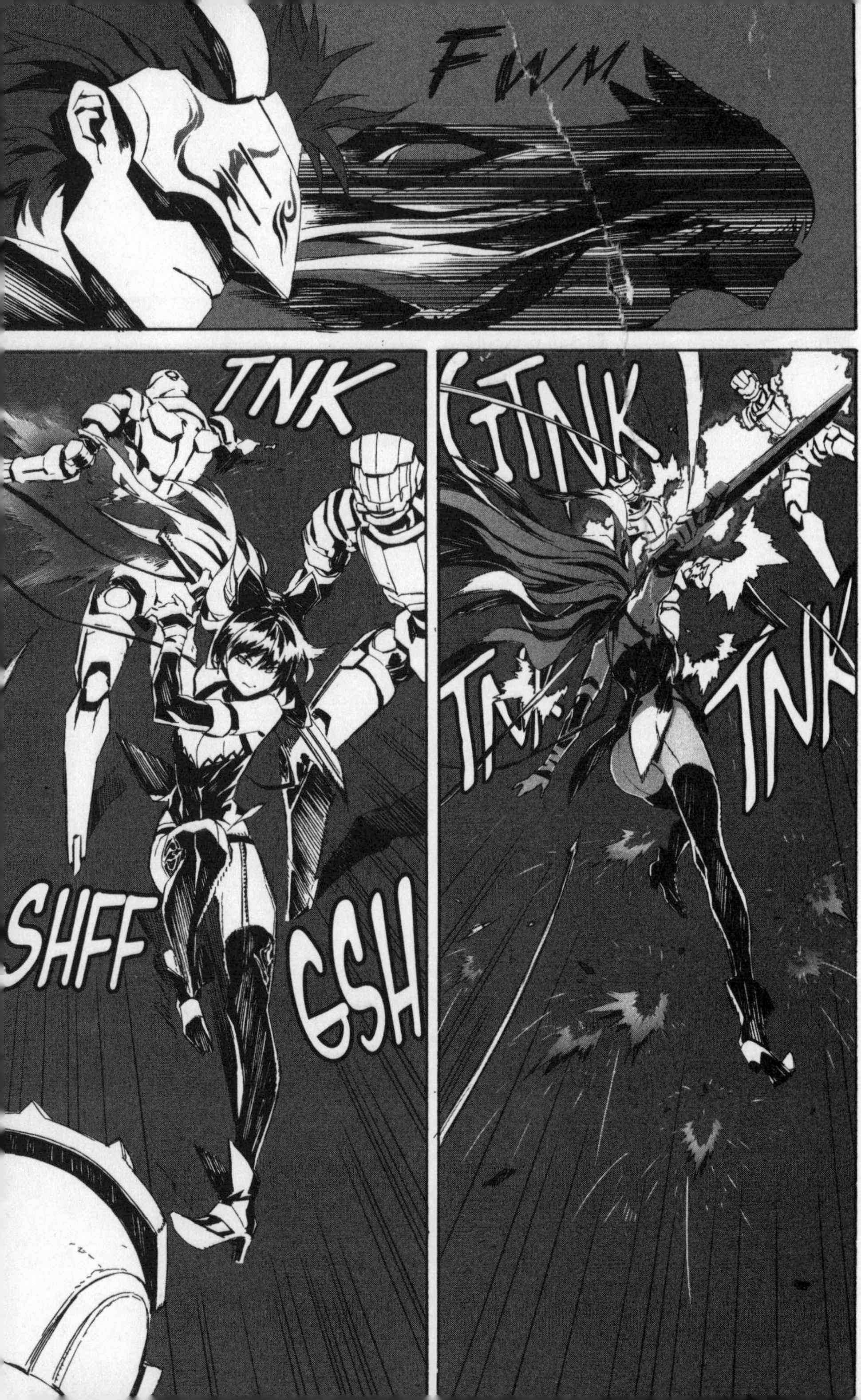
FWM
TINK
TNK
TNK
TNK
GSH
SHFF

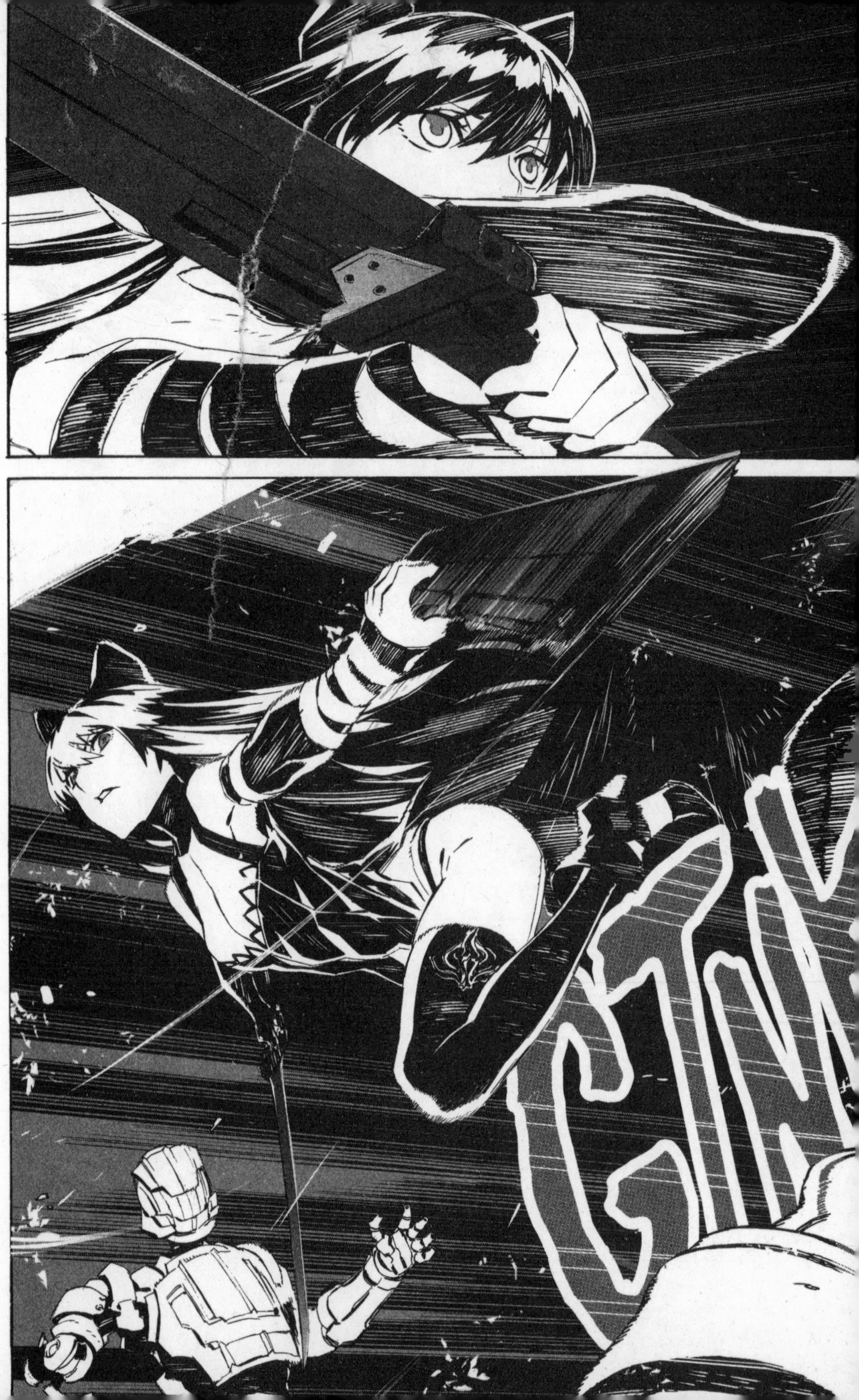

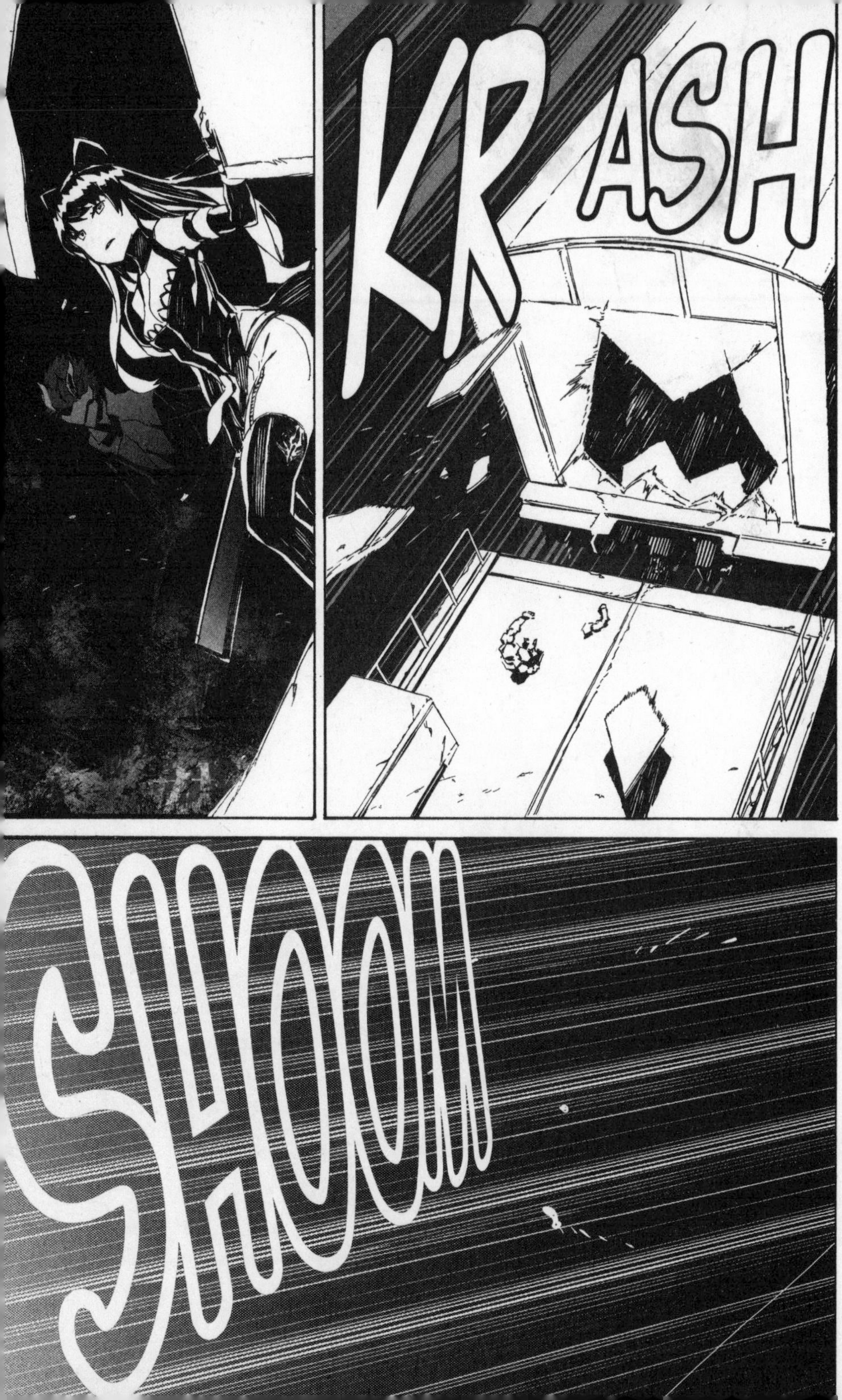
KRASH
SHOOOM

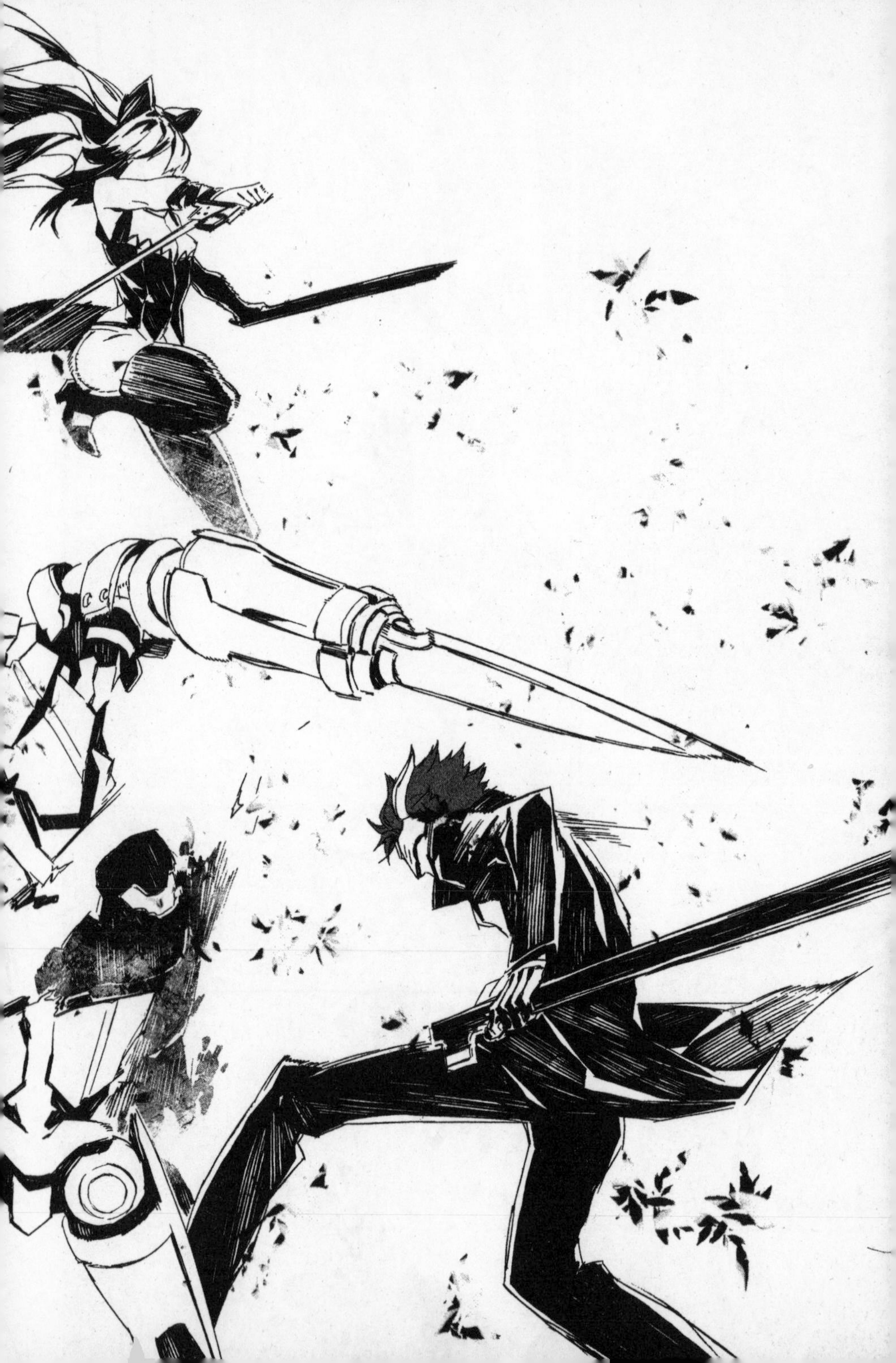

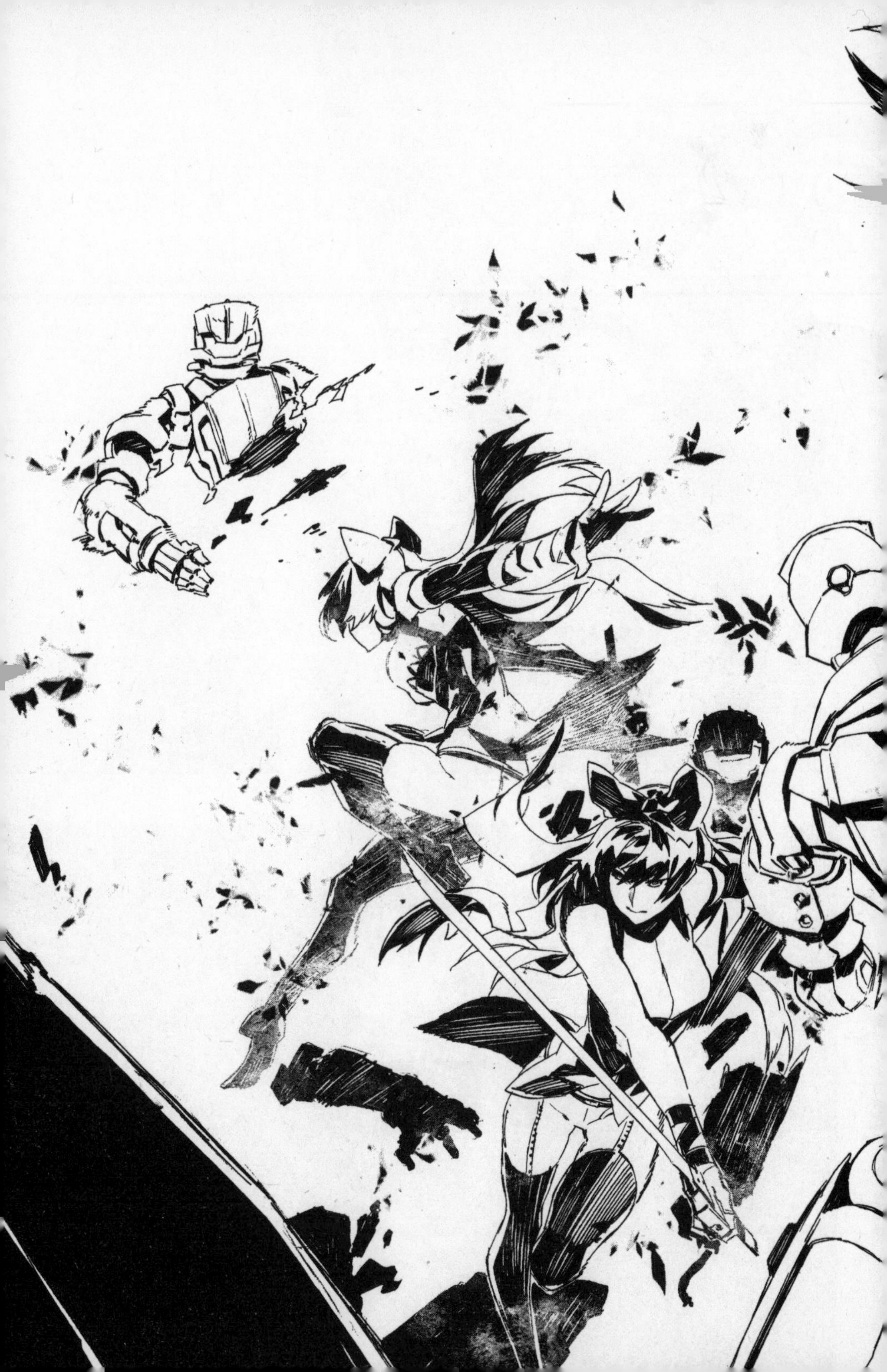

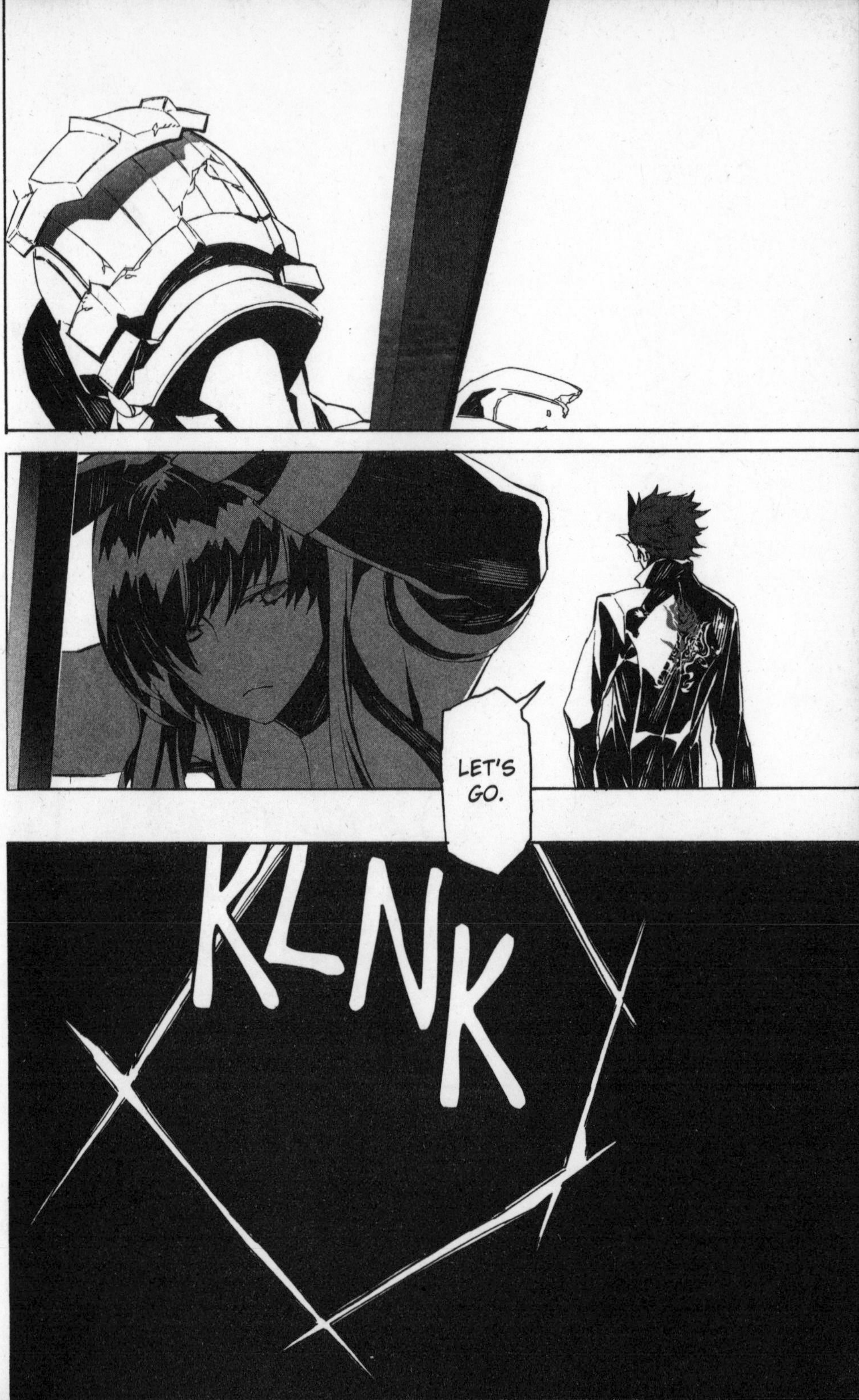
LET'S GO.
KLNK

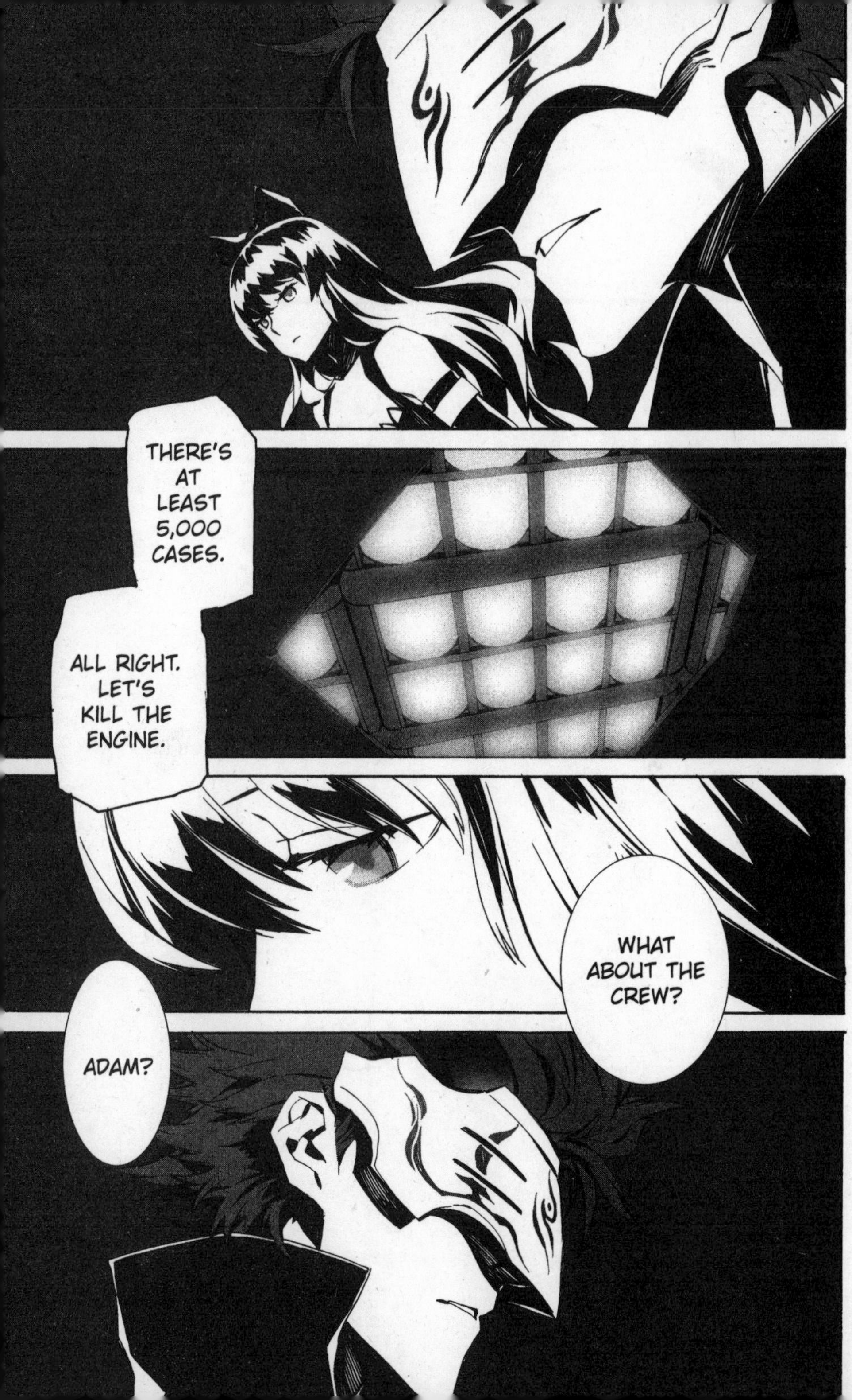
THERE'S AT LEAST 5,000 CASES.
ALL RIGHT. LET'S KILL THE ENGINE.
WHAT ABOUT THE CREW?
ADAM?

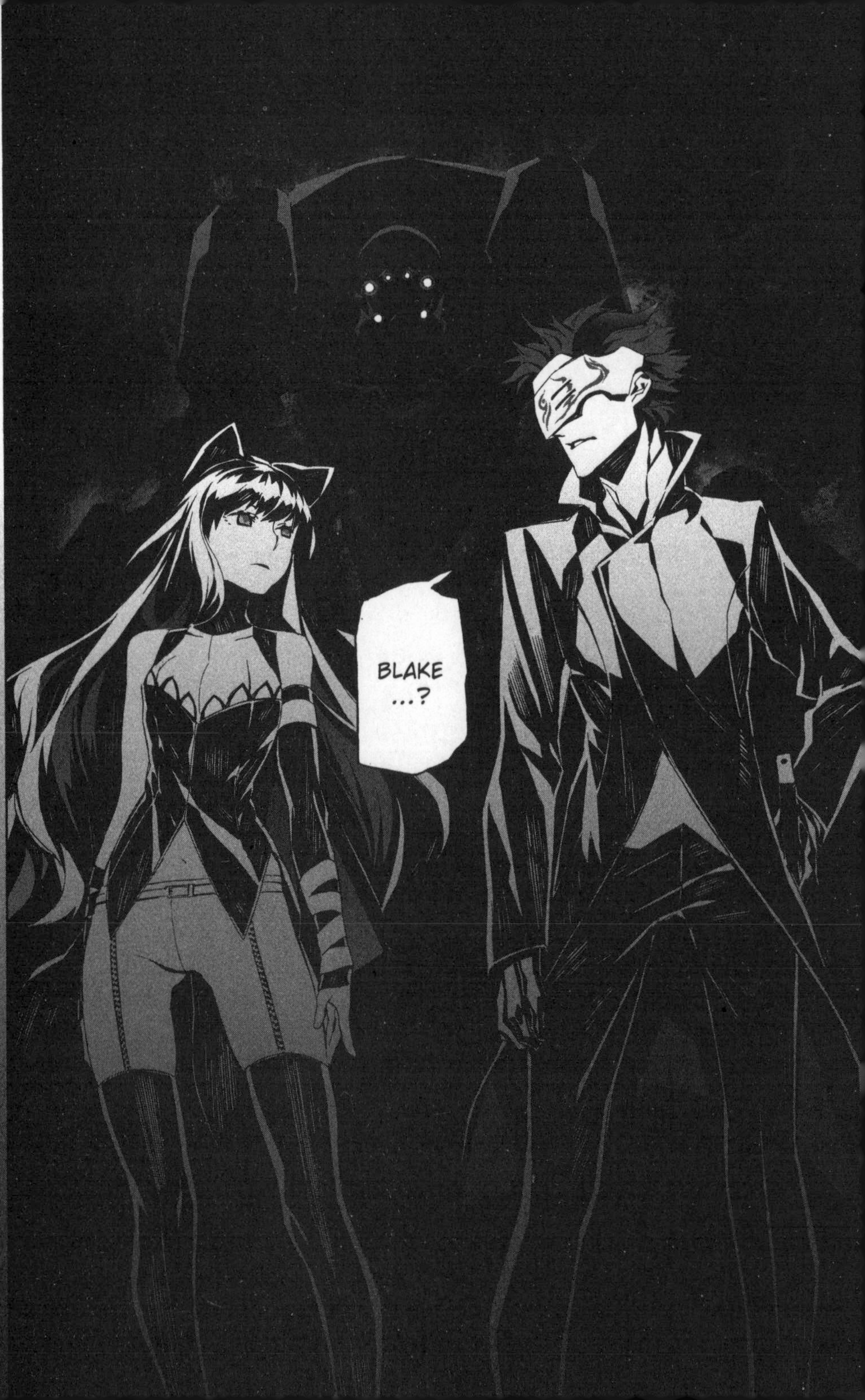
BLAKE ...?

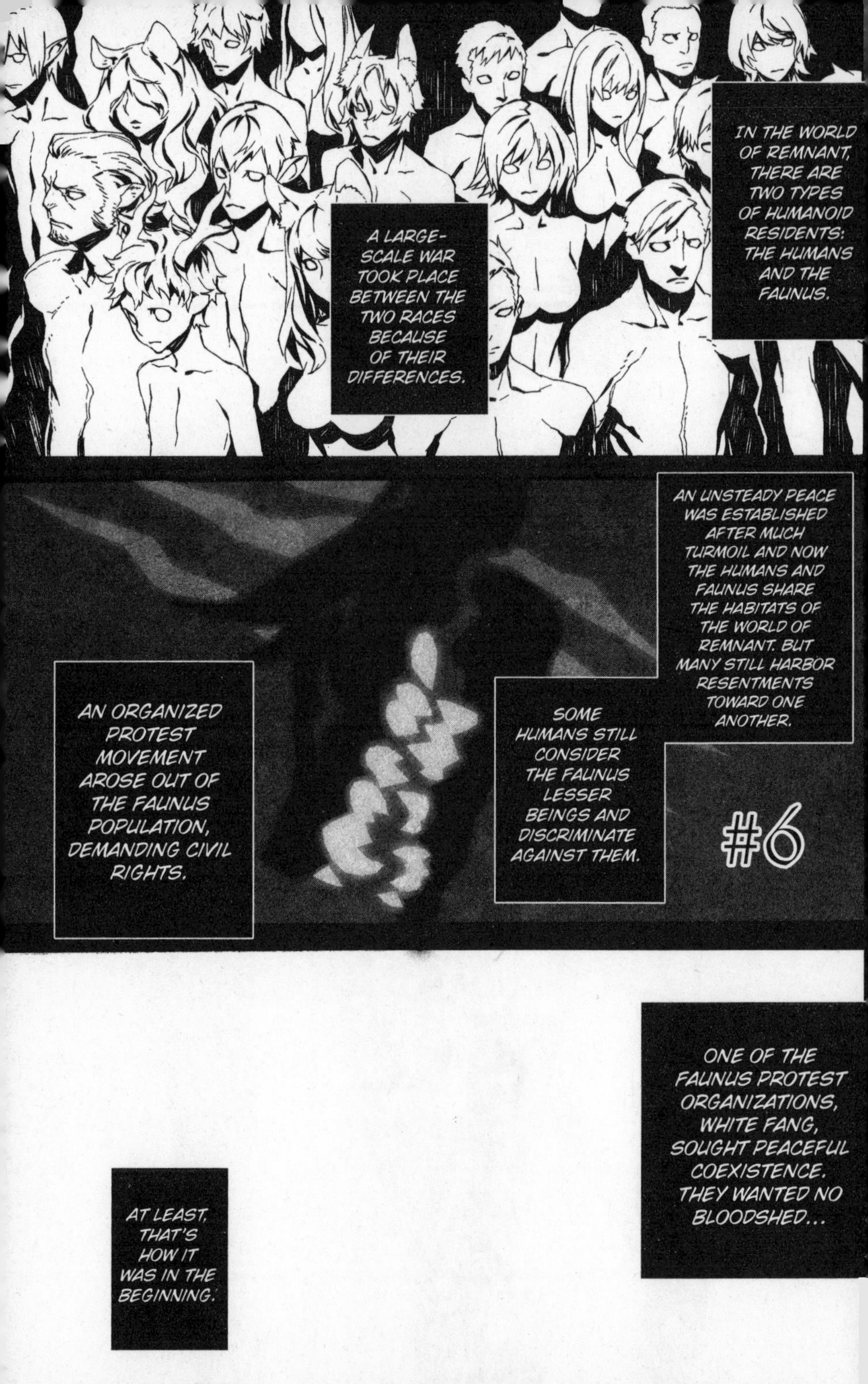
IN THE WORLD OF REMNANT, THERE ARE TWO TYPES OF HUMANOID RESIDENTS: THE HUMANS AND THE FAUNUS.
A LARGE-SCALE WAR TOOK PLACE BETWEEN THE TWO RACES BECAUSE OF THEIR DIFFERENCES.
AN UNSTEADY PEACE WAS ESTABLISHED AFTER MUCH TURMOIL AND NOW THE HUMANS AND FAUNUS SHARE THE HABITATS OF THE WORLD OF REMNANT. BUT MANY STILL HARBOR RESENTMENTS TOWARD ONE ANOTHER.
SOME HUMANS STILL CONSIDER THE FAUNUS LESSER BEINGS AND DISCRIMINATE AGAINST THEM.
#6
AN ORGANIZED PROTEST MOVEMENT AROSE OUT OF THE FAUNUS POPULATION, DEMANDING CIVIL RIGHTS.
ONE OF THE FAUNUS PROTEST ORGANIZATIONS, WHITE FANG, SOUGHT PEACEFUL COEXISTENCE. THEY WANTED NO BLOODSHED...
AT LEAST, THAT'S HOW IT WAS IN THE BEGINNING.

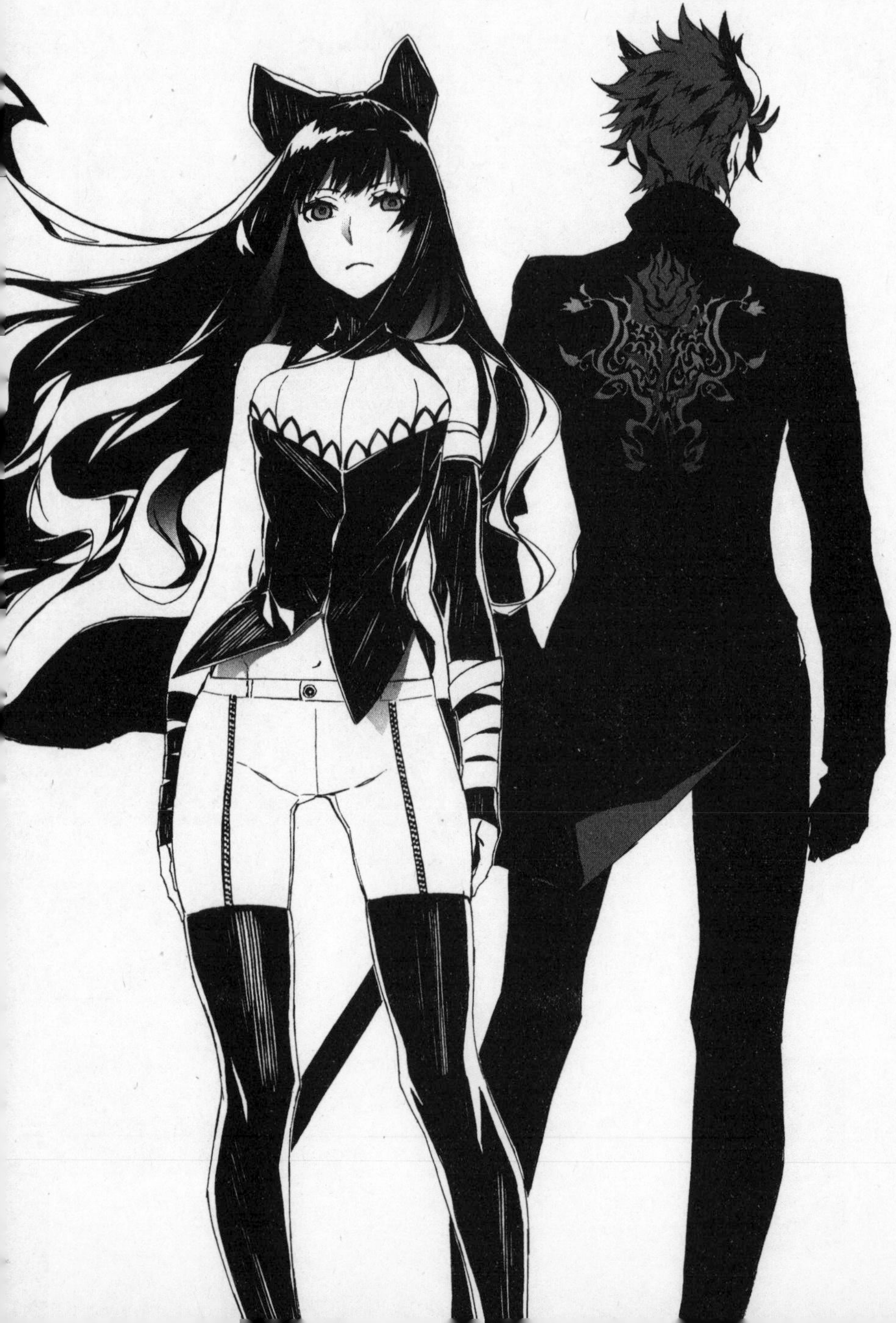

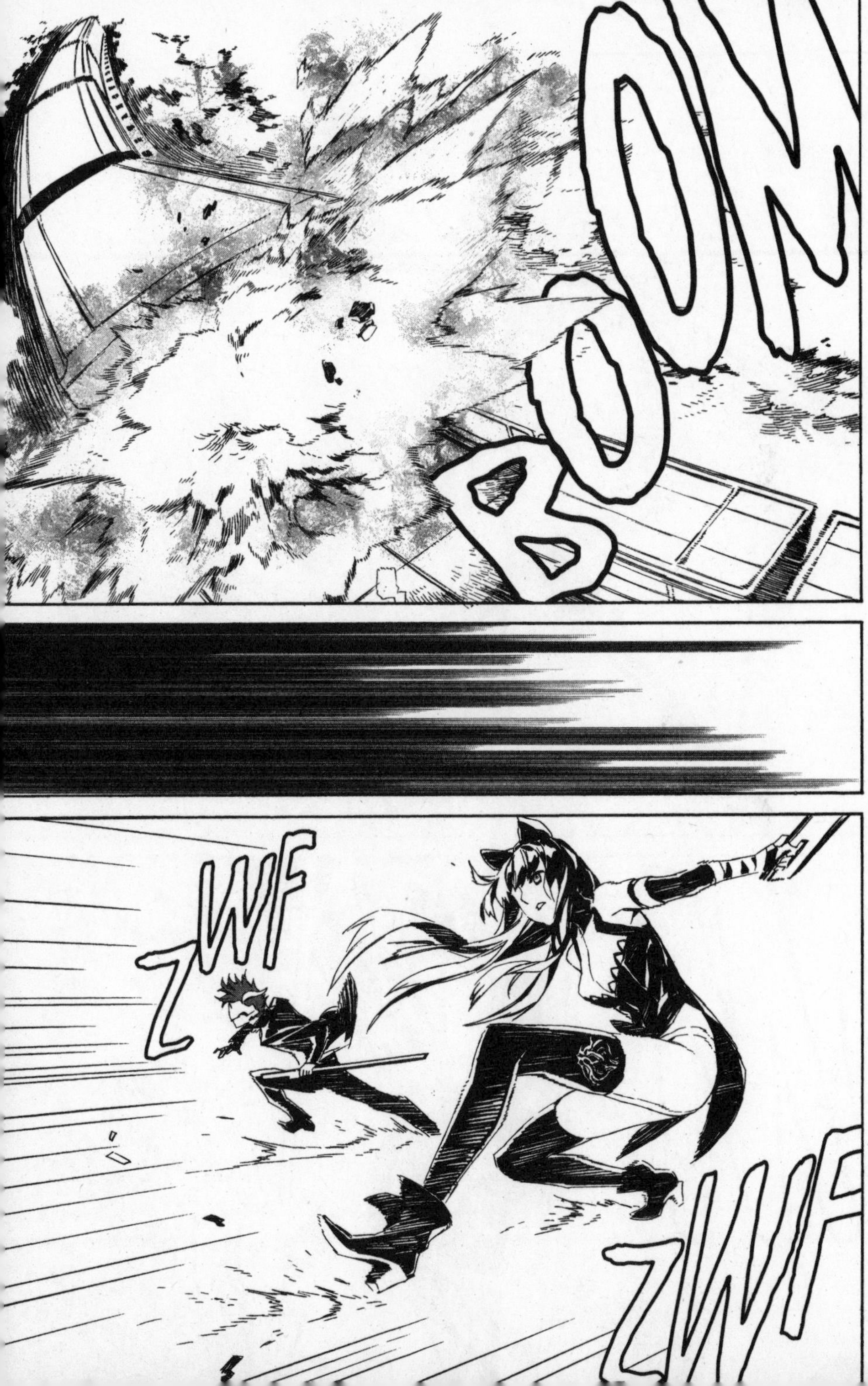
BOOM
ZWF
ZWF

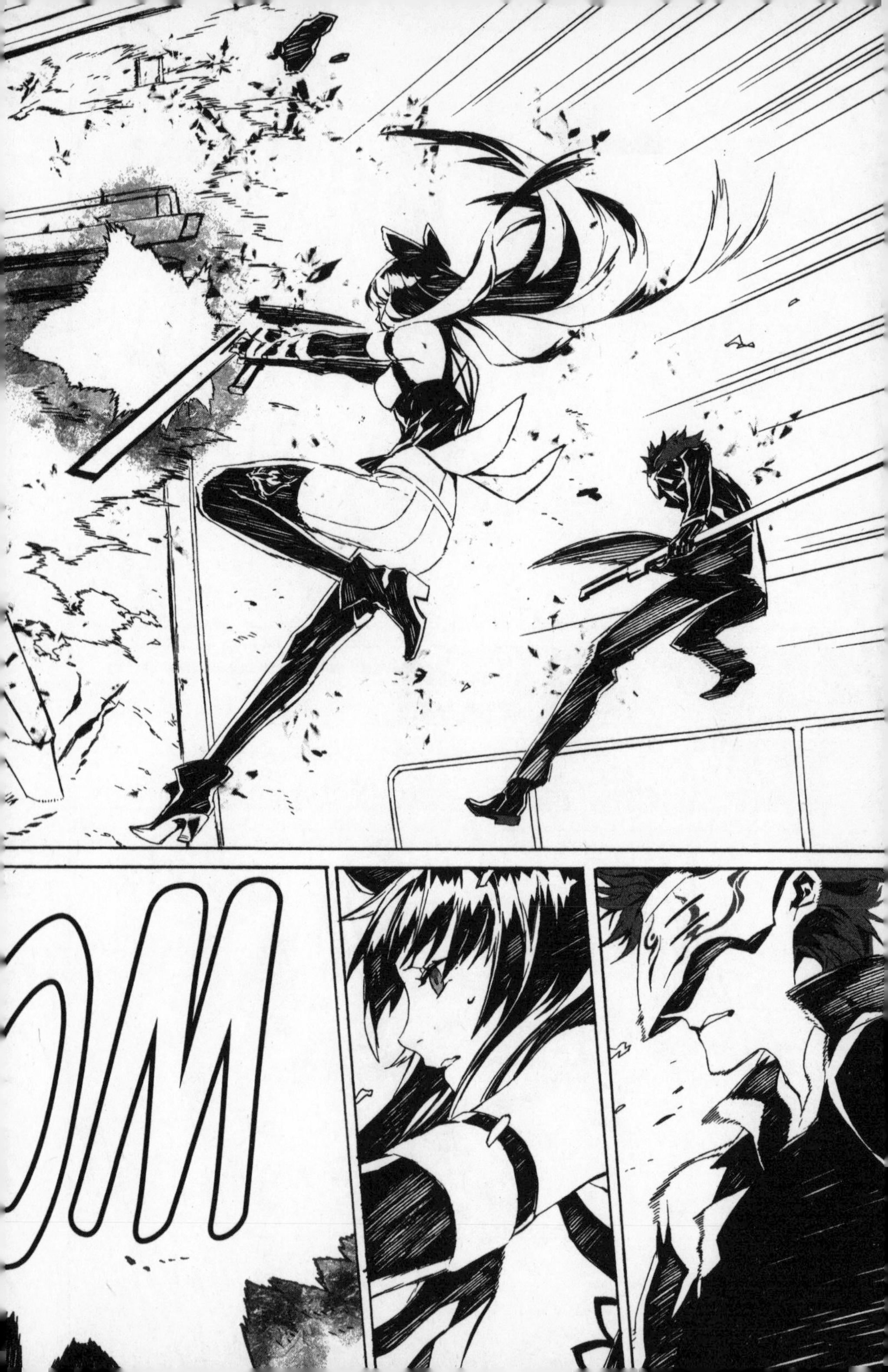
OM

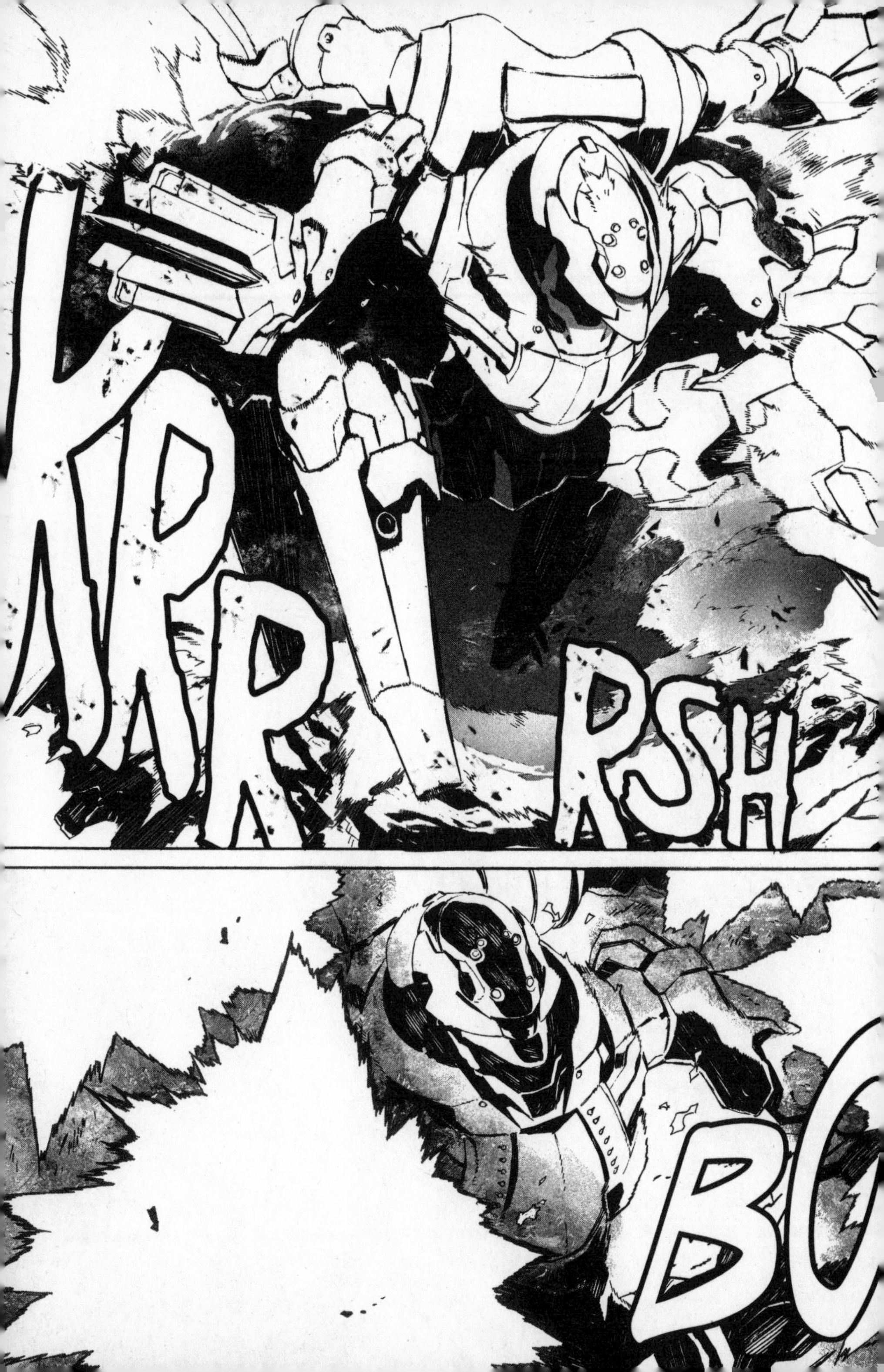
WRRSH
BO

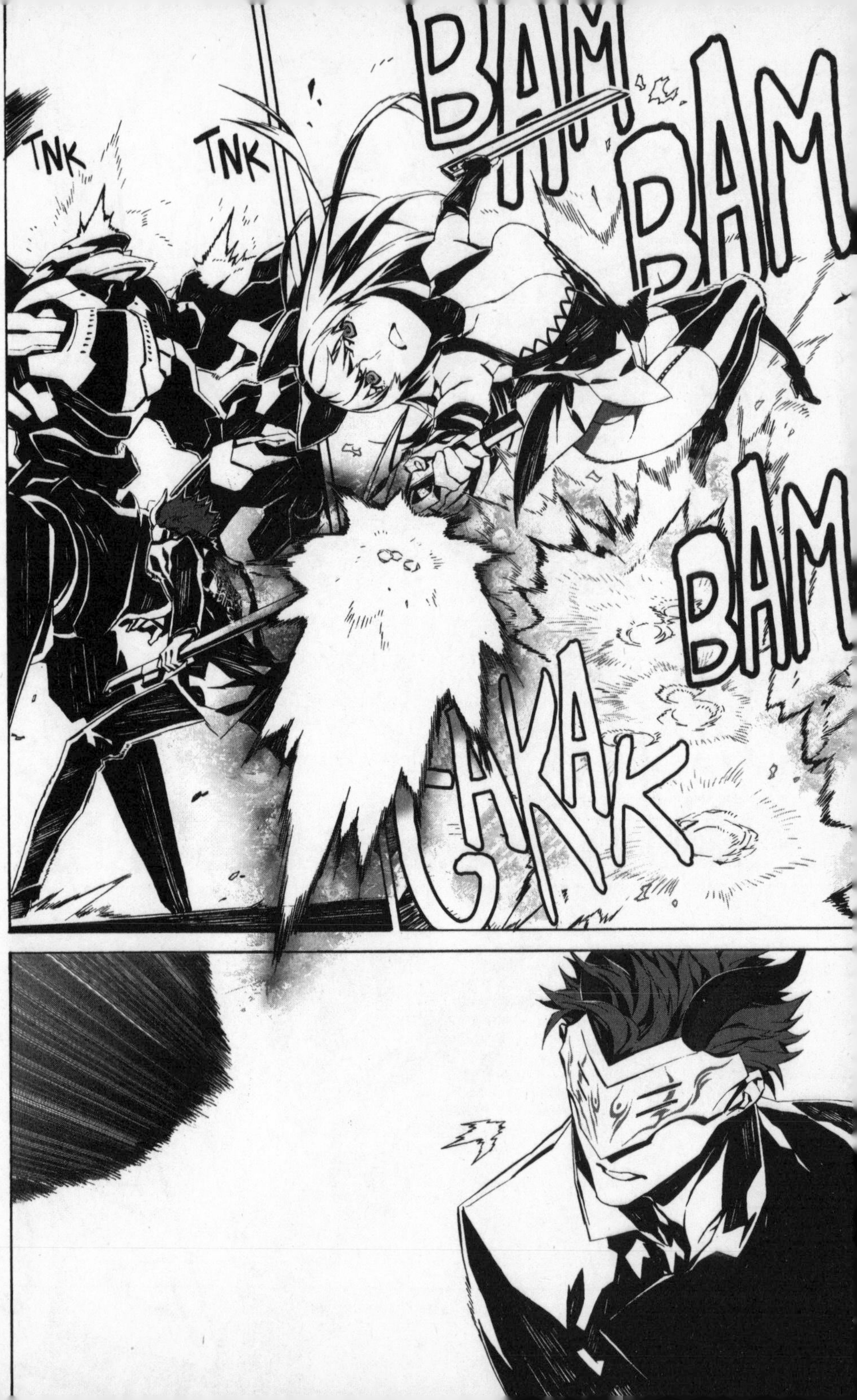
BAM
BAM
BAM
GAKAK
TNK
TNK

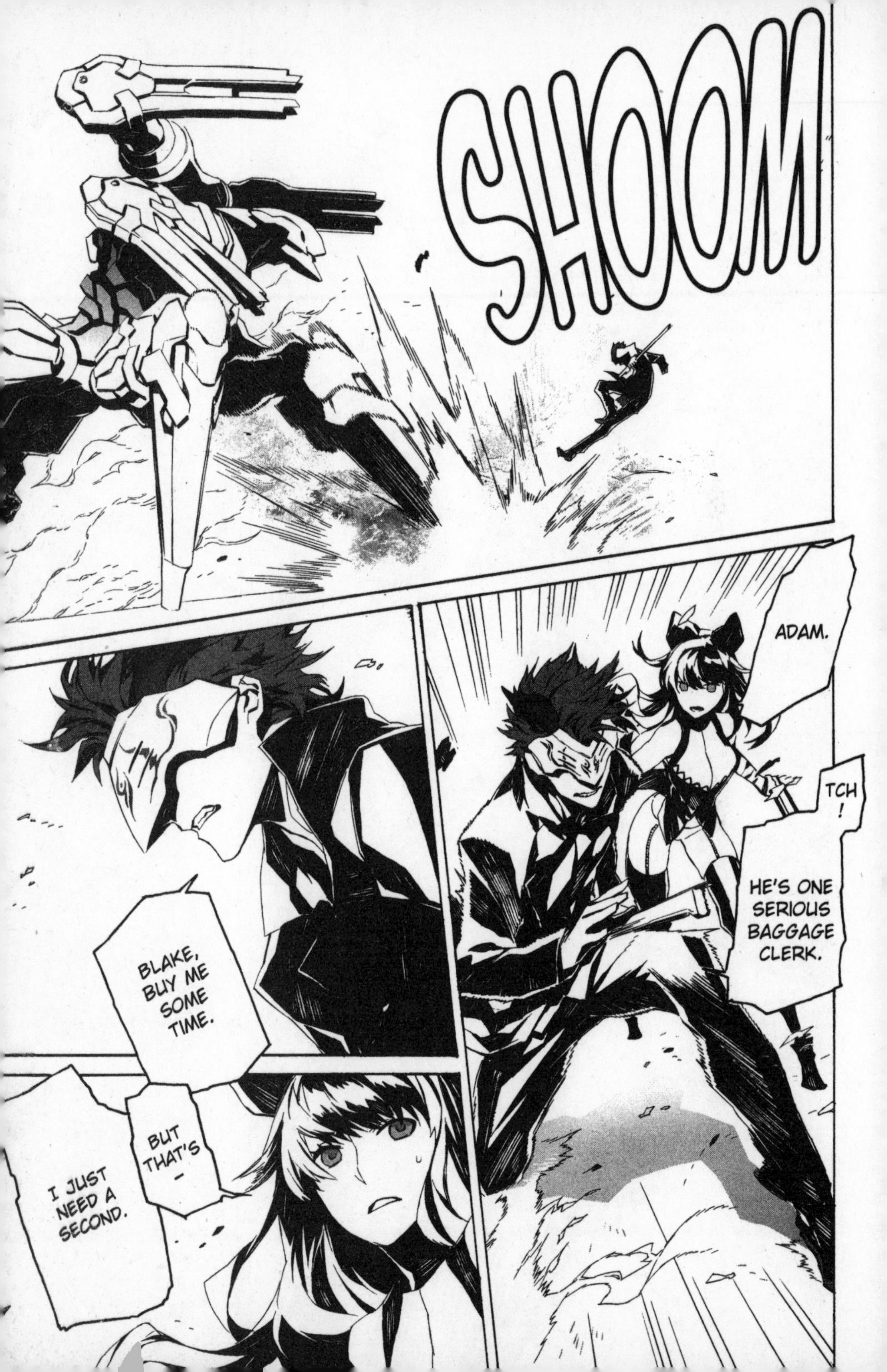
SHOOM
ADAM.
TCH!
HE'S ONE SERIOUS BAGGAGE CLERK.
BLAKE, BUY ME SOME TIME.
BUT THAT'S –
I JUST NEED A SECOND.

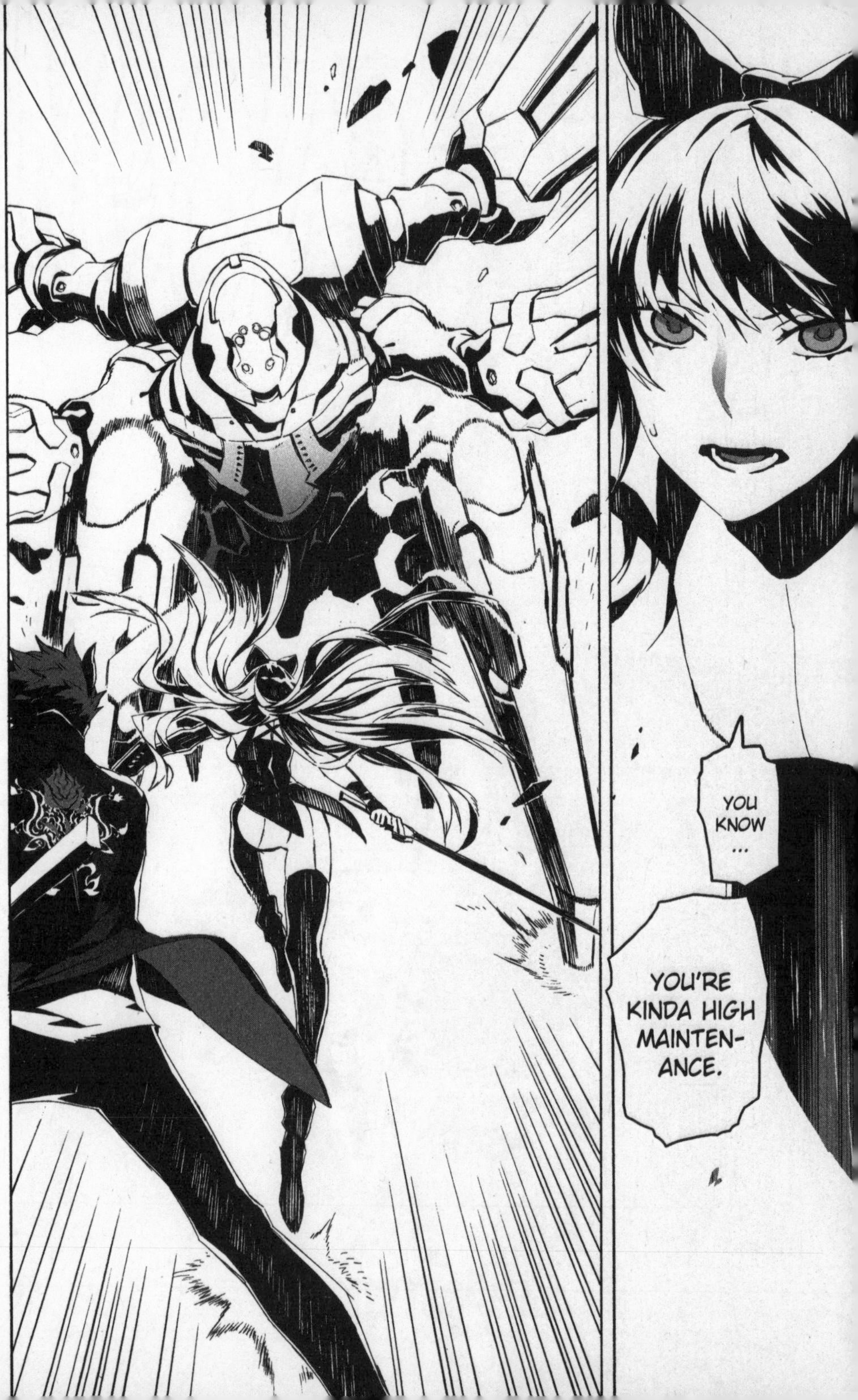
YOU KNOW ...
YOU'RE KINDA HIGH MAINTEN-ANCE.

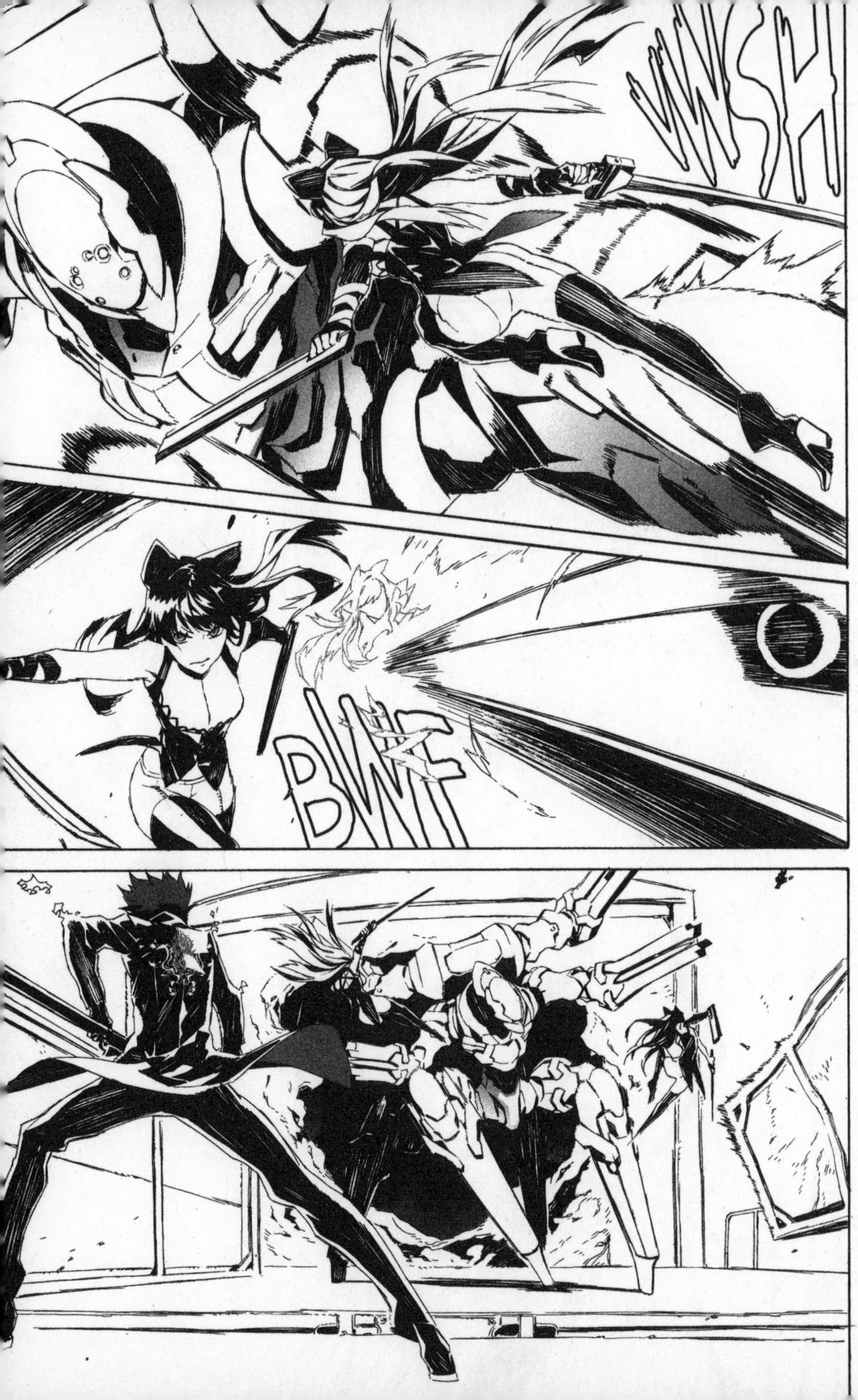
VWSH
BWF

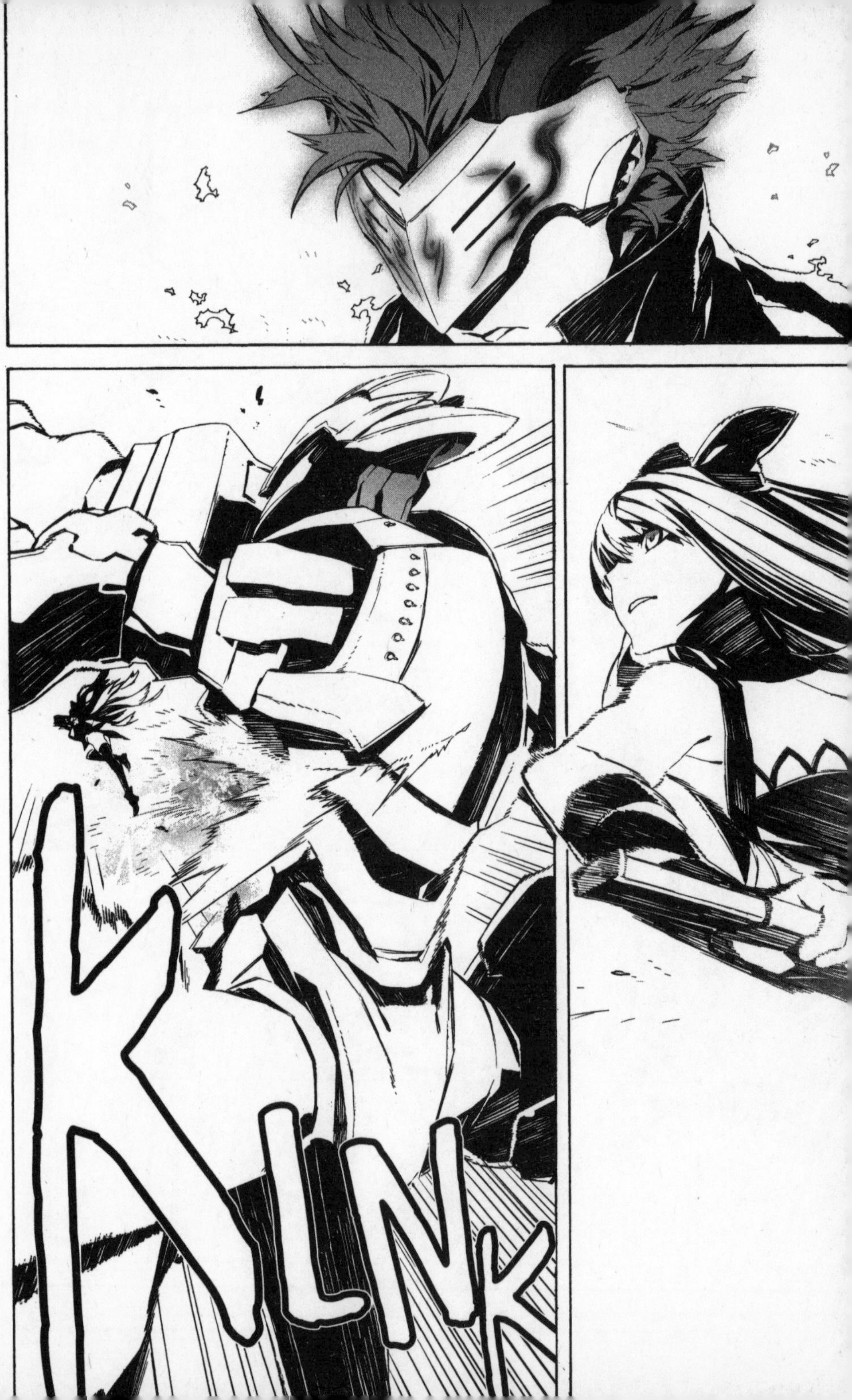
KLINK

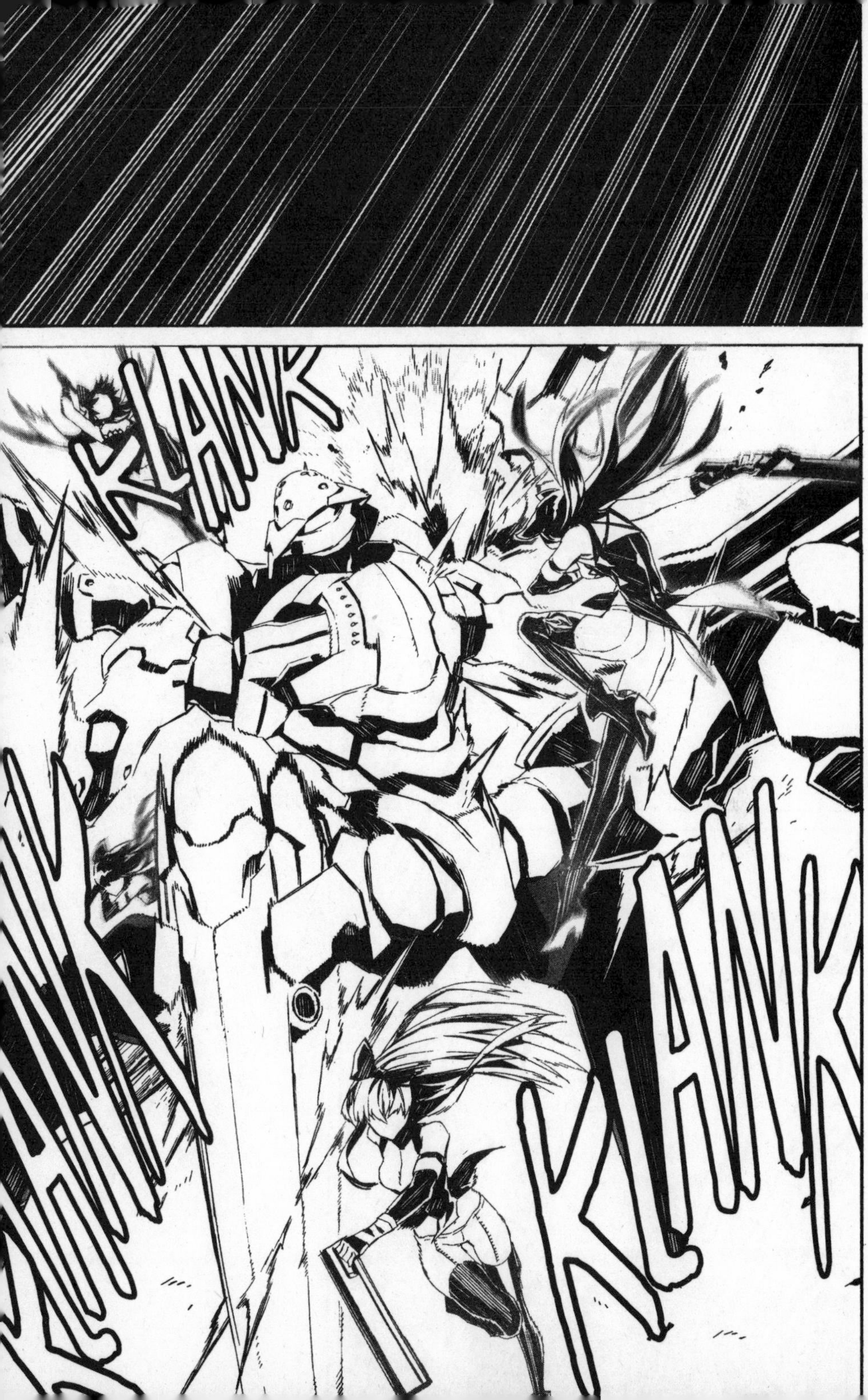
KLANK
KLANK

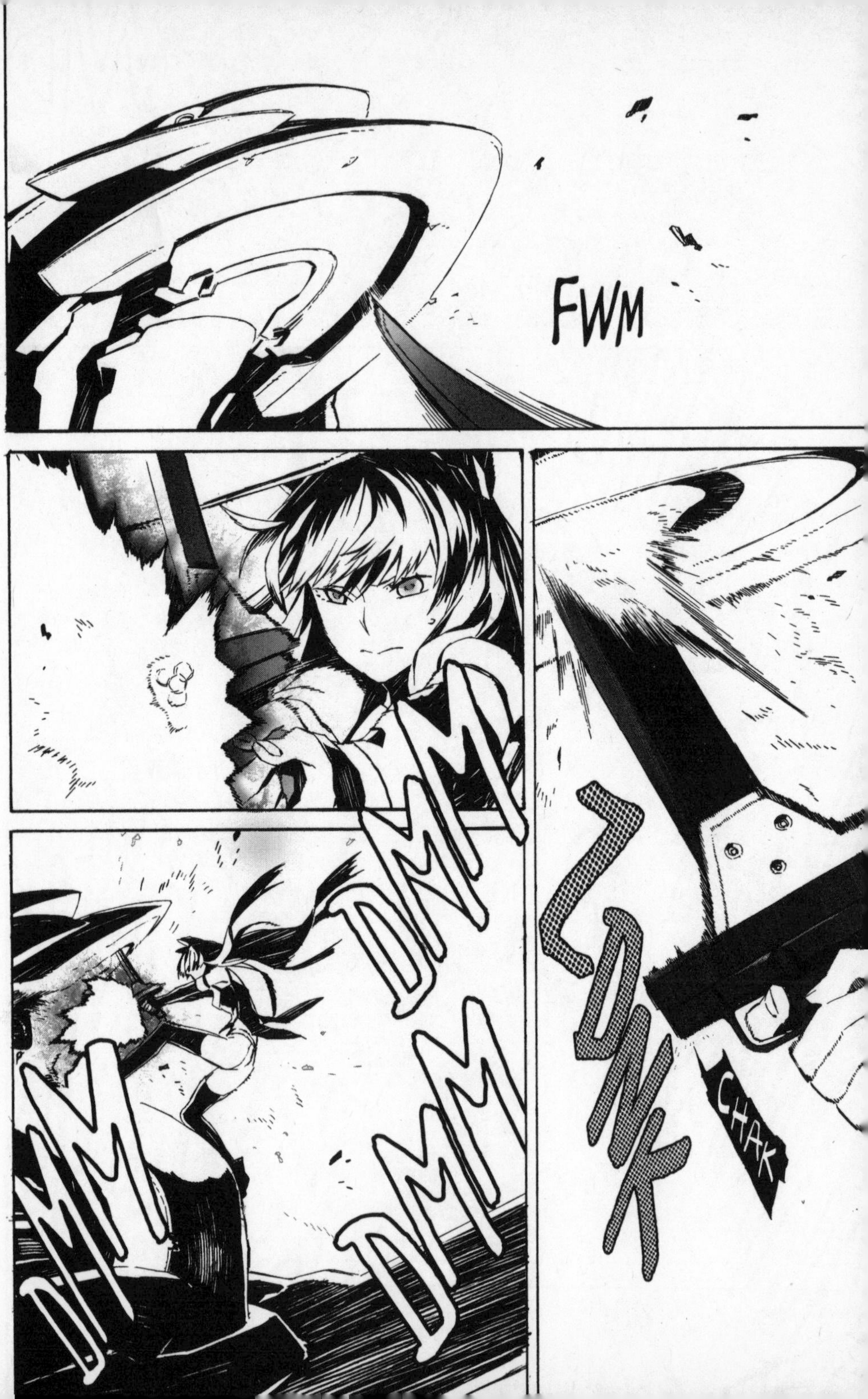
FWM
CLNK
CHAK
DMM
DMM
DMM

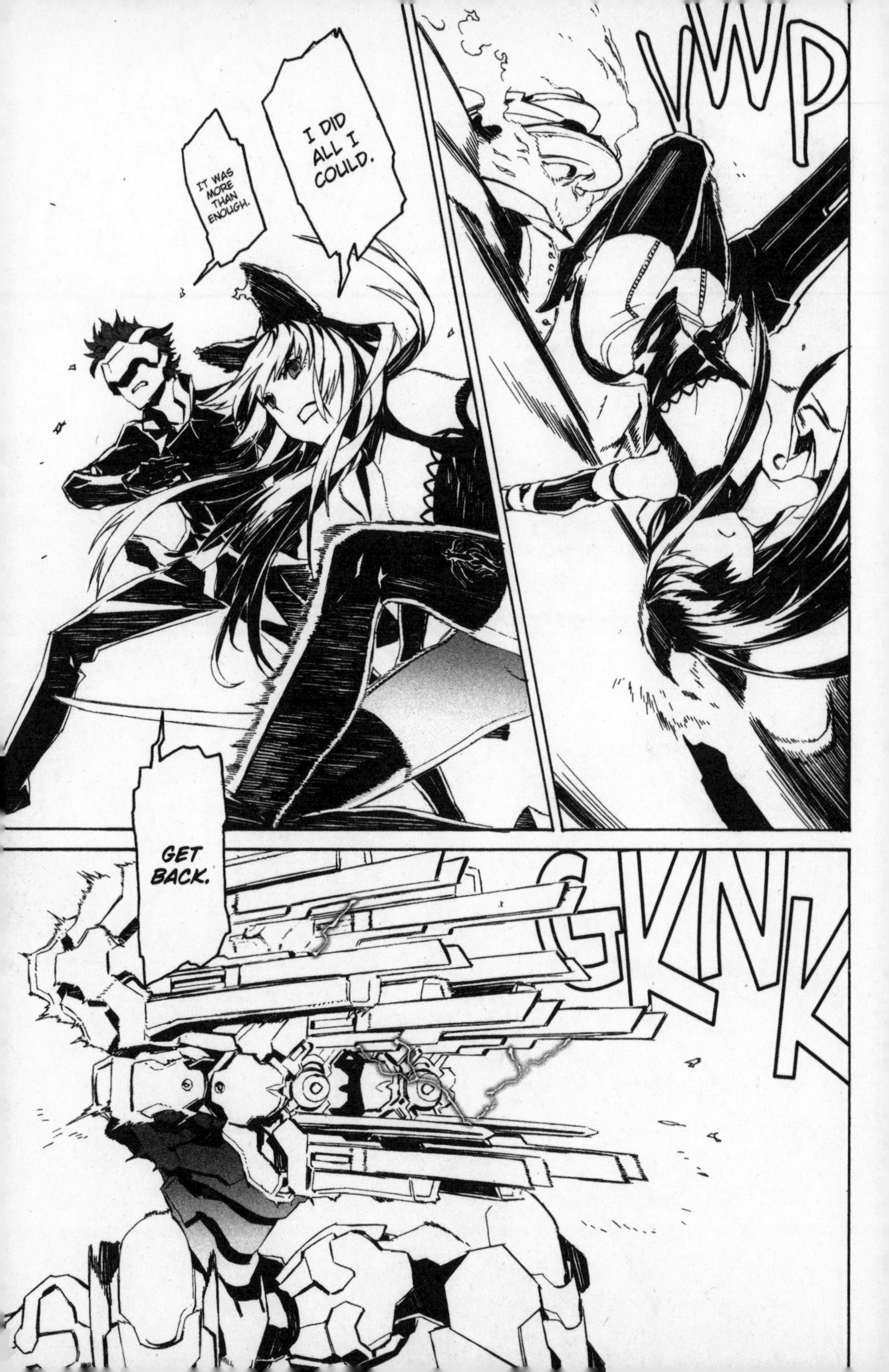
VWP
I DID ALL I COULD.
IT WAS MORE THAN ENOUGH.
GKNK
GET BACK.

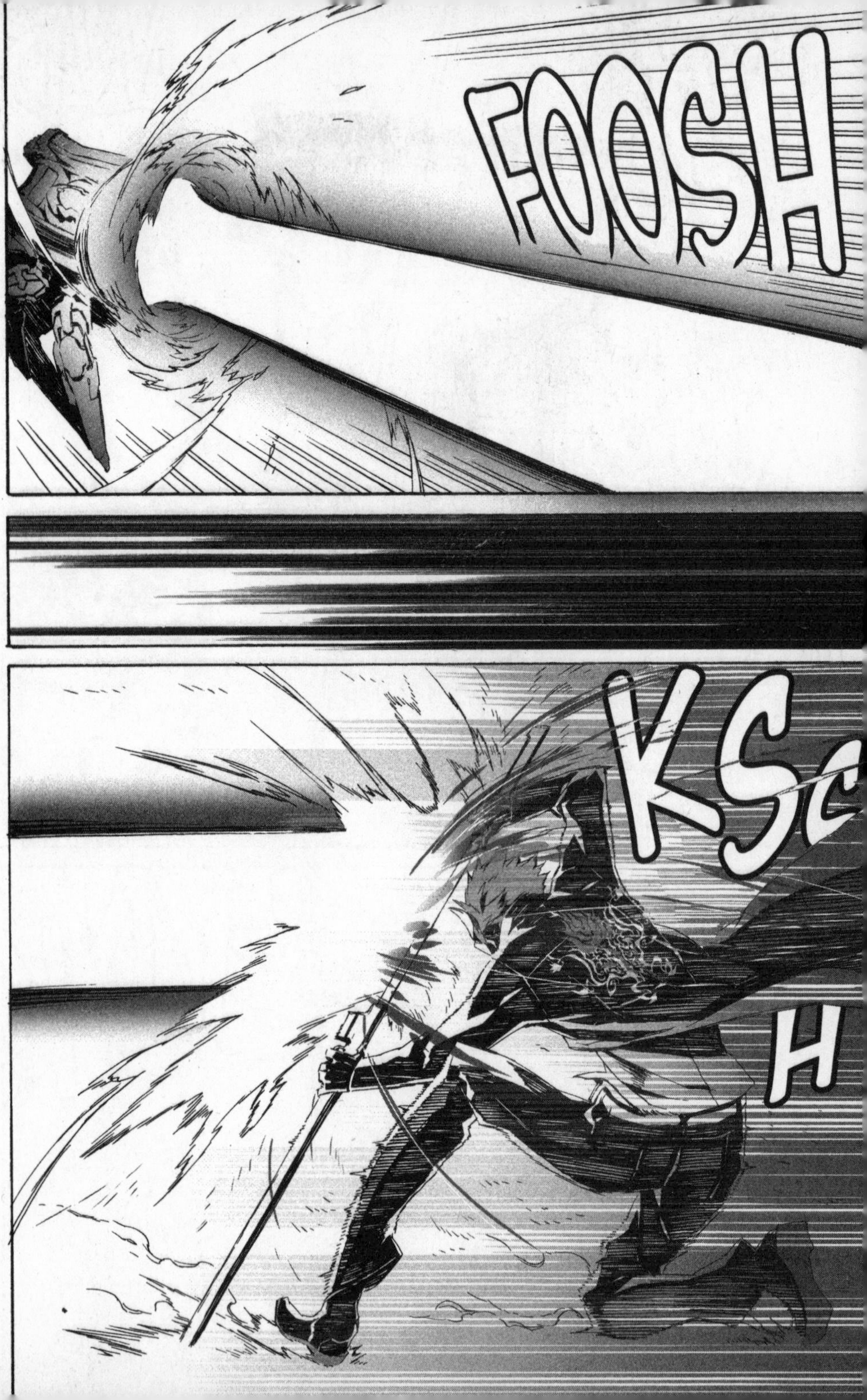
FOOSH
KSc
H

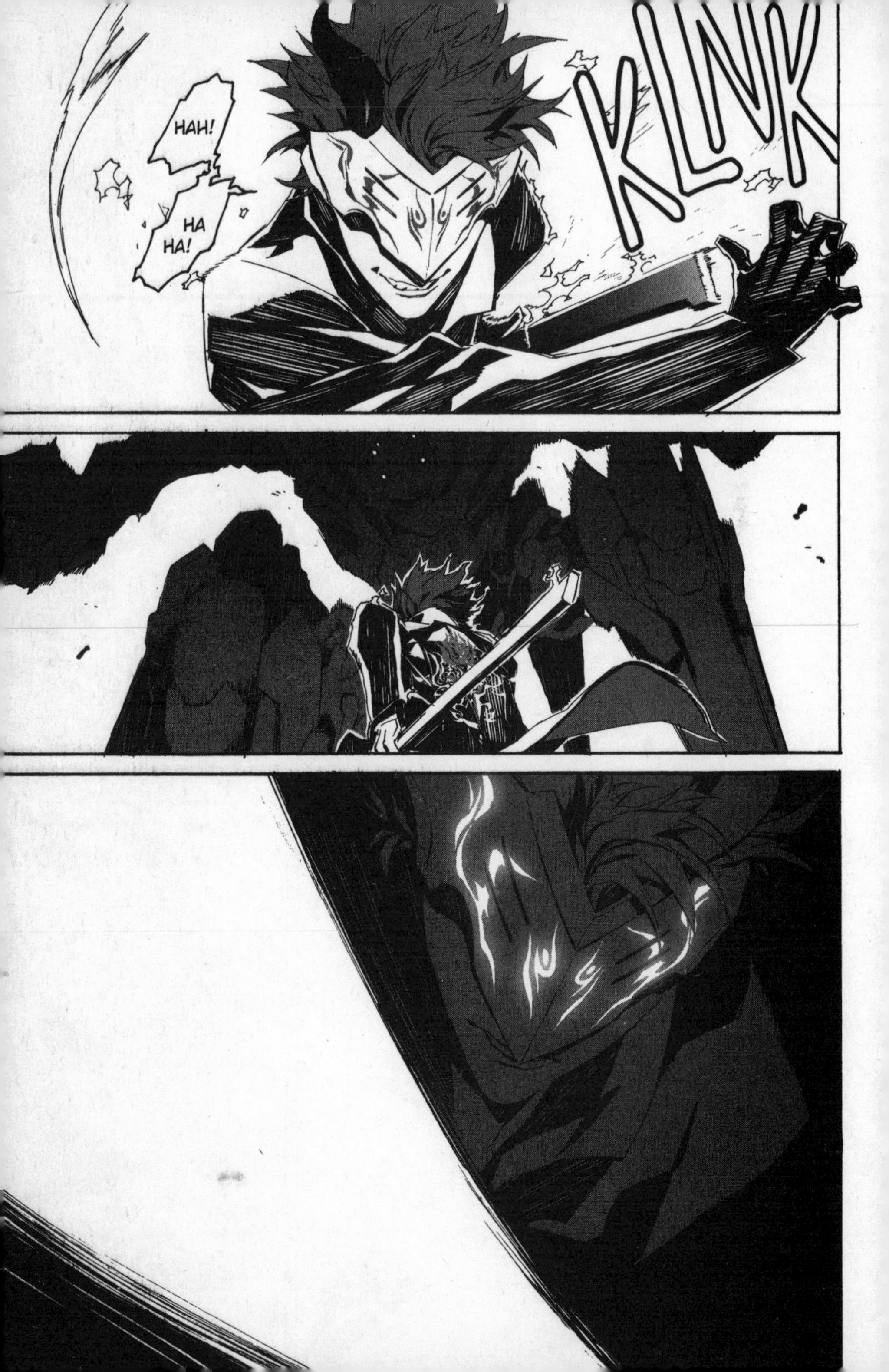
KLNK
HAH!
HA HA!

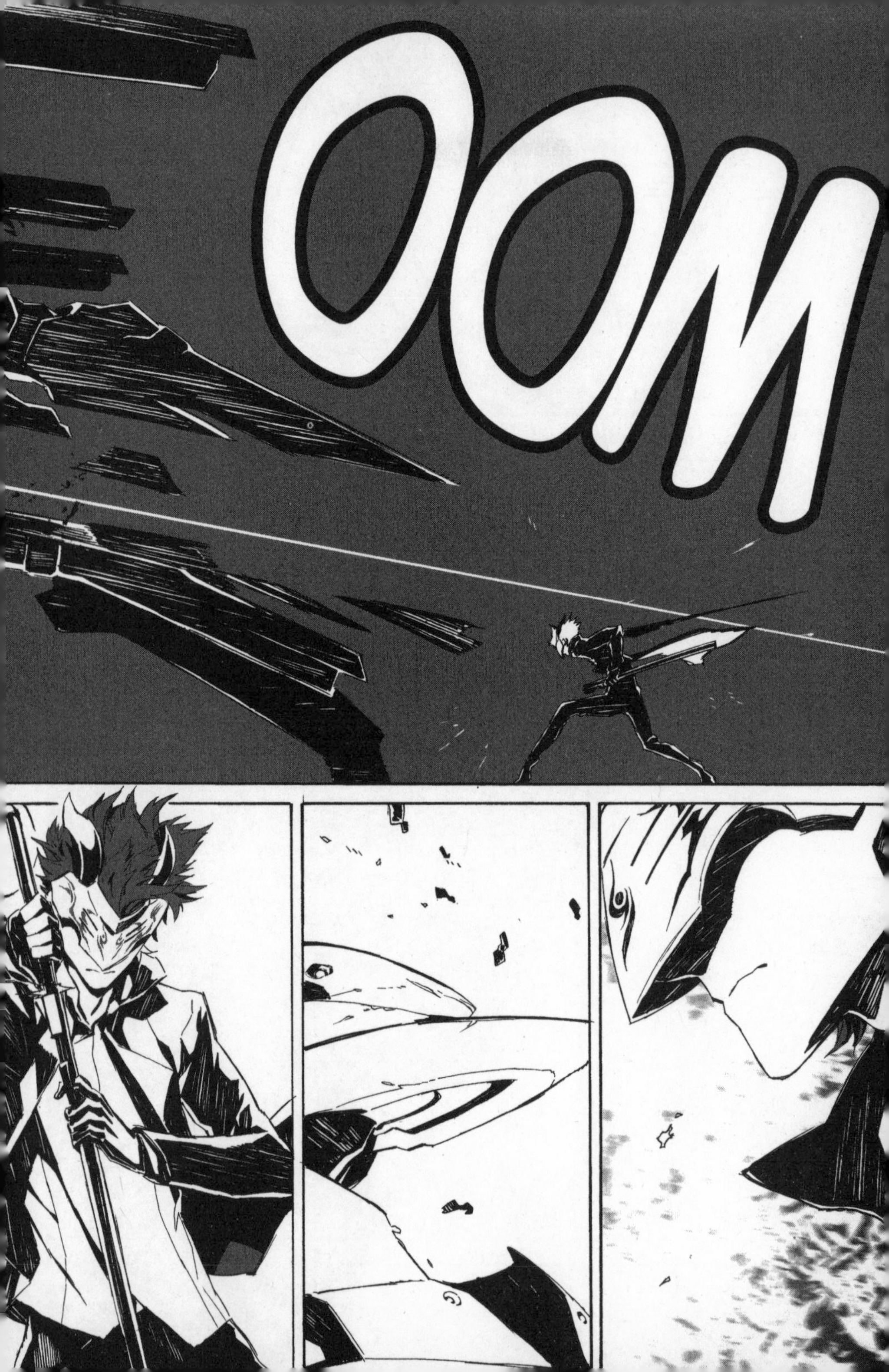
OOM

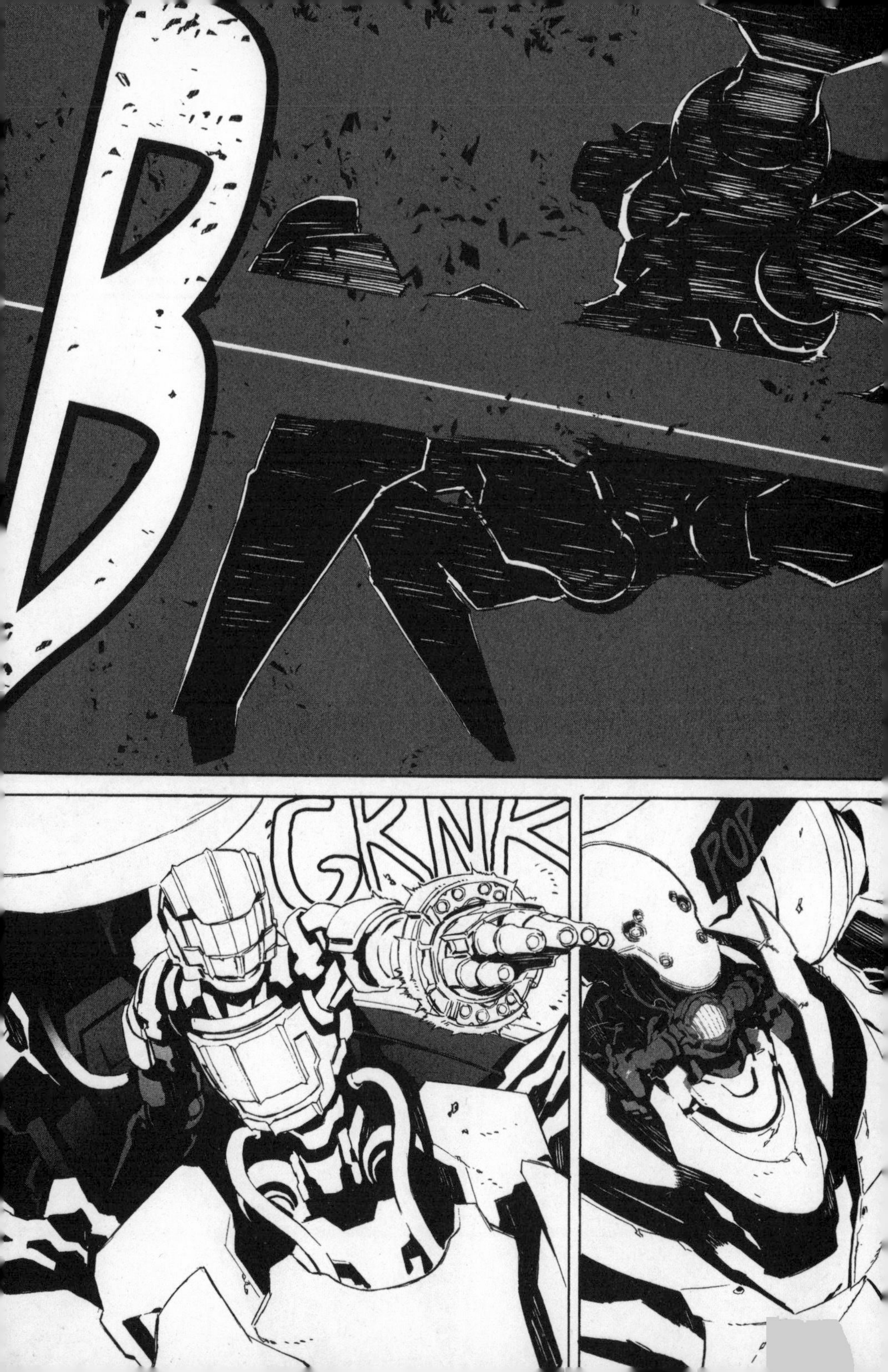
B
POP
GRNK

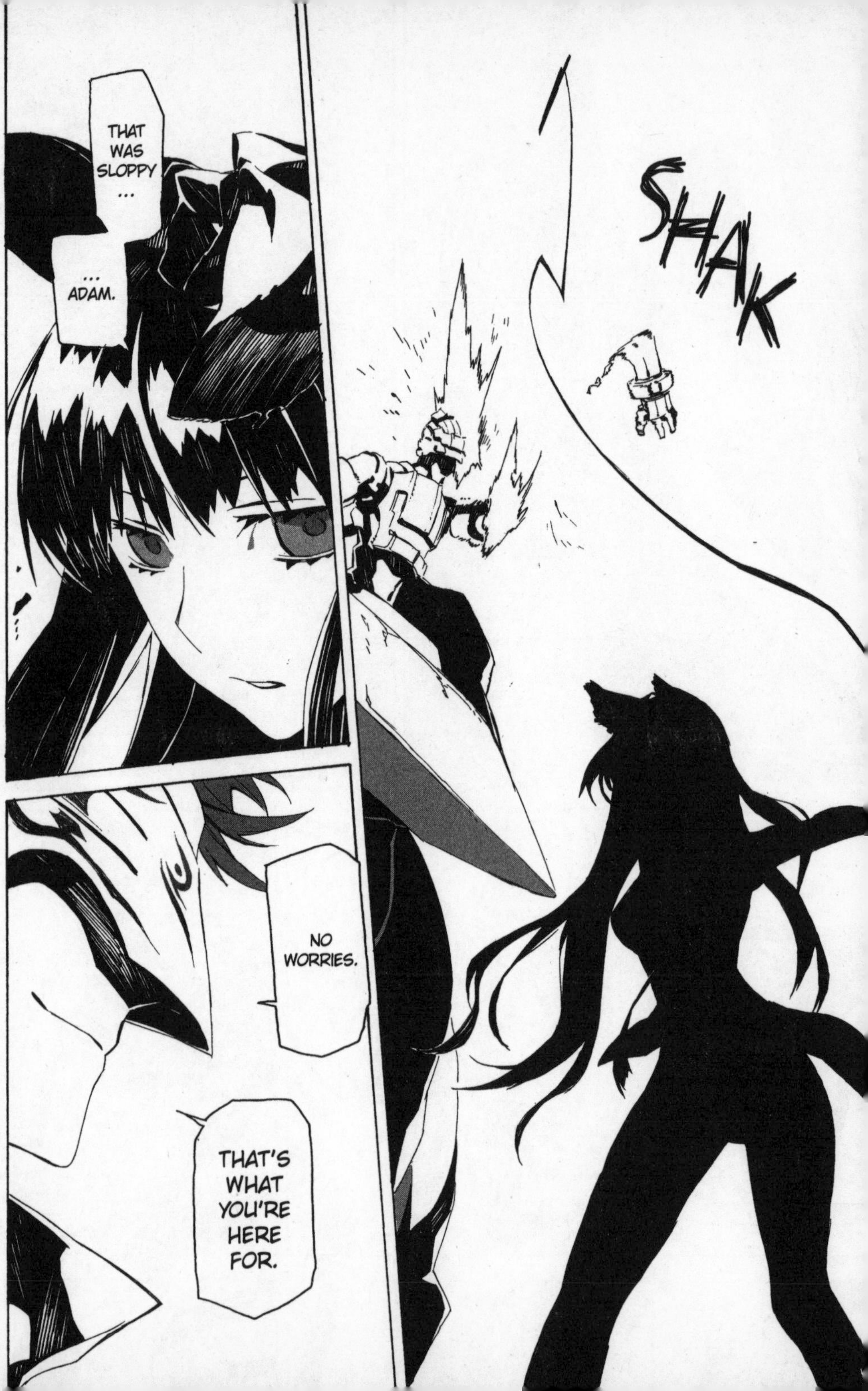
SHAK
THAT WAS SLOPPY ...
... ADAM.
NO WORRIES.
THAT'S WHAT YOU'RE HERE FOR.

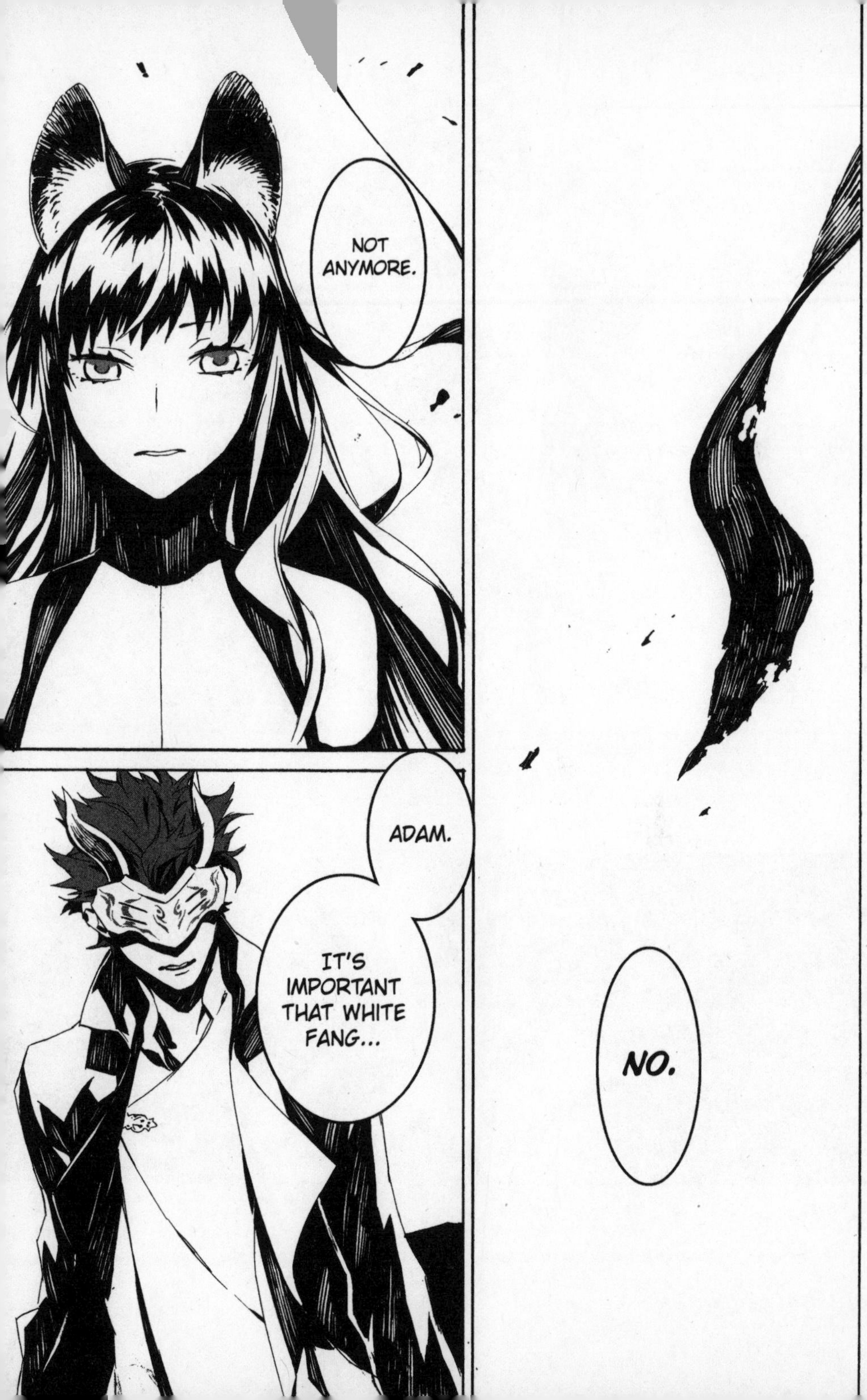
NO.
NOT ANYMORE.
ADAM.
IT'S IMPORTANT THAT WHITE FANG...

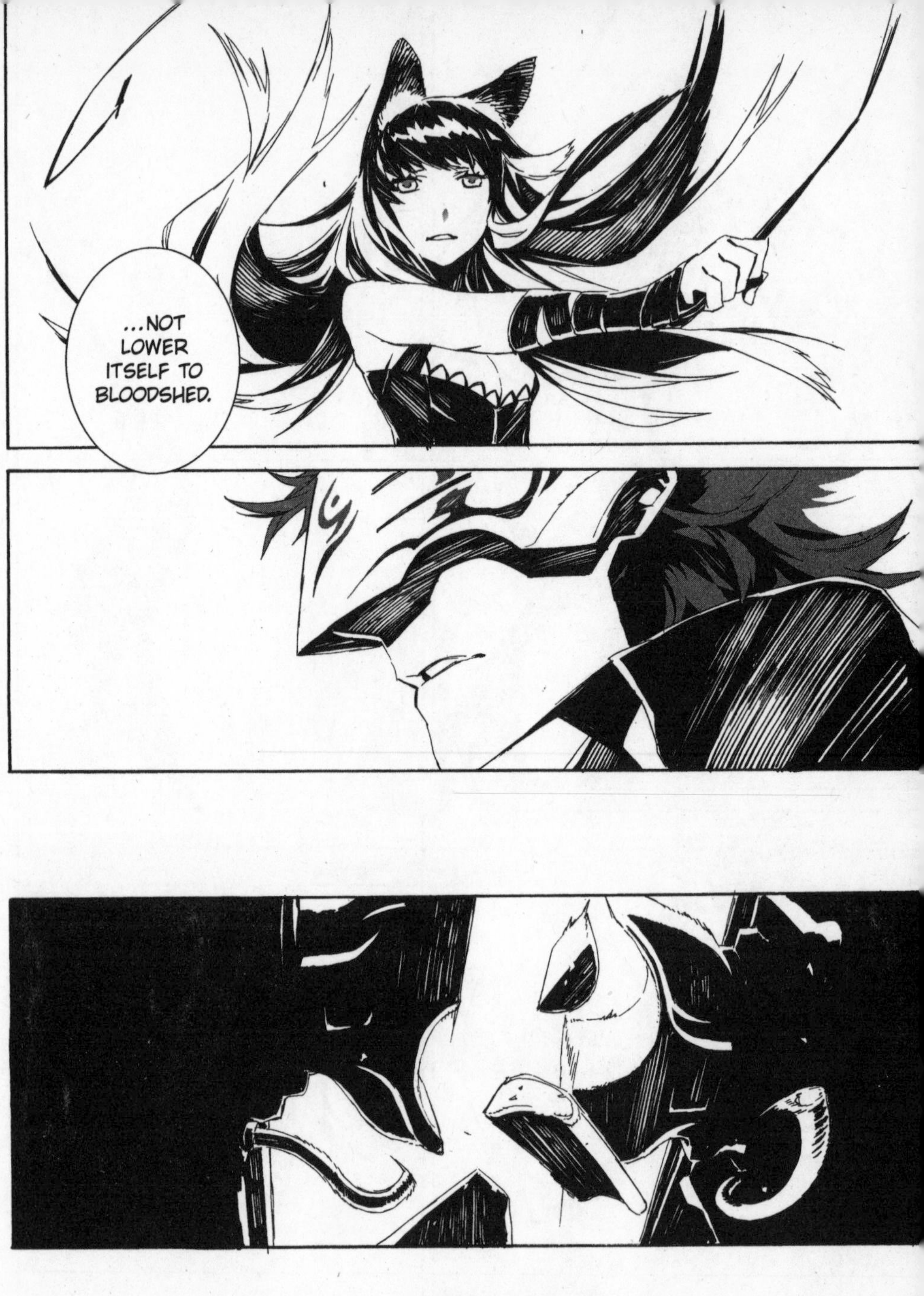
...NOT LOWER ITSELF TO BLOODSHED.

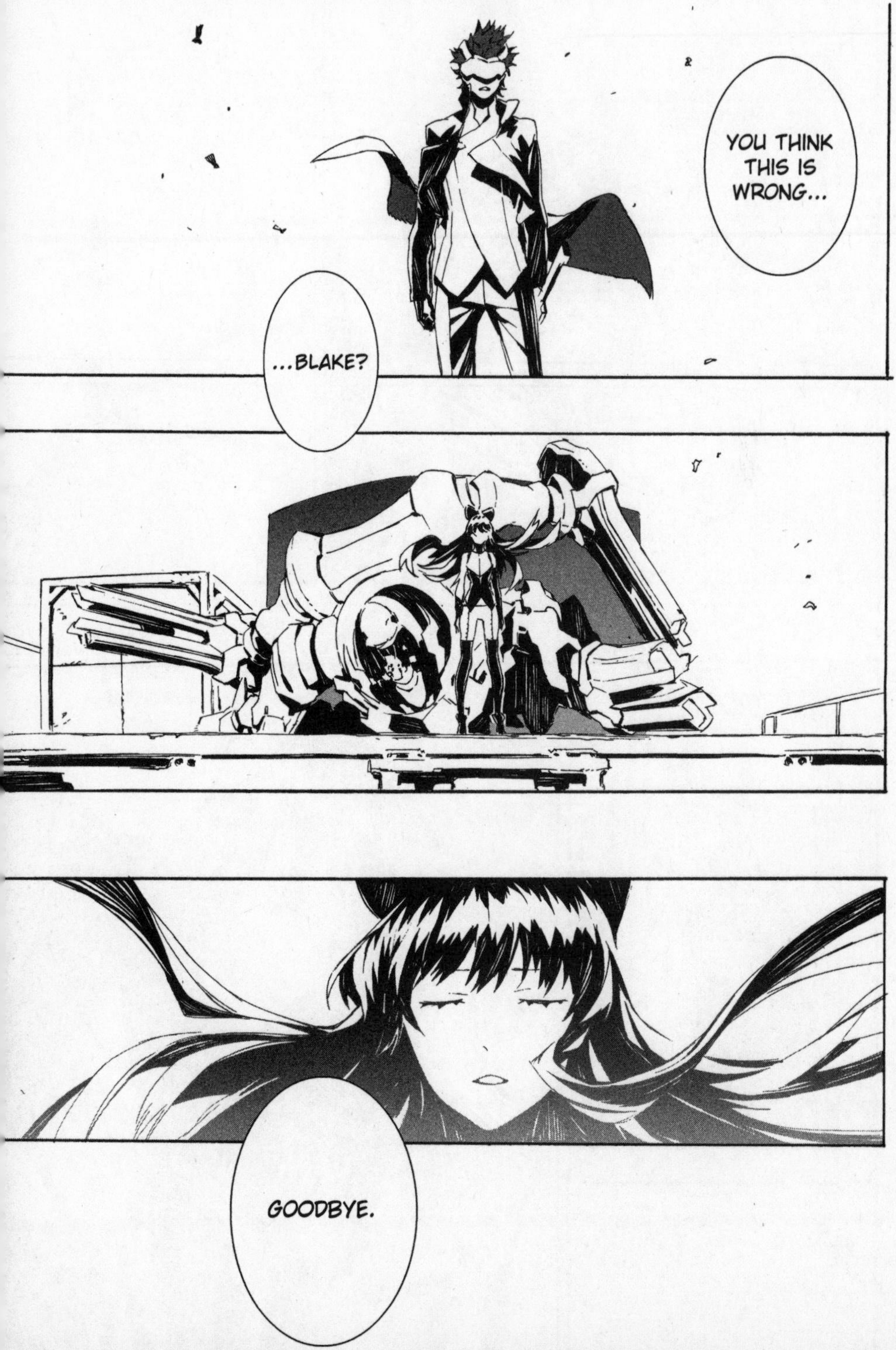
YOU THINK THIS IS WRONG...
...BLAKE?
GOODBYE.

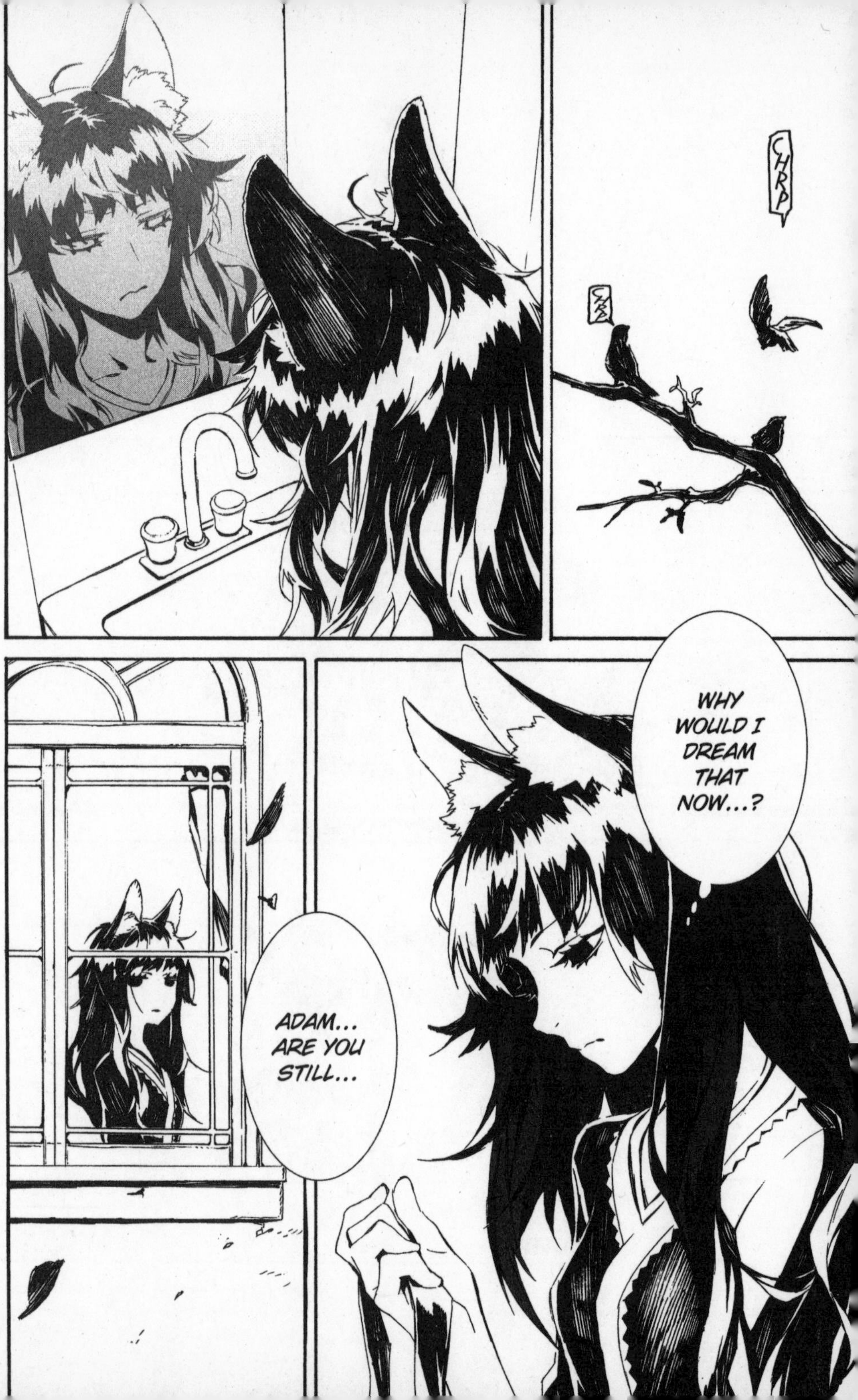
CHRP
WHY WOULD I DREAM THAT NOW...?
ADAM... ARE YOU STILL...

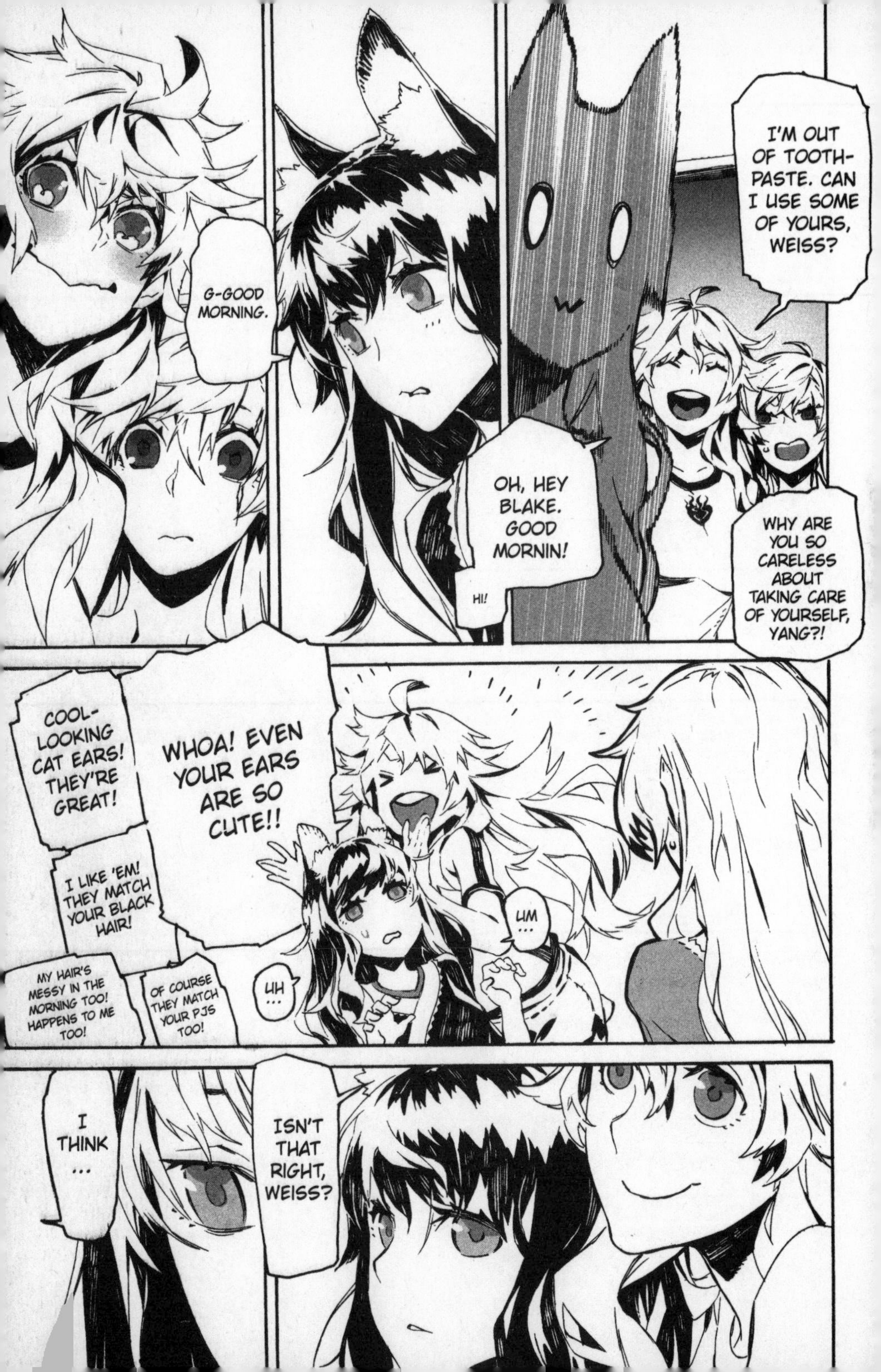
I'M OUT OF TOOTH-PASTE. CAN I USE SOME OF YOURS, WEISS?
OH, HEY BLAKE. GOOD MORNIN!
HI!
WHY ARE YOU SO CARELESS ABOUT TAKING CARE OF YOURSELF, YANG?!
G-GOOD MORNING.
WHOA! EVEN YOUR EARS ARE SO CUTE!!
COOL-LOOKING CAT EARS! THEY'RE GREAT!
I LIKE 'EM! THEY MATCH YOUR BLACK HAIR!
UM ...
UH ...
OF COURSE THEY MATCH YOUR PJS TOO!
MY HAIR'S MESSY IN THE MORNING TOO! HAPPENS TO ME TOO!
ISN'T THAT RIGHT, WEISS?
I THINK ...

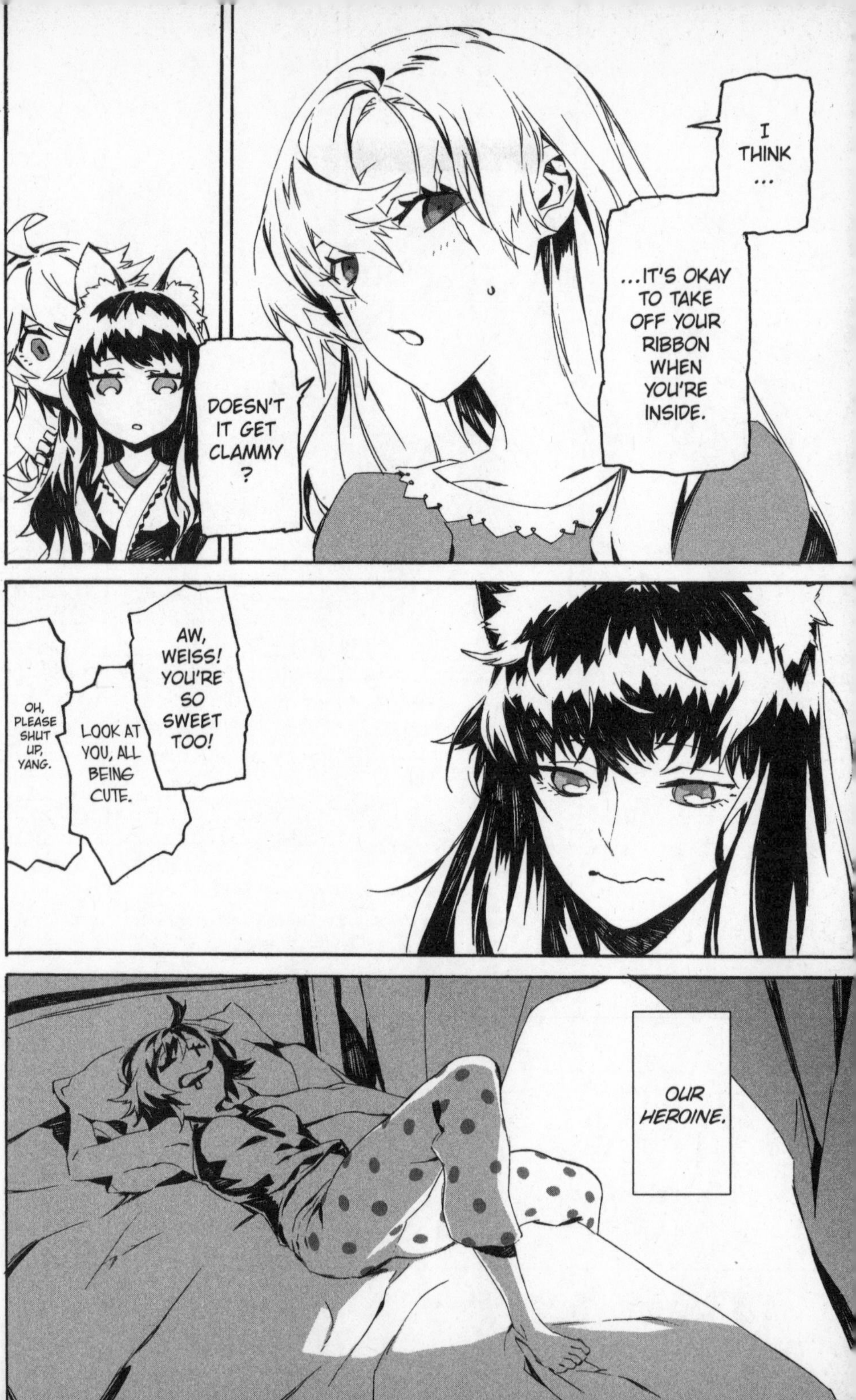
I THINK ...
...IT'S OKAY TO TAKE OFF YOUR RIBBON WHEN YOU'RE INSIDE.
DOESN'T IT GET CLAMMY?
AW, WEISS! YOU'RE SO SWEET TOO!
LOOK AT YOU, ALL BEING CUTE.
OH, PLEASE SHUT UP, YANG.
OUR HEROINE.

Blake Belladonna

B

RWBY

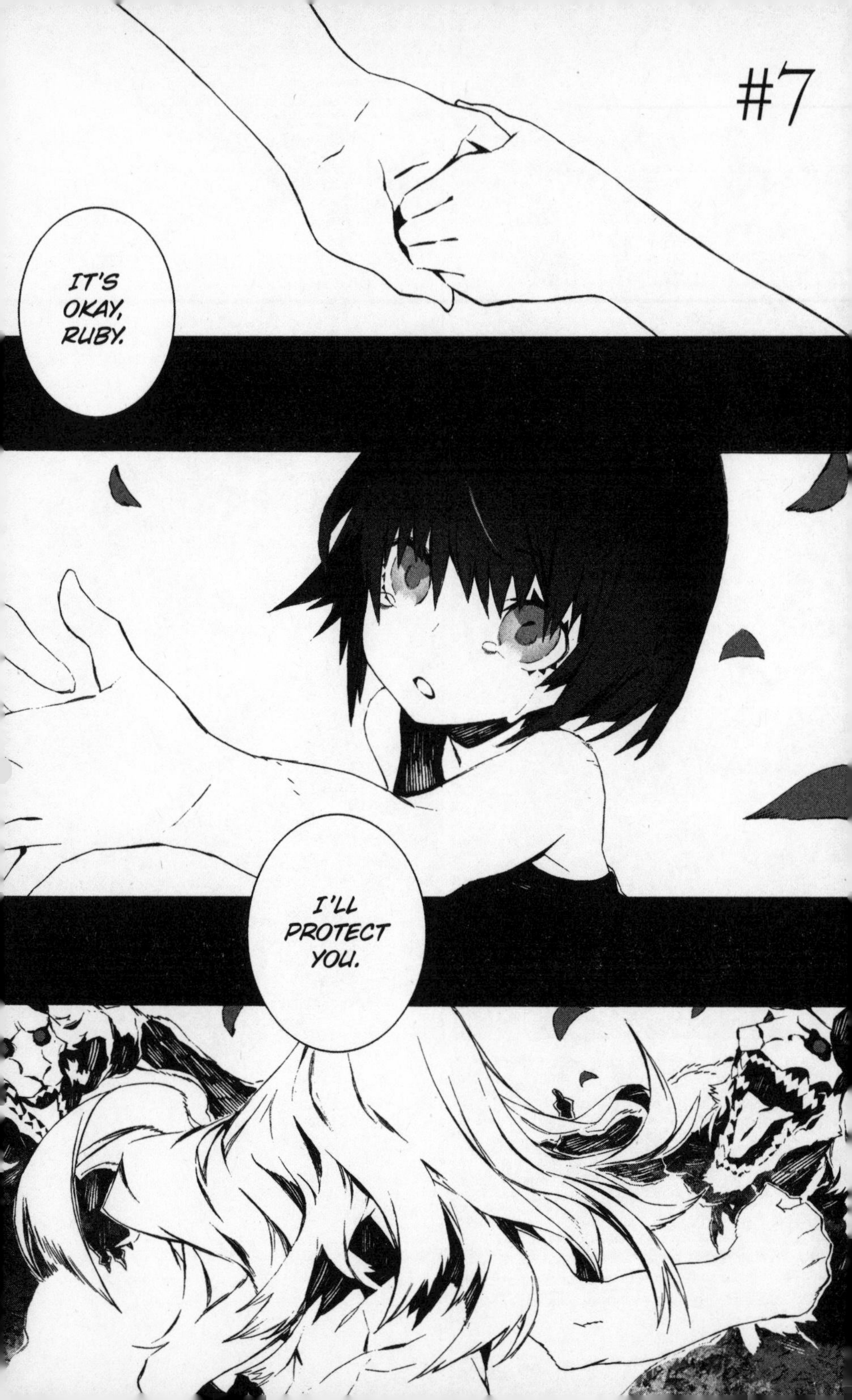
#7
IT'S OKAY, RUBY.
I'LL PROTECT YOU.

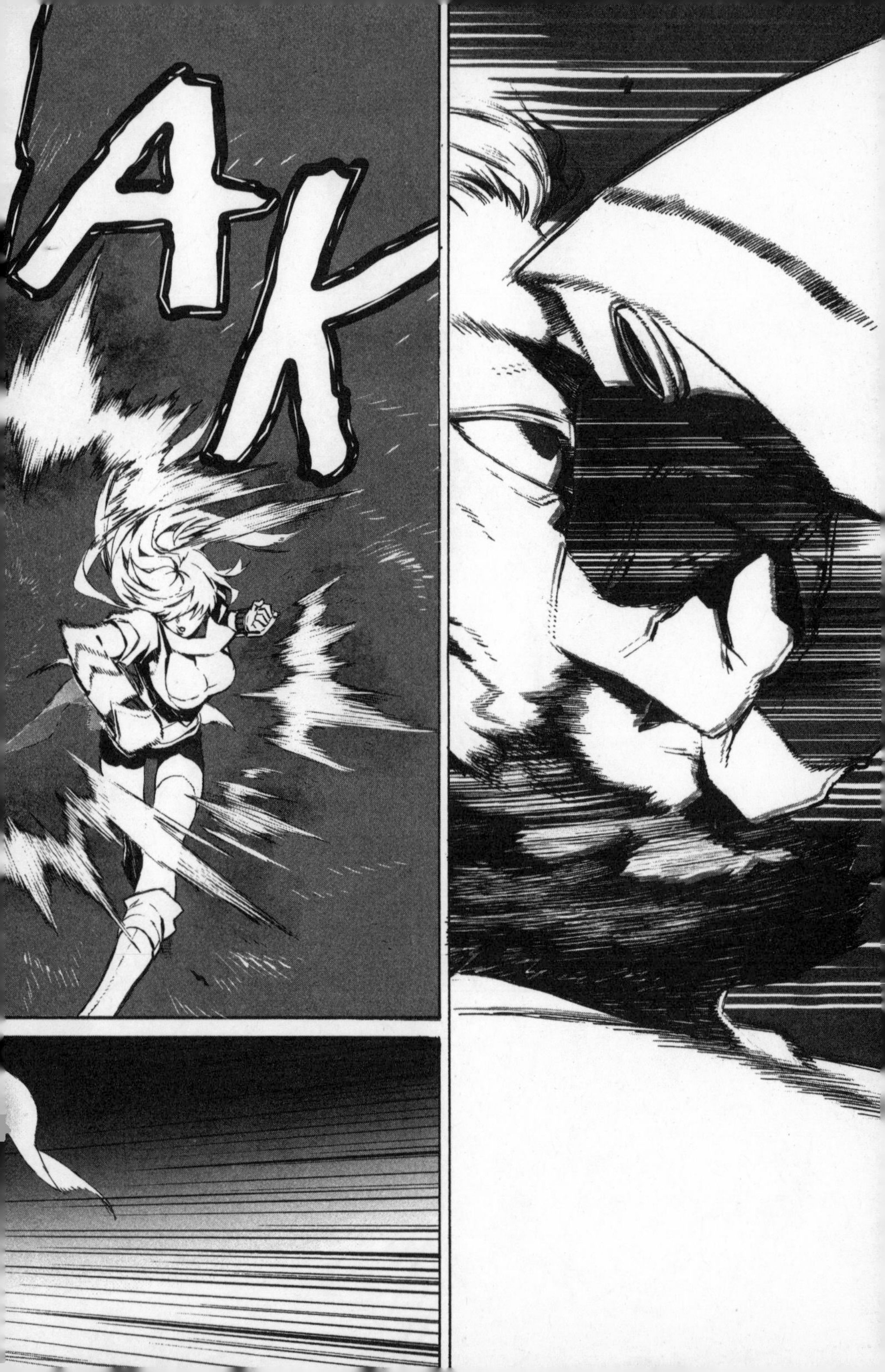
AK

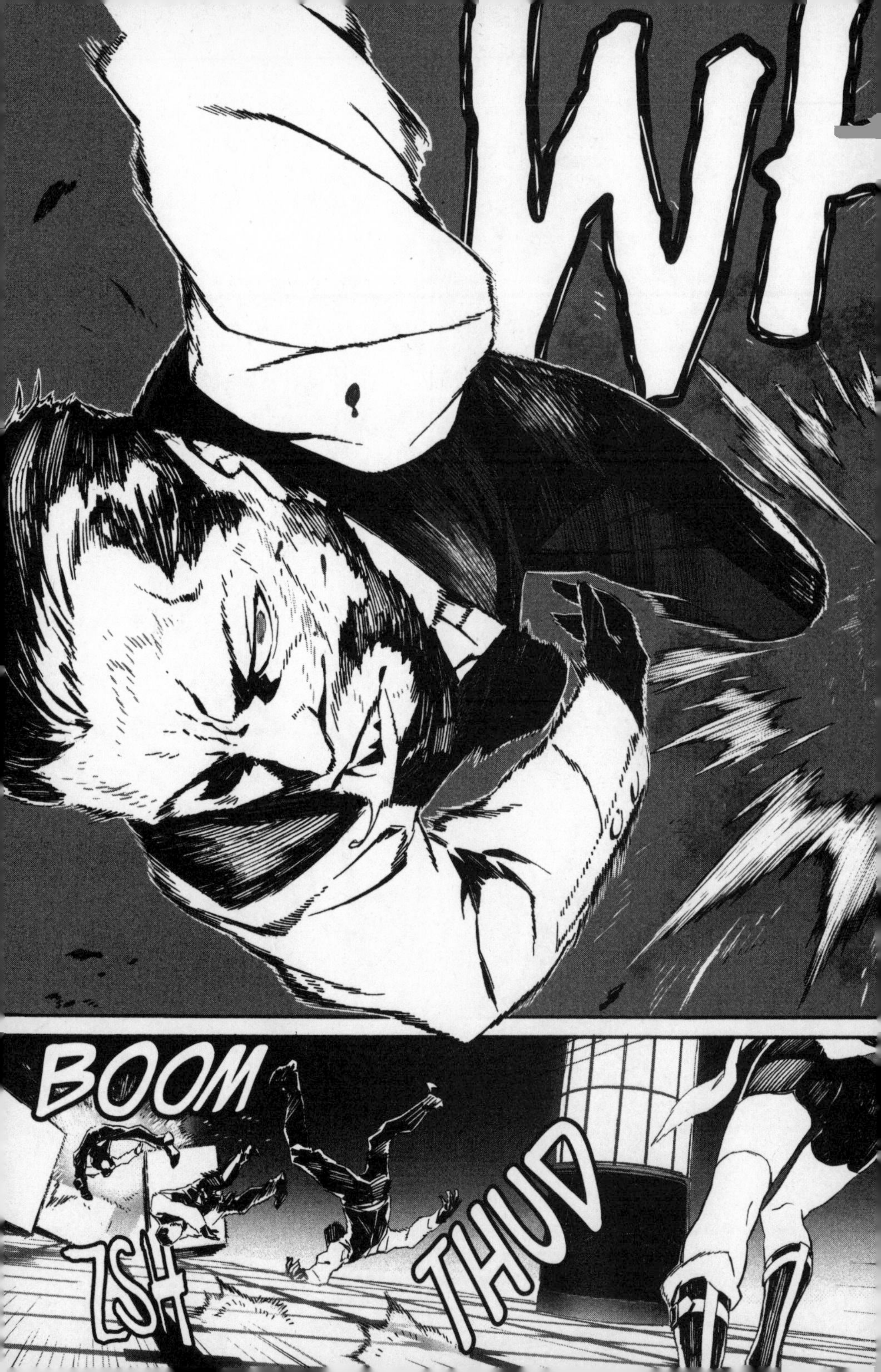
WH
THUD
BOOM
TSH

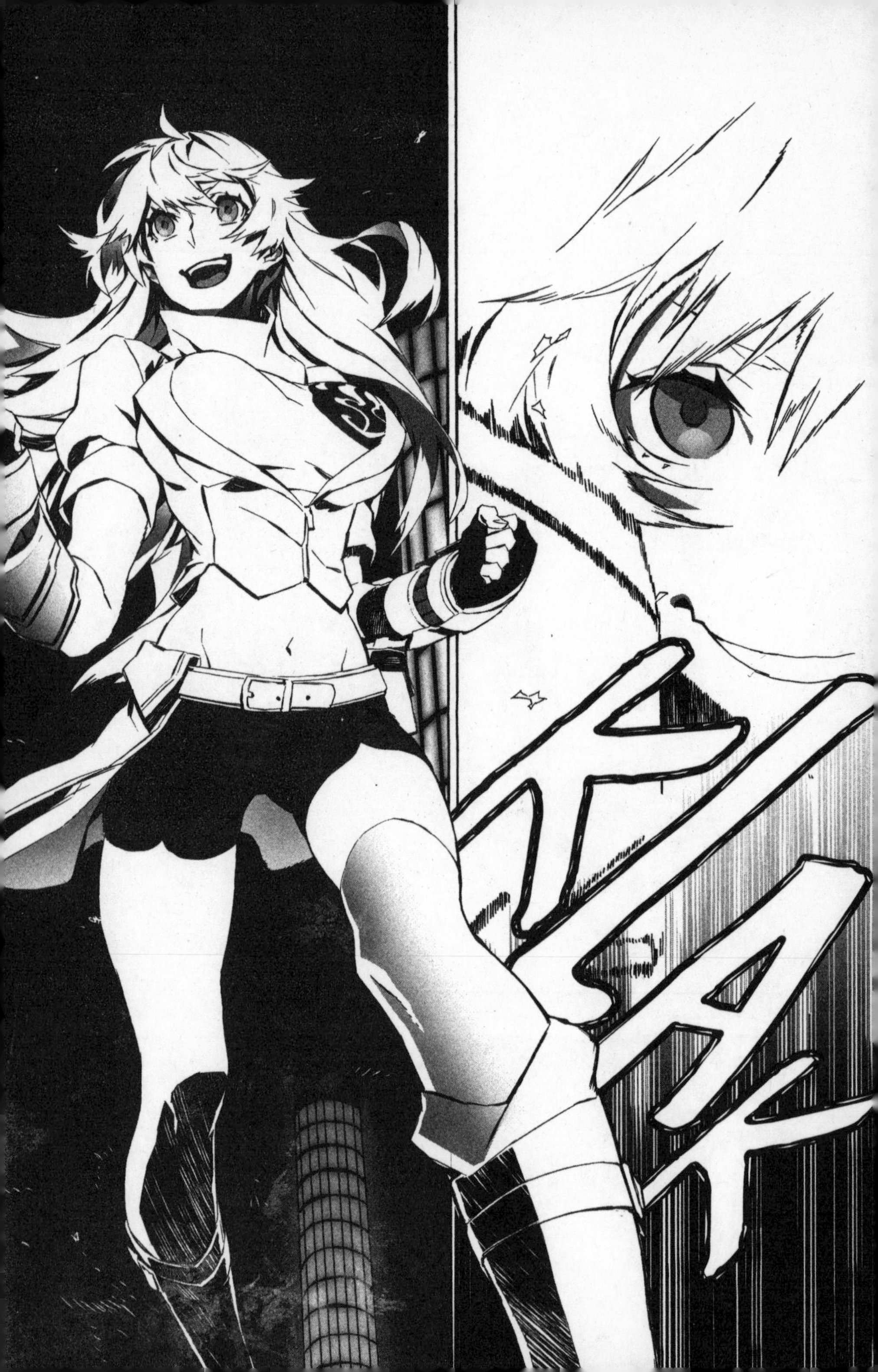

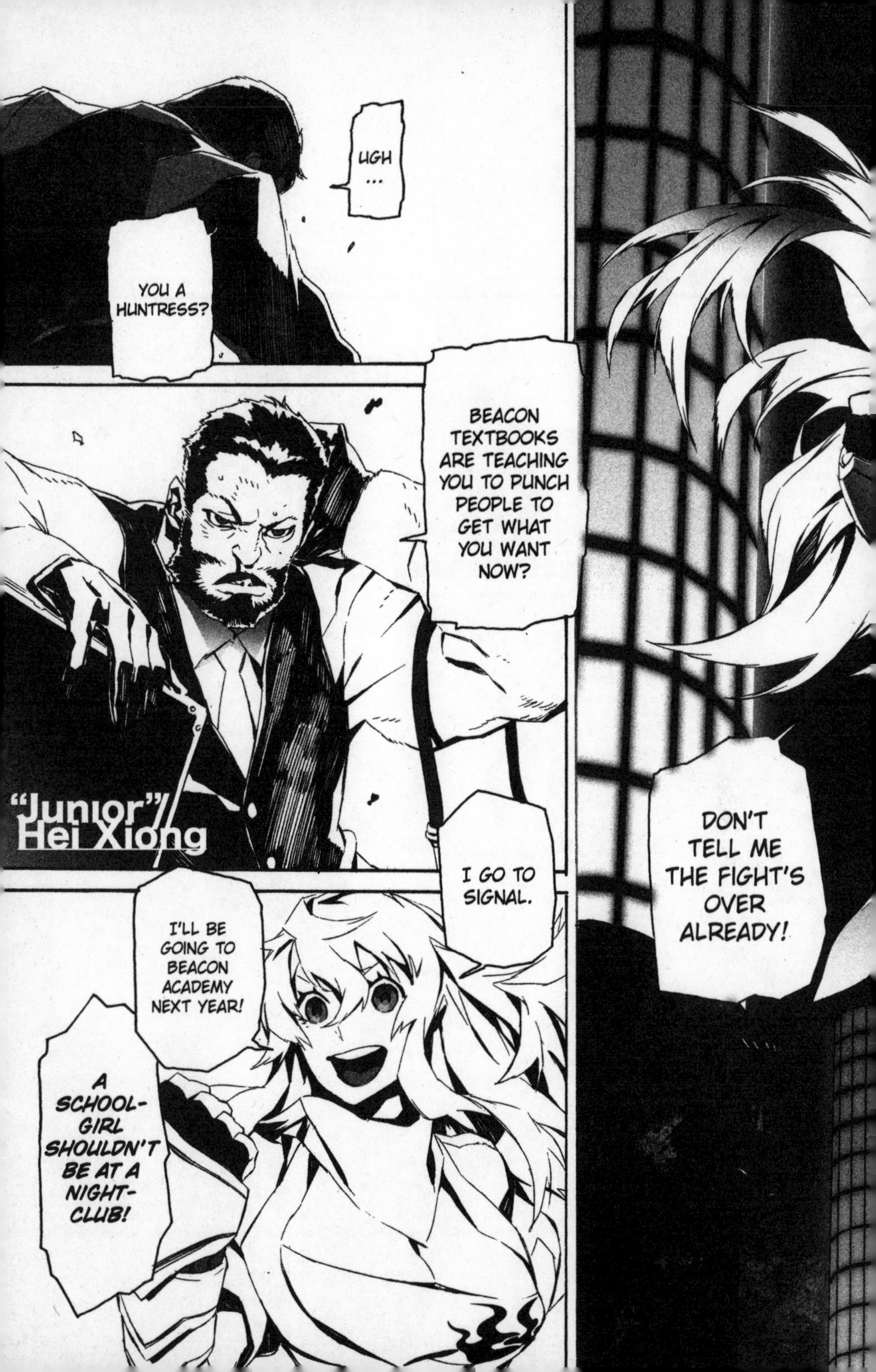
DON'T TELL ME THE FIGHT'S OVER ALREADY!
UGH ...
YOU A HUNTRESS?
BEACON TEXTBOOKS ARE TEACHING YOU TO PUNCH PEOPLE TO GET WHAT YOU WANT NOW?
"Junior"/ Hei Xiong
I GO TO SIGNAL.
I'LL BE GOING TO BEACON ACADEMY NEXT YEAR!
A SCHOOL-GIRL SHOULDN'T BE AT A NIGHT-CLUB!

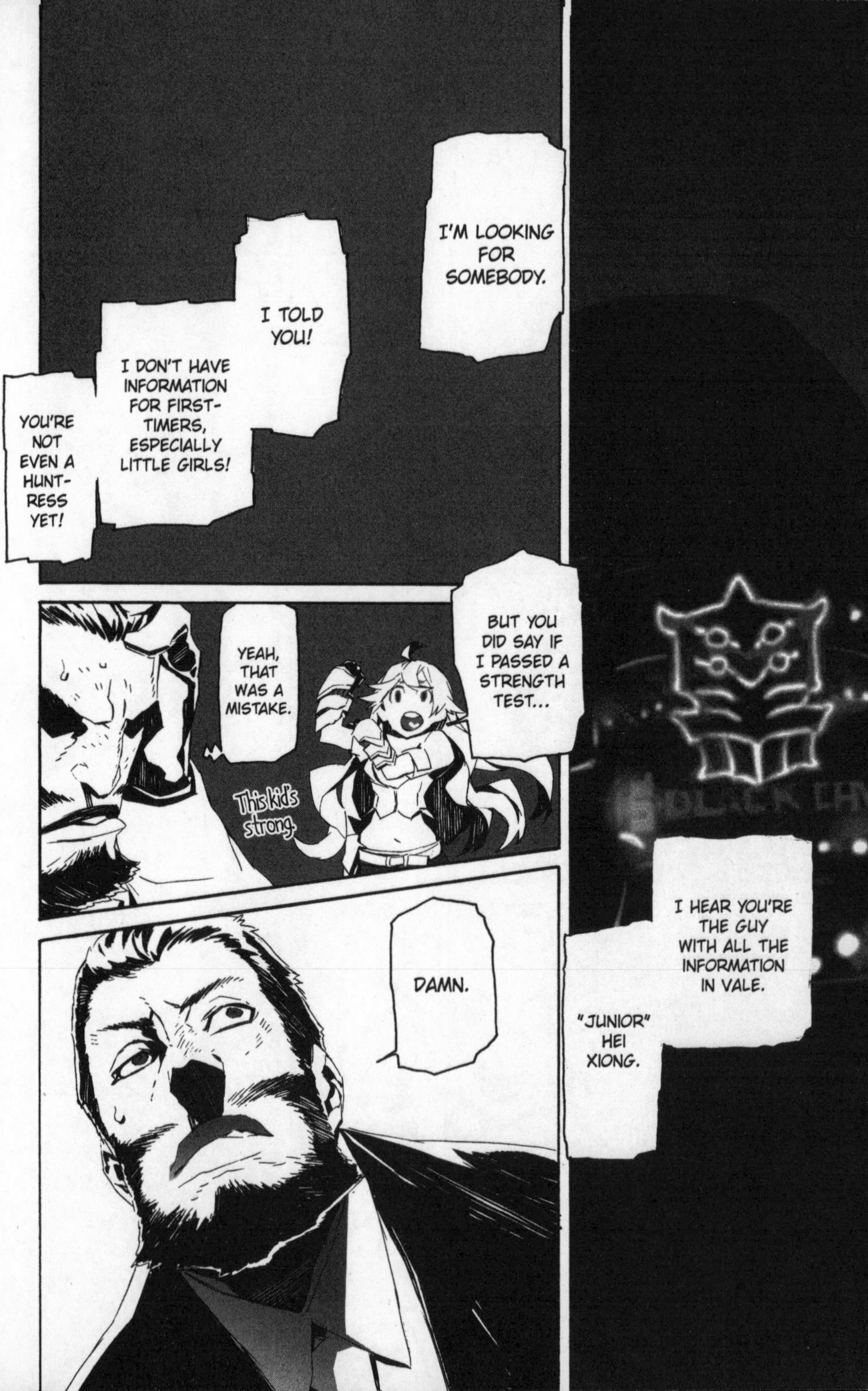

I HEAR YOU'RE THE GUY WITH ALL THE INFORMATION IN VALE.
"JUNIOR" HEI XIONG.
I'M LOOKING FOR SOMEBODY.
I TOLD YOU!
I DON'T HAVE INFORMATION FOR FIRST-TIMERS, ESPECIALLY LITTLE GIRLS!
YOU'RE NOT EVEN A HUNT-RESS YET!
BUT YOU DID SAY IF I PASSED A STRENGTH TEST...
YEAH, THAT WAS A MISTAKE.
This kid's strong.
DAMN.

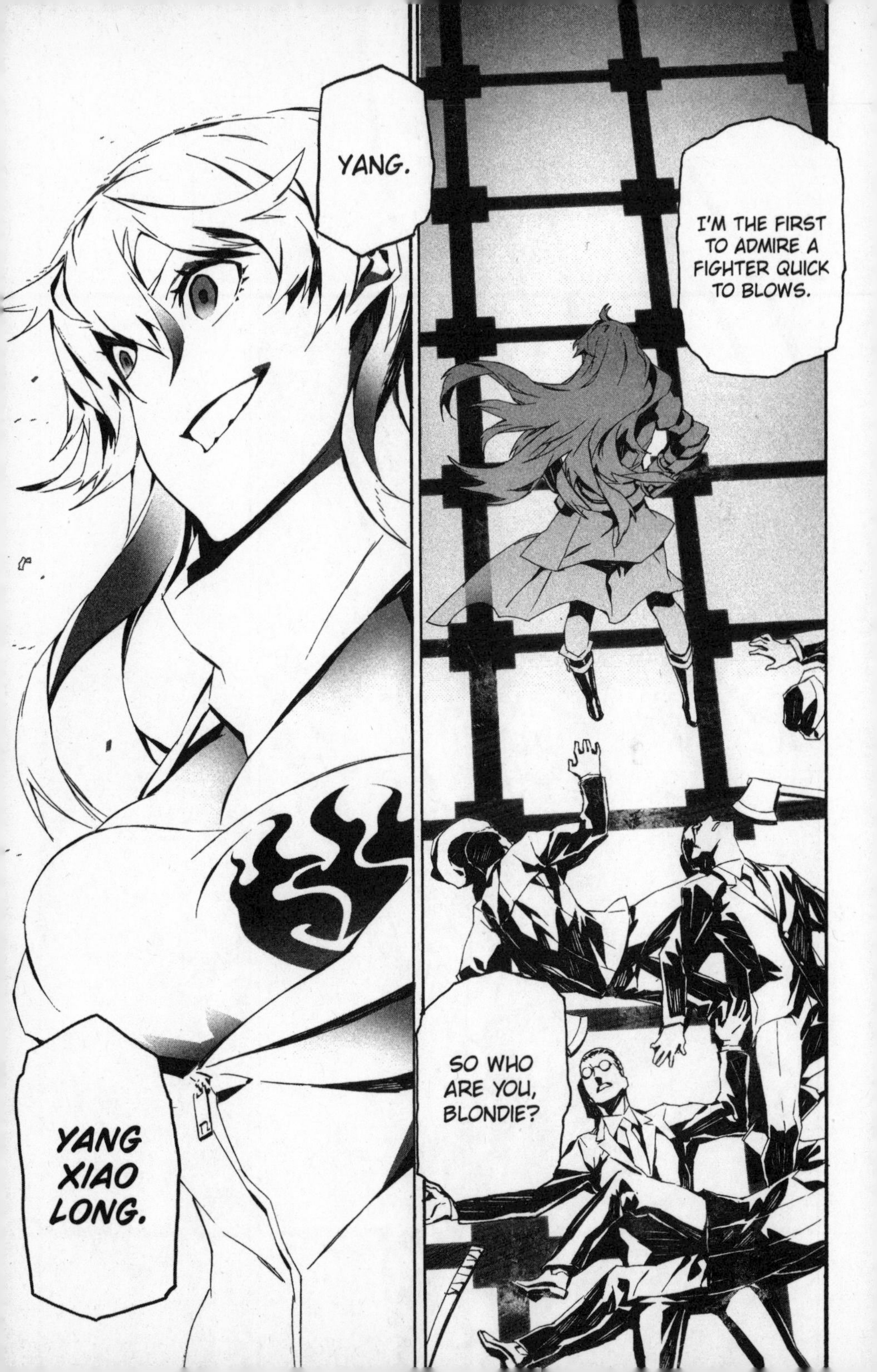
I'M THE FIRST TO ADMIRE A FIGHTER QUICK TO BLOWS.
SO WHO ARE YOU, BLONDIE?
YANG.
YANG XIAO LONG.

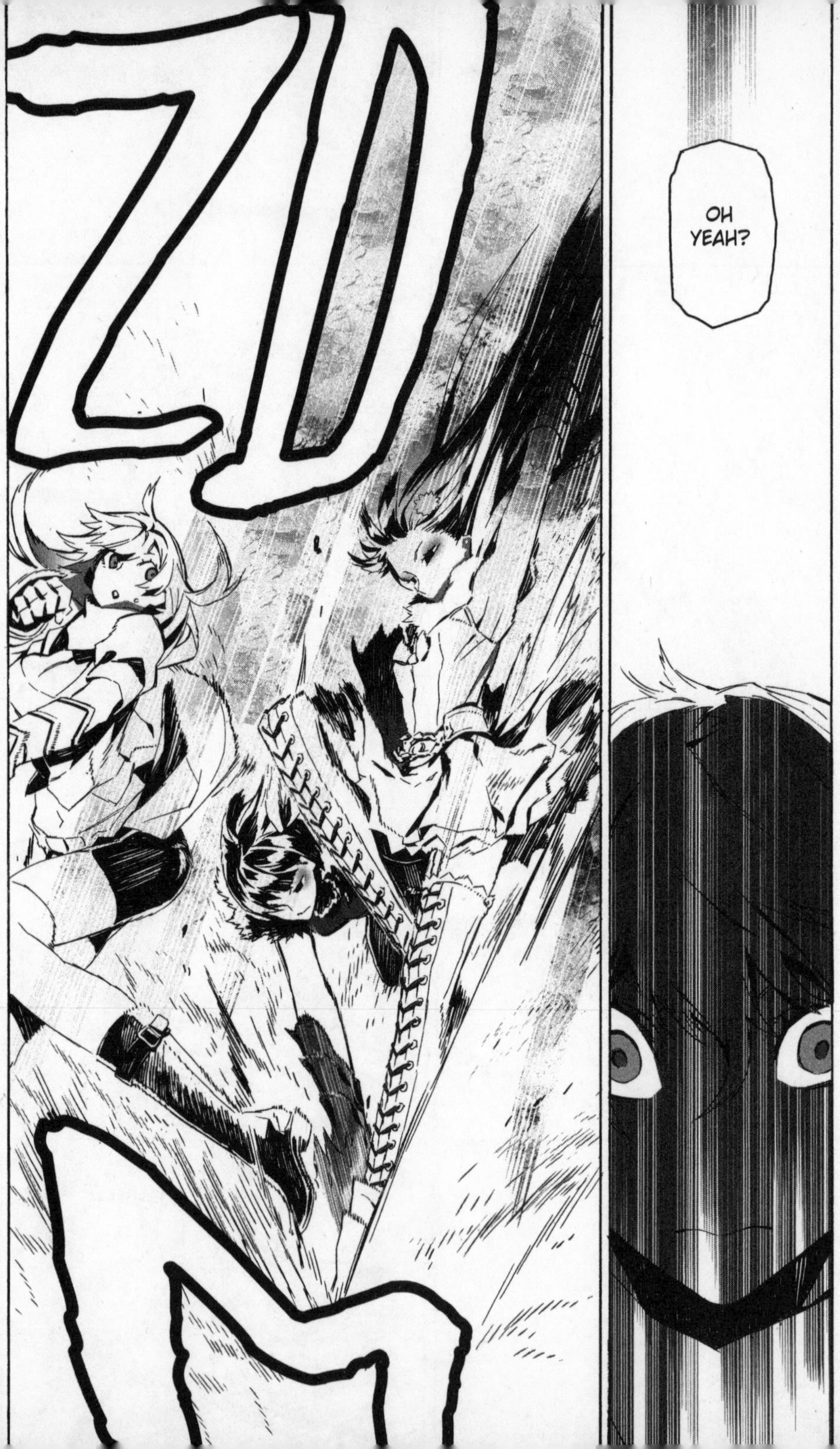
OH YEAH?

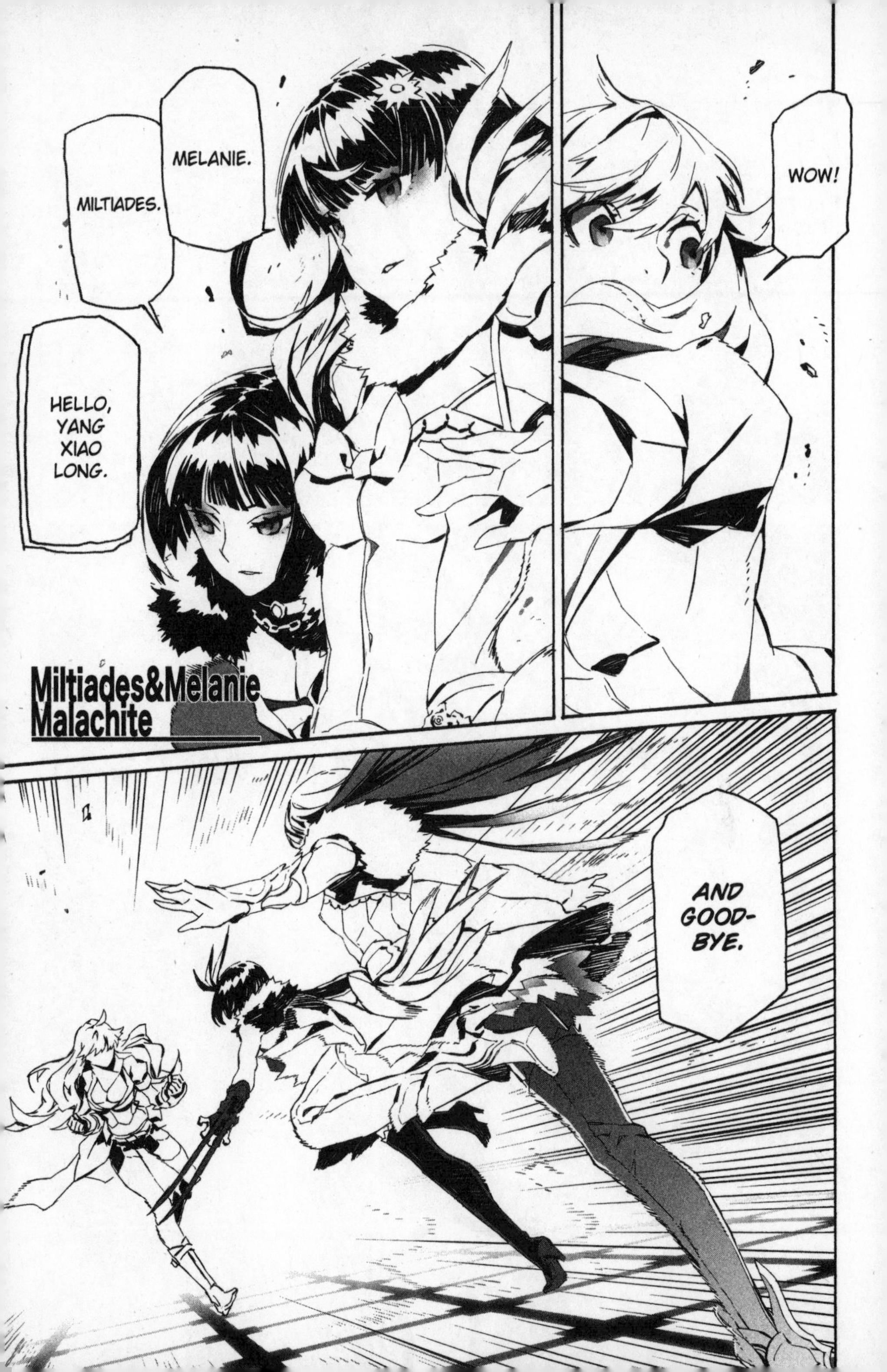
WOW!
MELANIE.
MILTIADES.
HELLO, YANG XIAO LONG.
Miltiades&Melanie Malachite
AND GOOD-BYE.

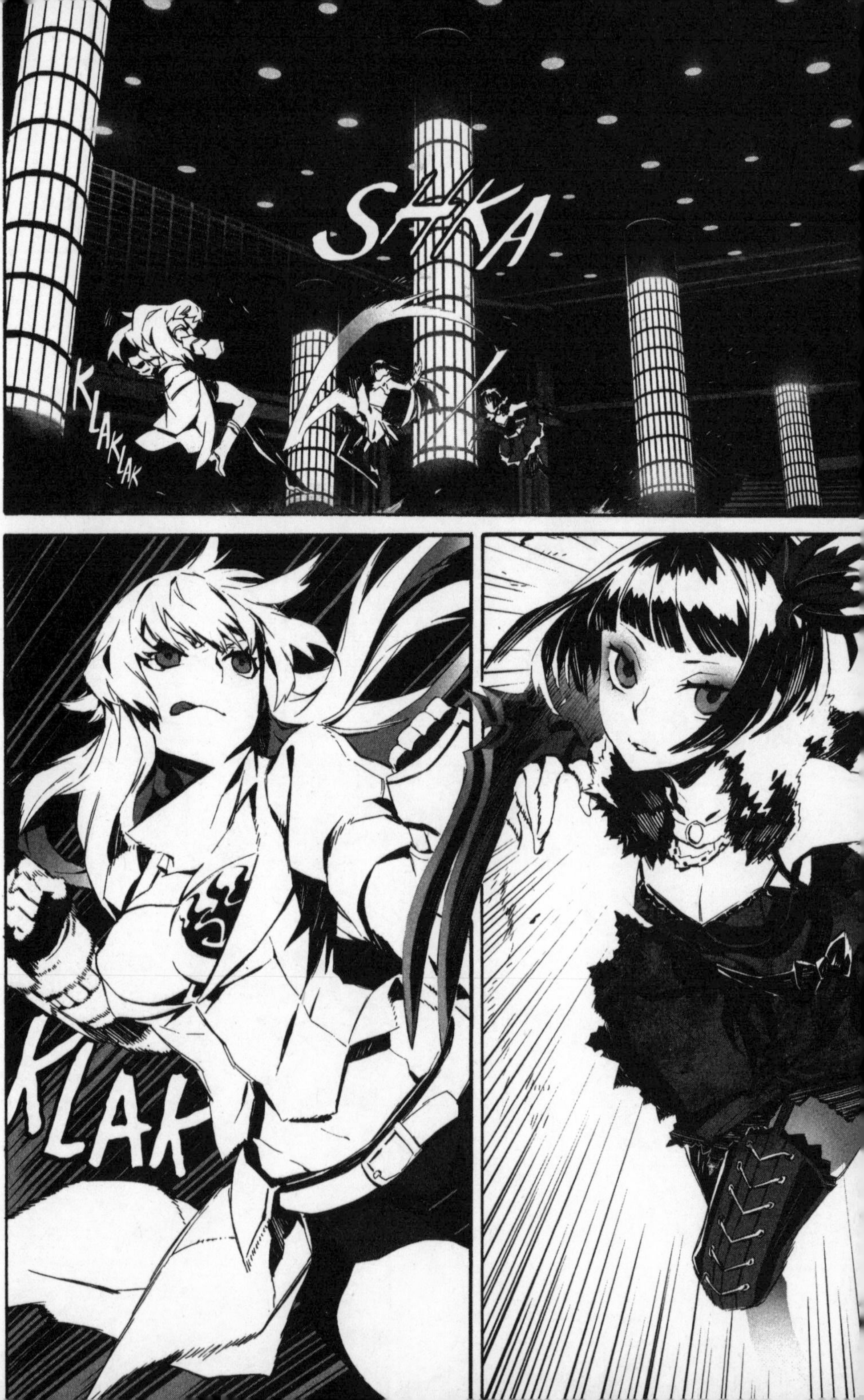
SHKA
KLAKKLAK
KLAK

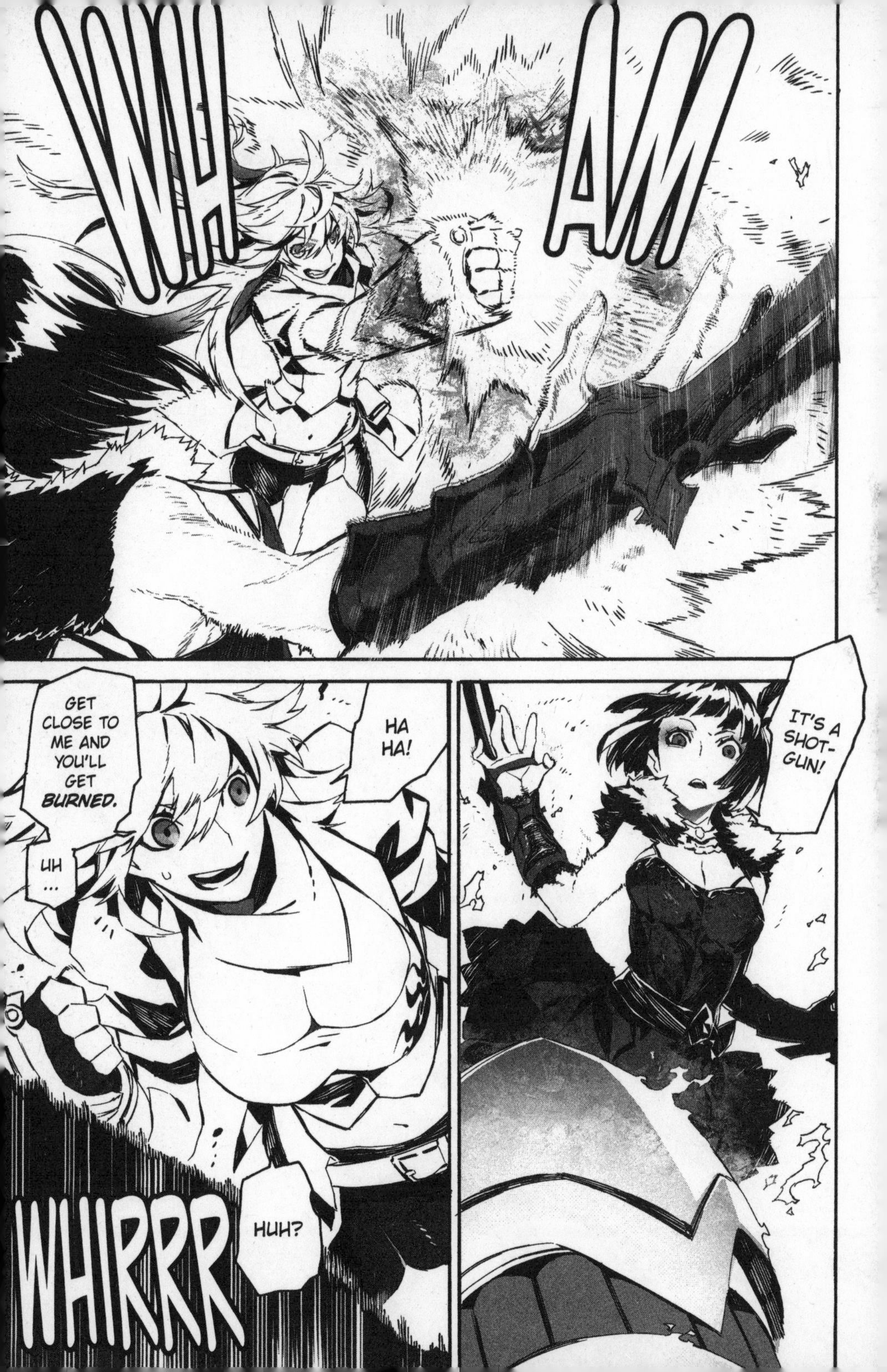
WHAM
IT'S A SHOT-GUN!
HA HA!
GET CLOSE TO ME AND YOU'LL GET BURNED.
UH ...
HUH?
WHIRRR

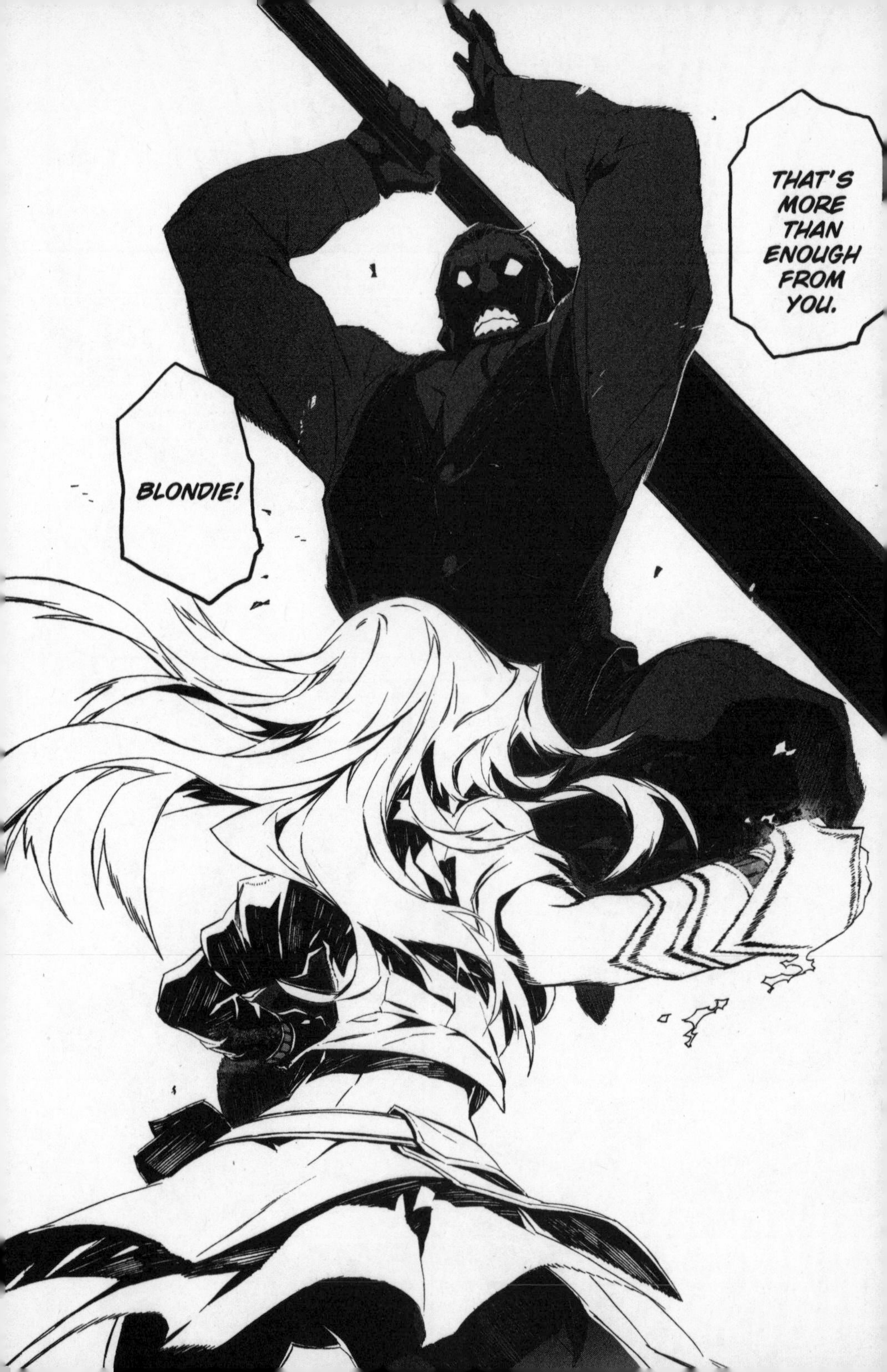
THAT'S MORE THAN ENOUGH FROM YOU.
BLONDIE!

#8

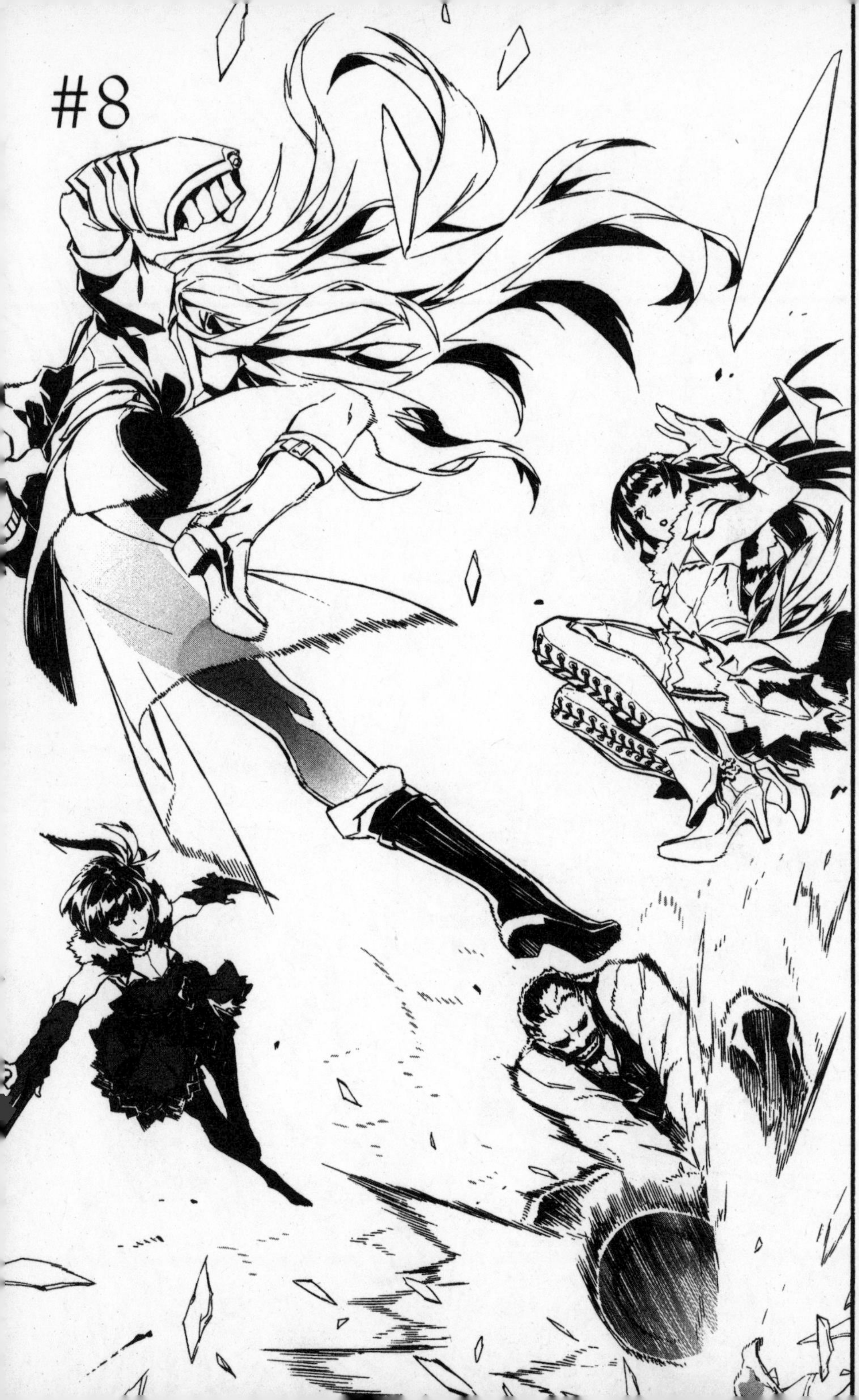

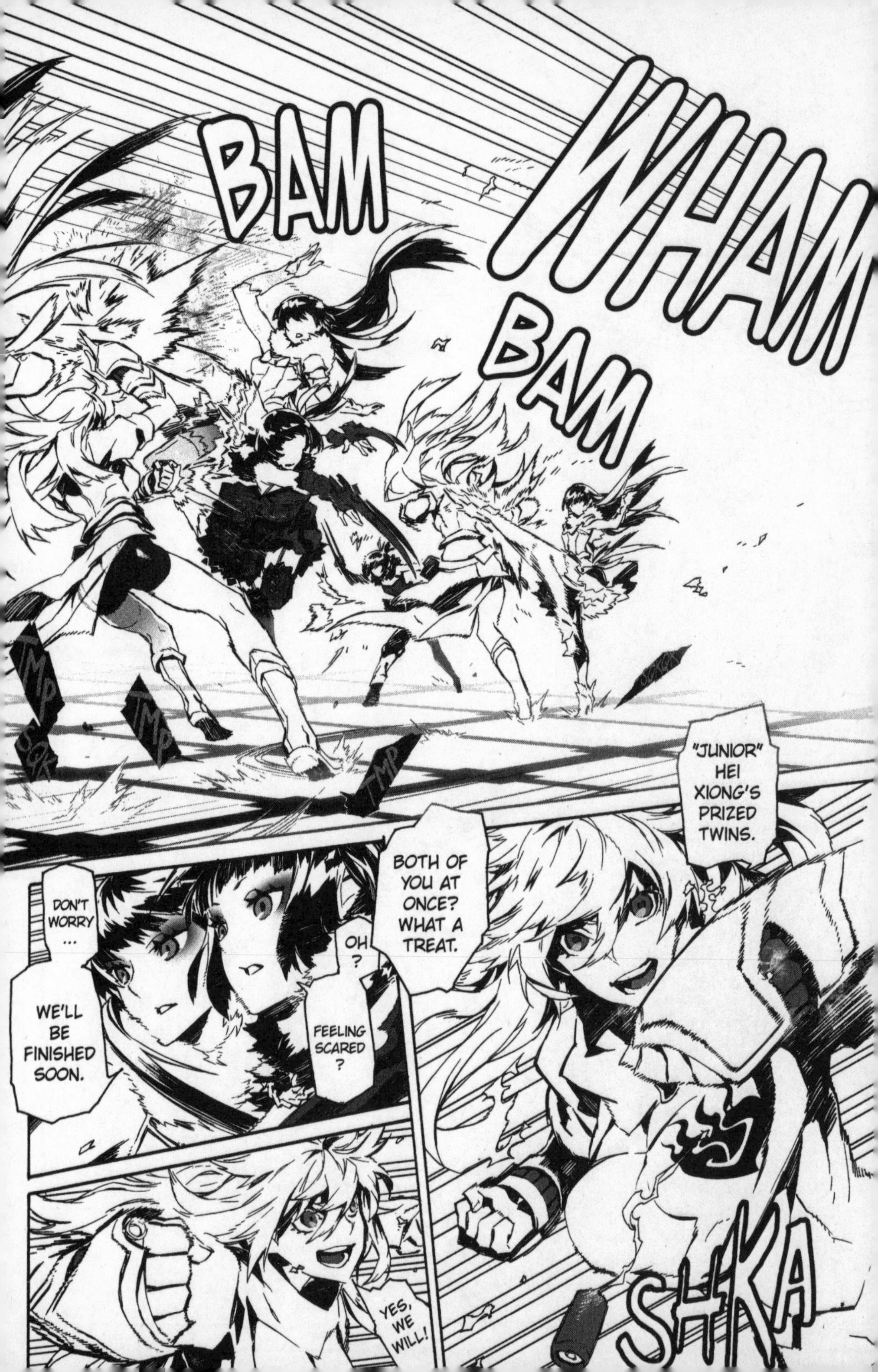
WHAM
BAM
BAM
TMP
TMP
TMP
"JUNIOR" HEI XIONG'S PRIZED TWINS.
BOTH OF YOU AT ONCE? WHAT A TREAT.
OH? FEELING SCARED?
DON'T WORRY...
WE'LL BE FINISHED SOON.
SHKA
YES, WE WILL!

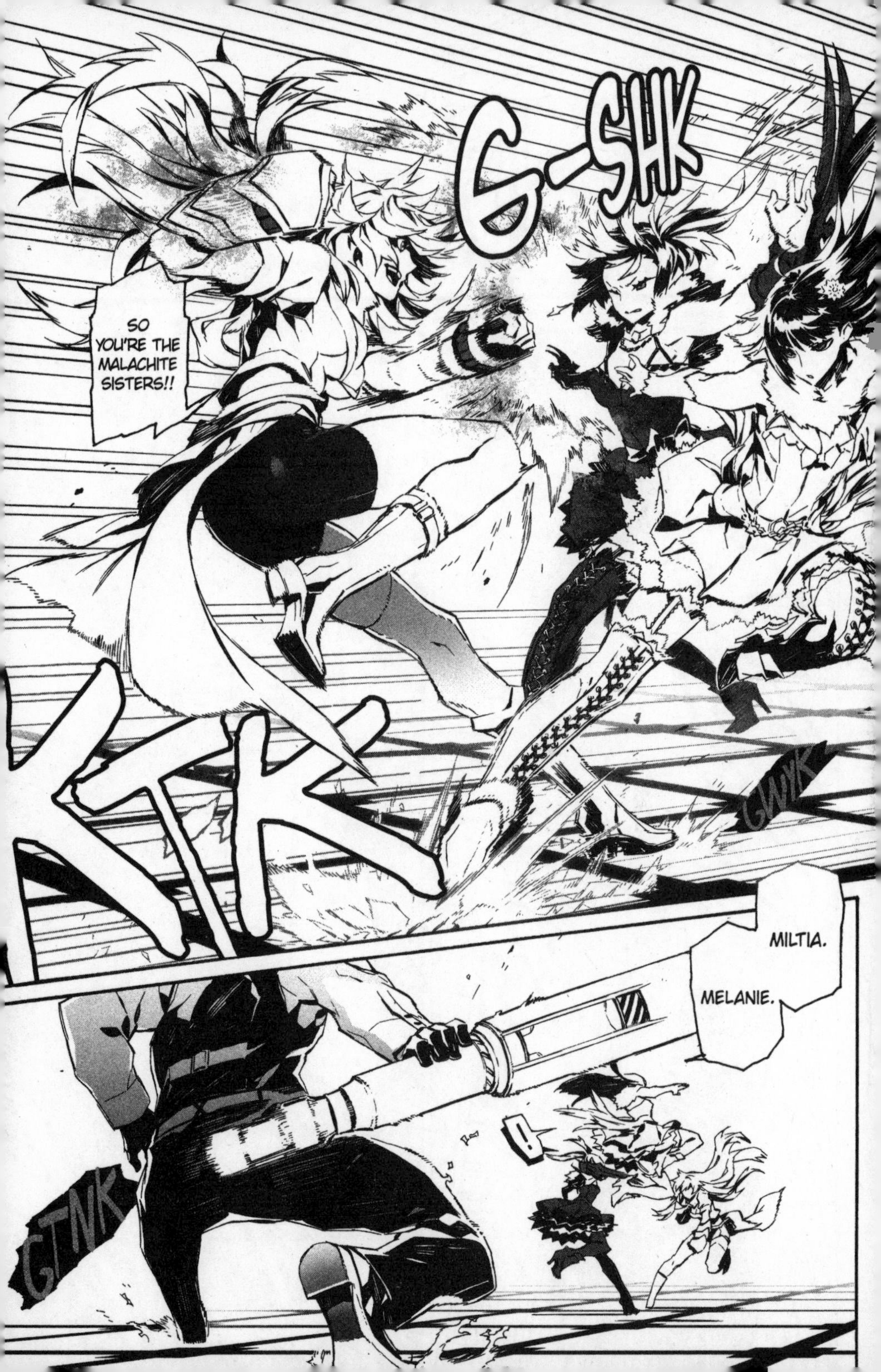
G-SHK
SO YOU'RE THE MALACHITE SISTERS!!
GWYK
MILTIA.
MELANIE.
!
GTNK

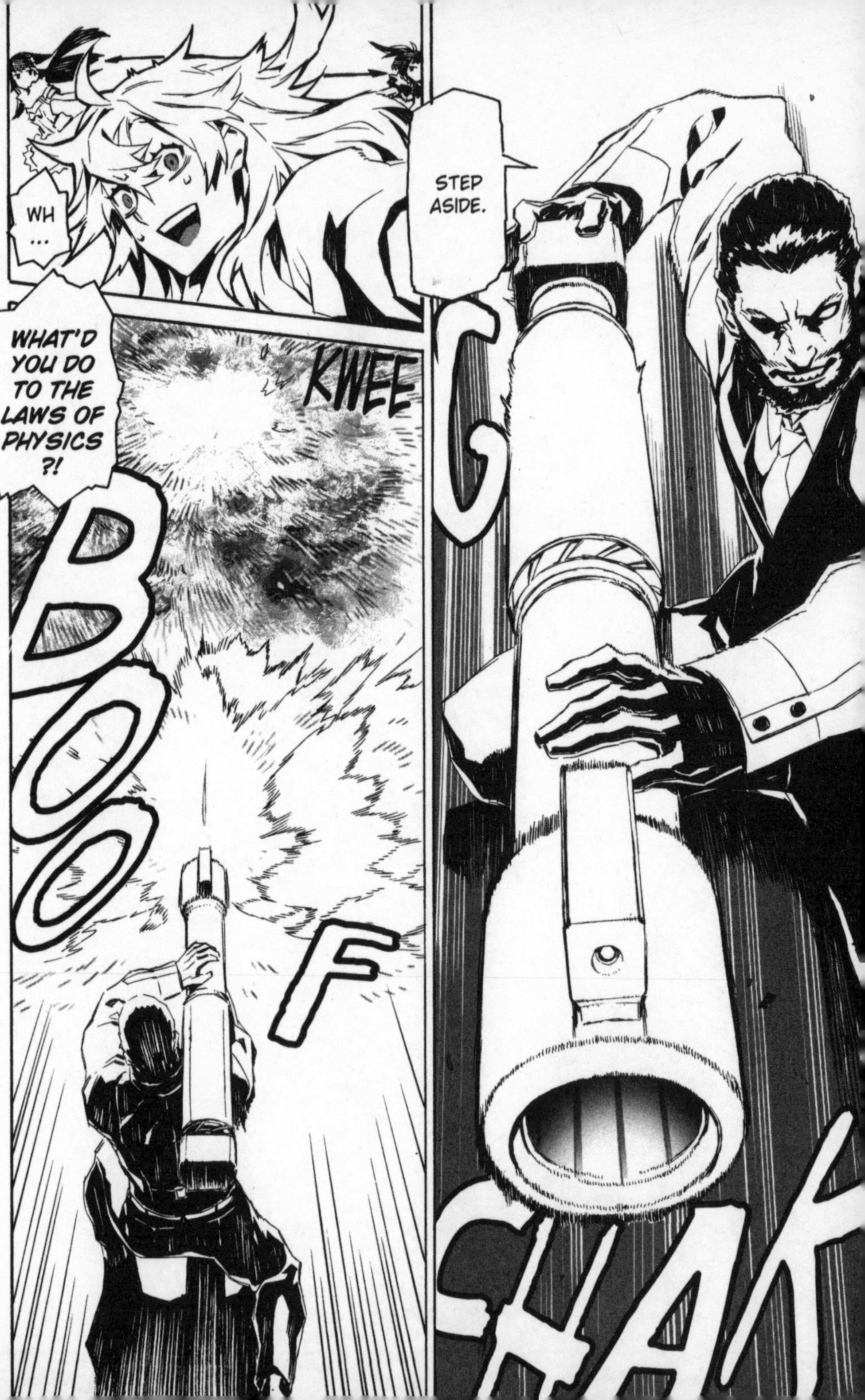
STEP ASIDE.
WH...
WHAT'D YOU DO TO THE LAWS OF PHYSICS?!
KWEE
BOOOF

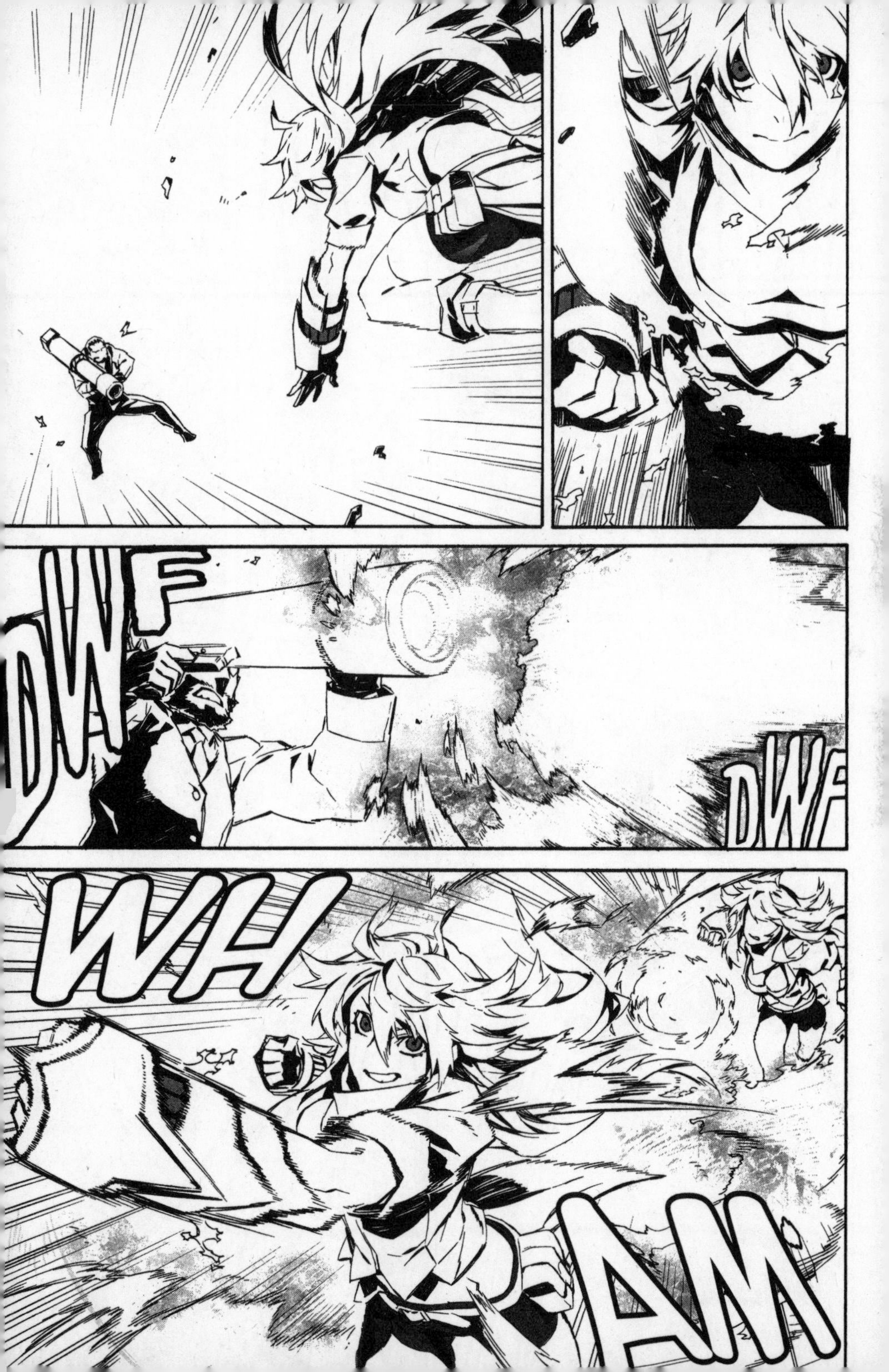
DWF
DWF
WH
AM

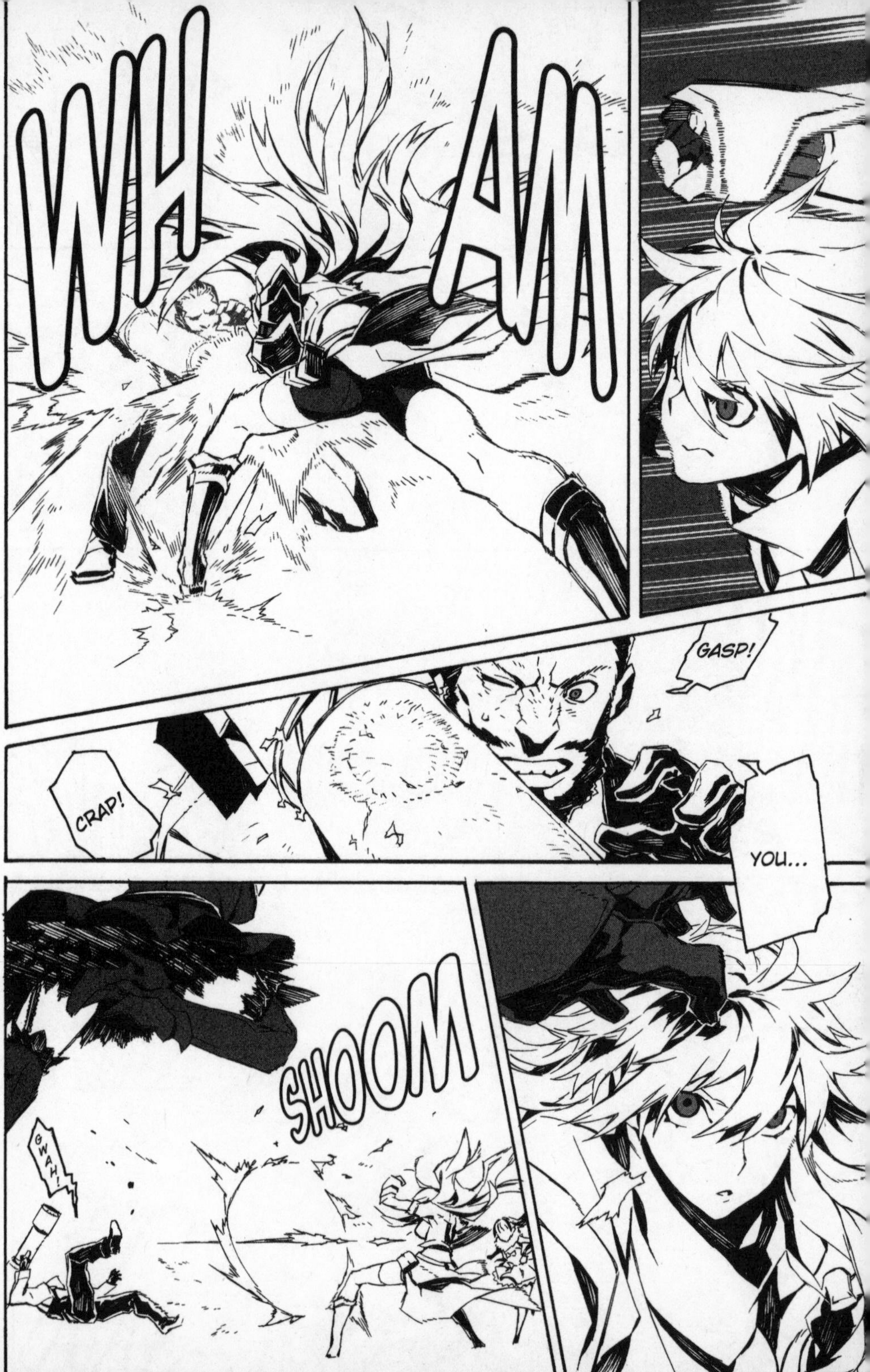
WH AM
GASP!
CRAP!
YOU...
SHOOM
GWAH!

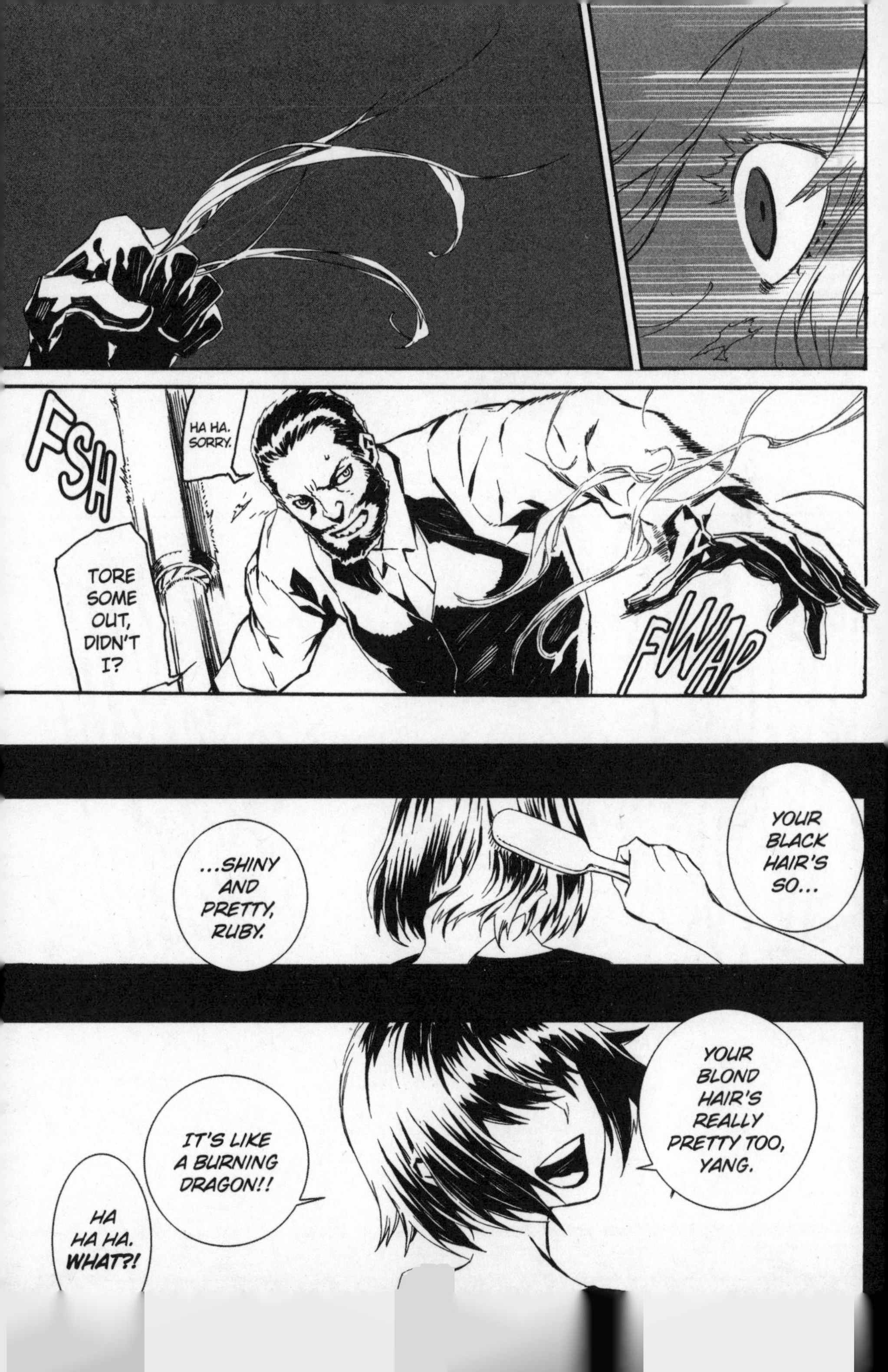
HA HA. SORRY.
FSH
FWAP
TORE SOME OUT, DIDN'T I?
YOUR BLACK HAIR'S SO...
...SHINY AND PRETTY, RUBY.
YOUR BLOND HAIR'S REALLY PRETTY TOO, YANG.
IT'S LIKE A BURNING DRAGON!!
HA HA HA. WHAT?!

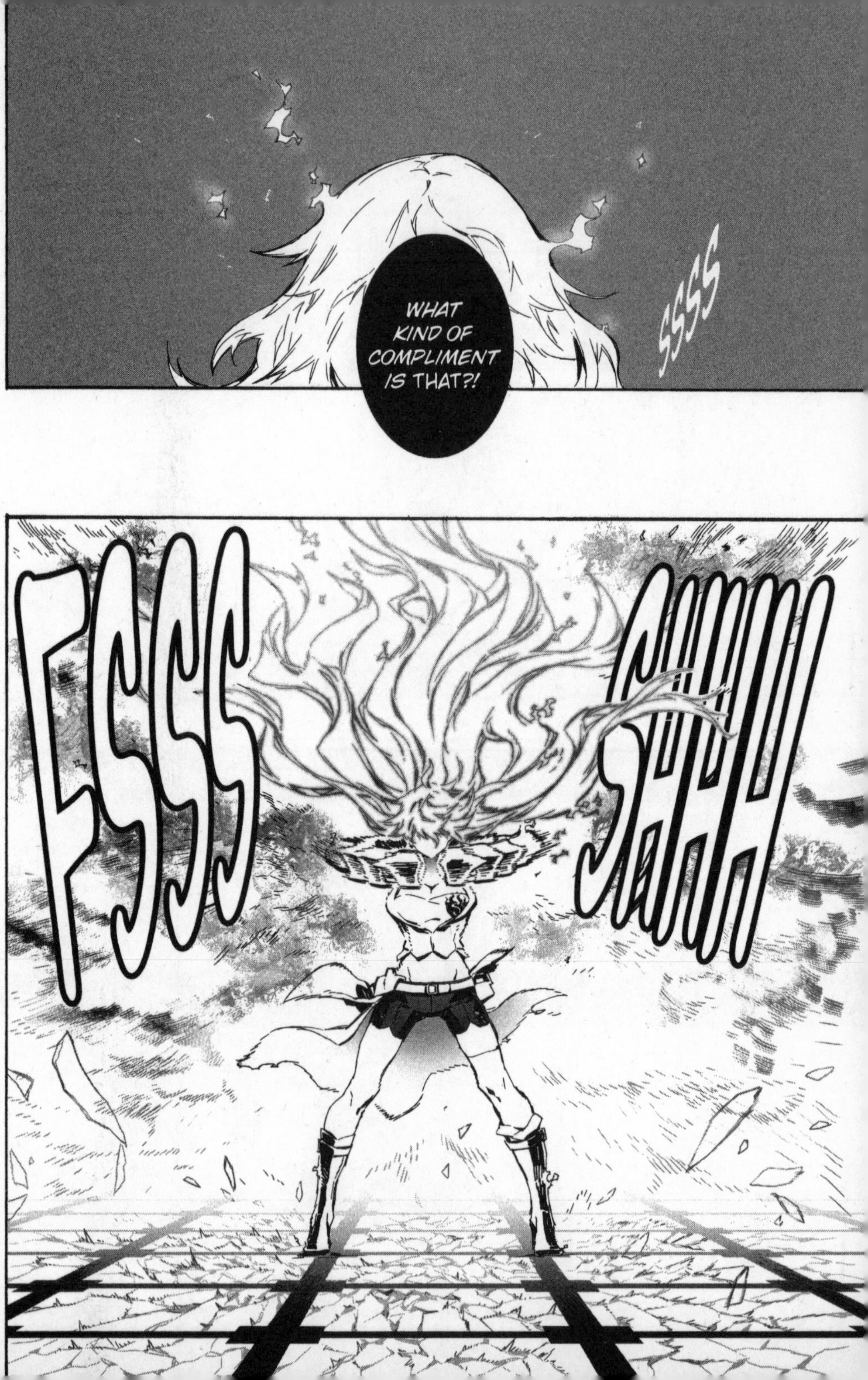
SSSS
WHAT KIND OF COMPLIMENT IS THAT?!
FSSS SHHH

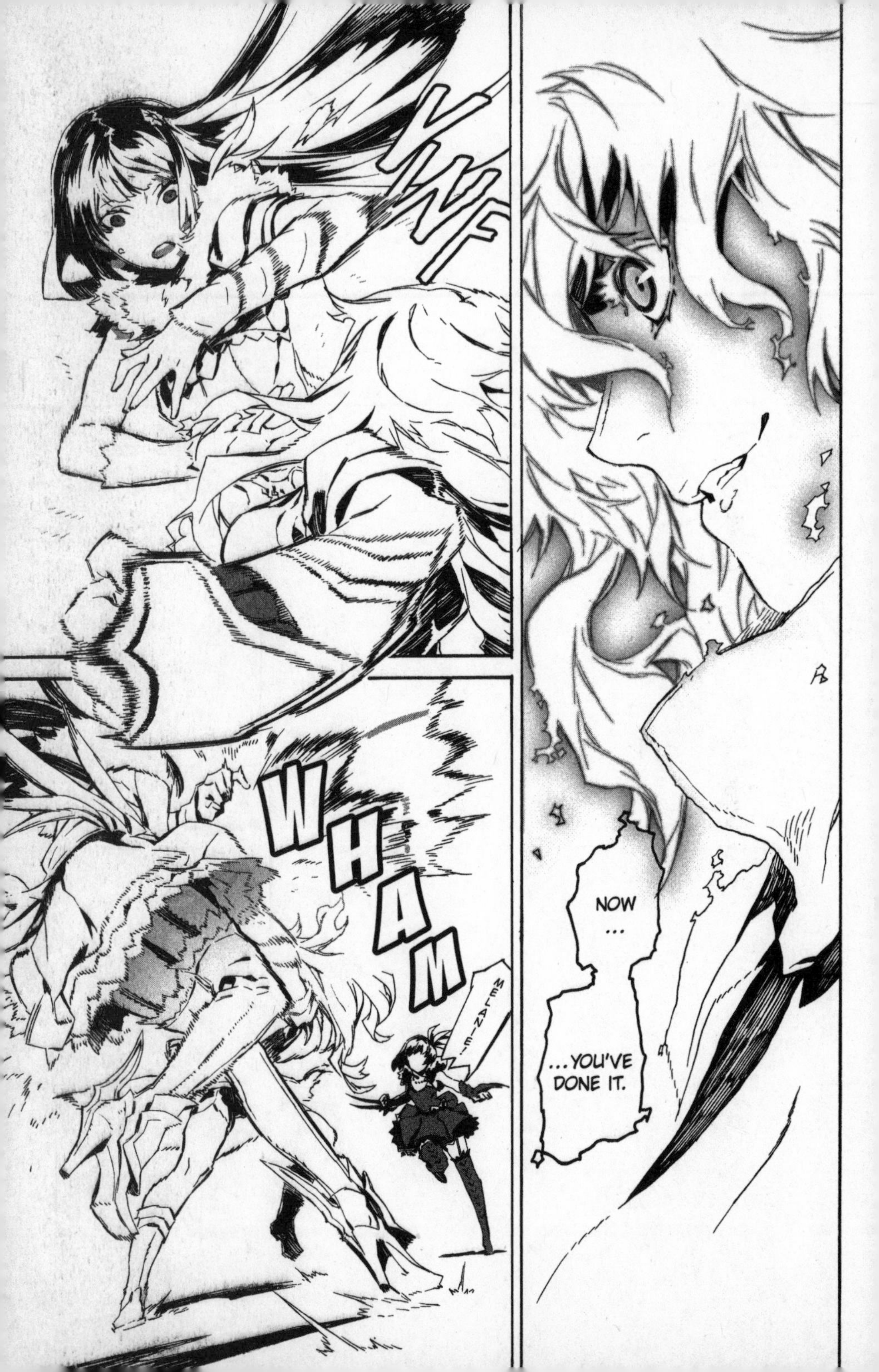
NOW ...
...YOU'VE DONE IT.
WHAM
MELANIE!

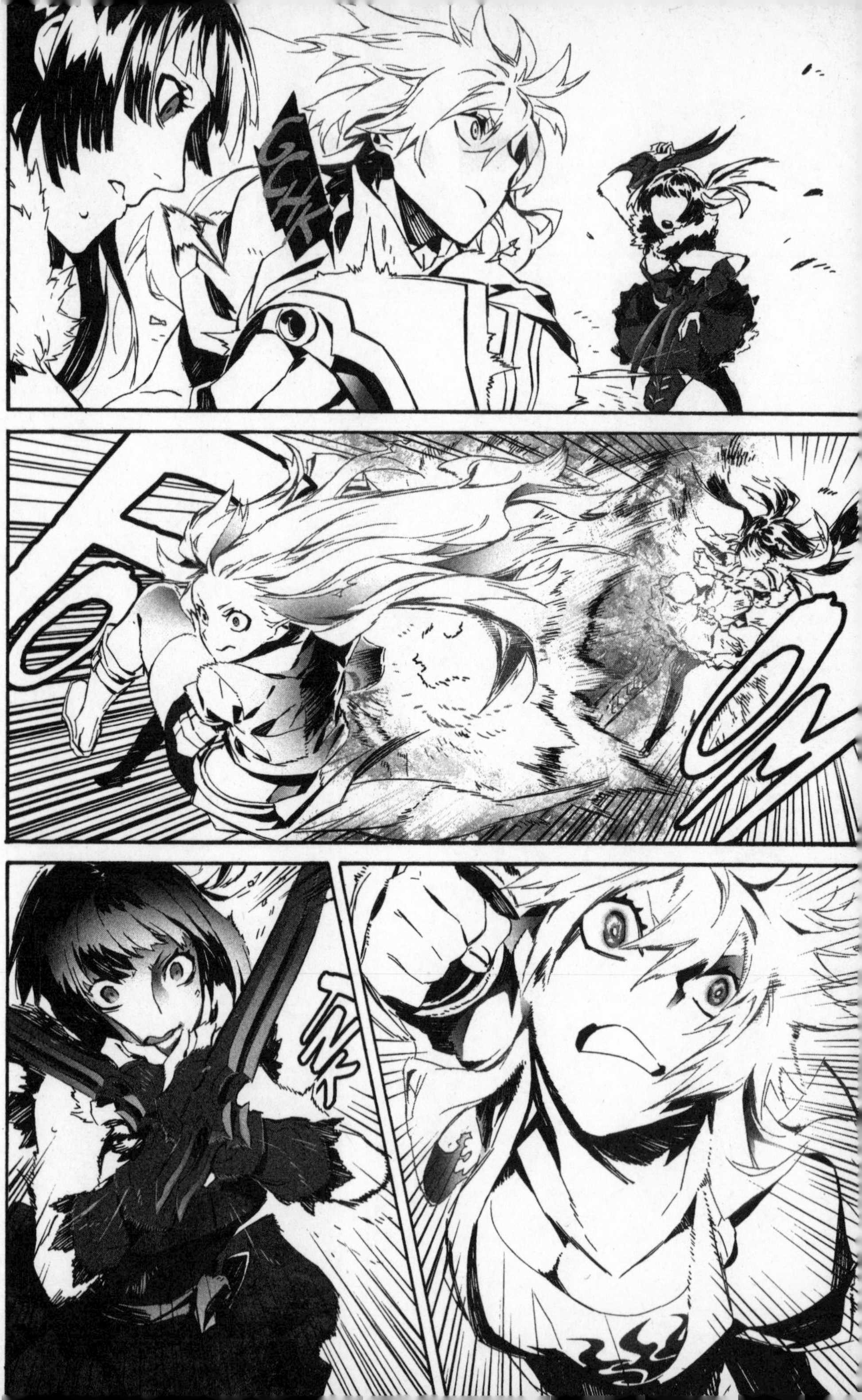
GUHK
OM
TINK

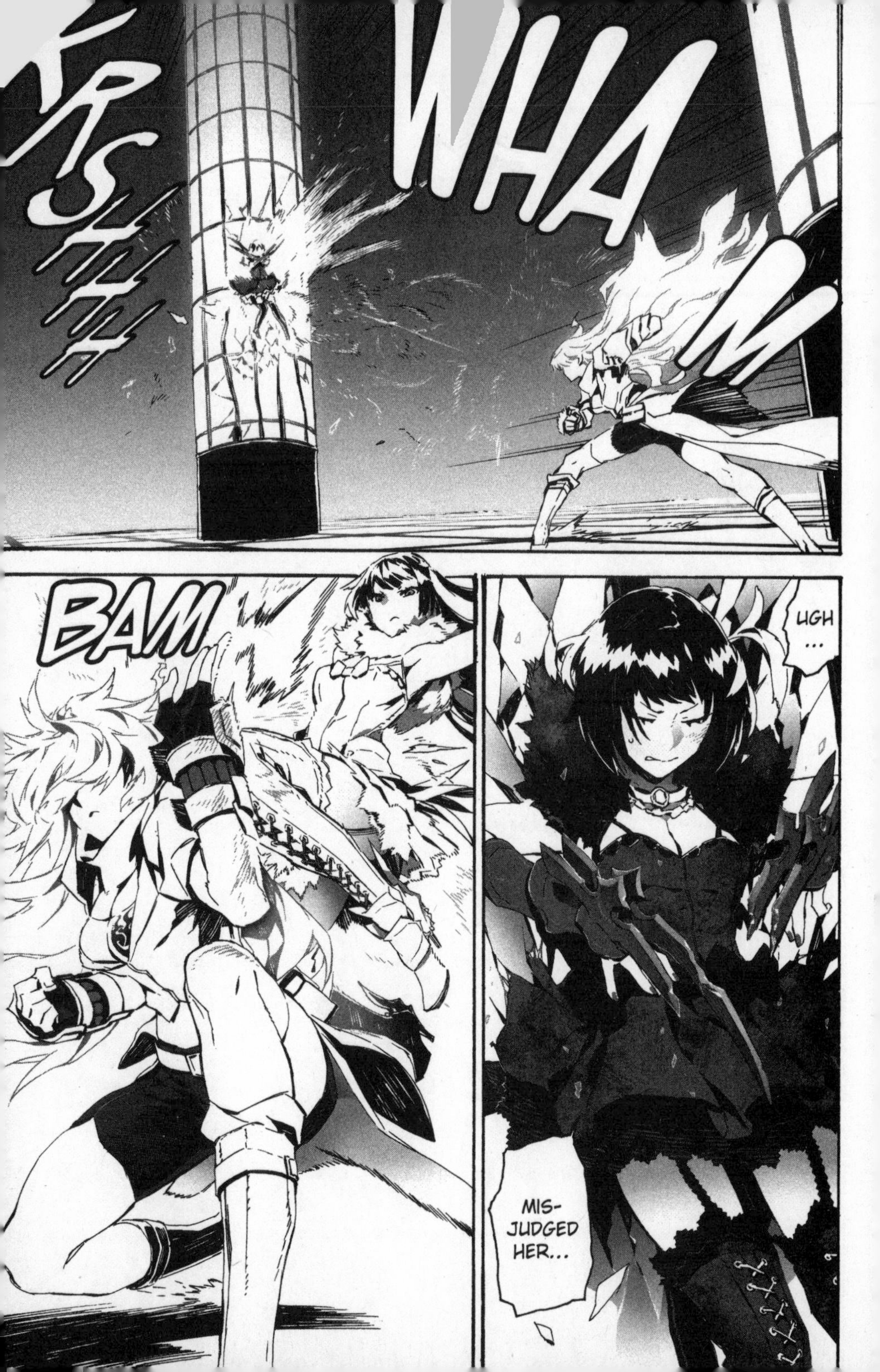
WHAM
KRSHHH
UGH ...
MIS-JUDGED HER...
BAM

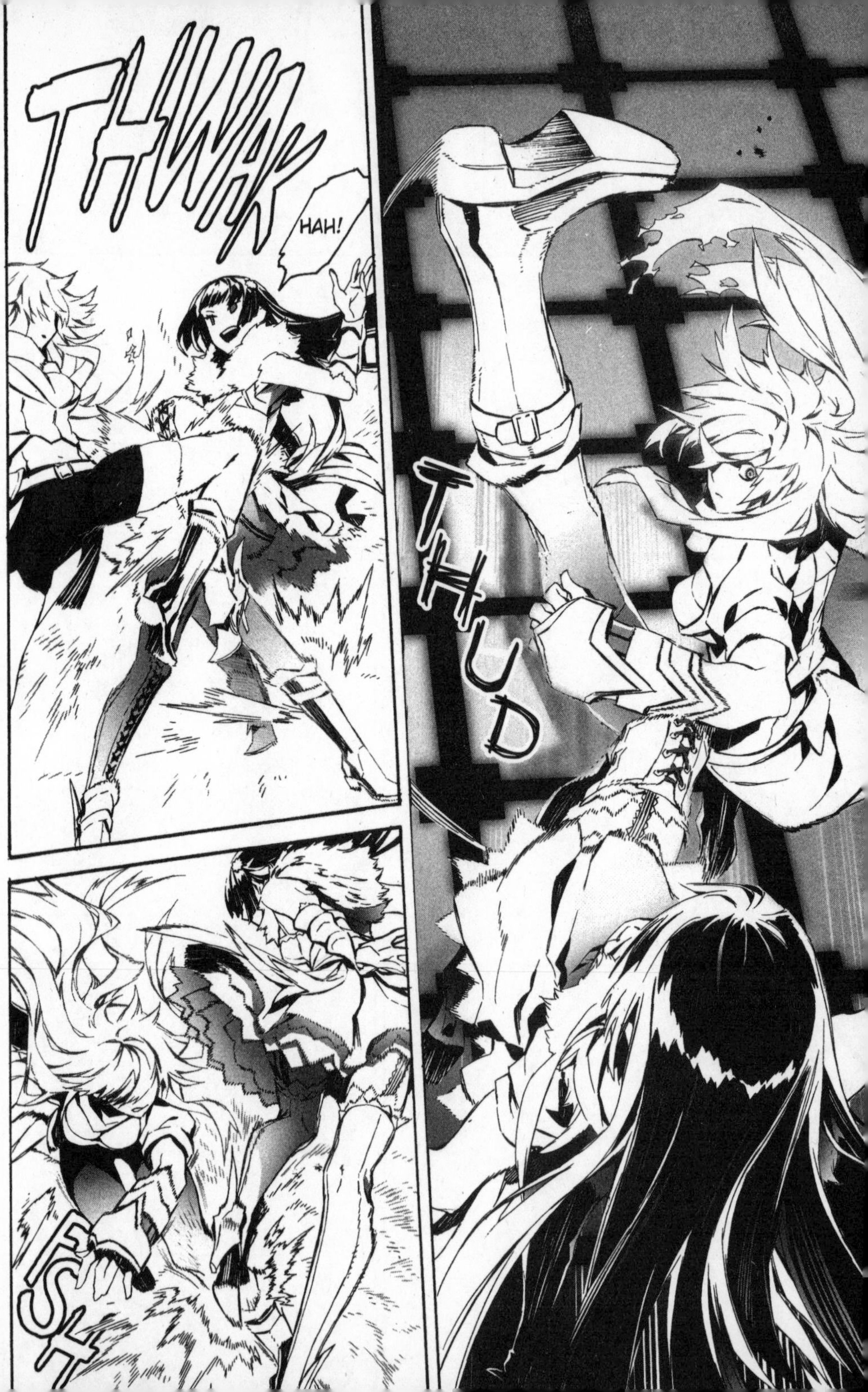
THUD
THWAK
HAH!
FSH

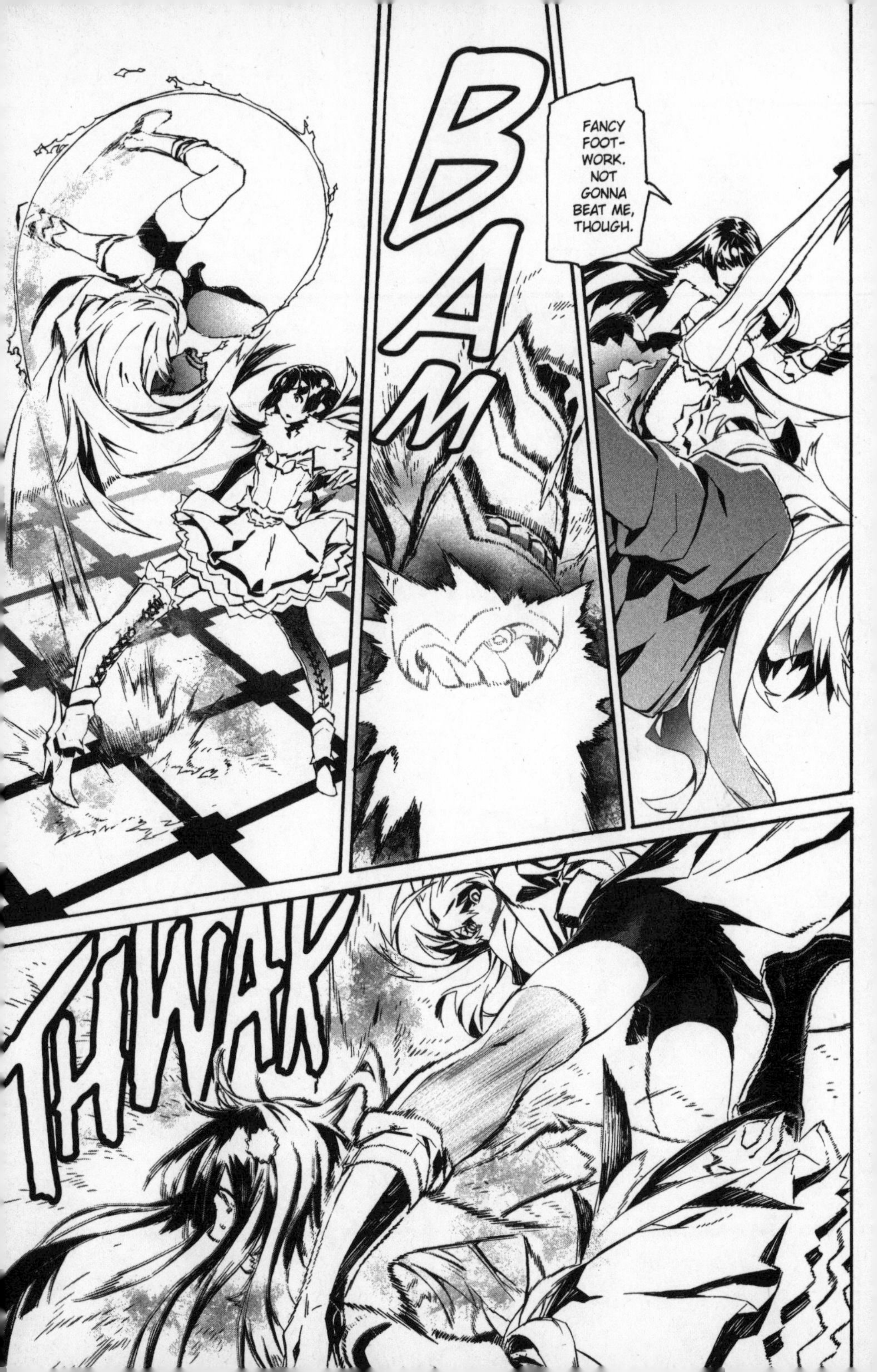
FANCY FOOT-WORK. NOT GONNA BEAT ME, THOUGH.
BAM
THWAK

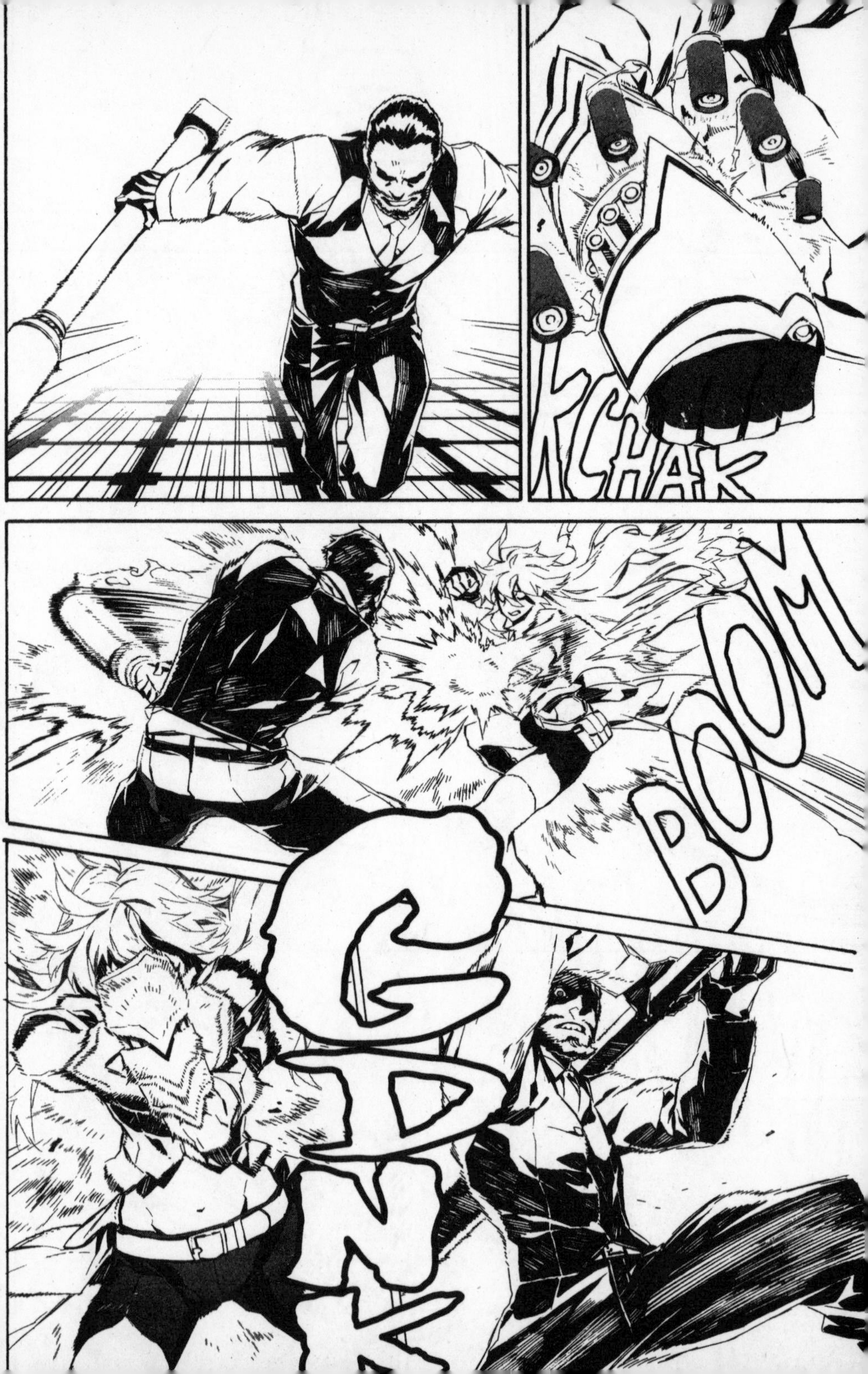
KCHAK
BOOM
GDNK

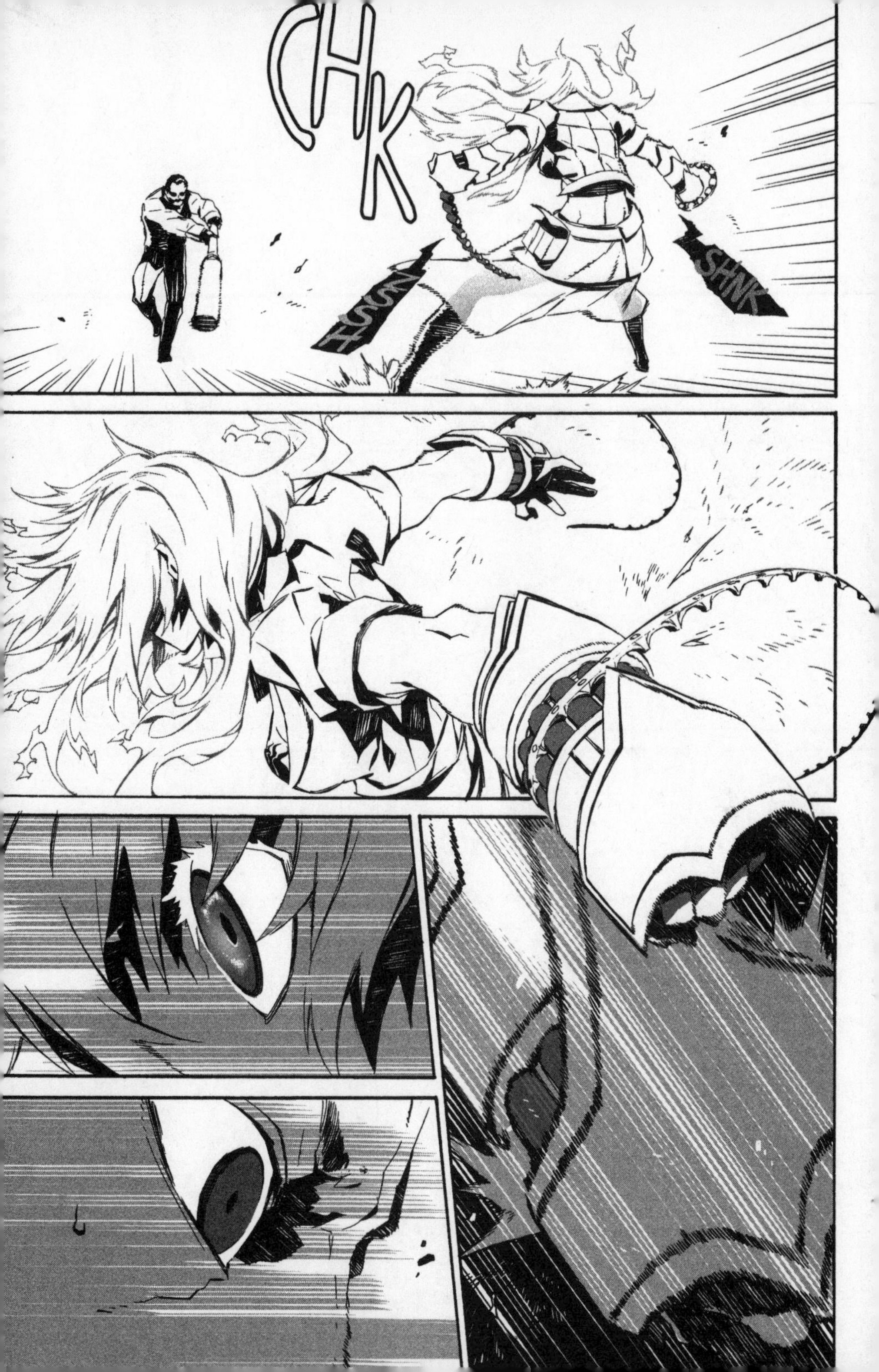
CHK
SHNK
FSSSH

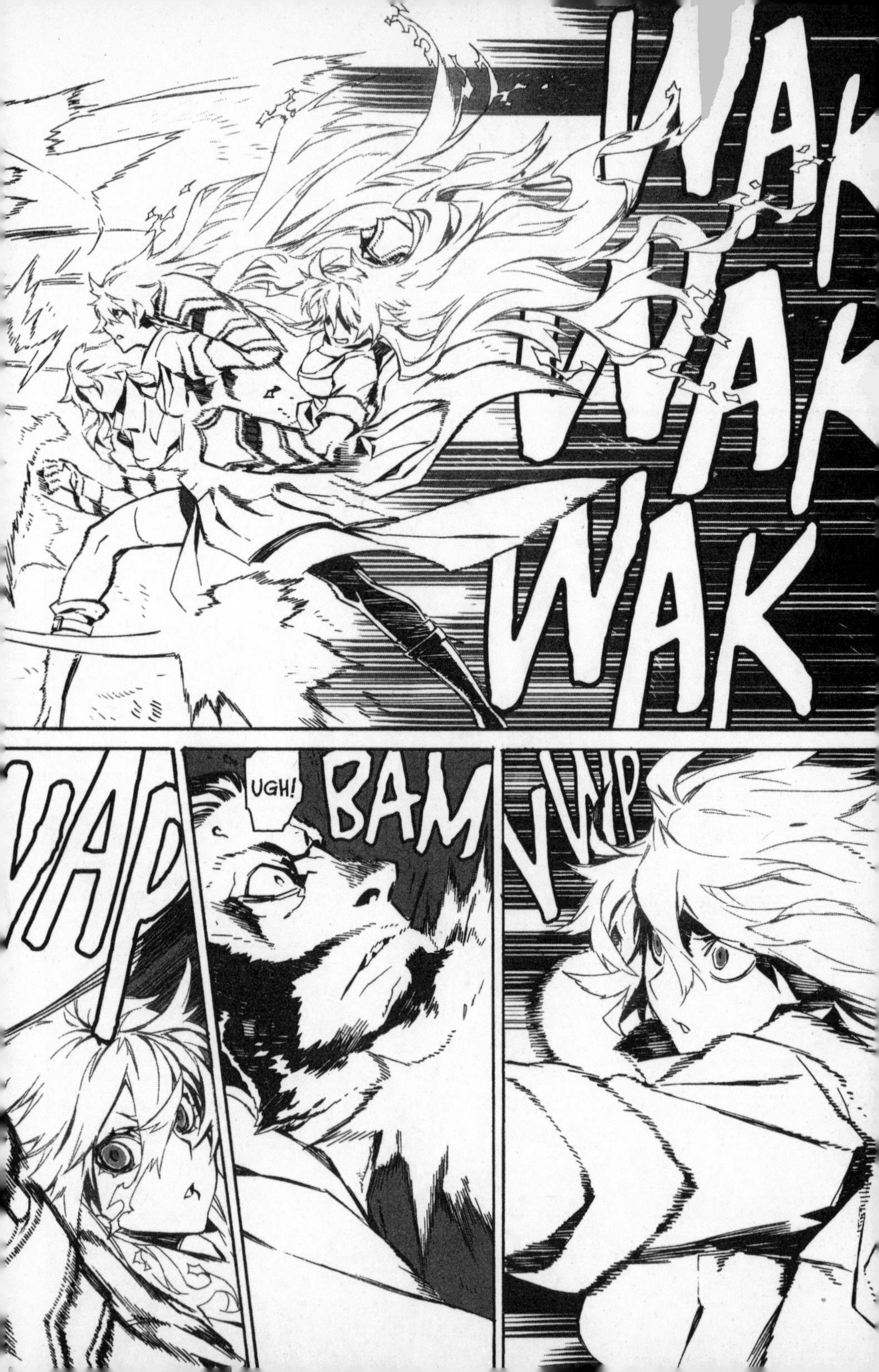
WAK
WAK
VWIP
UGH!
BAM

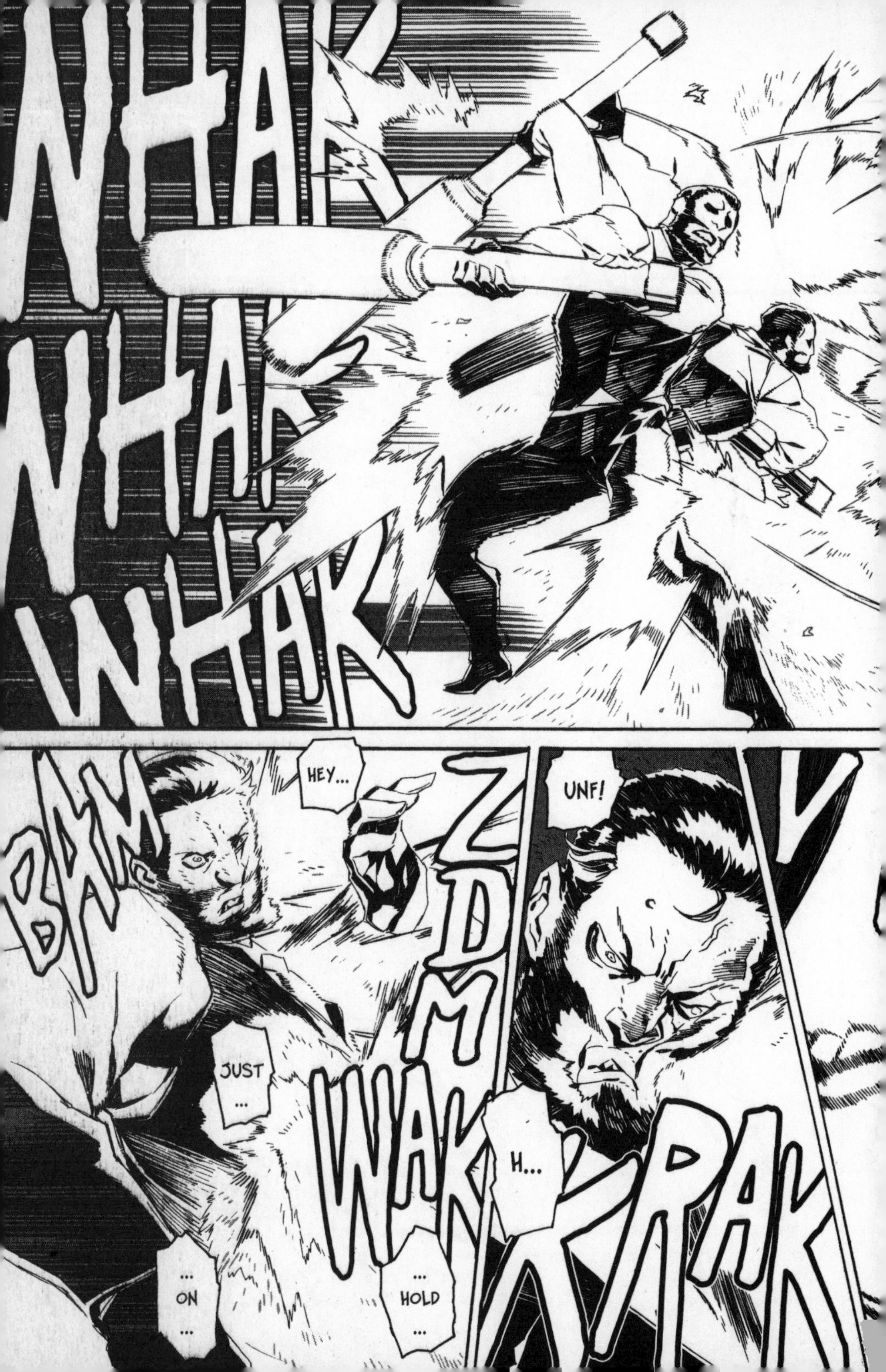
WHAK
WHAK
WHAK
UNF!
KRAK
HEY...
JUST
...
H...
...
HOLD
...
...
ON
...
ZDM
WAK
BAM

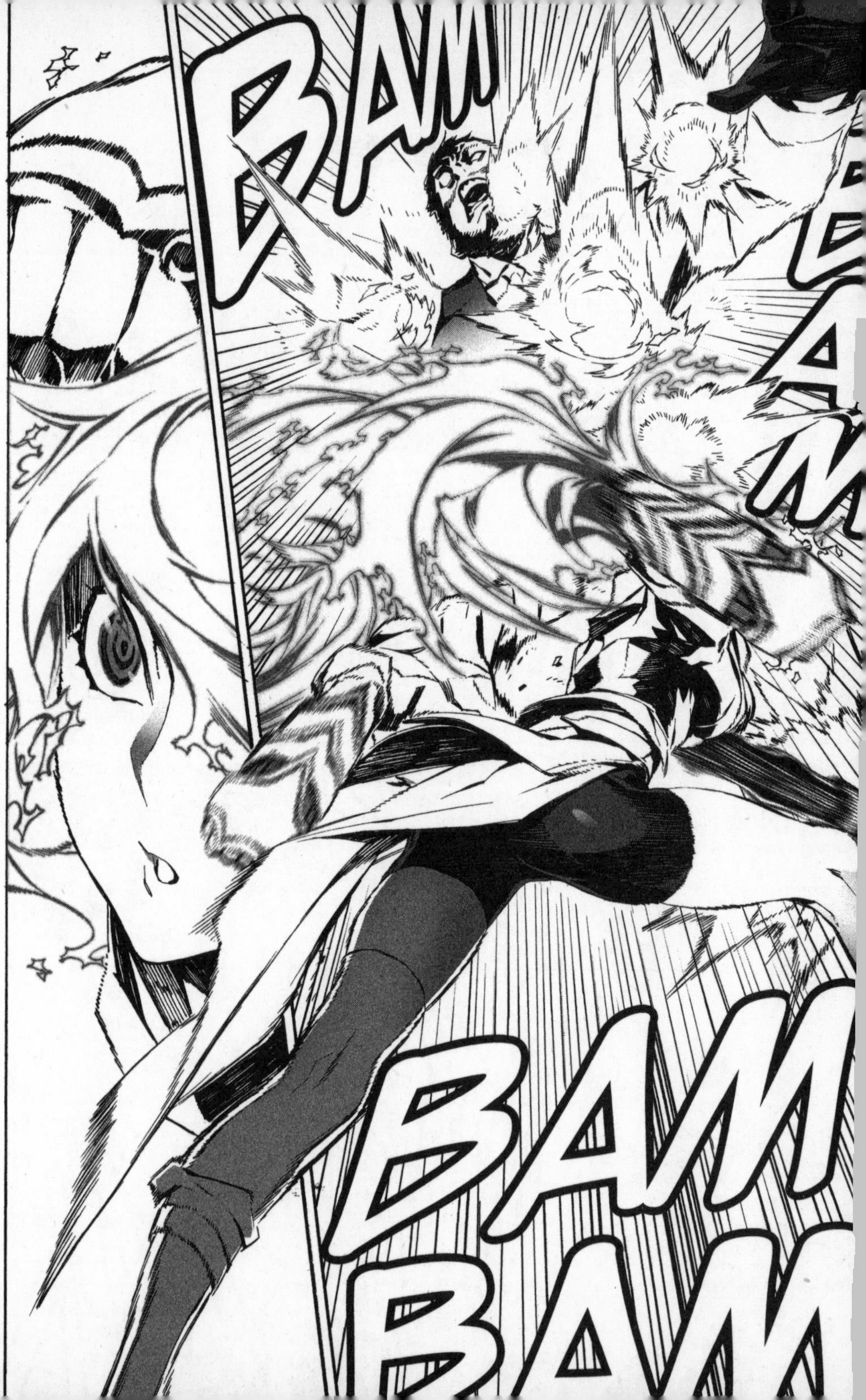
BAM
BAM
BAM
BAM

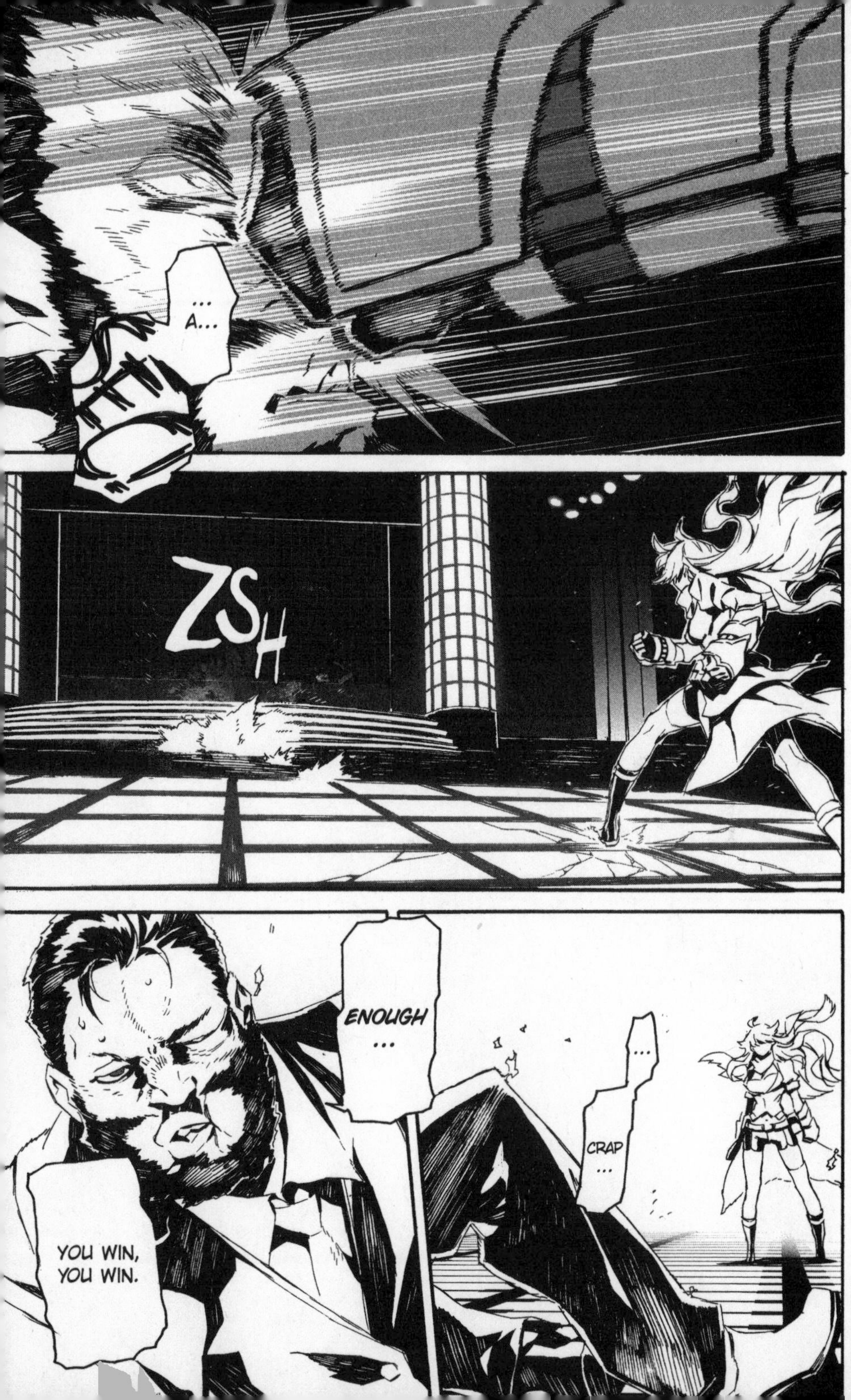
... A...
ZSH
... CRAP ...
ENOUGH ...
YOU WIN, YOU WIN.

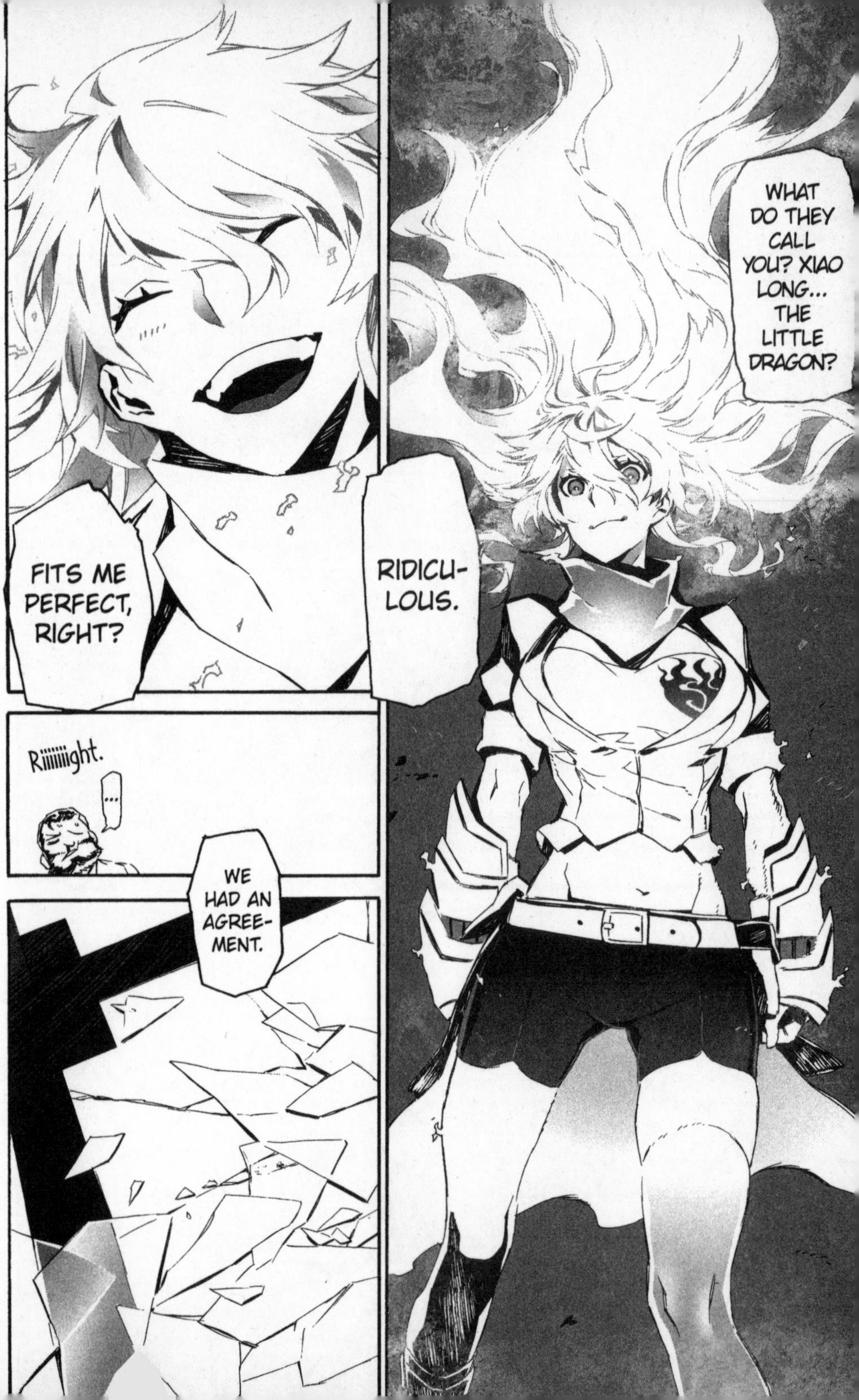
WHAT DO THEY CALL YOU? XIAO LONG... THE LITTLE DRAGON?
RIDICULOUS.
FITS ME PERFECT, RIGHT?
Riiiiiiight.
...
WE HAD AN AGREEMENT.

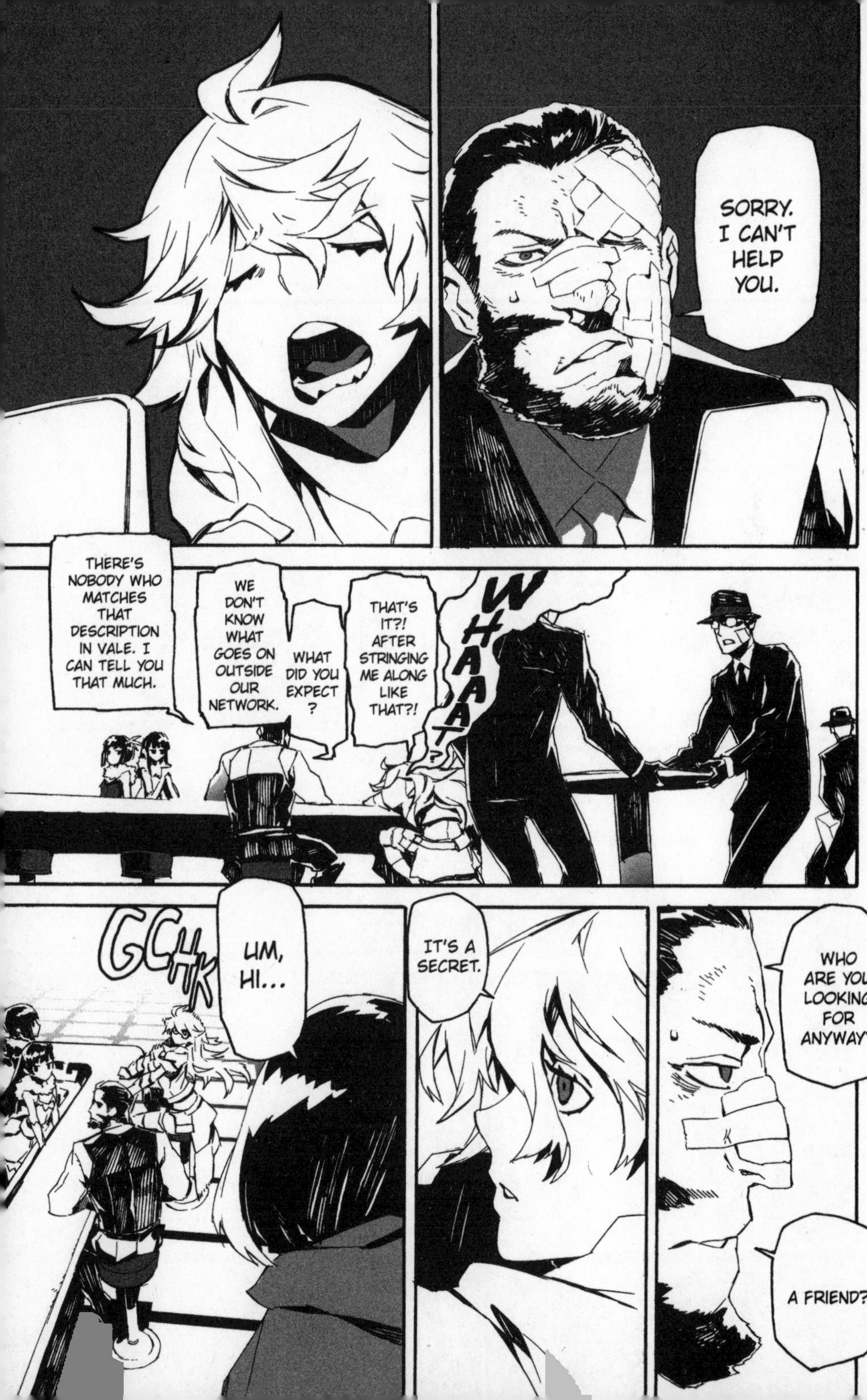
SORRY. I CAN'T HELP YOU.
WHAAAT?
THAT'S IT?! AFTER STRINGING ME ALONG LIKE THAT?!
WHAT DID YOU EXPECT?
WE DON'T KNOW WHAT GOES ON OUTSIDE OUR NETWORK.
THERE'S NOBODY WHO MATCHES THAT DESCRIPTION IN VALE. I CAN TELL YOU THAT MUCH.
WHO ARE YOU LOOKING FOR ANYWAY?
A FRIEND?
IT'S A SECRET.
UM, HI...
GCHK

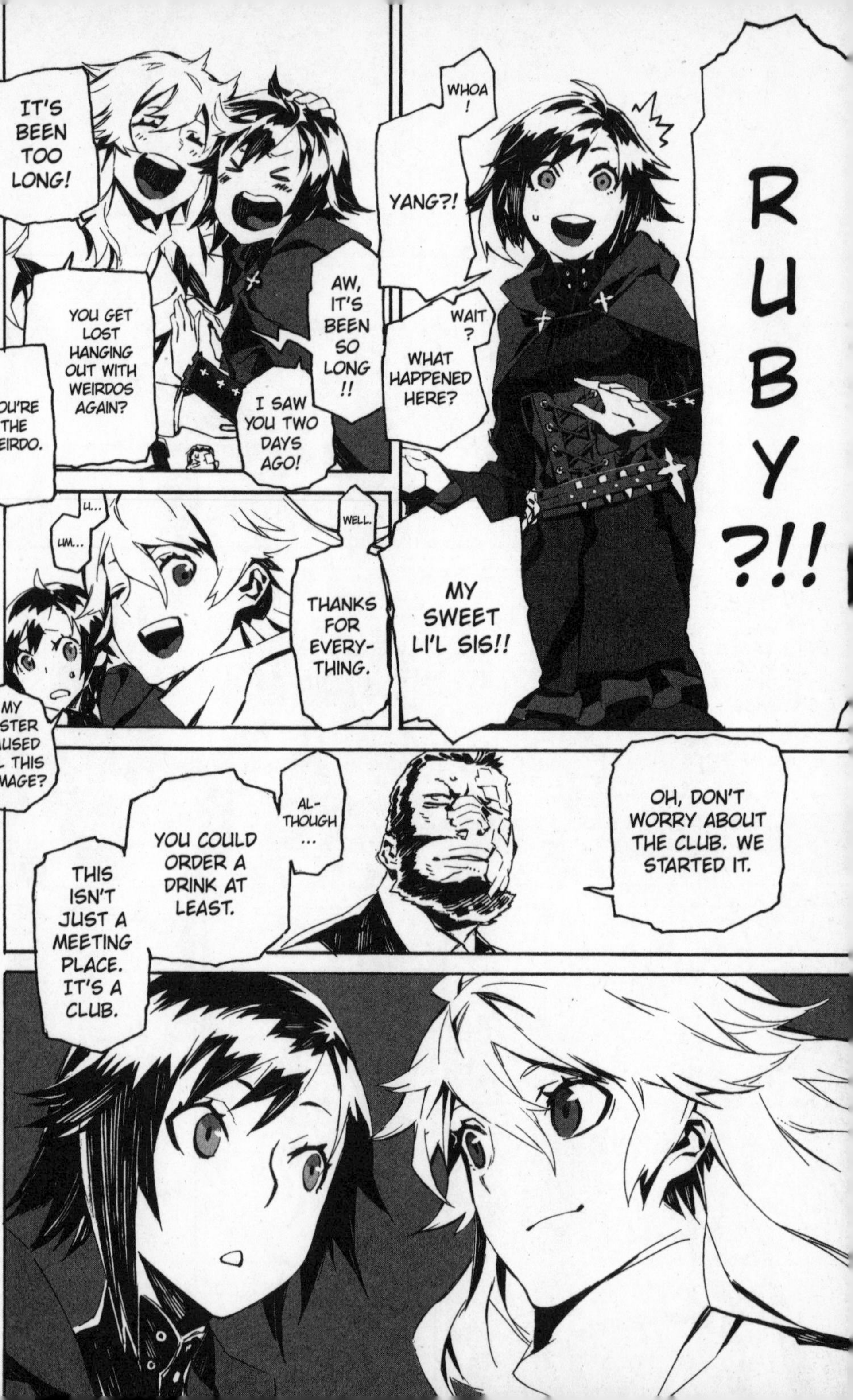
RUBY?!!
WHOA!
YANG?!
WAIT?
WHAT HAPPENED HERE?
MY SWEET LI'L SIS!!
IT'S BEEN TOO LONG!
AW, IT'S BEEN SO LONG!!
I SAW YOU TWO DAYS AGO!
YOU GET LOST HANGING OUT WITH WEIRDOS AGAIN?
YOU'RE THE WEIRDO.
WELL.
THANKS FOR EVERY-THING.
U...
UM...
MY SISTER CAUSED ALL THIS DAMAGE?
OH, DON'T WORRY ABOUT THE CLUB. WE STARTED IT.
AL-THOUGH...
YOU COULD ORDER A DRINK AT LEAST.
THIS ISN'T JUST A MEETING PLACE. IT'S A CLUB.

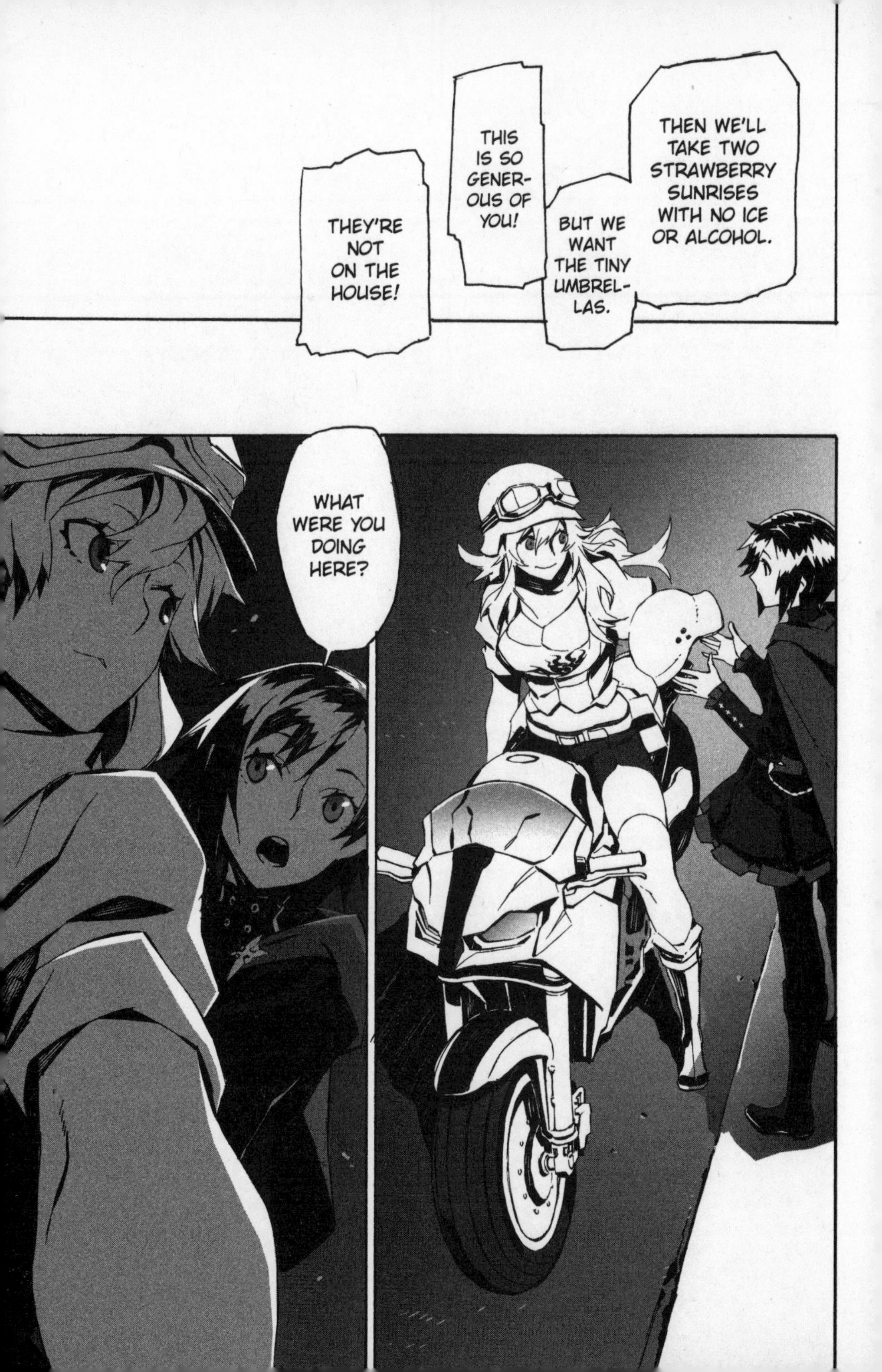
THEN WE'LL TAKE TWO STRAWBERRY SUNRISES WITH NO ICE OR ALCOHOL.
BUT WE WANT THE TINY UMBREL-LAS.
THIS IS SO GENER-OUS OF YOU!
THEY'RE NOT ON THE HOUSE!
WHAT WERE YOU DOING HERE?

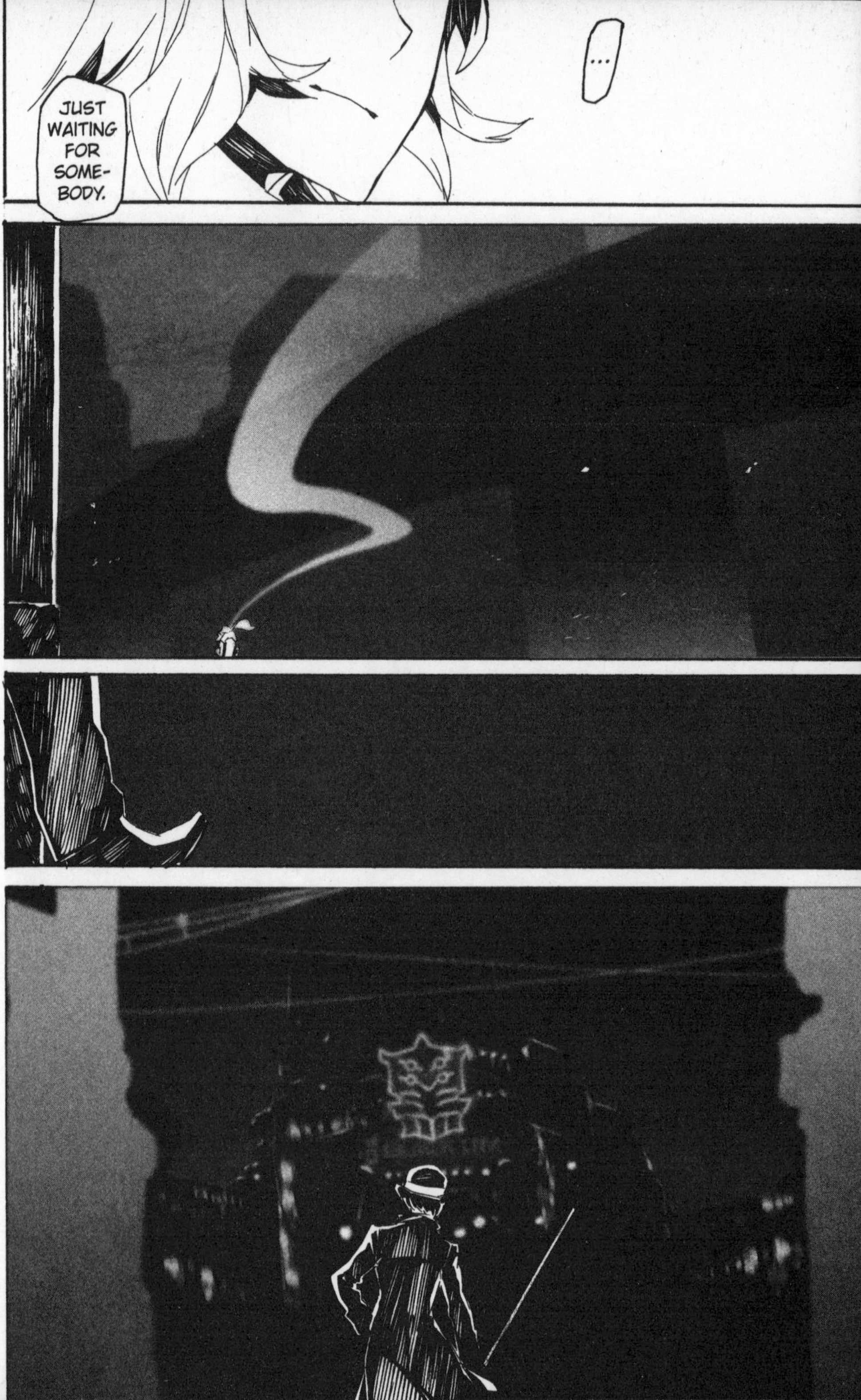
...
JUST WAITING FOR SOMEBODY.

Yang Xiao Long

y

RWBY

#9

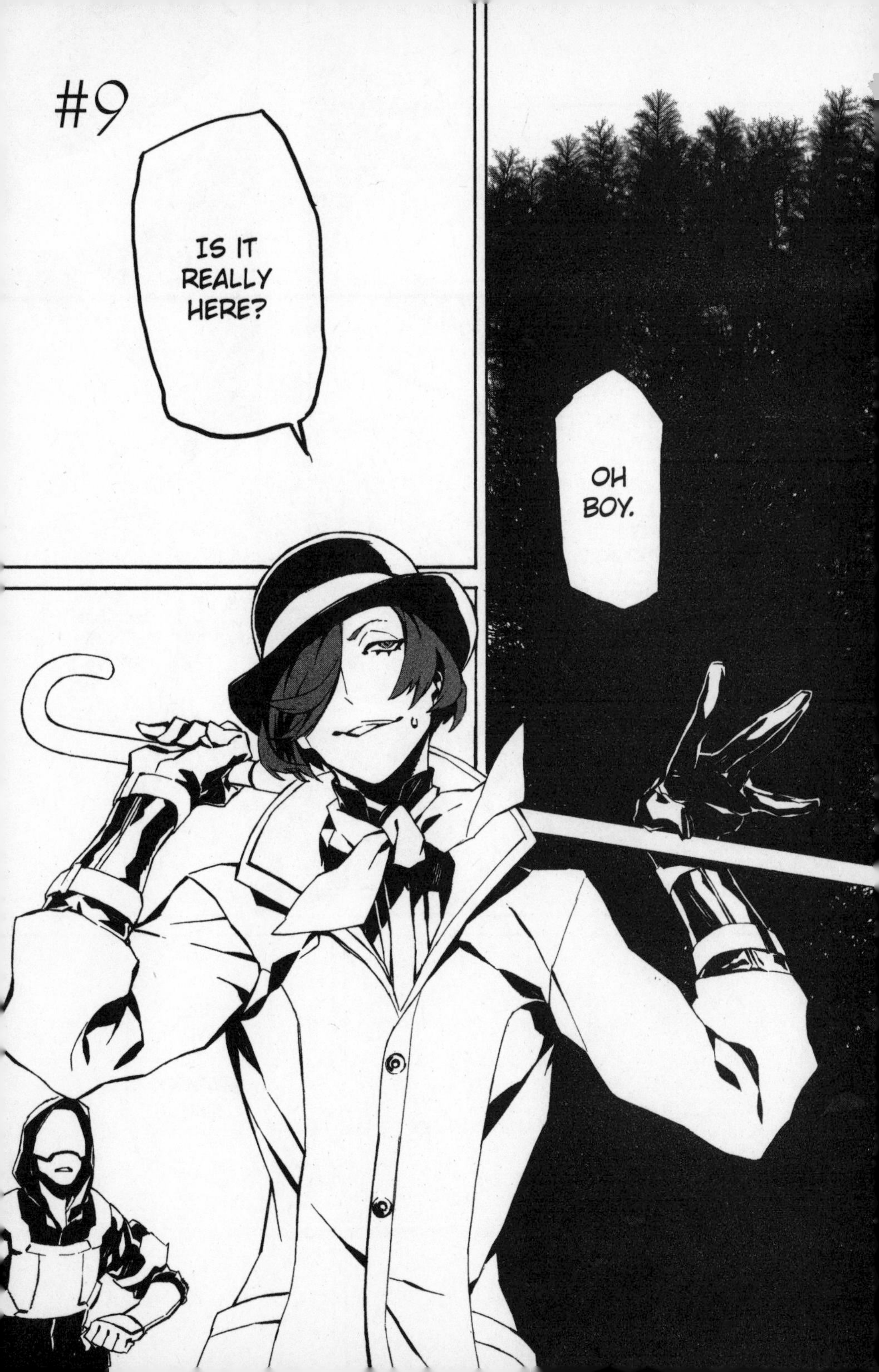
OH BOY.
IS IT REALLY HERE?

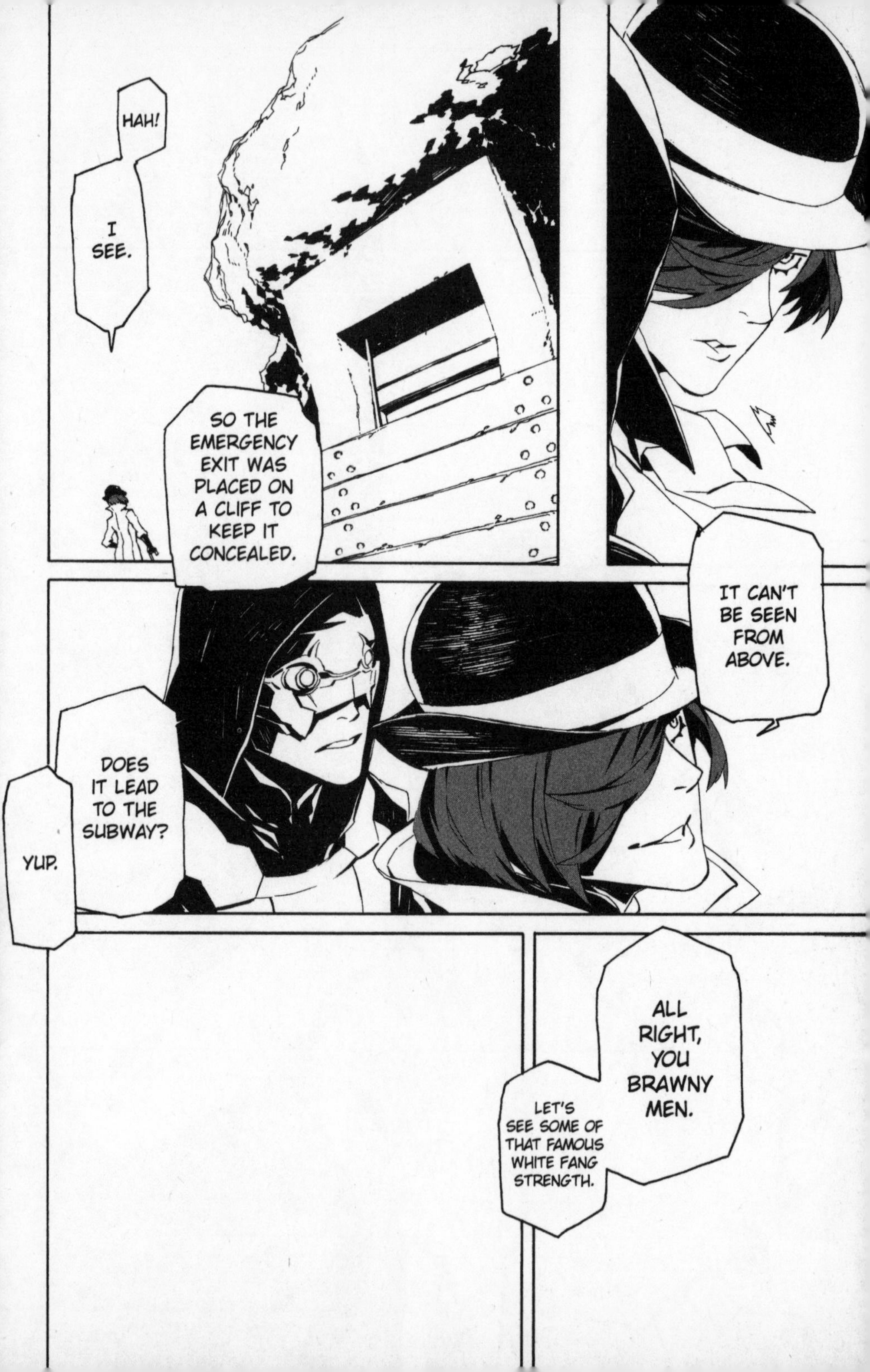
HAH!
I SEE.
SO THE EMERGENCY EXIT WAS PLACED ON A CLIFF TO KEEP IT CONCEALED.
IT CAN'T BE SEEN FROM ABOVE.
DOES IT LEAD TO THE SUBWAY?
YUP.
ALL RIGHT, YOU BRAWNY MEN.
LET'S SEE SOME OF THAT FAMOUS WHITE FANG STRENGTH.

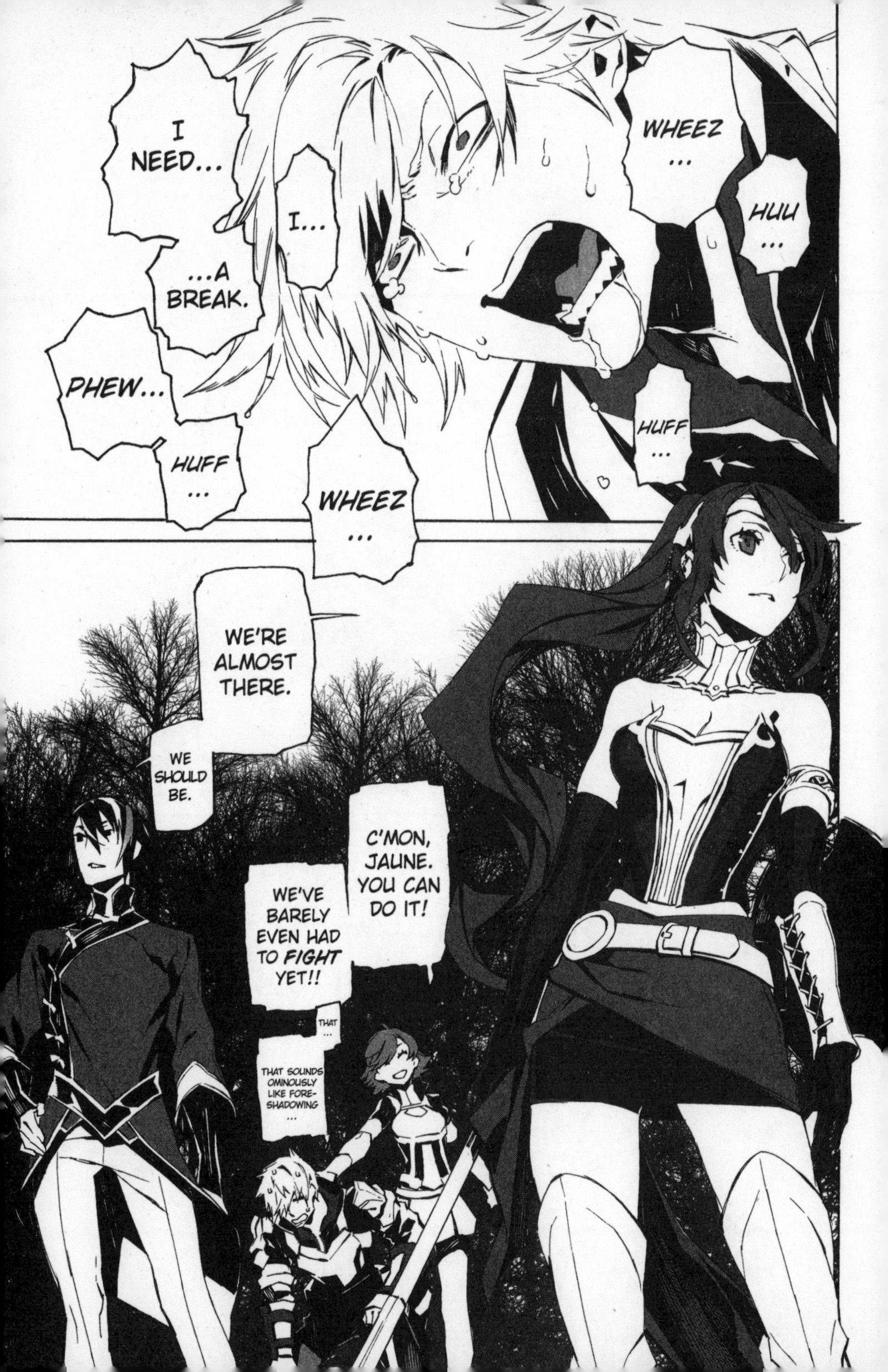
WHEEZ...
HUU...
I...
I NEED...
...A BREAK.
HUFF...
PHEW...
WHEEZ...
HUFF...
WE'RE ALMOST THERE.
WE SHOULD BE.
C'MON, JAUNE. YOU CAN DO IT!
WE'VE BARELY EVEN HAD TO FIGHT YET!!
THAT...
THAT SOUNDS OMINOUSLY LIKE FORE-SHADOWING...

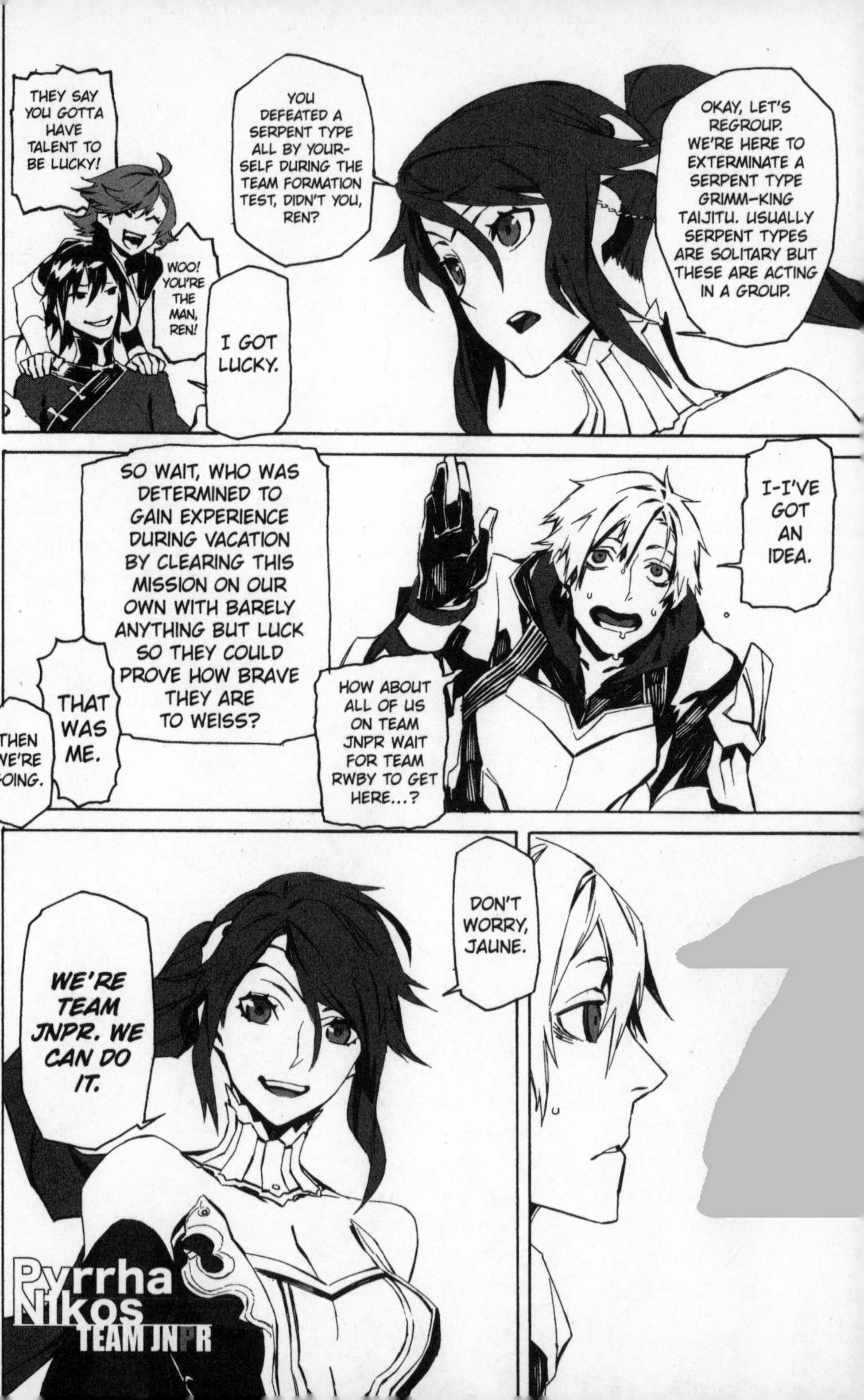
OKAY, LET'S REGROUP. WE'RE HERE TO EXTERMINATE A SERPENT TYPE GRIMM—KING TAIJITU. USUALLY SERPENT TYPES ARE SOLITARY BUT THESE ARE ACTING IN A GROUP.
YOU DEFEATED A SERPENT TYPE ALL BY YOURSELF DURING THE TEAM FORMATION TEST, DIDN'T YOU, REN?
I GOT LUCKY.
THEY SAY YOU GOTTA HAVE TALENT TO BE LUCKY!
WOO! YOU'RE THE MAN, REN!
I-I'VE GOT AN IDEA.
HOW ABOUT ALL OF US ON TEAM JNPR WAIT FOR TEAM RWBY TO GET HERE...?
SO WAIT, WHO WAS DETERMINED TO GAIN EXPERIENCE DURING VACATION BY CLEARING THIS MISSION ON OUR OWN WITH BARELY ANYTHING BUT LUCK SO THEY COULD PROVE HOW BRAVE THEY ARE TO WEISS?
THAT WAS ME.
THEN WE'RE GOING.
DON'T WORRY, JAUNE.
WE'RE TEAM JNPR. WE CAN DO IT.
Pyrrha Nikos
TEAM JNPR

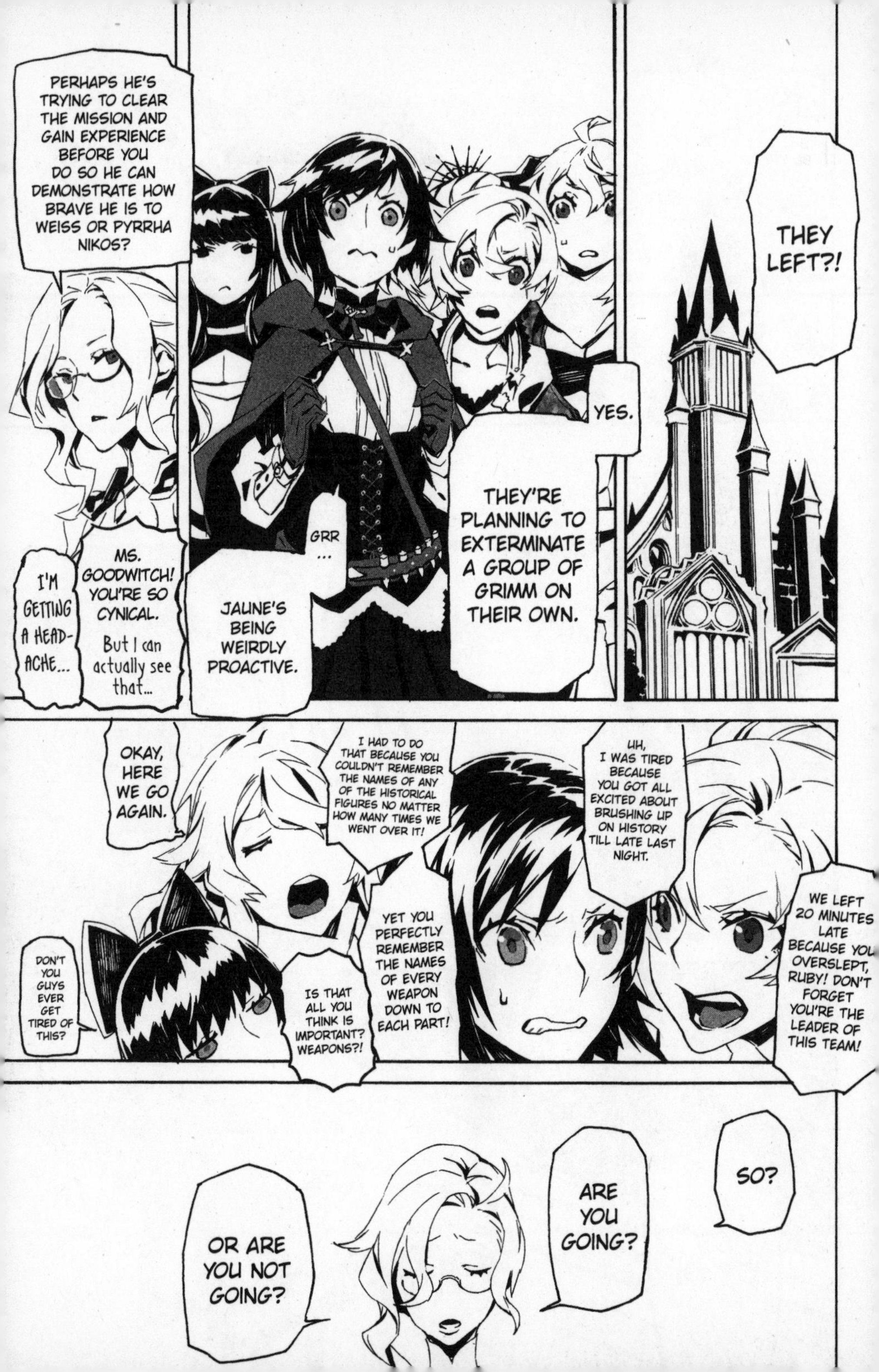
THEY LEFT?!
YES.
THEY'RE PLANNING TO EXTERMINATE A GROUP OF GRIMM ON THEIR OWN.
GRR...
JAUNE'S BEING WEIRDLY PROACTIVE.
PERHAPS HE'S TRYING TO CLEAR THE MISSION AND GAIN EXPERIENCE BEFORE YOU DO SO HE CAN DEMONSTRATE HOW BRAVE HE IS TO WEISS OR PYRRHA NIKOS?
MS. GOODWITCH! YOU'RE SO CYNICAL.
But I can actually see that...
I'M GETTING A HEAD-ACHE...
WE LEFT 20 MINUTES LATE BECAUSE YOU OVERSLEPT, RUBY! DON'T FORGET YOU'RE THE LEADER OF THIS TEAM!
UH, I WAS TIRED BECAUSE YOU GOT ALL EXCITED ABOUT BRUSHING UP ON HISTORY TILL LATE LAST NIGHT.
I HAD TO DO THAT BECAUSE YOU COULDN'T REMEMBER THE NAMES OF ANY OF THE HISTORICAL FIGURES NO MATTER HOW MANY TIMES WE WENT OVER IT!
YET YOU PERFECTLY REMEMBER THE NAMES OF EVERY WEAPON DOWN TO EACH PART!
IS THAT ALL YOU THINK IS IMPORTANT? WEAPONS?!
OKAY, HERE WE GO AGAIN.
DON'T YOU GUYS EVER GET TIRED OF THIS?
SO?
ARE YOU GOING?
OR ARE YOU NOT GOING?

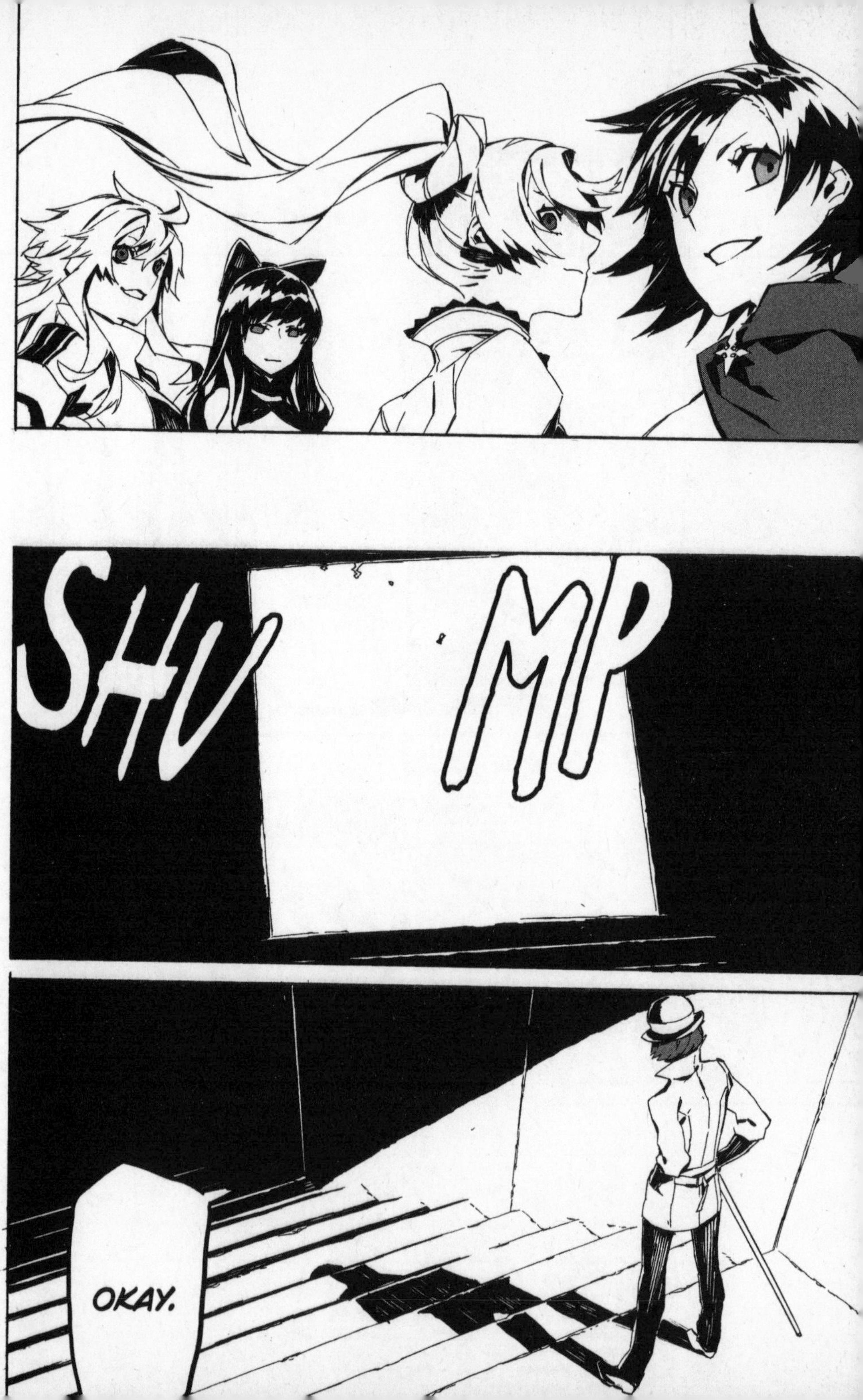
SHUMP
OKAY.

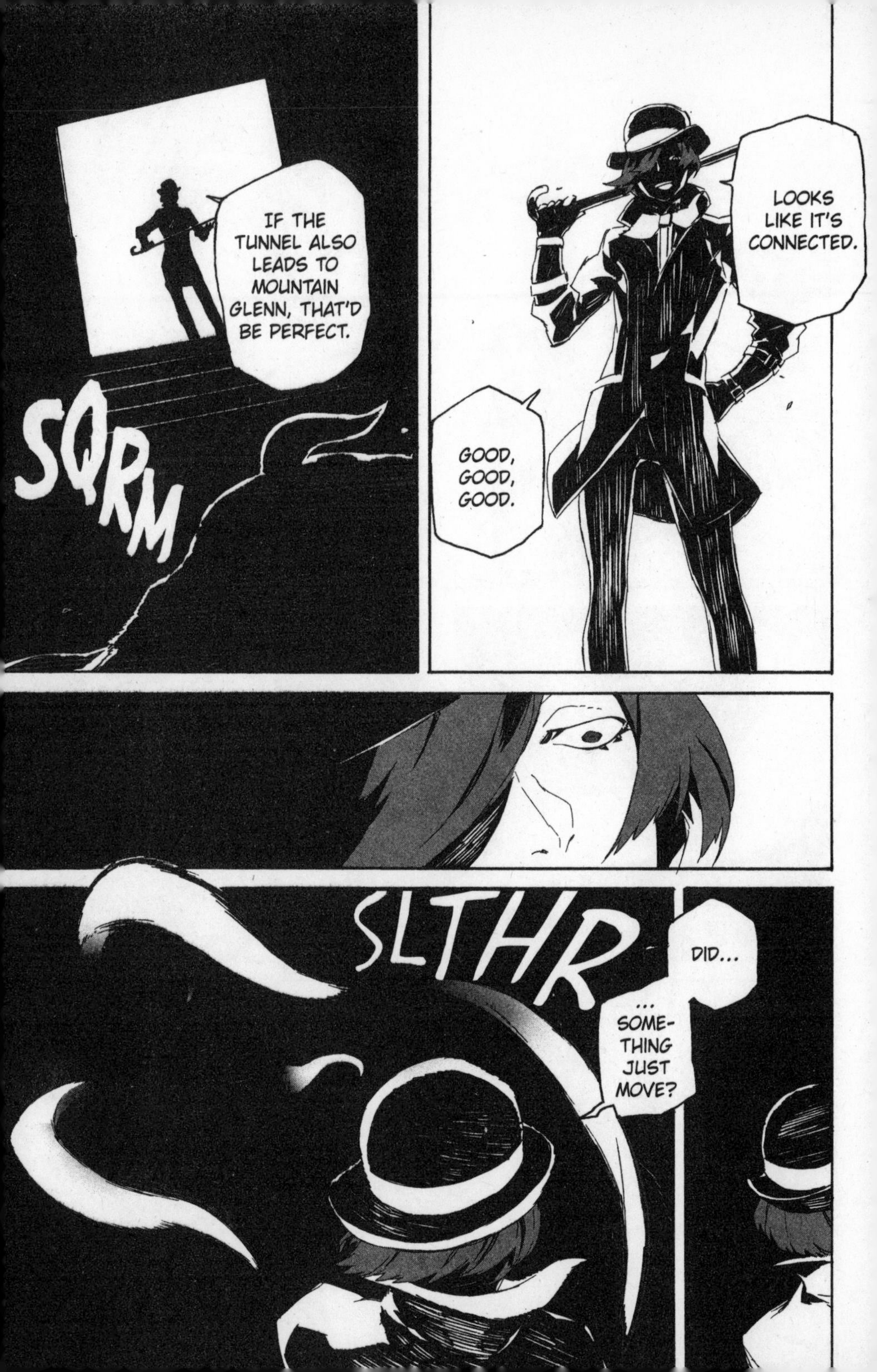
LOOKS LIKE IT'S CONNECTED.
GOOD, GOOD, GOOD.
IF THE TUNNEL ALSO LEADS TO MOUNTAIN GLENN, THAT'D BE PERFECT.
SQRM
SLTHR
DID...
...SOMETHING JUST MOVE?

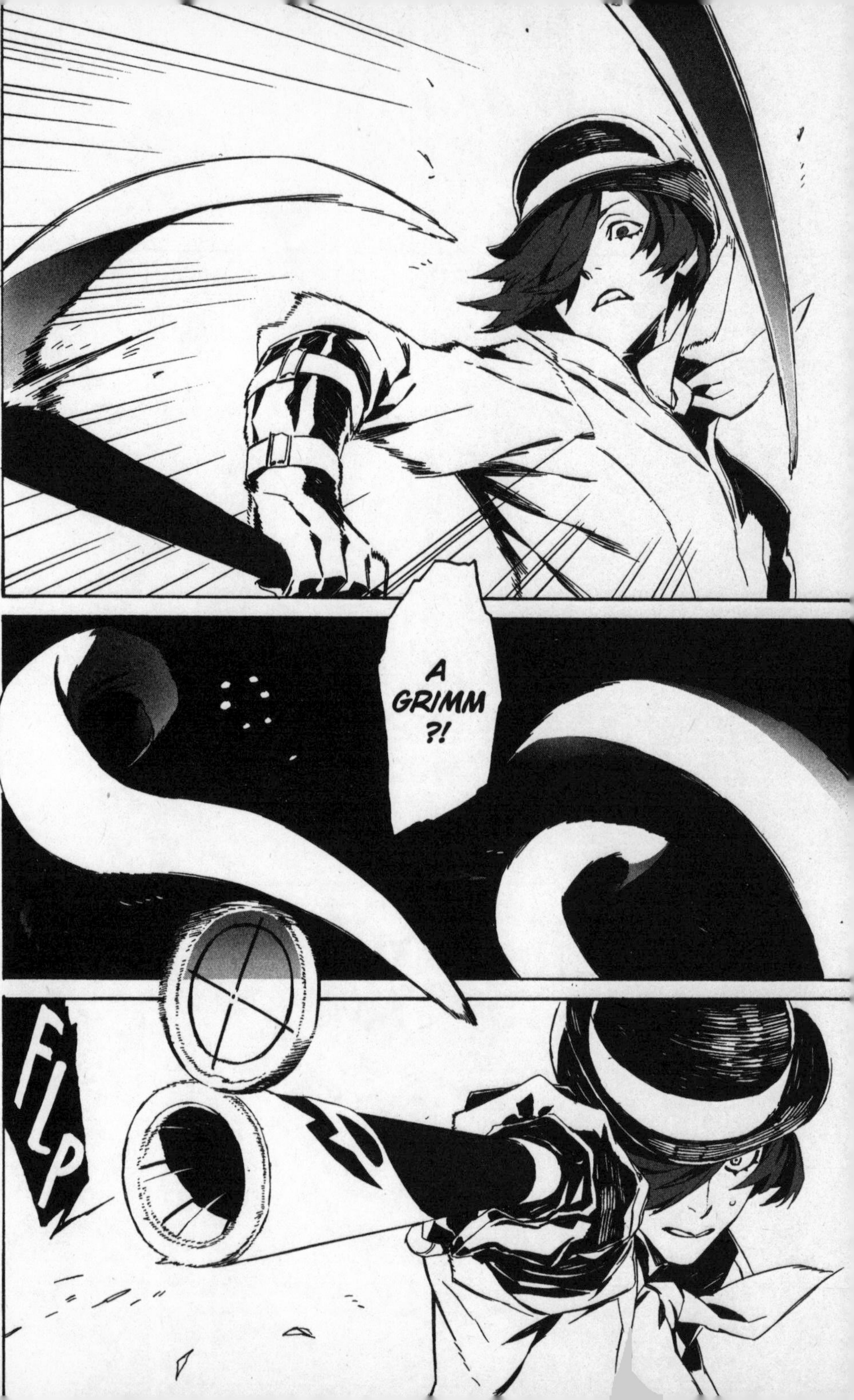
A GRIMM ?!
FLP

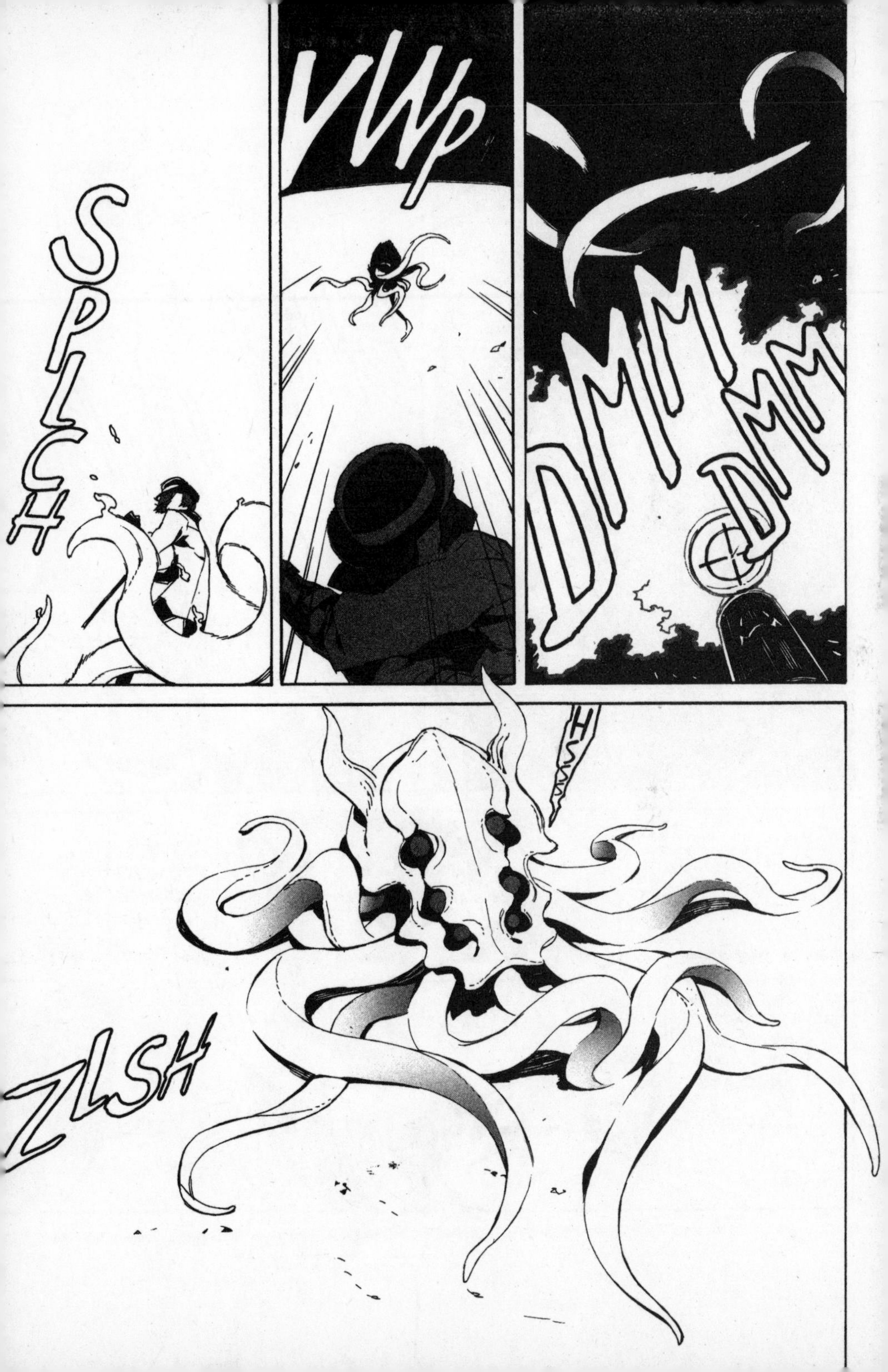
DMM DMM
VWP
SPLCH
HSSSS
ZLSH

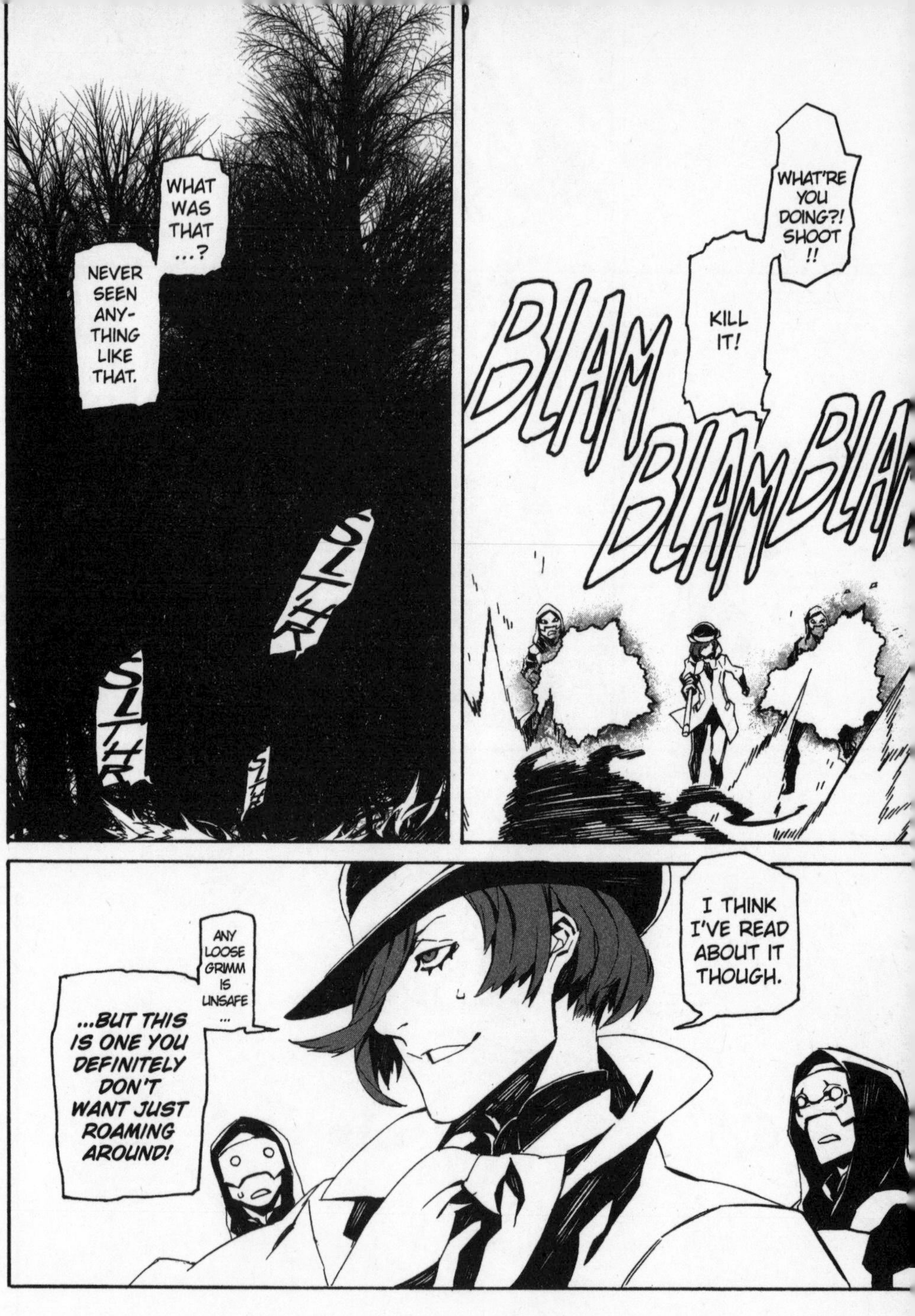
WHAT'RE YOU DOING?! SHOOT !!
KILL IT!
BLAM
BLAM BLA
WHAT WAS THAT ...?
NEVER SEEN ANY-THING LIKE THAT.
SLTHR
SLTHR
I THINK I'VE READ ABOUT IT THOUGH.
ANY LOOSE GRIMM IS UNSAFE ...
...BUT THIS IS ONE YOU DEFINITELY DON'T WANT JUST ROAMING AROUND!

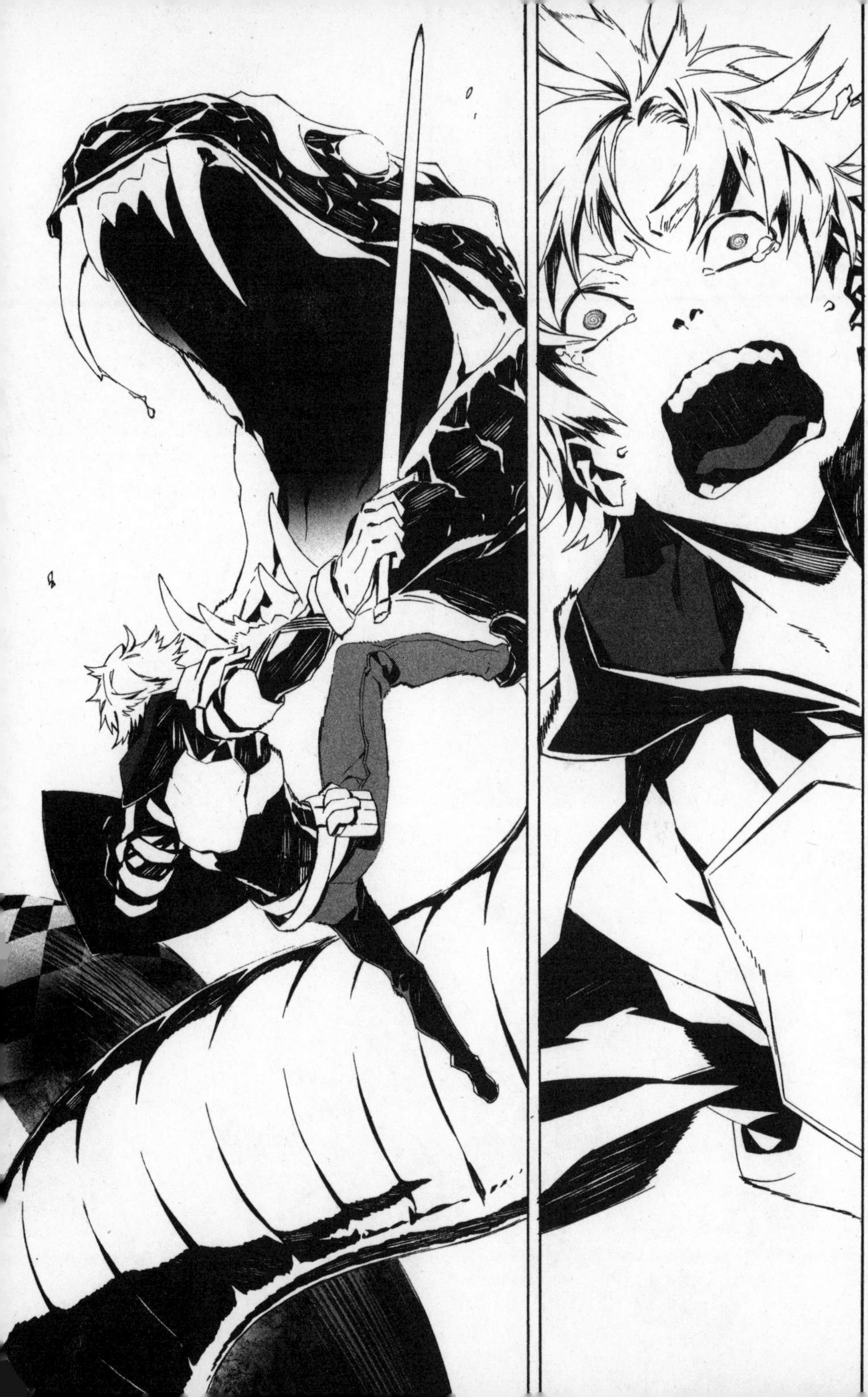

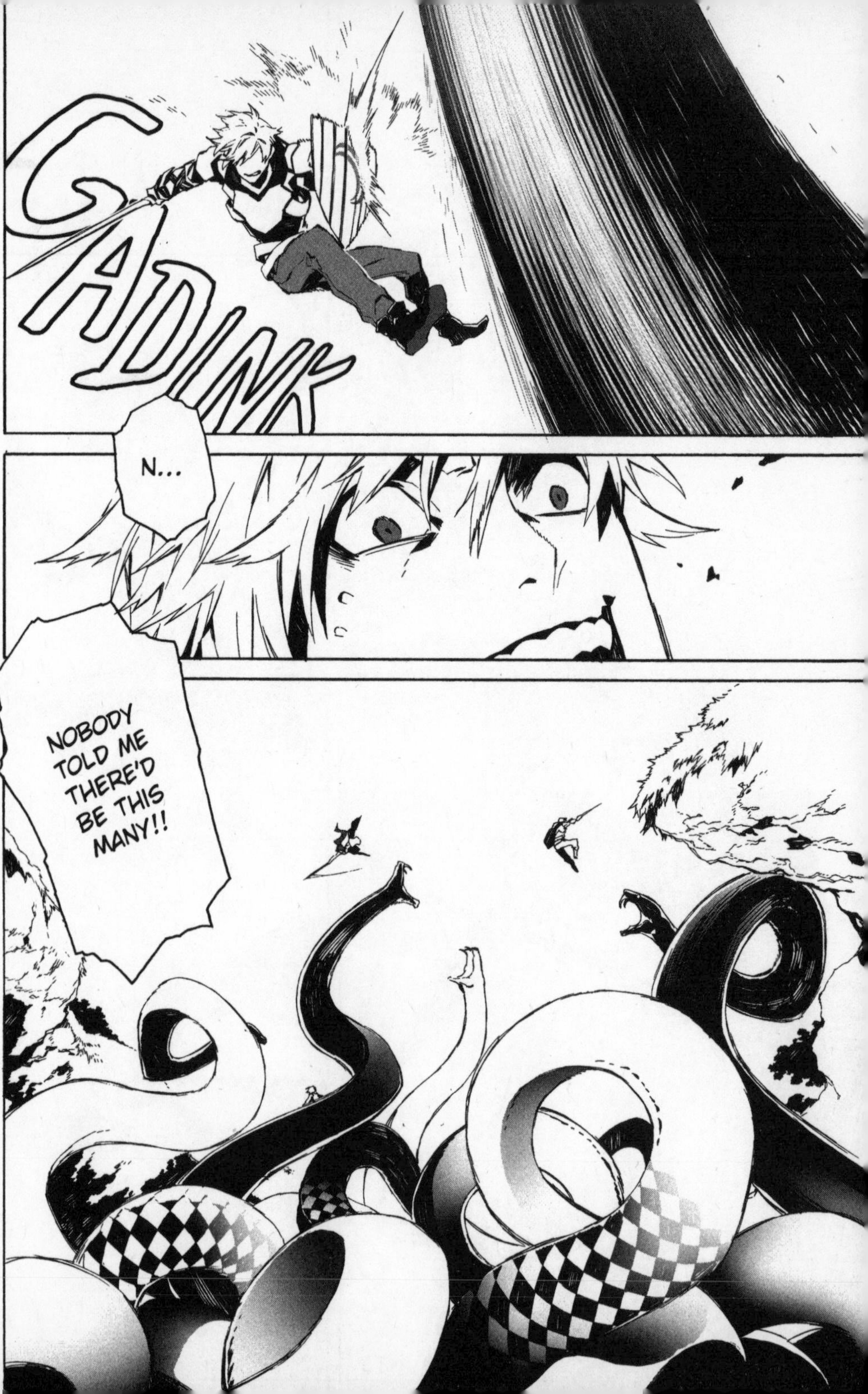
GADINK
N...
NOBODY TOLD ME THERE'D BE THIS MANY!!

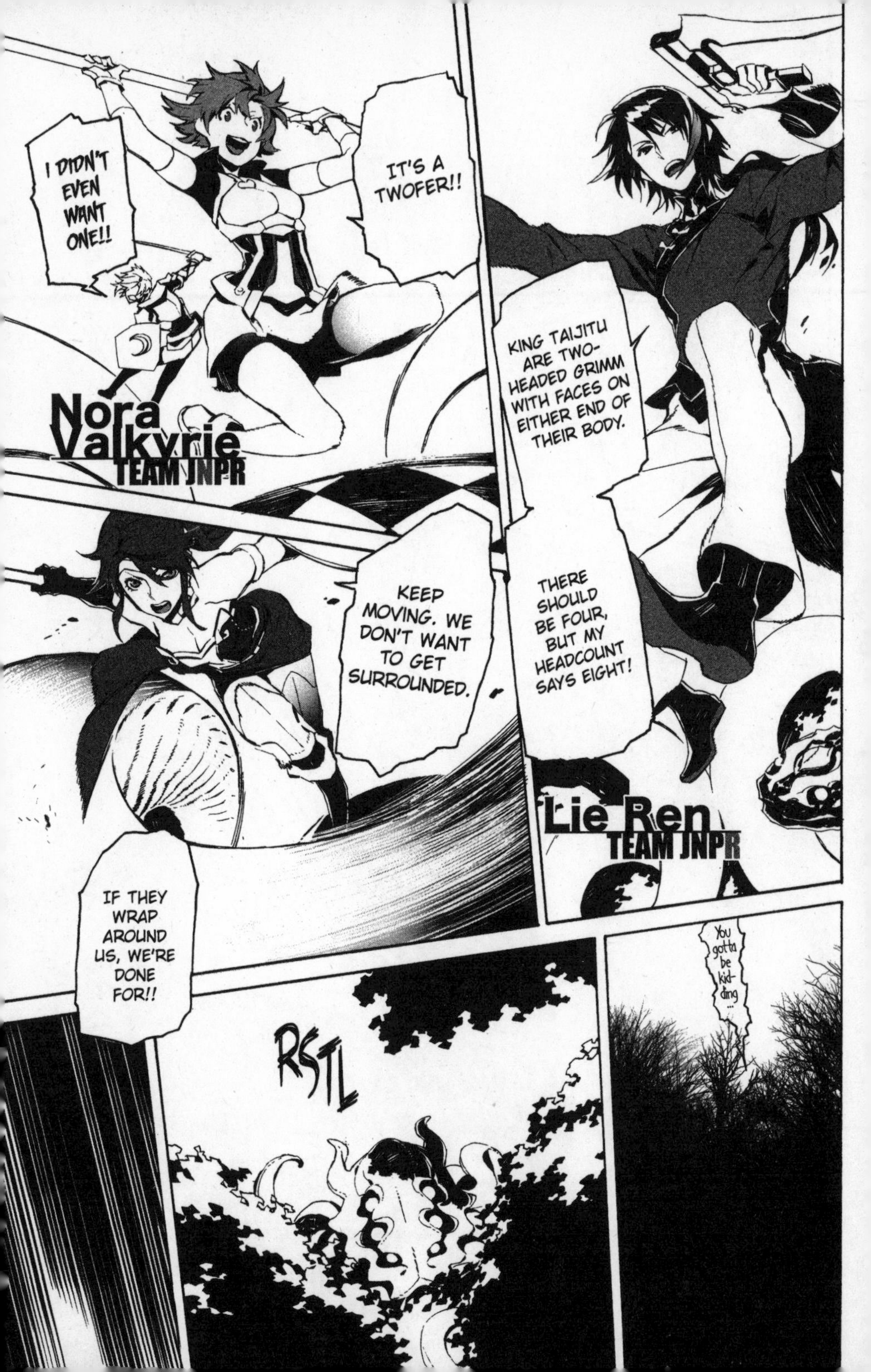

KING TAIJITU ARE TWO-HEADED GRIMM WITH FACES ON EITHER END OF THEIR BODY.
THERE SHOULD BE FOUR, BUT MY HEADCOUNT SAYS EIGHT!
Lie Ren
TEAM JNPR
IT'S A TWOFER!!
I DIDN'T EVEN WANT ONE!!
Nora Valkyrie
TEAM JNPR
KEEP MOVING. WE DON'T WANT TO GET SURROUNDED.
IF THEY WRAP AROUND US, WE'RE DONE FOR!!
You gotta be kid-ding...
RSTL

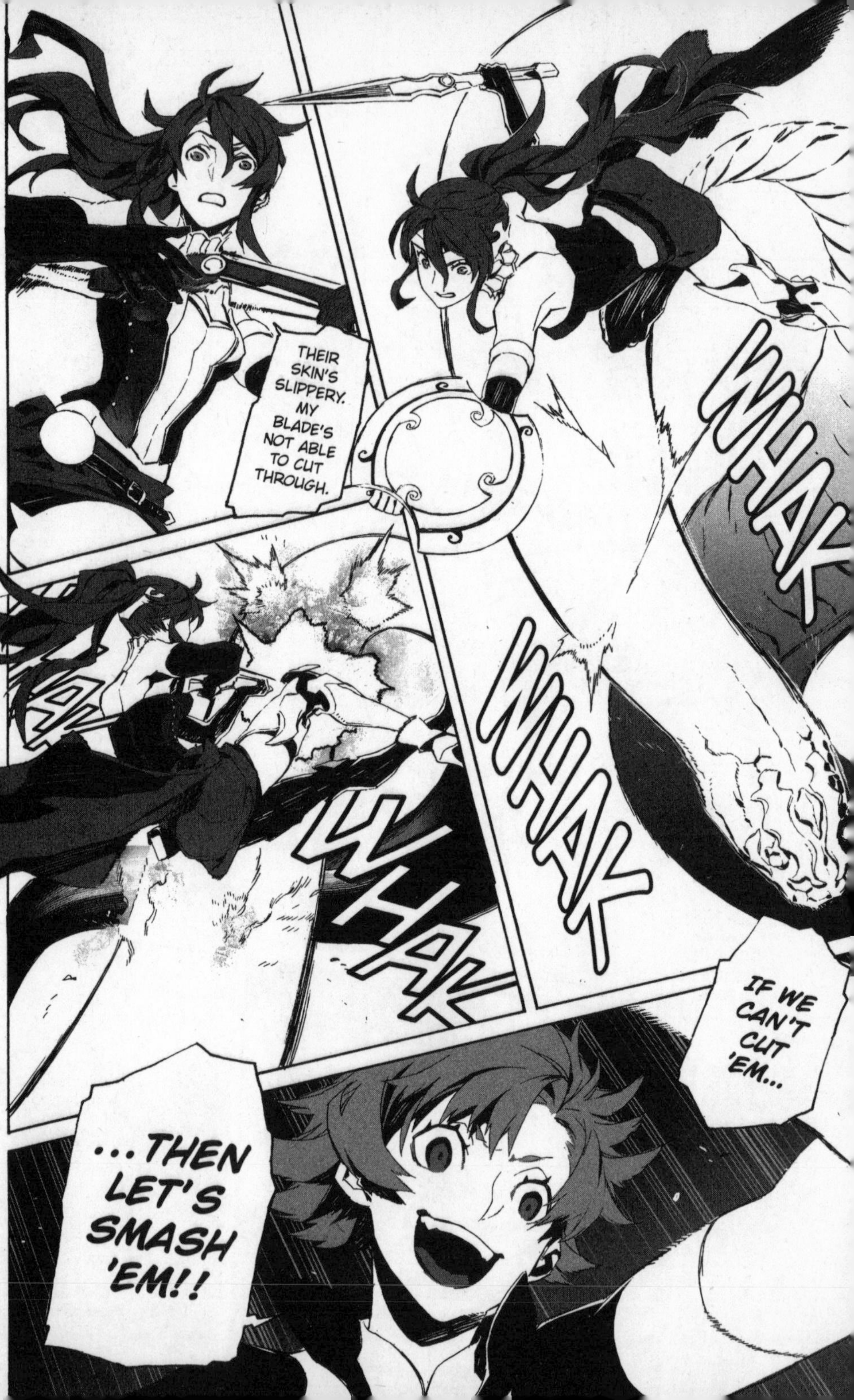
WHAK
THEIR SKIN'S SLIPPERY. MY BLADE'S NOT ABLE TO CUT THROUGH.
WHAK
WHAK
IF WE CAN'T CUT 'EM...
...THEN LET'S SMASH 'EM!!

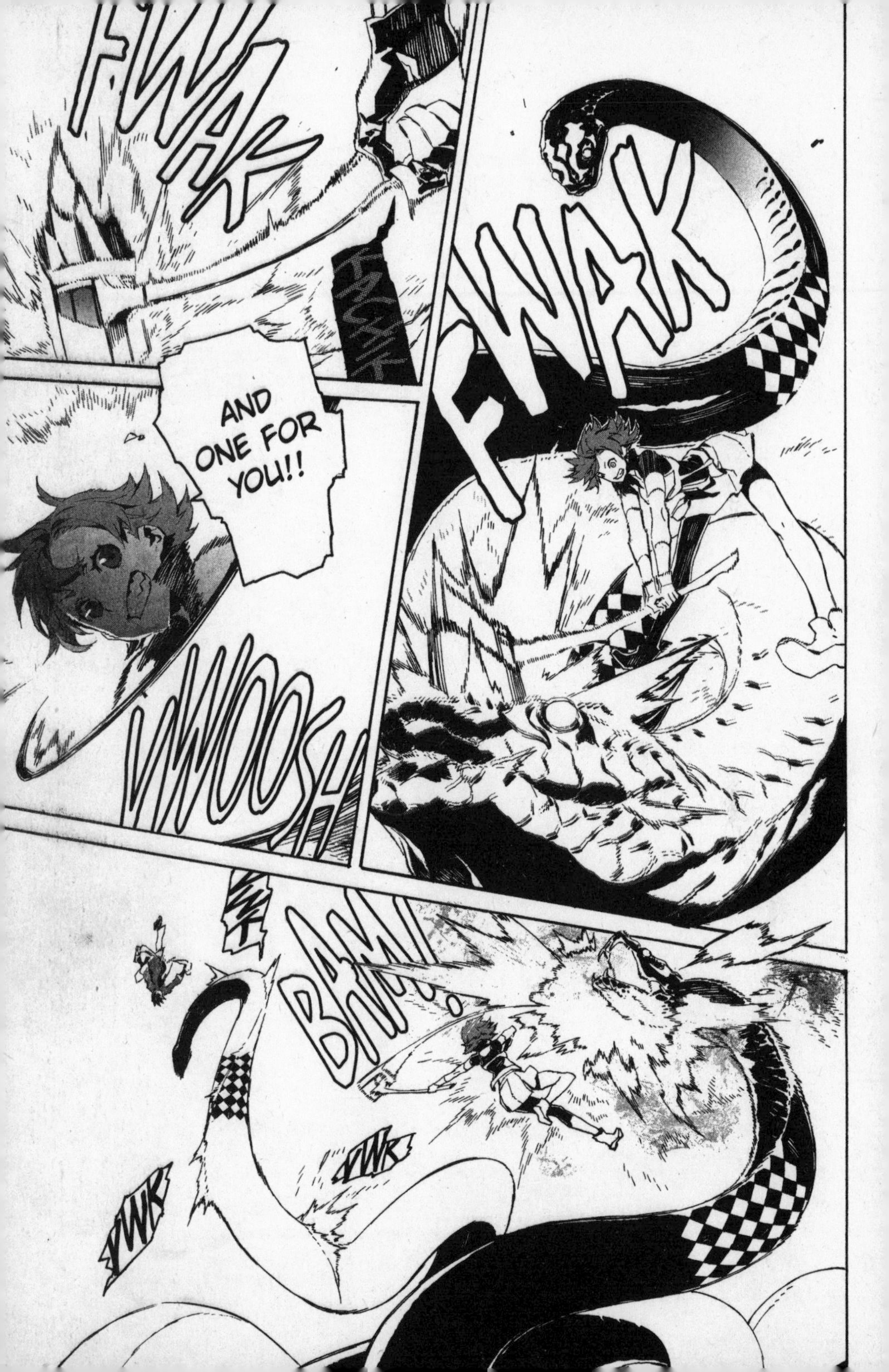
FWAK
FWAK
AND ONE FOR YOU!!
WHOOSH
BAM!!
VWR
VWR

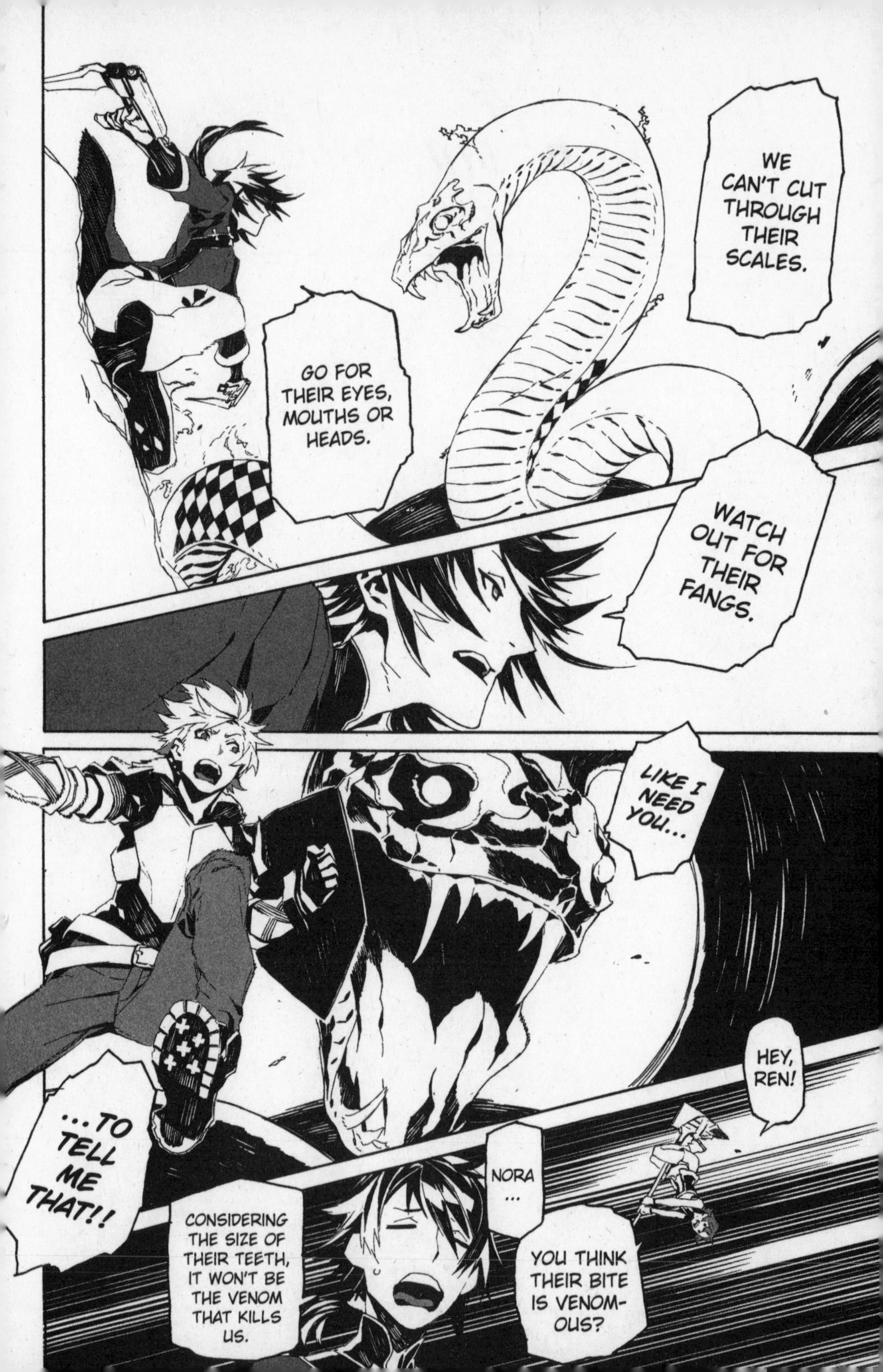
WE CAN'T CUT THROUGH THEIR SCALES.
GO FOR THEIR EYES, MOUTHS OR HEADS.
WATCH OUT FOR THEIR FANGS.
LIKE I NEED YOU...
...TO TELL ME THAT!!
HEY, REN!
NORA ...
YOU THINK THEIR BITE IS VENOM-OUS?
CONSIDERING THE SIZE OF THEIR TEETH, IT WON'T BE THE VENOM THAT KILLS US.

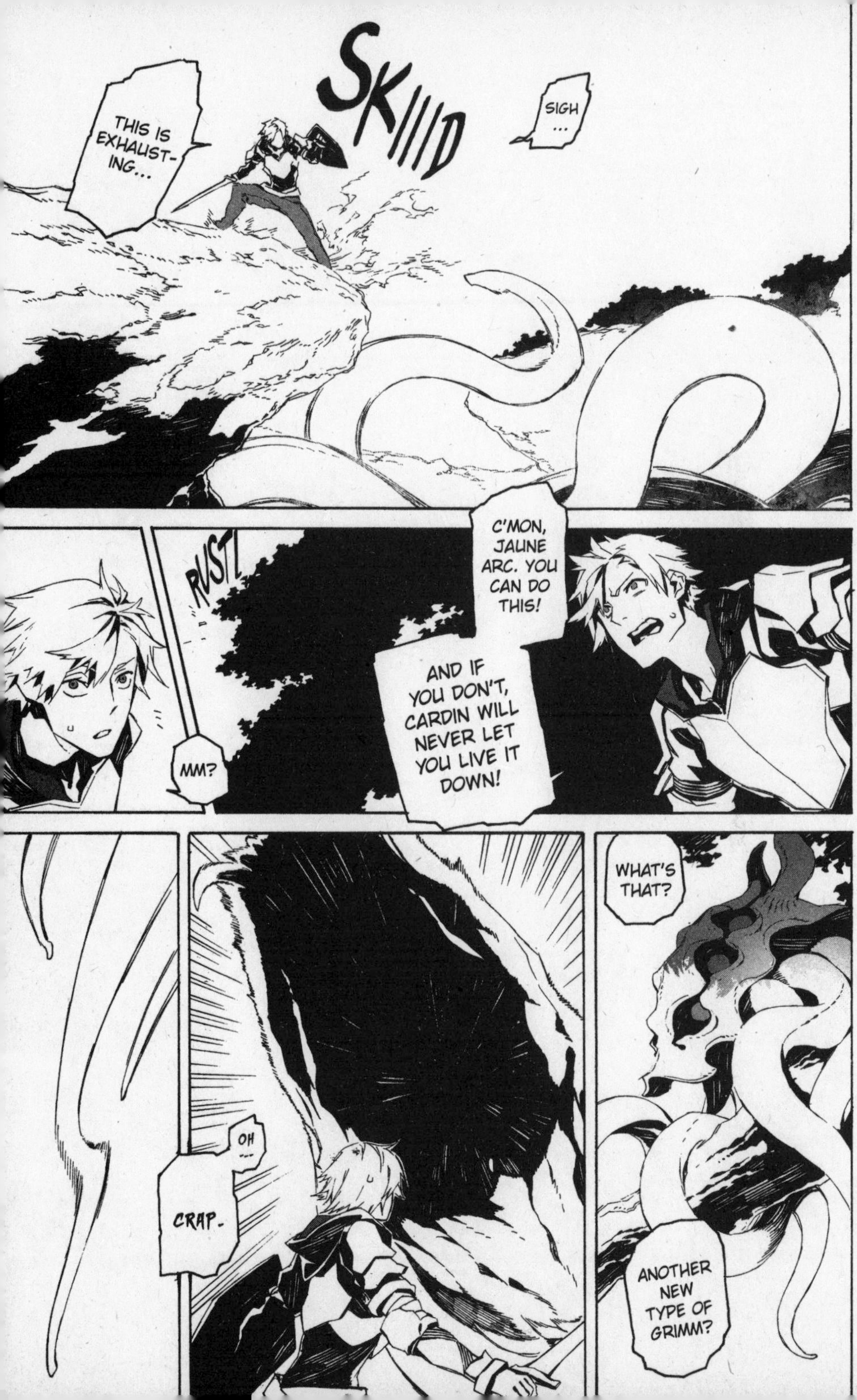
SIGH ...
SKIIID
THIS IS EXHAUSTING...
C'MON, JAUNE ARC. YOU CAN DO THIS!
AND IF YOU DON'T, CARDIN WILL NEVER LET YOU LIVE IT DOWN!
RUSTL
MM?
WHAT'S THAT?
ANOTHER NEW TYPE OF GRIMM?
OH ...
CRAP.

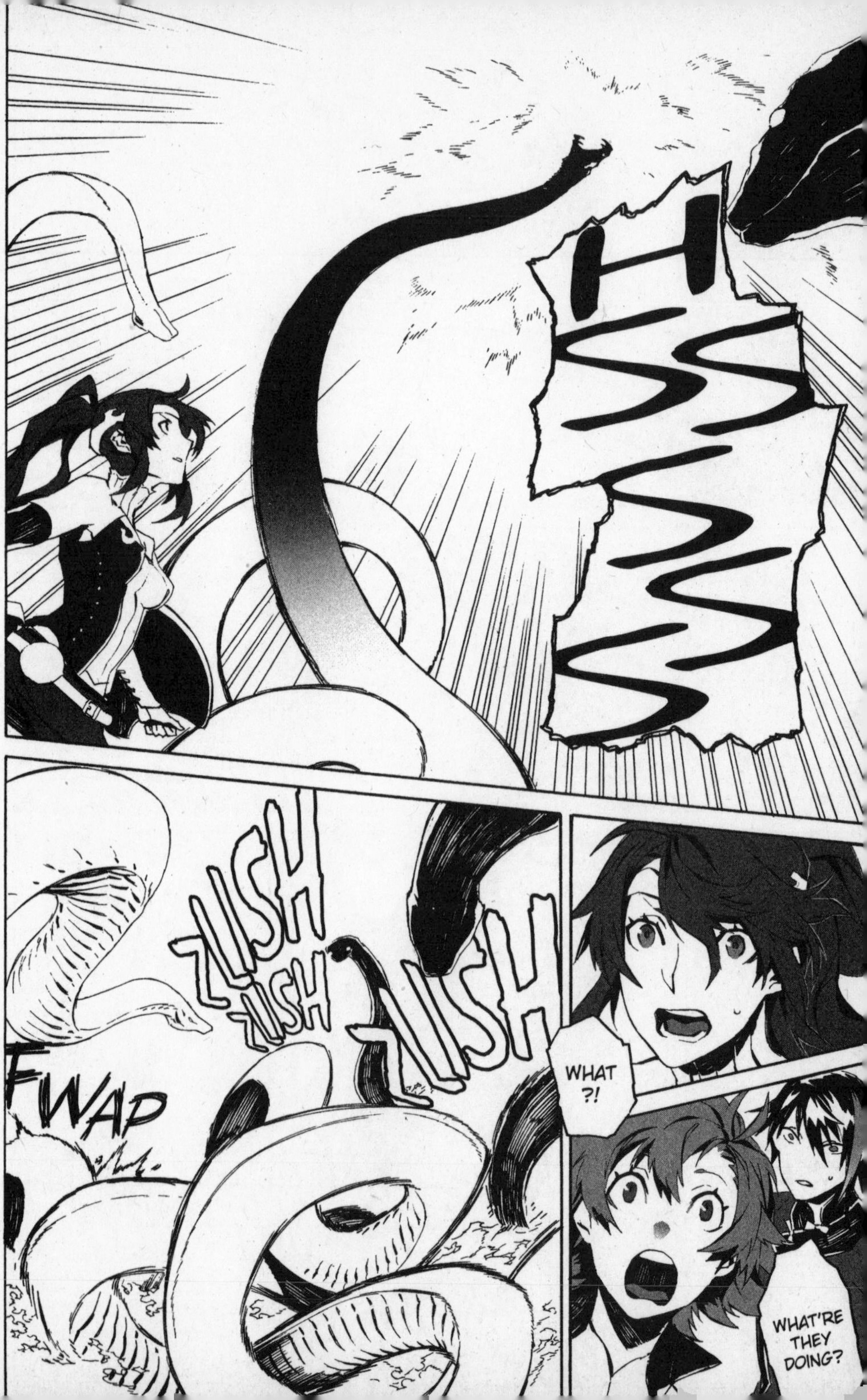
HISSSSS
WHAT ?!
WHAT'RE THEY DOING?
ZLISH
ZLISH
ZLISH
FWAP

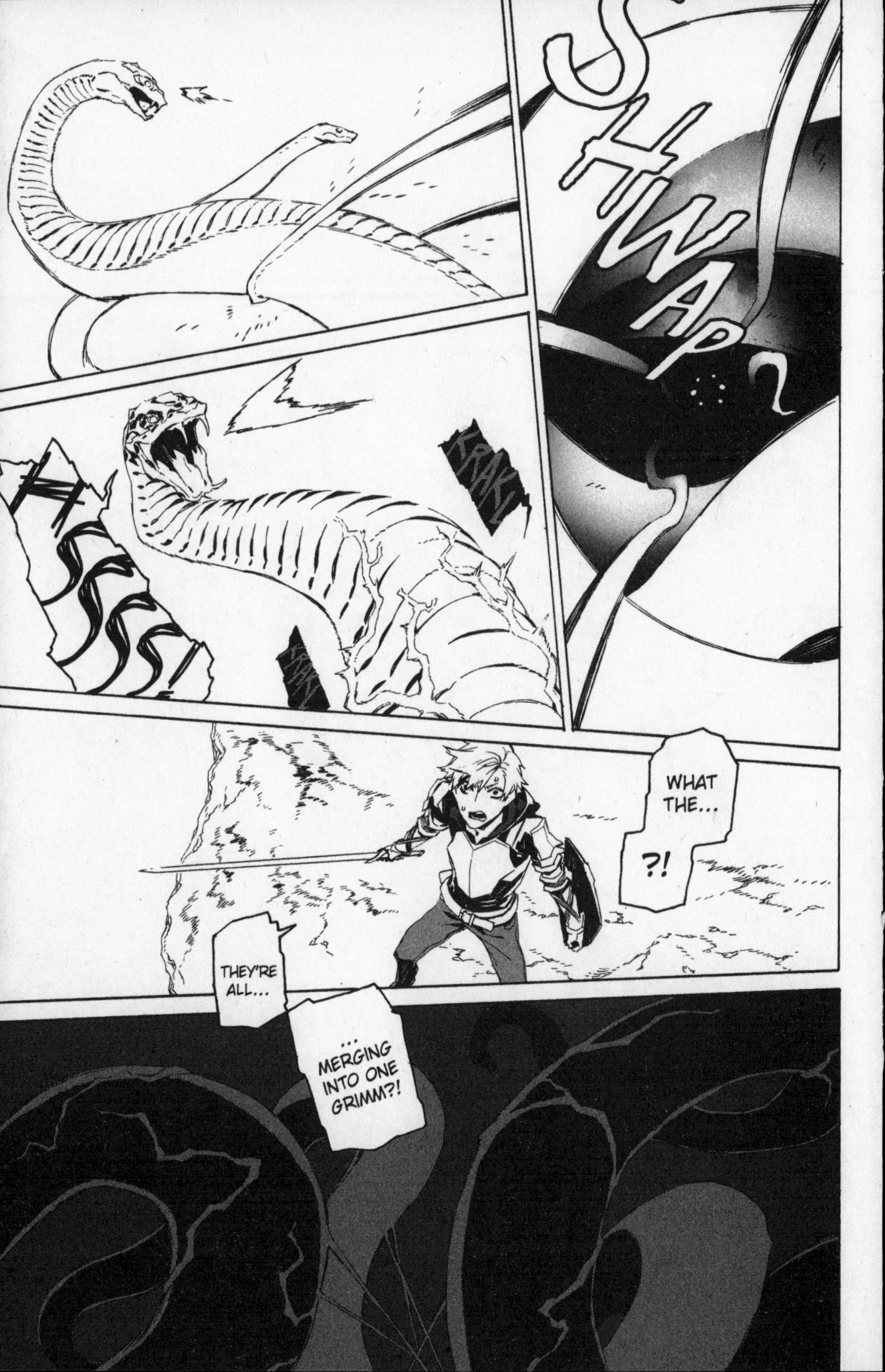
SHWAP
KRAK
KRAK
HSSSS!
WHAT THE...
?!
THEY'RE ALL...
...MERGING INTO ONE GRIMM?!

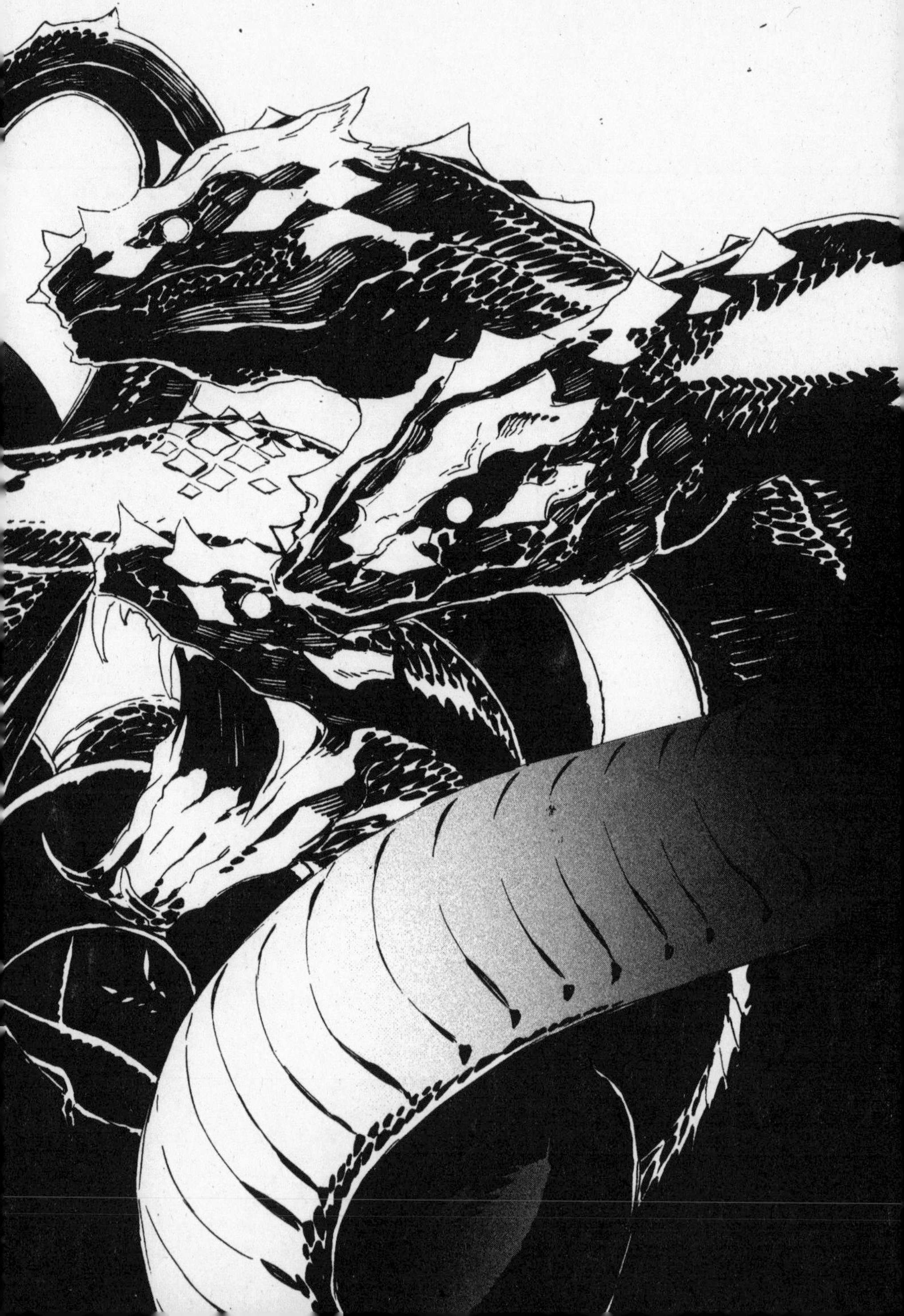

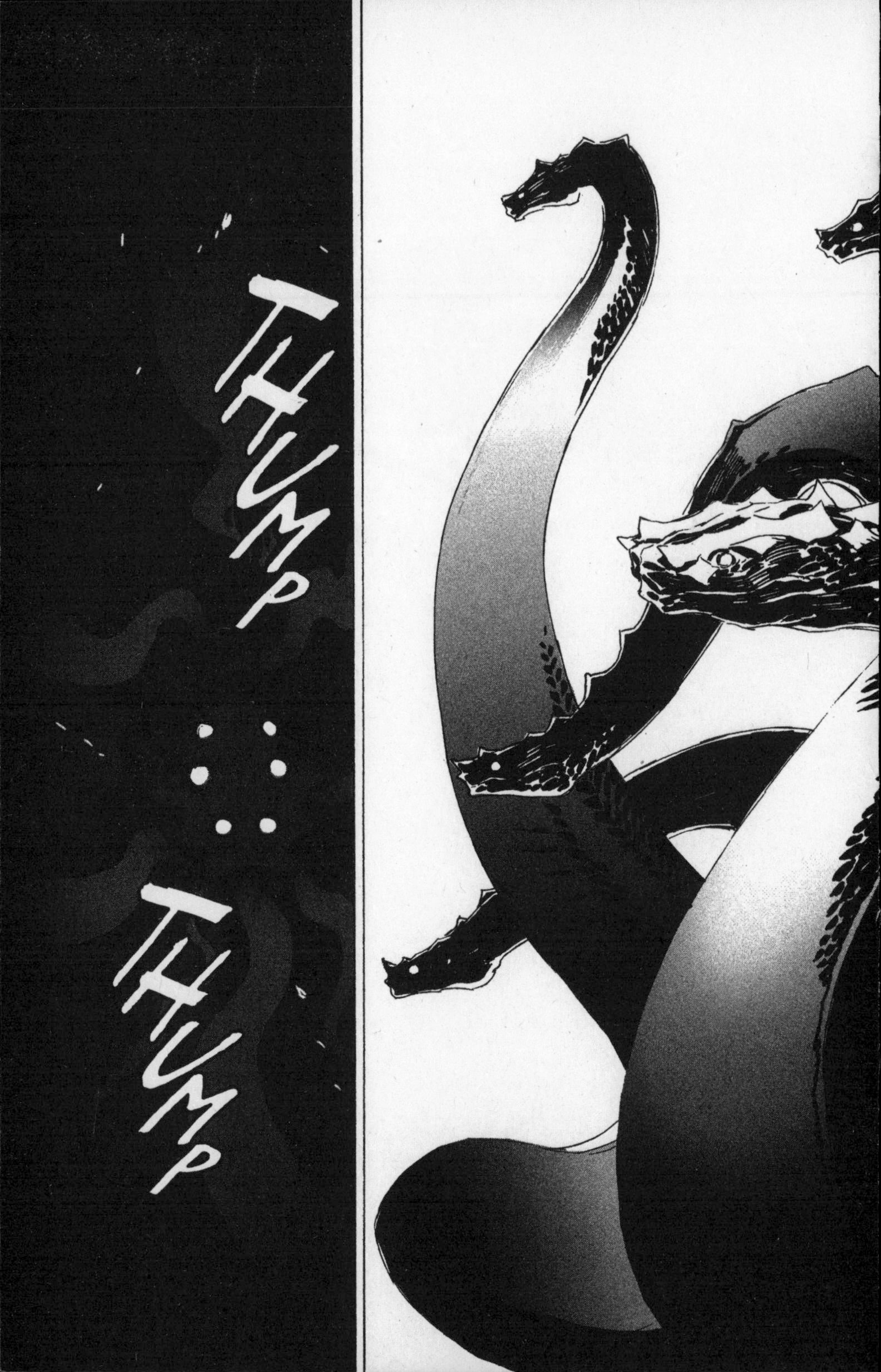
THUMP
THUMP

RWBY

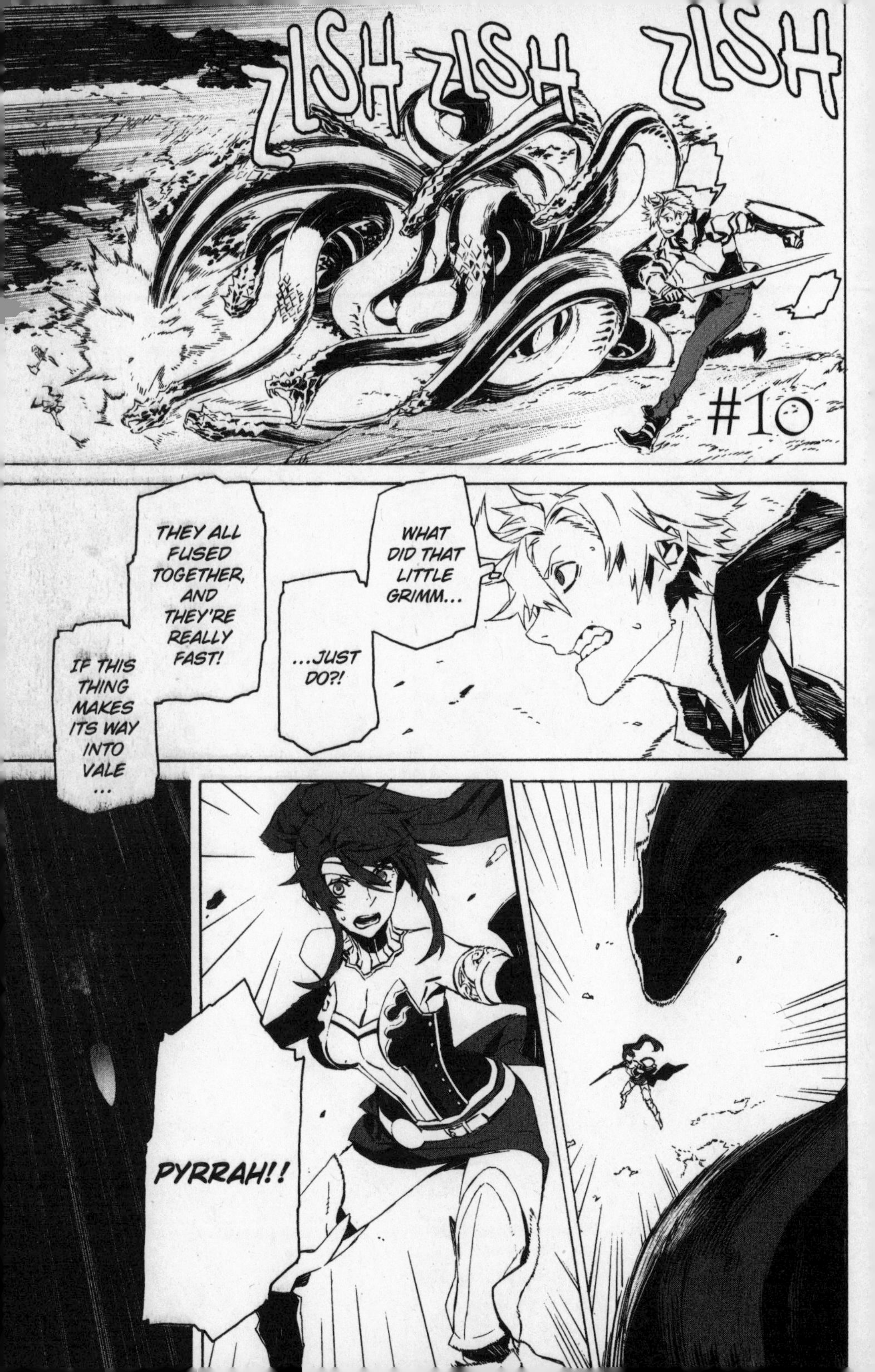
ZISH ZISH ZISH
#10
WHAT DID THAT LITTLE GRIMM...
...JUST DO?!
THEY ALL FUSED TOGETHER, AND THEY'RE REALLY FAST!
IF THIS THING MAKES ITS WAY INTO VALE ...
PYRRAH!!

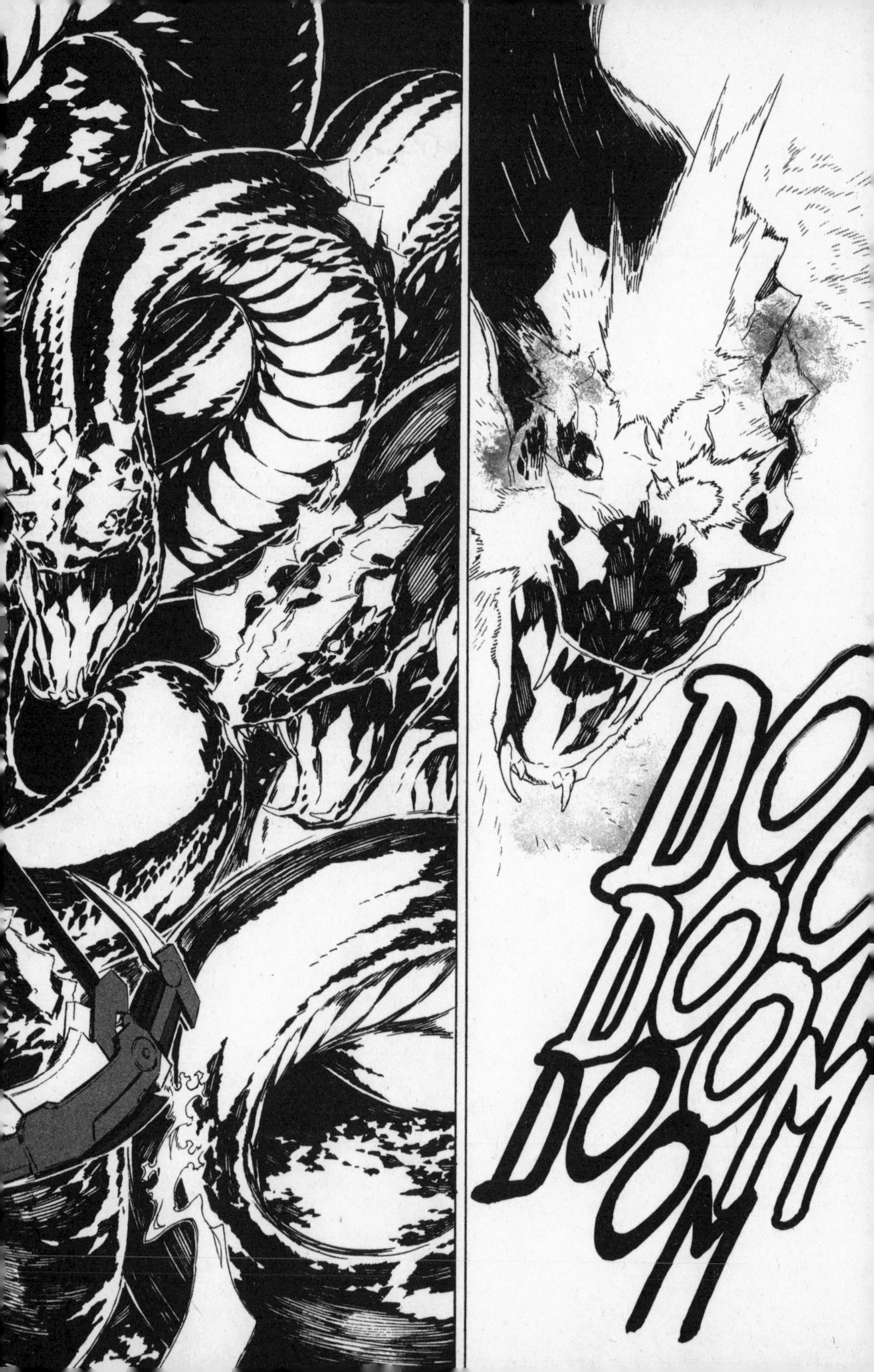
DOOM
DOOM

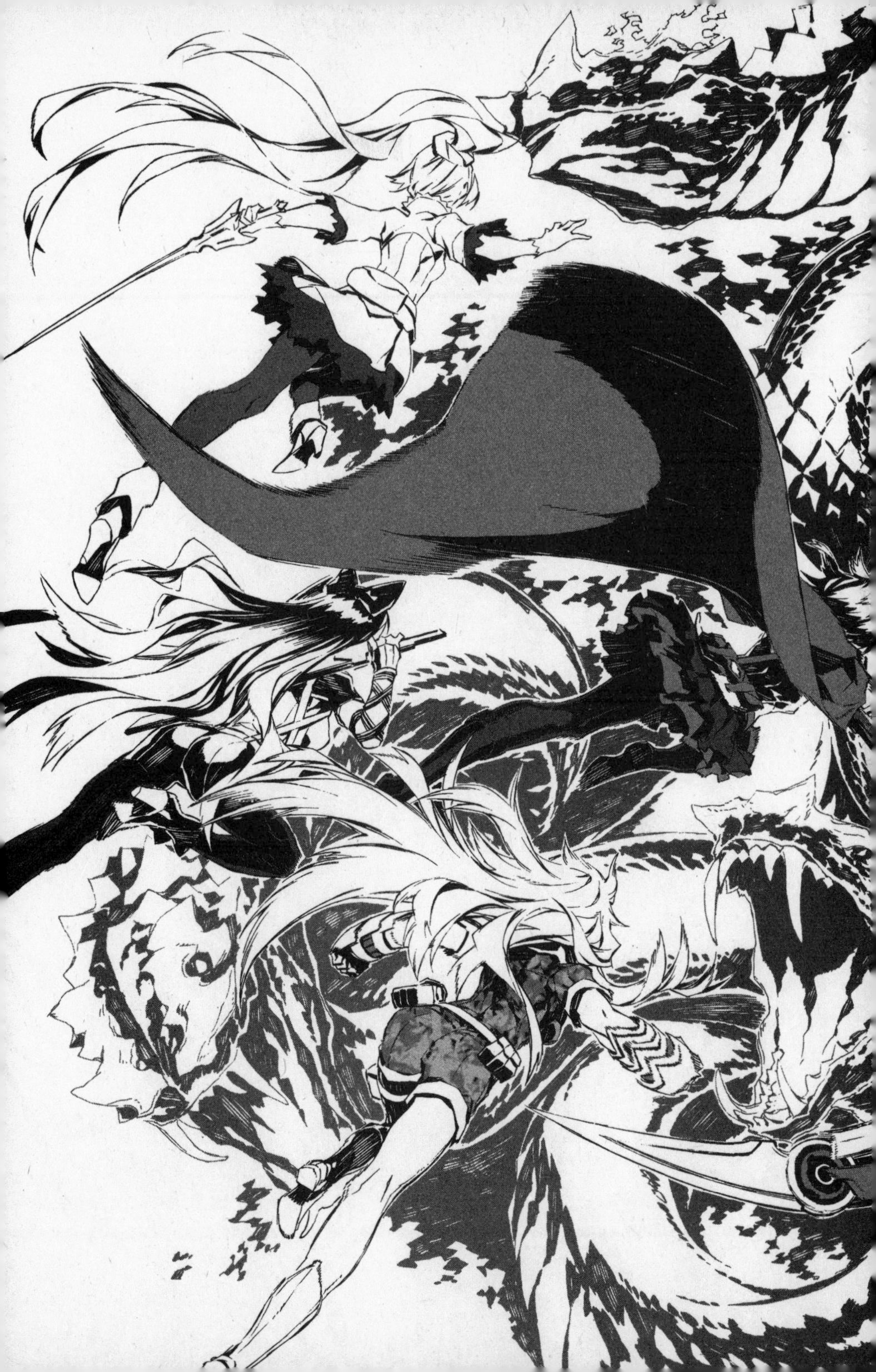

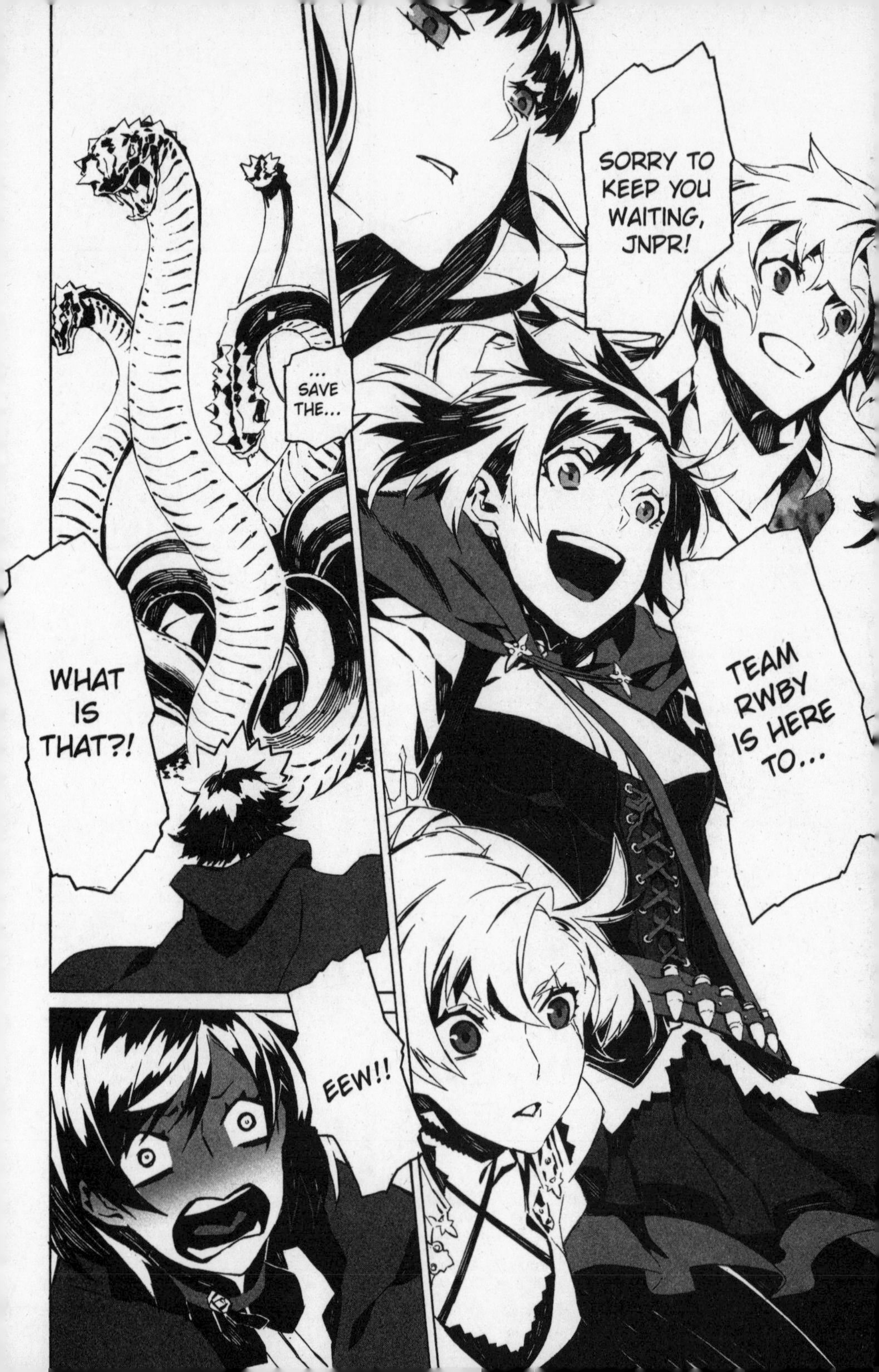
SORRY TO KEEP YOU WAITING, JNPR!
TEAM RWBY IS HERE TO...
... SAVE THE...
WHAT IS THAT?!
EEW!!

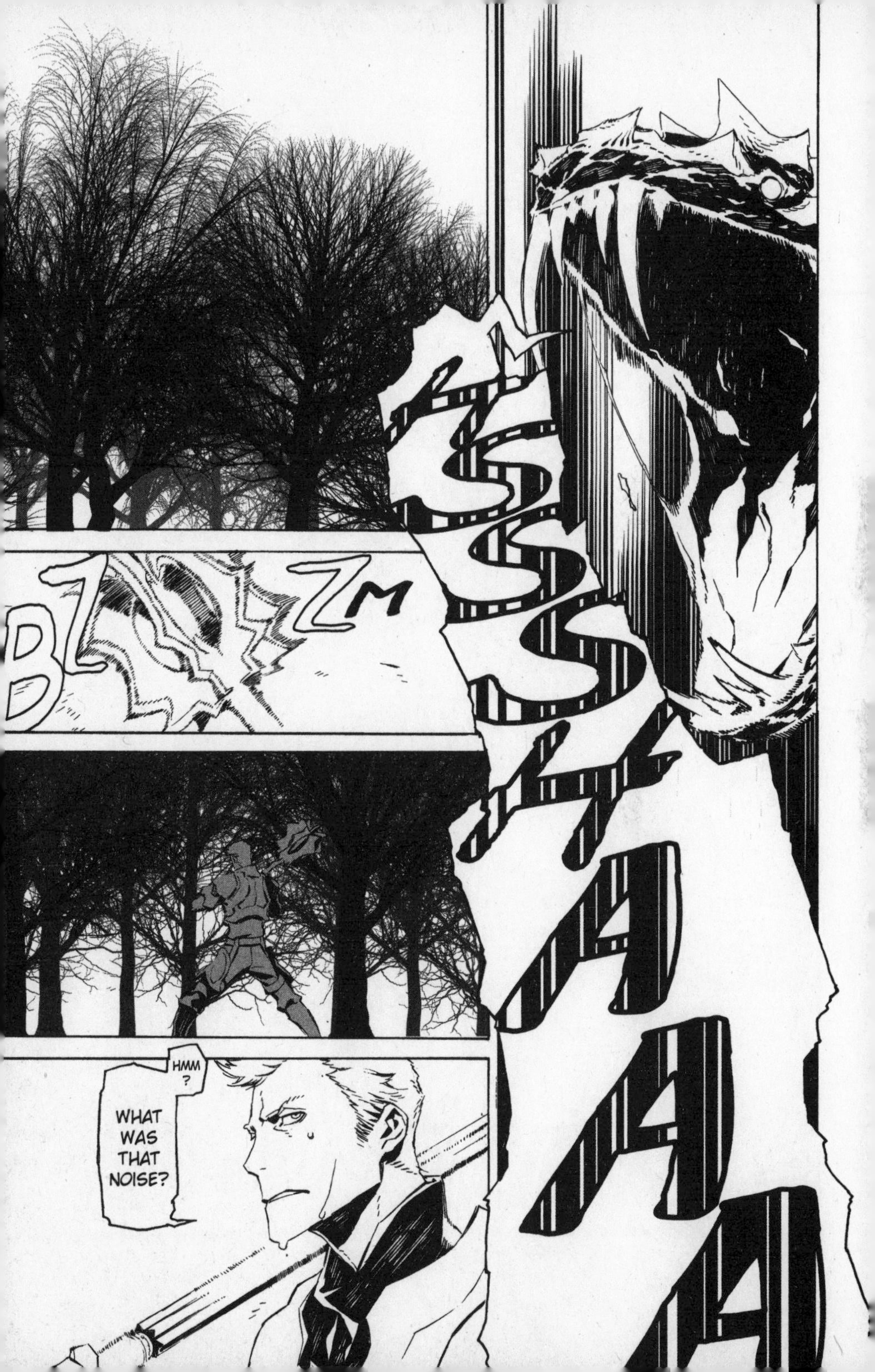
HSSSHAAAA
BZZZM
HMM?
WHAT WAS THAT NOISE?

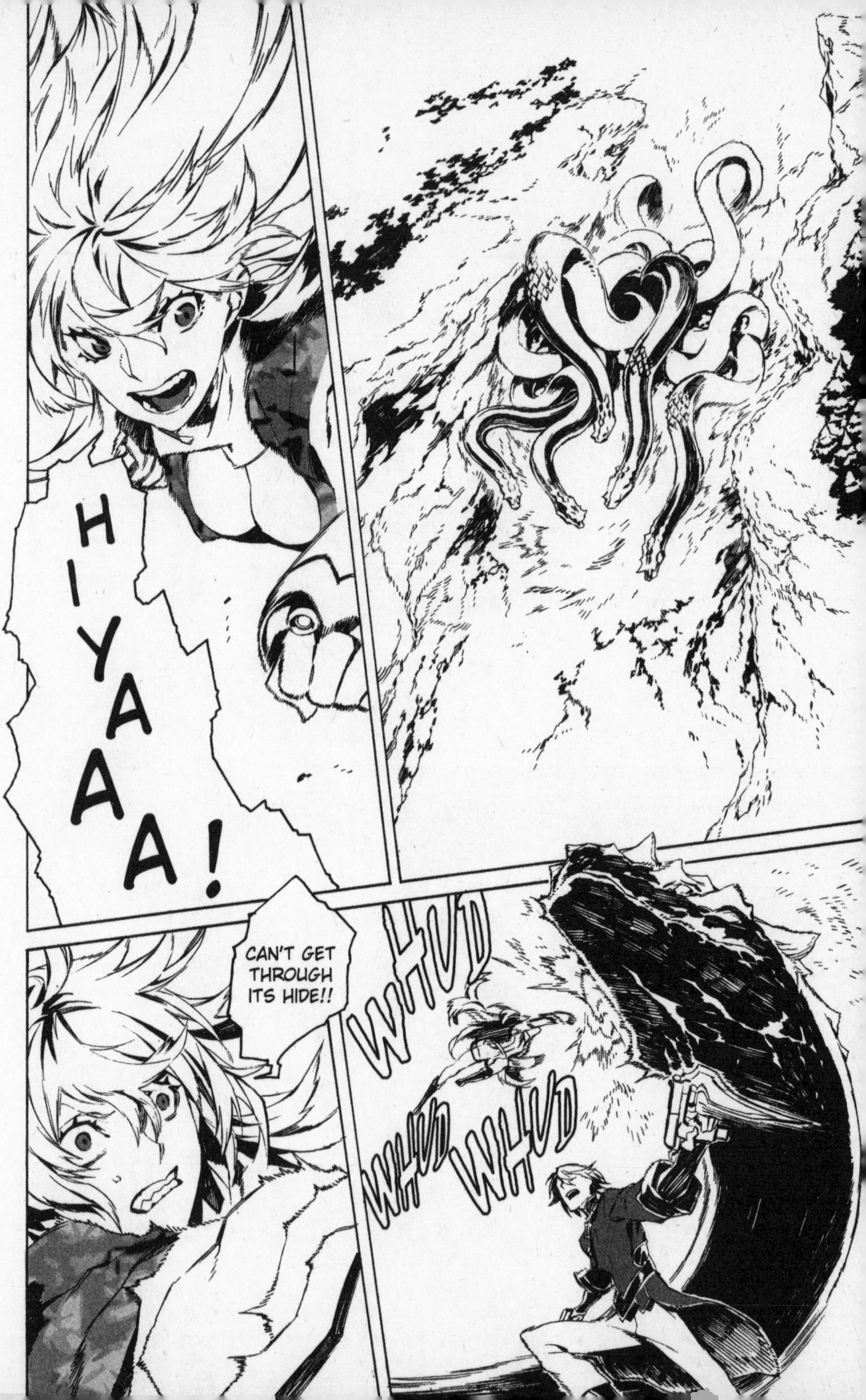
HIYAAA!
CAN'T GET THROUGH ITS HIDE!!
WHUD
WHUD WHUD

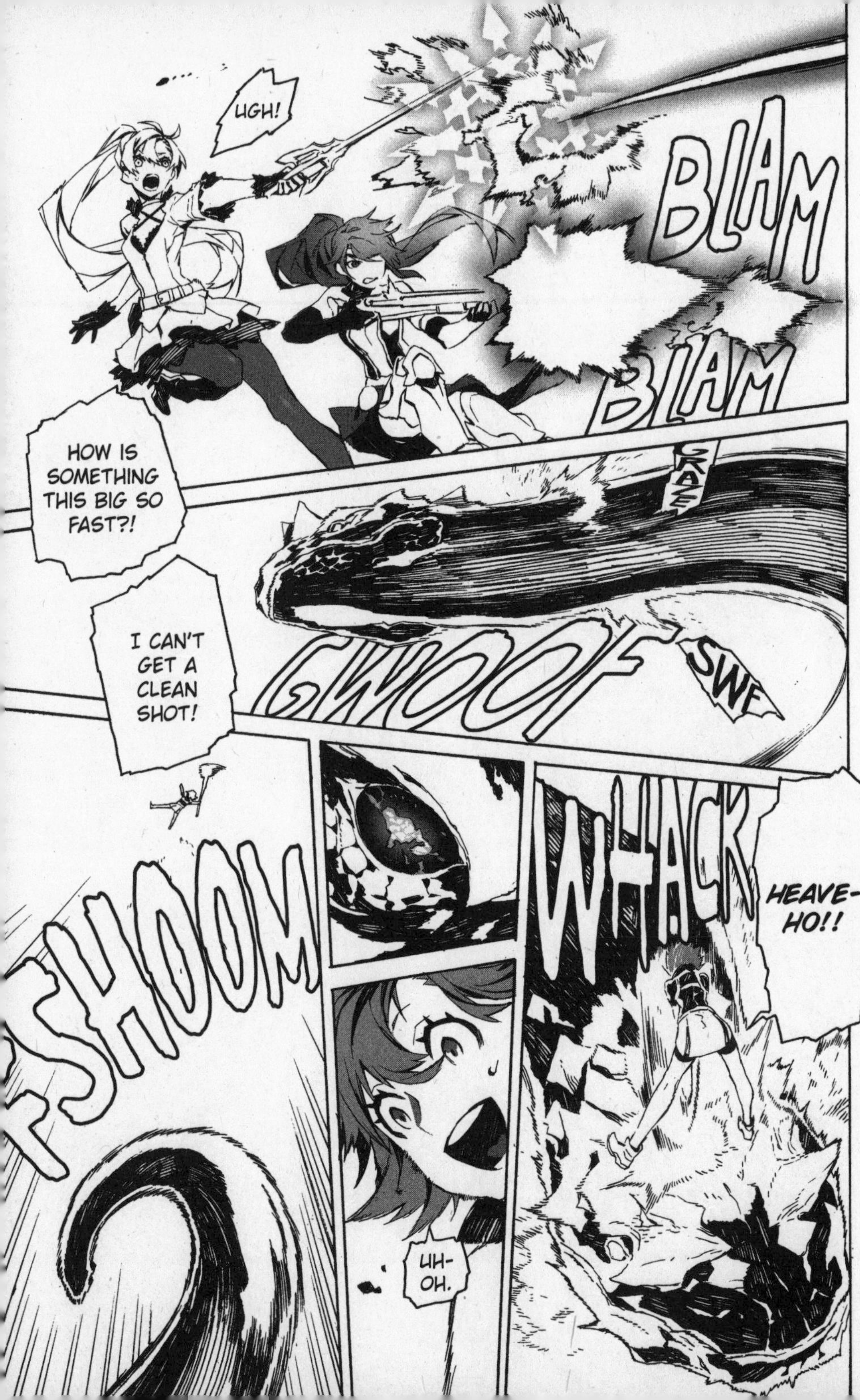

BLAM
BLAM
UGH!
GRAZE
HOW IS SOMETHING THIS BIG SO FAST?!
SWF
GWOOF
I CAN'T GET A CLEAN SHOT!
HEAVE-HO!!
WHACK
UH-OH.
FSHOOM

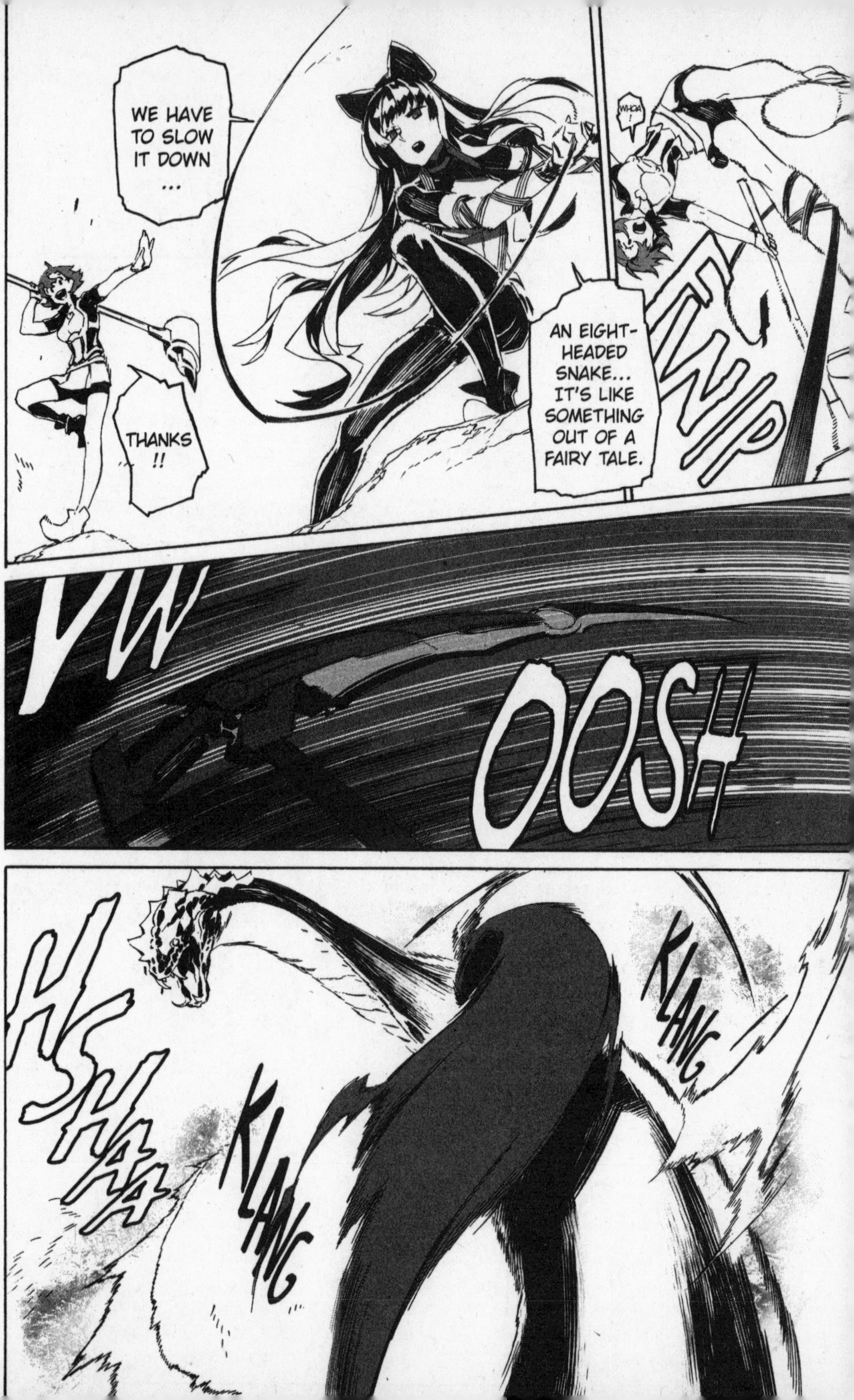
WHOA!
FWIP
AN EIGHT-HEADED SNAKE... IT'S LIKE SOMETHING OUT OF A FAIRY TALE.
WE HAVE TO SLOW IT DOWN...
THANKS!!
VWOOSH
KLANG
KLANG
HSHAAA

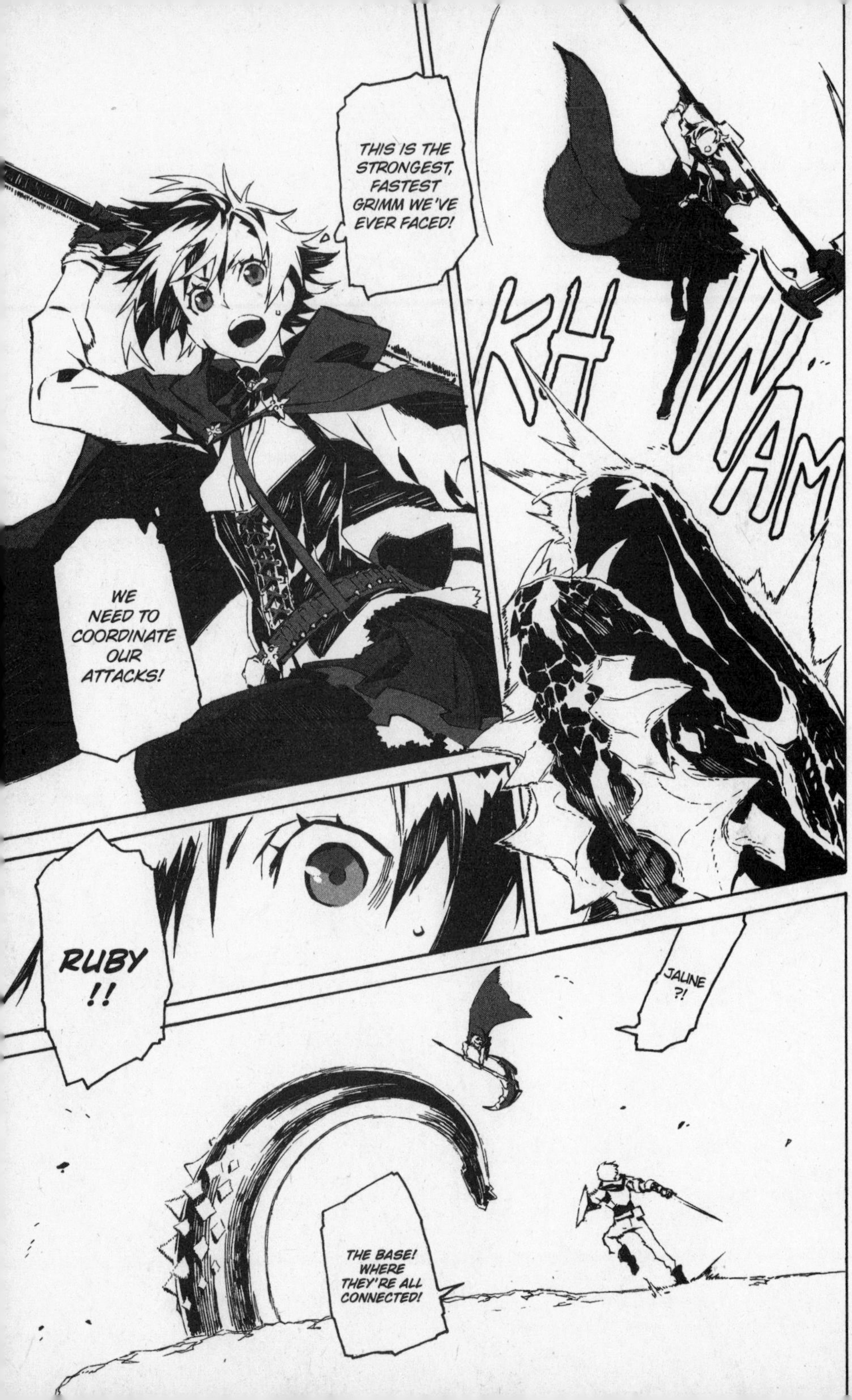

KHWAM
THIS IS THE STRONGEST, FASTEST GRIMM WE'VE EVER FACED!
WE NEED TO COORDINATE OUR ATTACKS!
RUBY !!
JAUNE ?!
THE BASE! WHERE THEY'RE ALL CONNECTED!

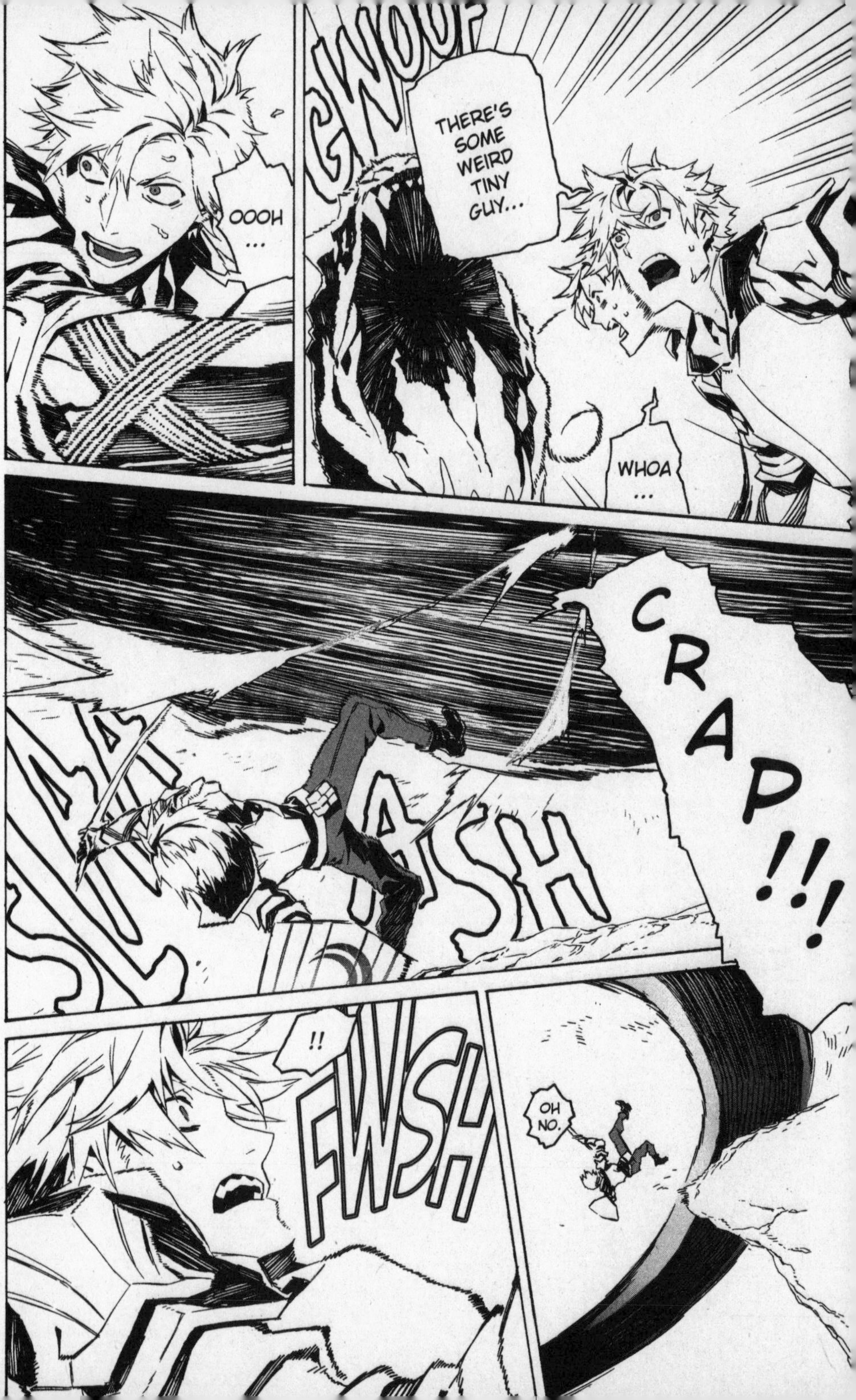
GWOOF
THERE'S SOME WEIRD TINY GUY...
WHOA ...
OOOH ...
CRAP!!!
OH NO.
!!
FWSH

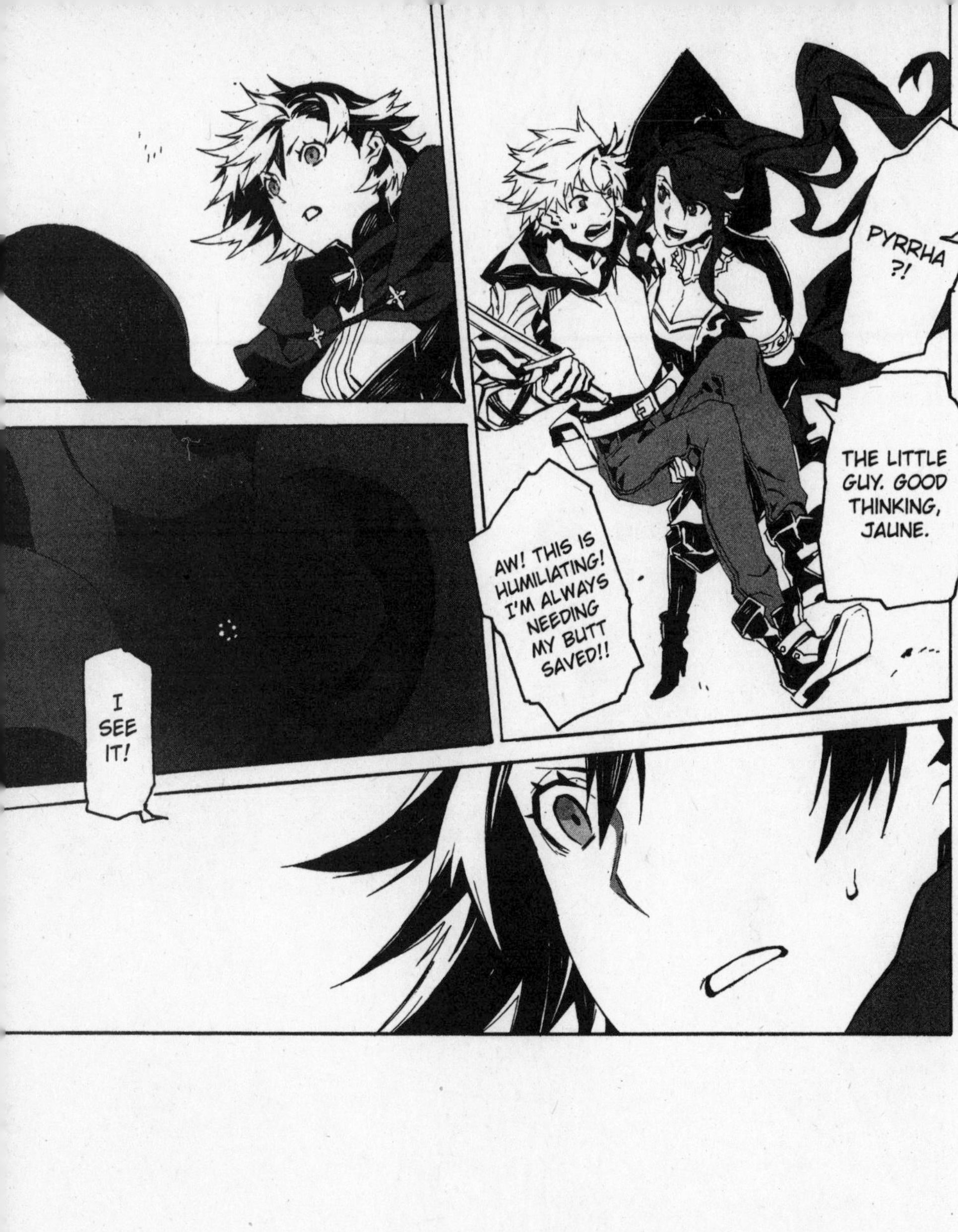
PYRRHA?!
THE LITTLE GUY. GOOD THINKING, JAUNE.
AW! THIS IS HUMILIATING! I'M ALWAYS NEEDING MY BUTT SAVED!!
I SEE IT!

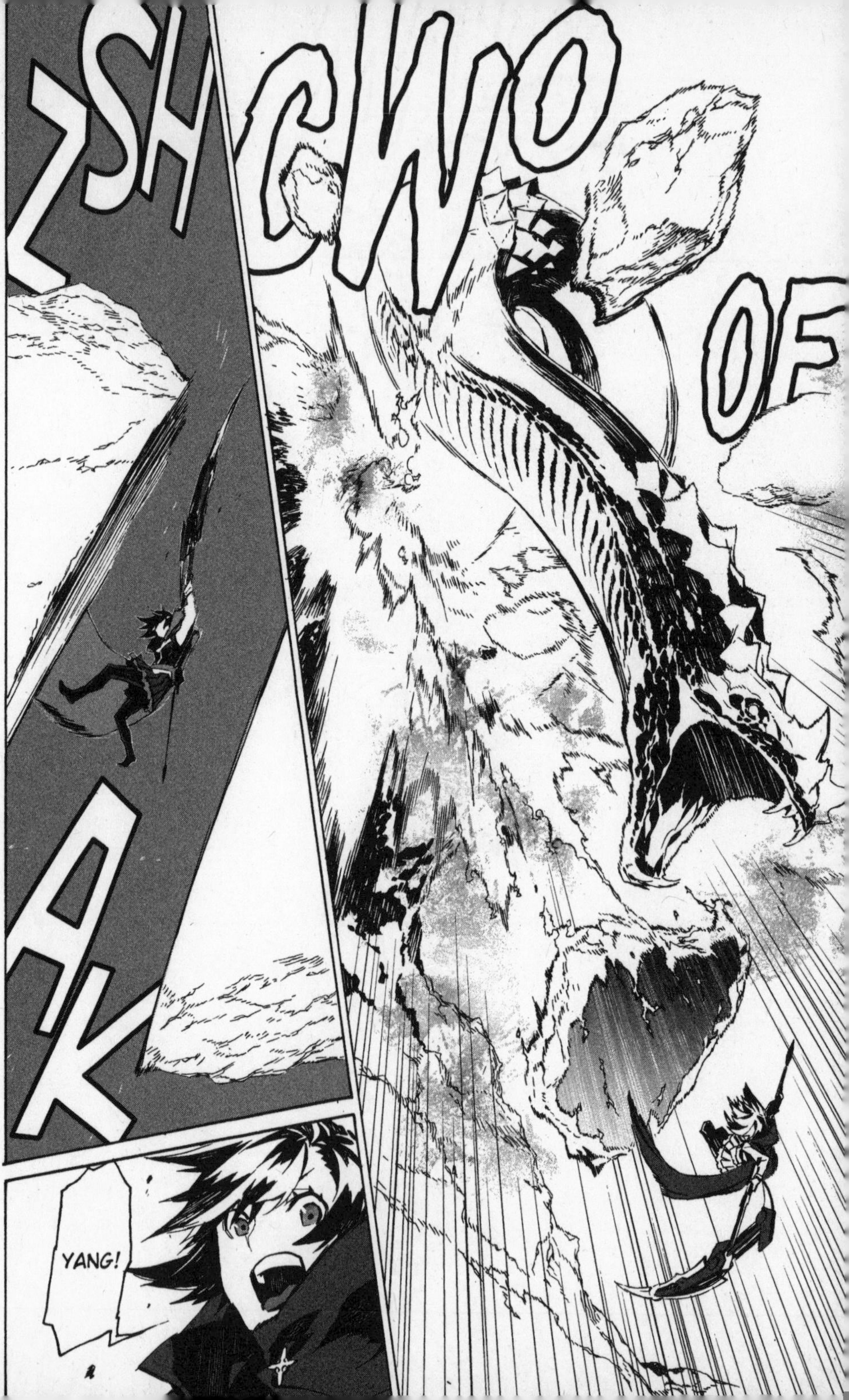
YANG!

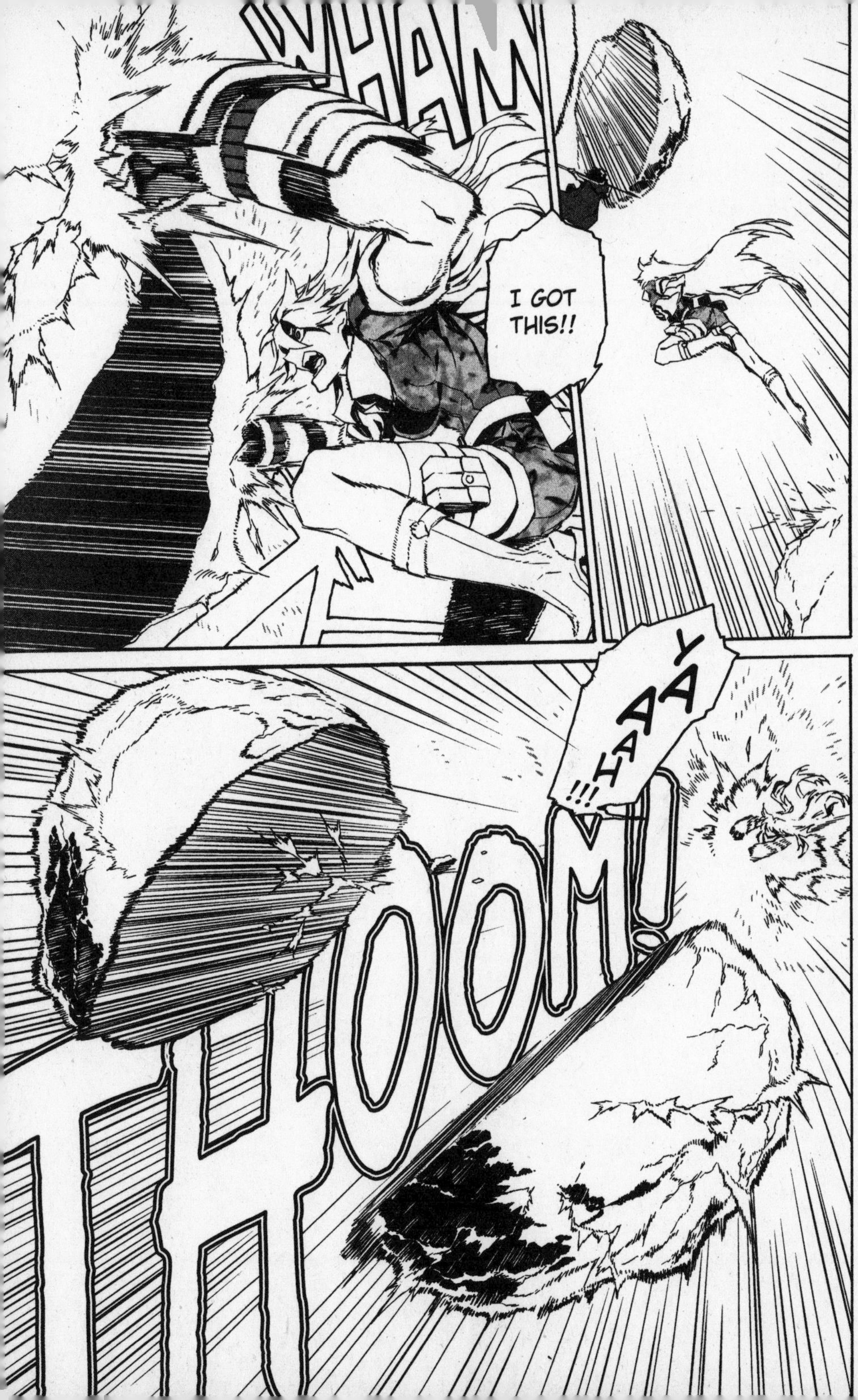
I GOT THIS!!
WHAM
YAAAH!!!
THOOOM!

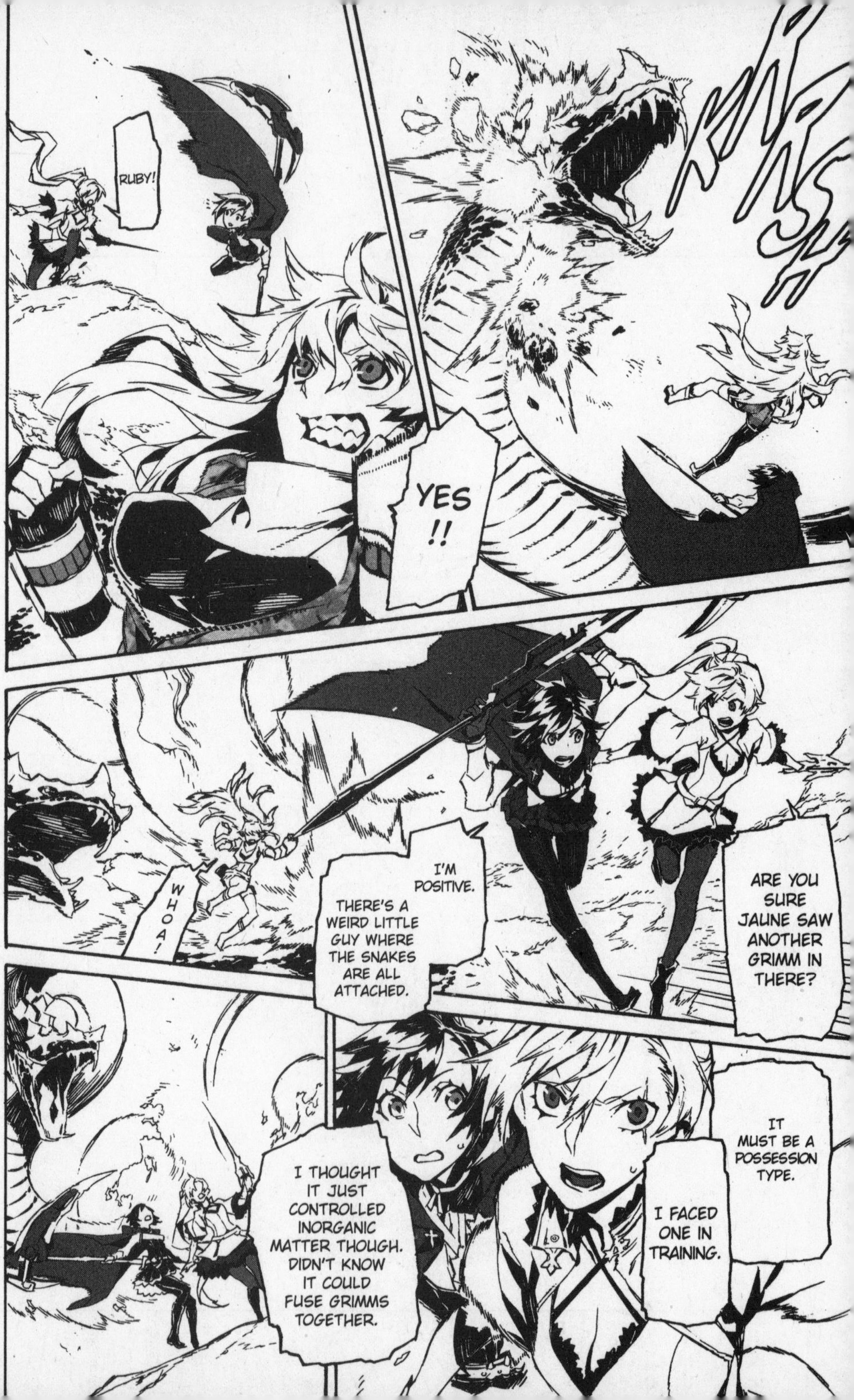
RUBY!
YES!!
ARE YOU SURE JAUNE SAW ANOTHER GRIMM IN THERE?
I'M POSITIVE.
THERE'S A WEIRD LITTLE GUY WHERE THE SNAKES ARE ALL ATTACHED.
WHOA!
IT MUST BE A POSSESSION TYPE.
I FACED ONE IN TRAINING.
I THOUGHT IT JUST CONTROLLED INORGANIC MATTER THOUGH. DIDN'T KNOW IT COULD FUSE GRIMMS TOGETHER.

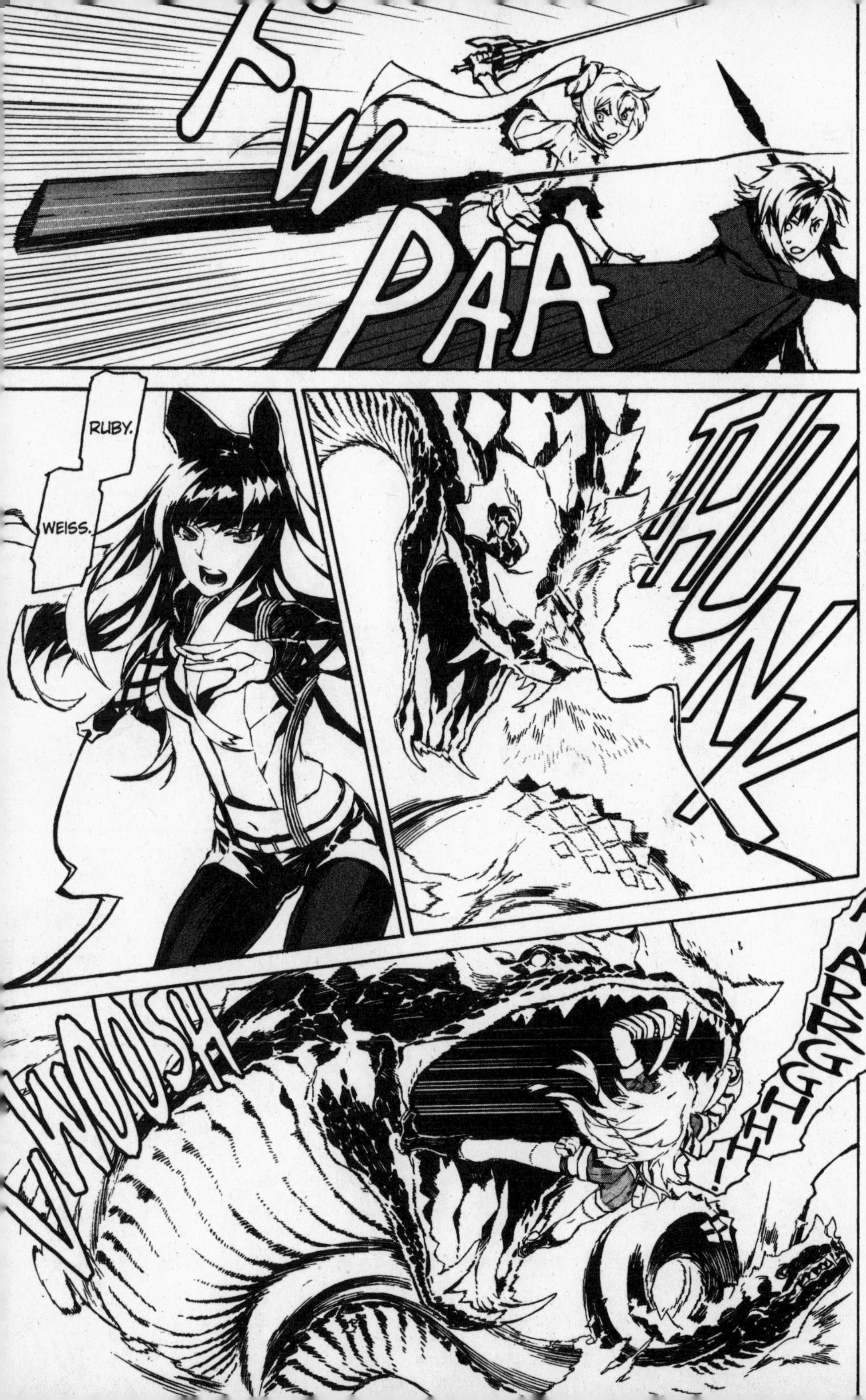
TWPAA
THUNK
RUBY.
WEISS.
AAARRGHHH!
WHOOSH

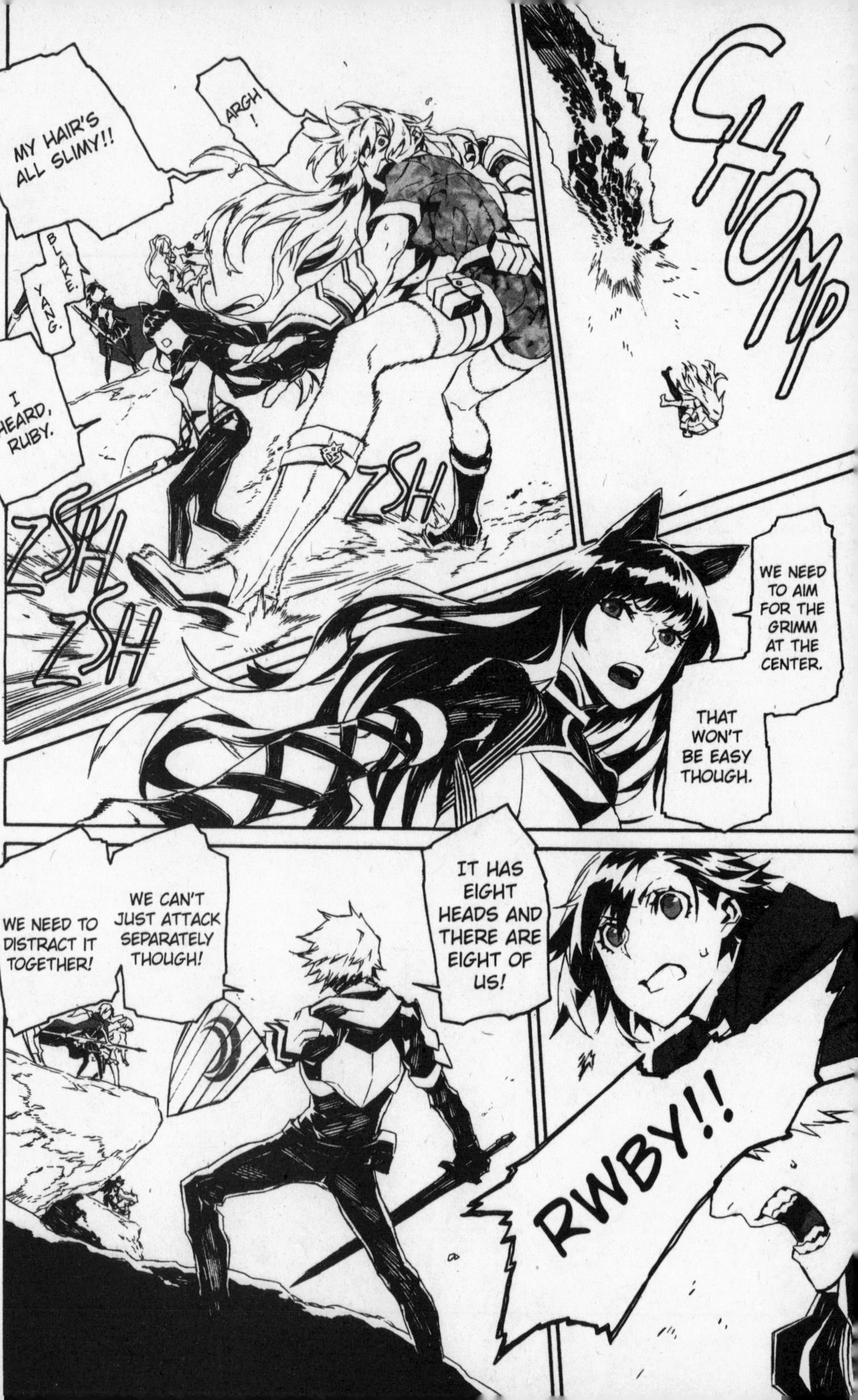
CHOMP
ARGH!
MY HAIR'S ALL SLIMY!!
BLAKE, YANG.
I HEARD, RUBY.
ZSH
ZSH
ZSH
ZSH
WE NEED TO AIM FOR THE GRIMM AT THE CENTER.
THAT WON'T BE EASY THOUGH.
IT HAS EIGHT HEADS AND THERE ARE EIGHT OF US!
RWBY!!
WE CAN'T JUST ATTACK SEPARATELY THOUGH!
WE NEED TO DISTRACT IT TOGETHER!

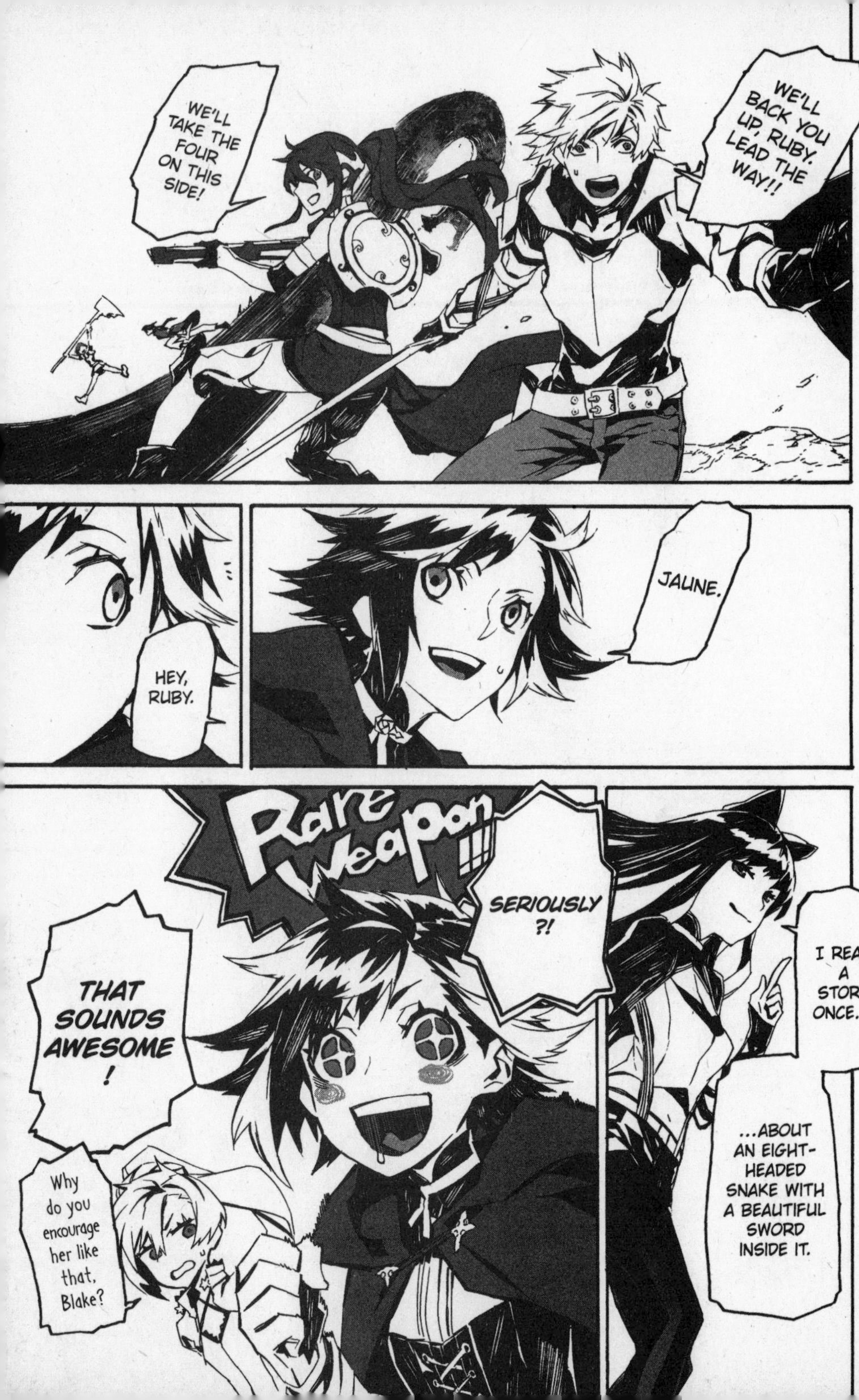
WE'LL BACK YOU UP, RUBY. LEAD THE WAY!!
WE'LL TAKE THE FOUR ON THIS SIDE!
JAUNE.
HEY, RUBY.
I READ A STORY ONCE...
...ABOUT AN EIGHT-HEADED SNAKE WITH A BEAUTIFUL SWORD INSIDE IT.
Rare Weapon
SERIOUSLY ?!
THAT SOUNDS AWESOME!
Why do you encourage her like that, Blake?

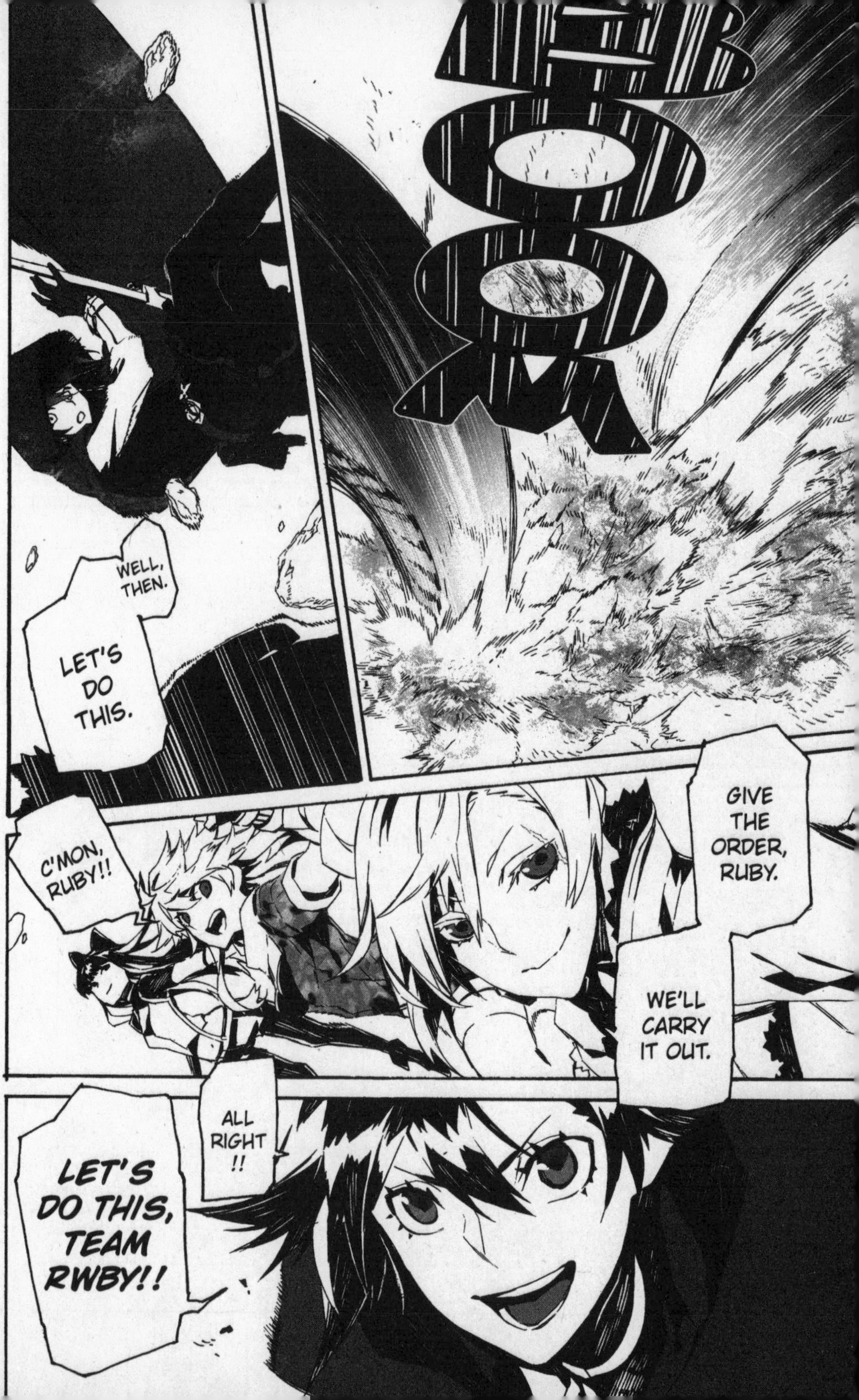
BOOM
WELL, THEN.
LET'S DO THIS.
GIVE THE ORDER, RUBY.
WE'LL CARRY IT OUT.
C'MON, RUBY!!
ALL RIGHT!!
LET'S DO THIS, TEAM RWBY!!

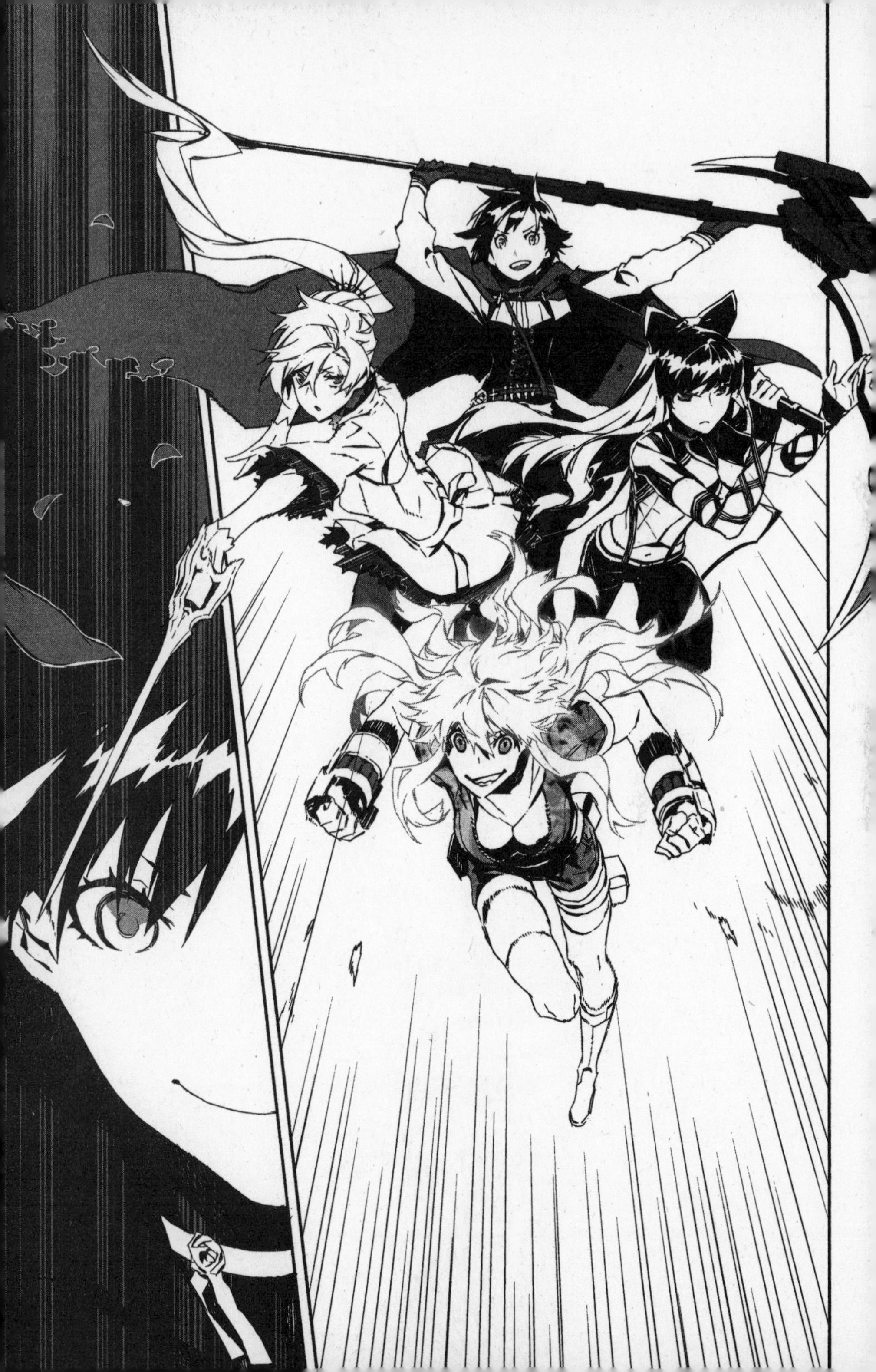

RWBY

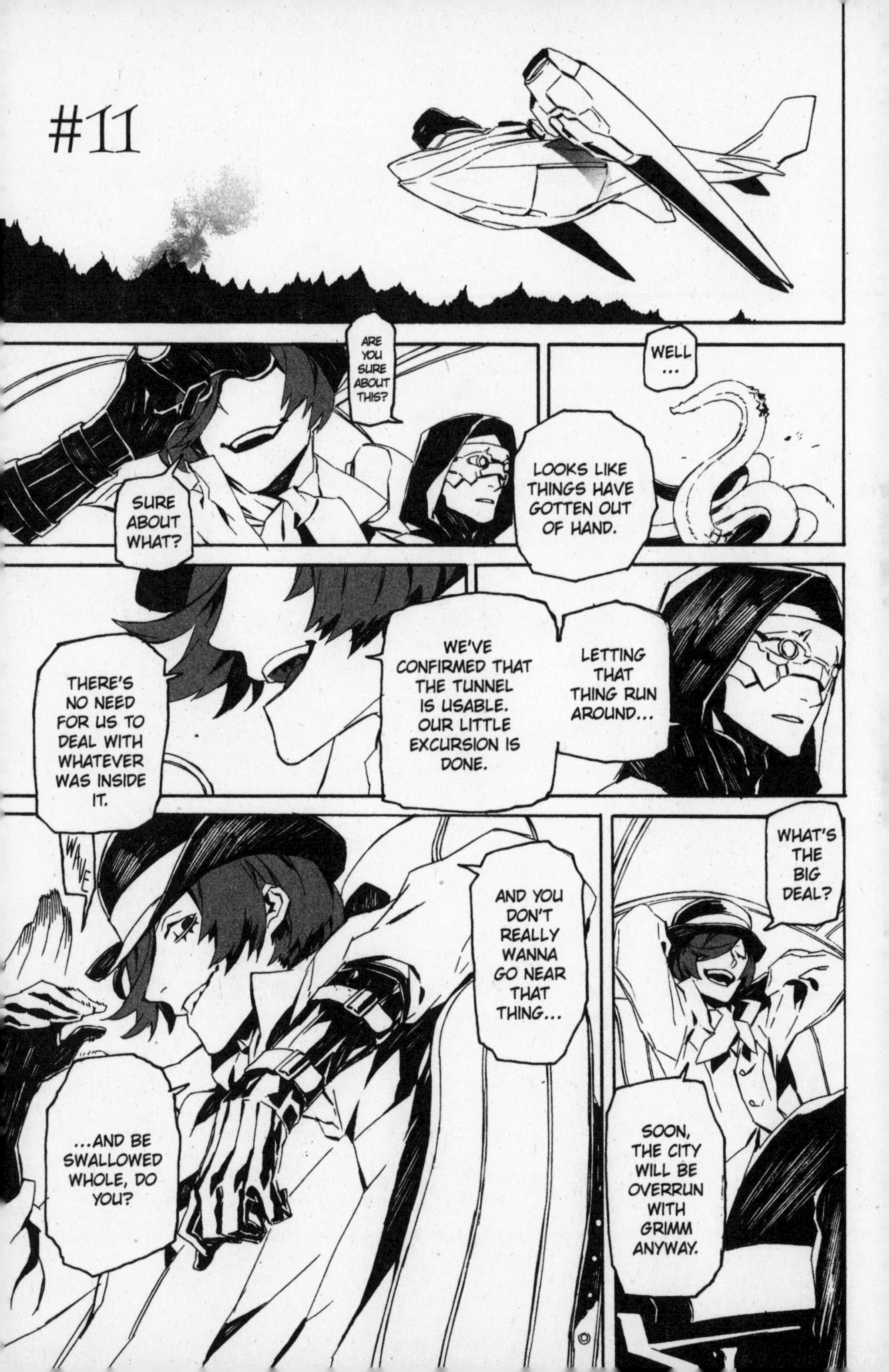
#11
WELL...
LOOKS LIKE THINGS HAVE GOTTEN OUT OF HAND.
ARE YOU SURE ABOUT THIS?
SURE ABOUT WHAT?
LETTING THAT THING RUN AROUND...
WE'VE CONFIRMED THAT THE TUNNEL IS USABLE. OUR LITTLE EXCURSION IS DONE.
THERE'S NO NEED FOR US TO DEAL WITH WHATEVER WAS INSIDE IT.
WHAT'S THE BIG DEAL?
SOON, THE CITY WILL BE OVERRUN WITH GRIMM ANYWAY.
WAVE
AND YOU DON'T REALLY WANNA GO NEAR THAT THING...
...AND BE SWALLOWED WHOLE, DO YOU?

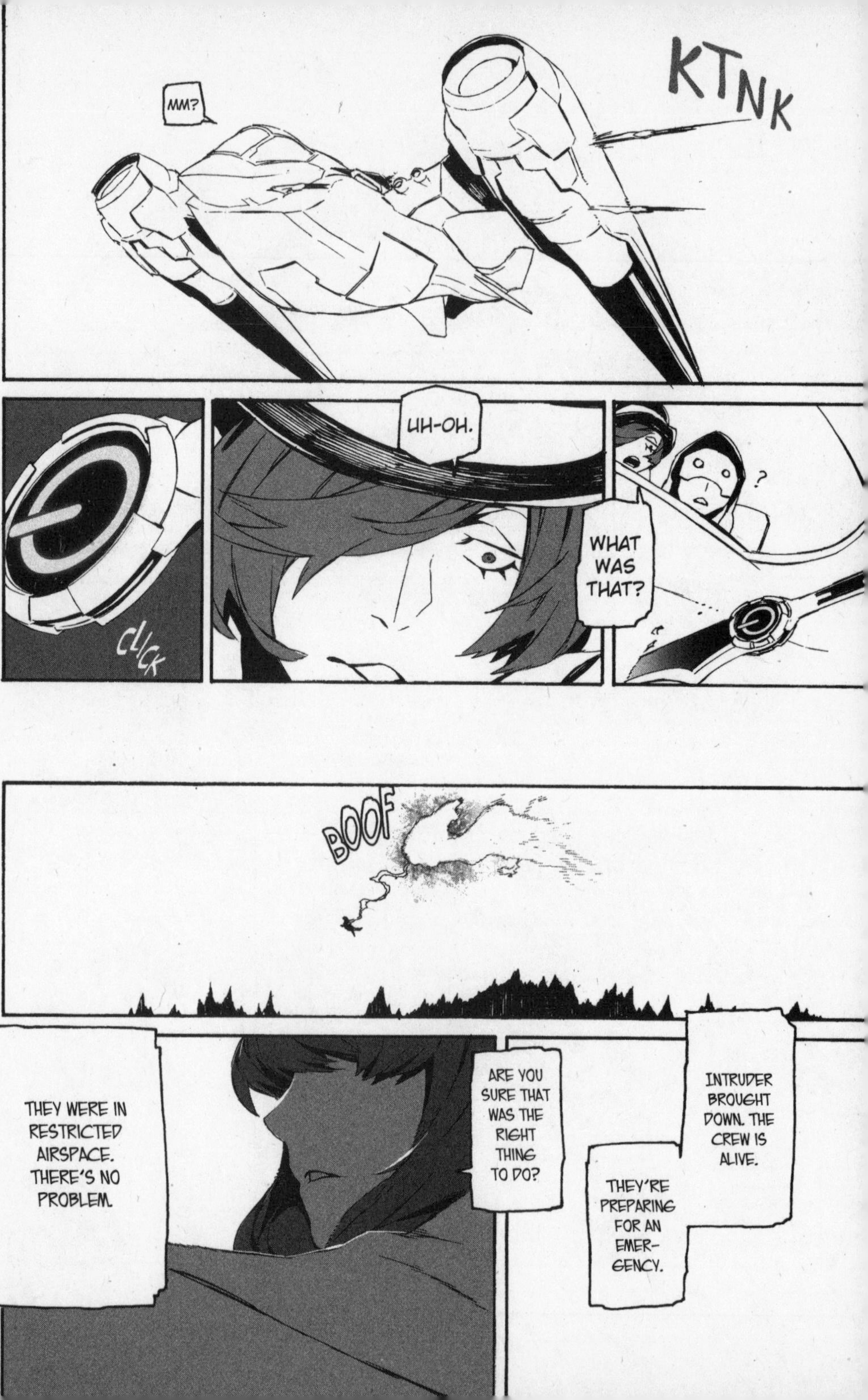
KTNK
MM?
?
WHAT WAS THAT?
UH-OH.
CLICK
BOOF
INTRUDER BROUGHT DOWN. THE CREW IS ALIVE.
THEY'RE PREPARING FOR AN EMERGENCY.
ARE YOU SURE THAT WAS THE RIGHT THING TO DO?
THEY WERE IN RESTRICTED AIRSPACE. THERE'S NO PROBLEM.

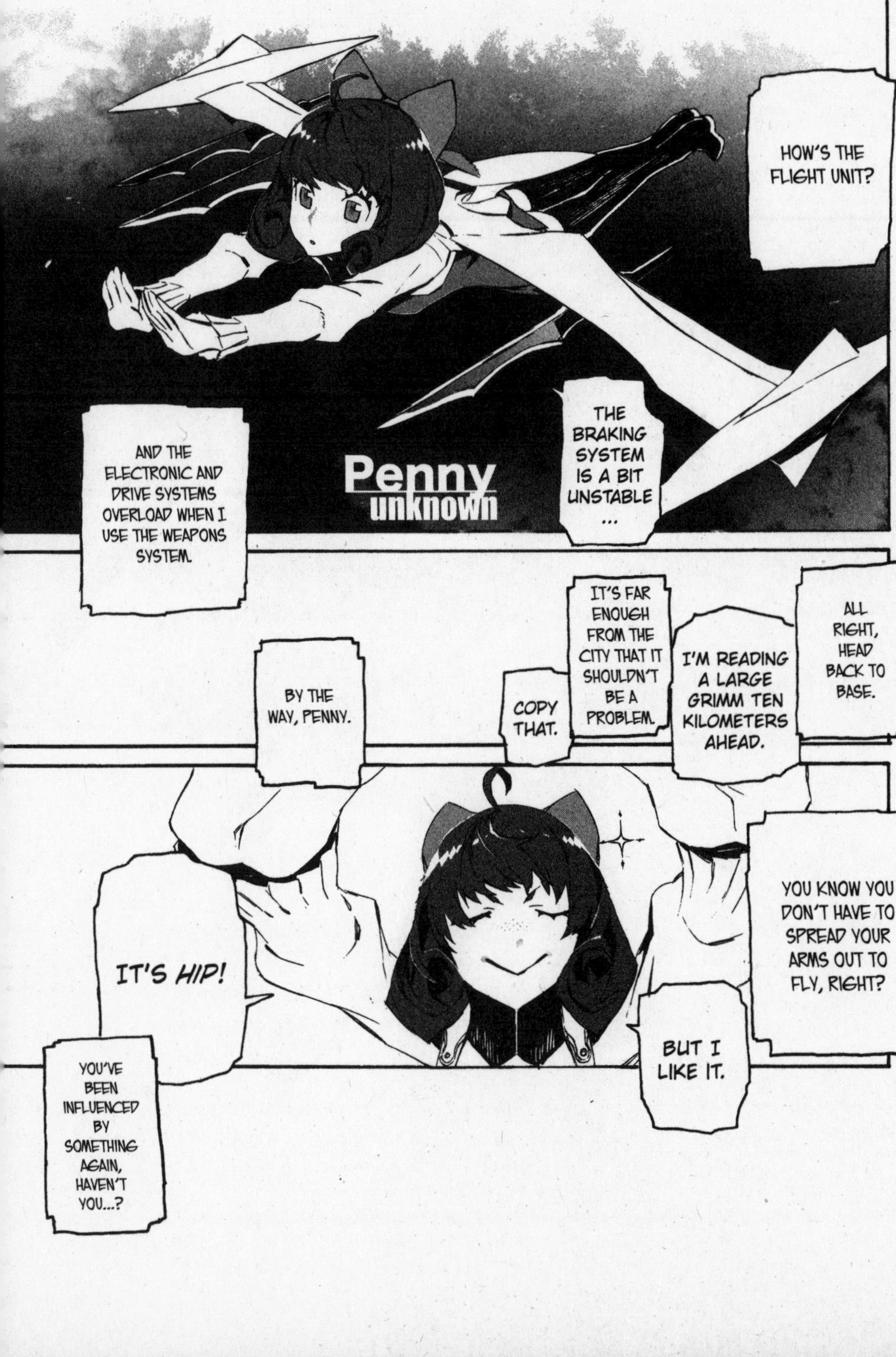
HOW'S THE FLIGHT UNIT?
THE BRAKING SYSTEM IS A BIT UNSTABLE ...
AND THE ELECTRONIC AND DRIVE SYSTEMS OVERLOAD WHEN I USE THE WEAPONS SYSTEM.
Penny unknown
ALL RIGHT, HEAD BACK TO BASE.
I'M READING A LARGE GRIMM TEN KILOMETERS AHEAD.
IT'S FAR ENOUGH FROM THE CITY THAT IT SHOULDN'T BE A PROBLEM.
COPY THAT.
BY THE WAY, PENNY.
YOU KNOW YOU DON'T HAVE TO SPREAD YOUR ARMS OUT TO FLY, RIGHT?
BUT I LIKE IT.
IT'S *HIP*!
YOU'VE BEEN INFLUENCED BY SOMETHING AGAIN, HAVEN'T YOU...?

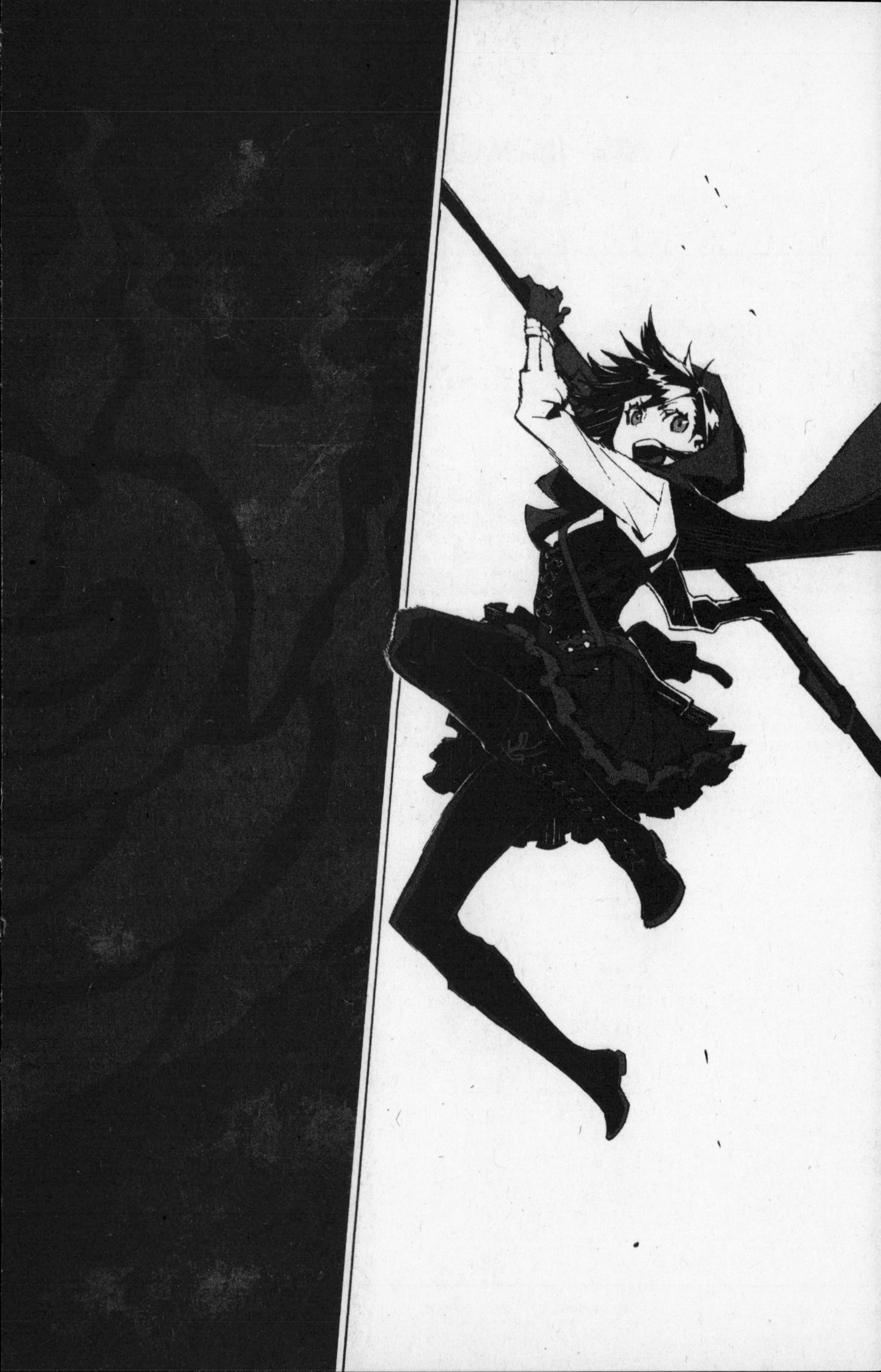

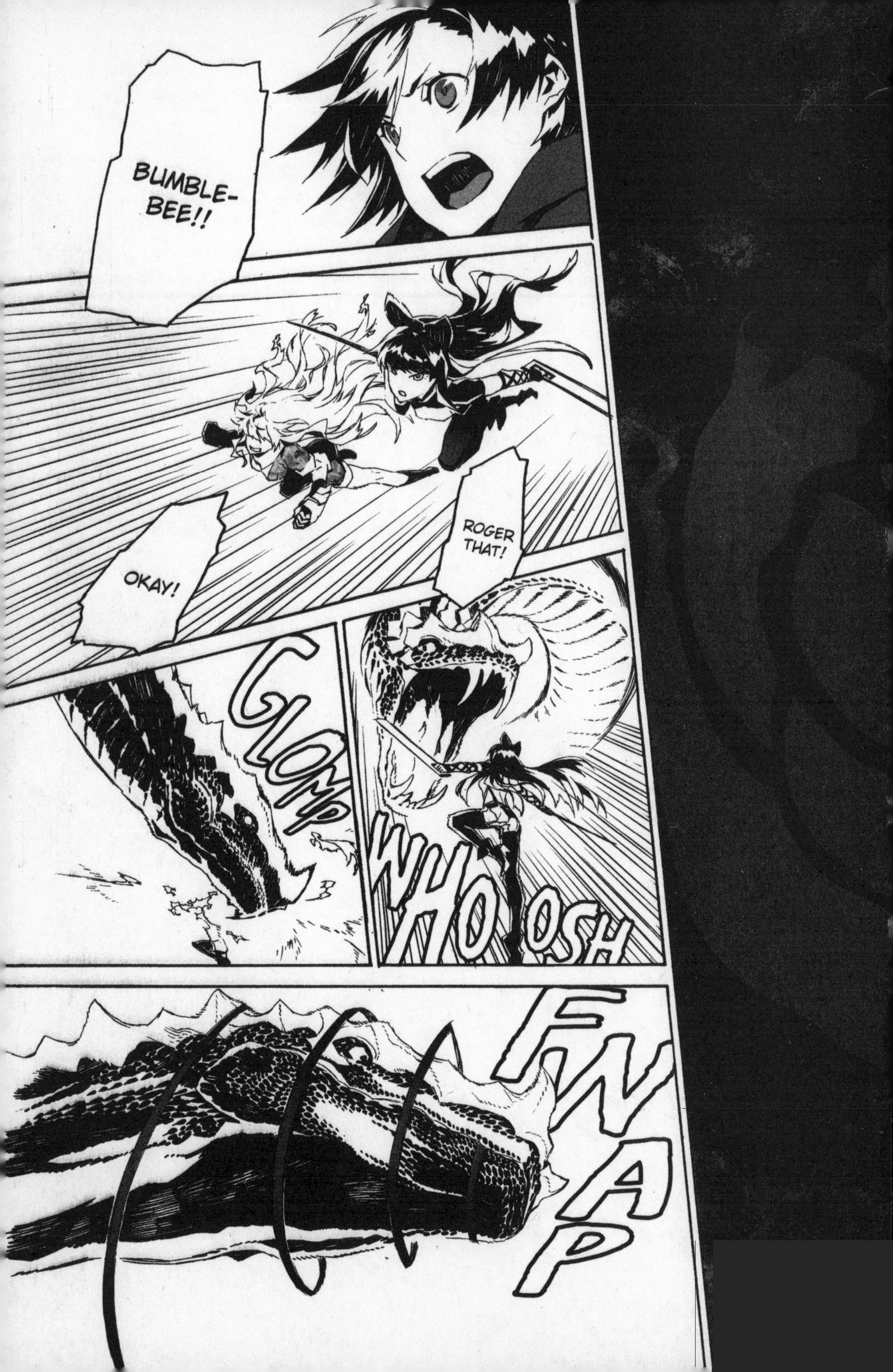
BUMBLE-BEE!!
ROGER THAT!
OKAY!
WHOOSH
GLOMP
FWAP

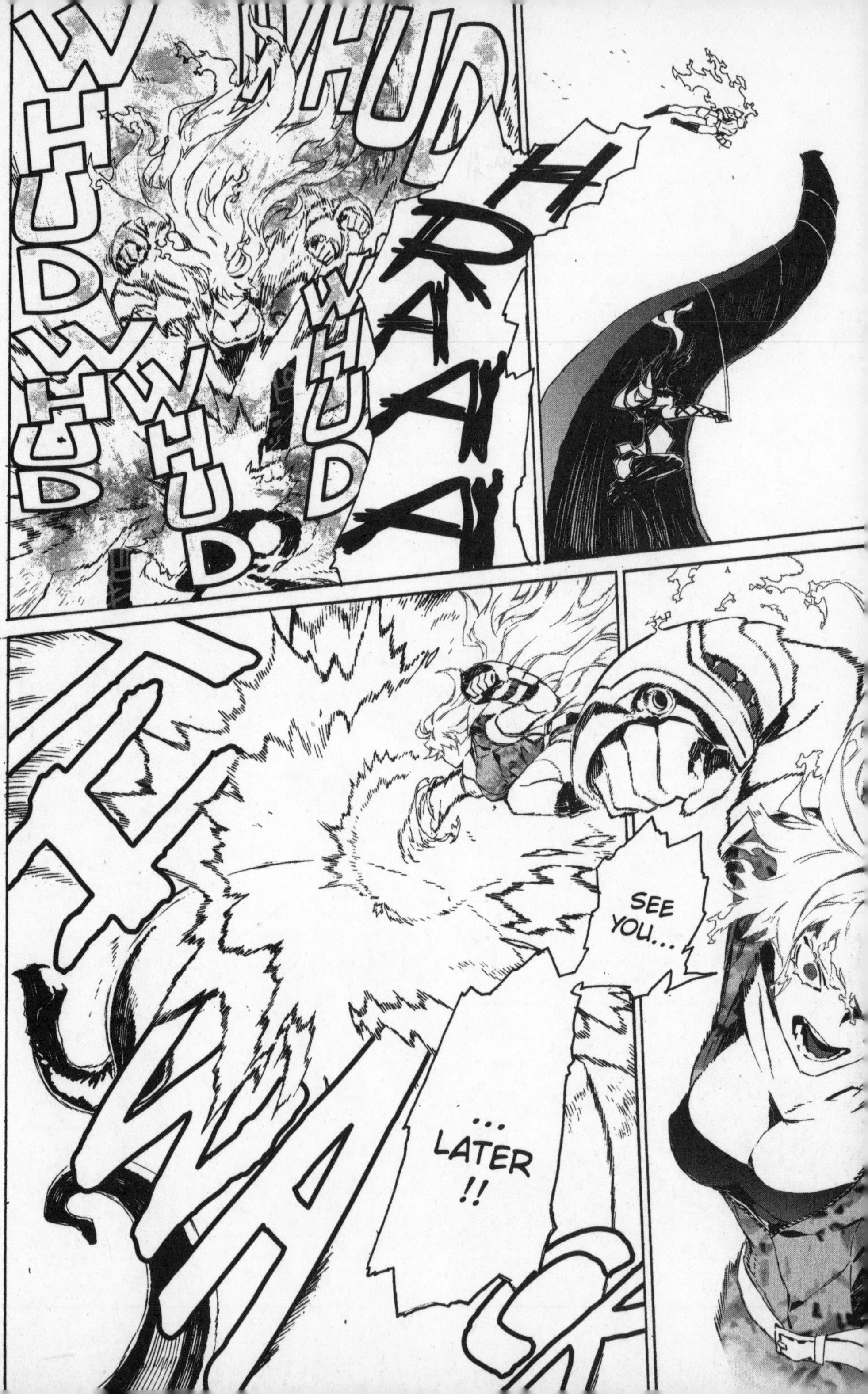
WHUD
HRAAAA
WHUD
WHUD
WHUD
WHUD
SEE YOU...
...LATER!!

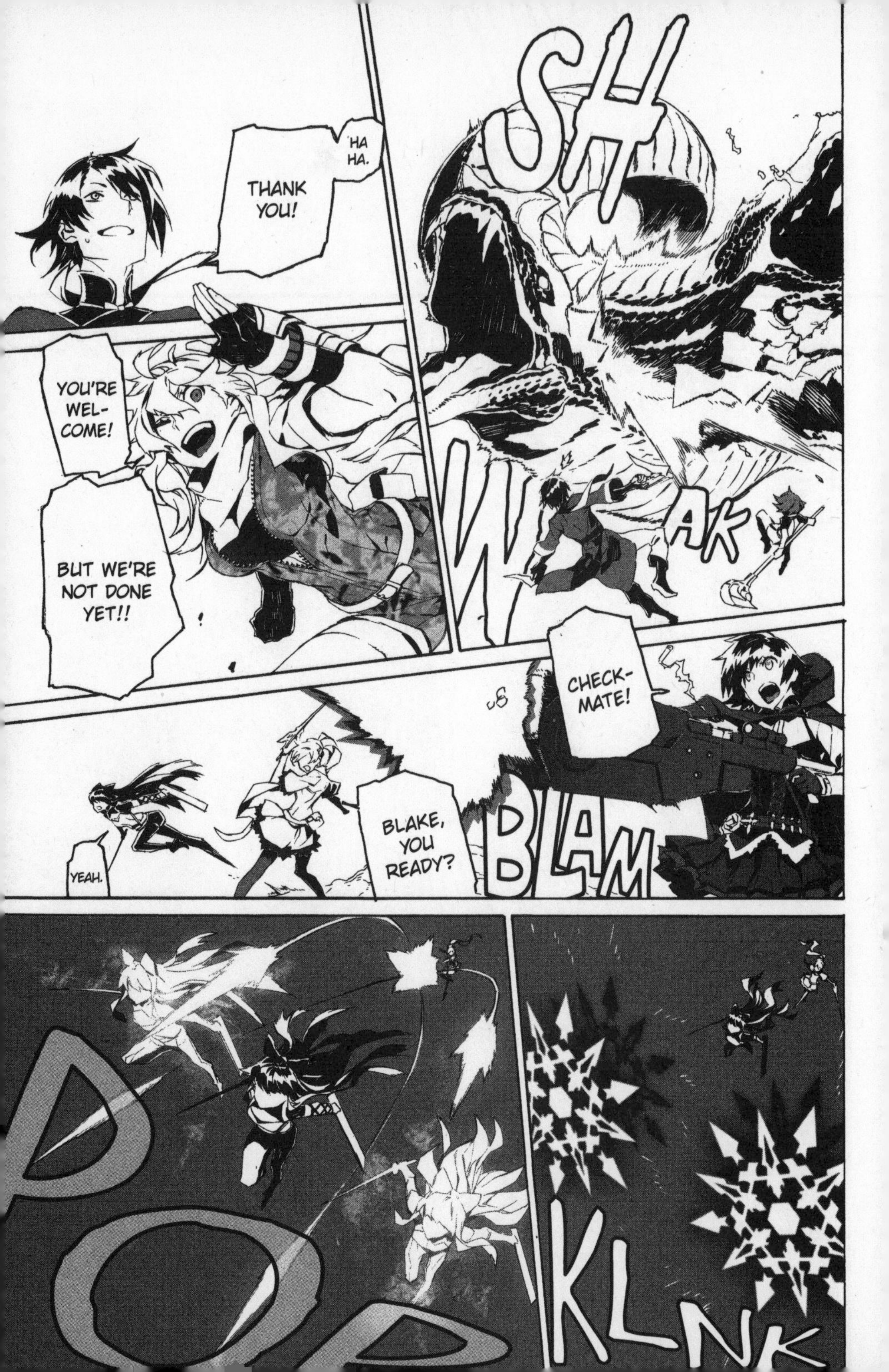
SH
WAK
HA HA.
THANK YOU!
YOU'RE WEL-COME!
BUT WE'RE NOT DONE YET!!
CHECK-MATE!
BLAM
BLAKE, YOU READY?
YEAH.
KLNK
PO

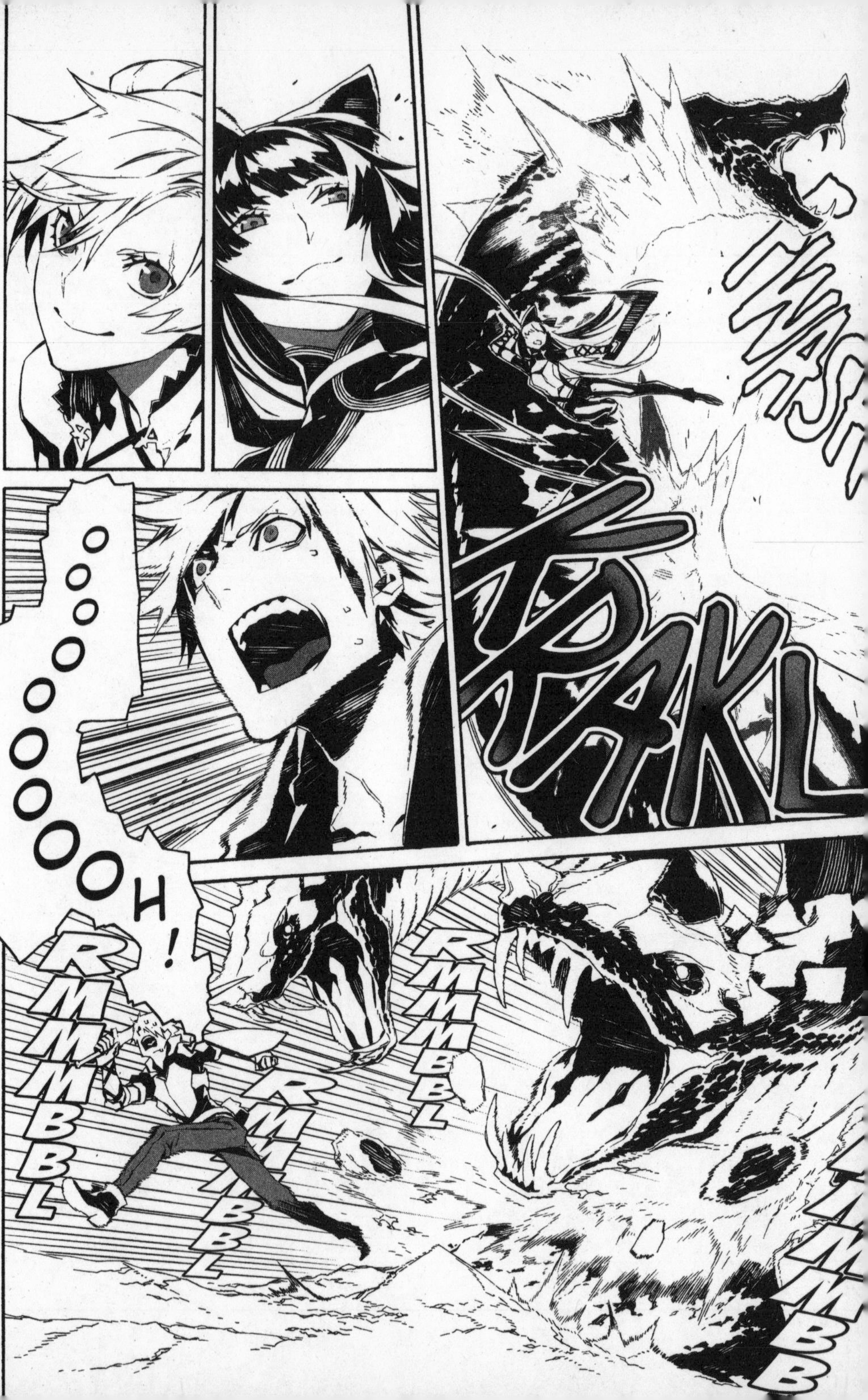
THWASH
KRAKL
MMBB
RMMMBBL
RMMMBBL
OOOOOOOOOOOOOH!
RMMMMBBL

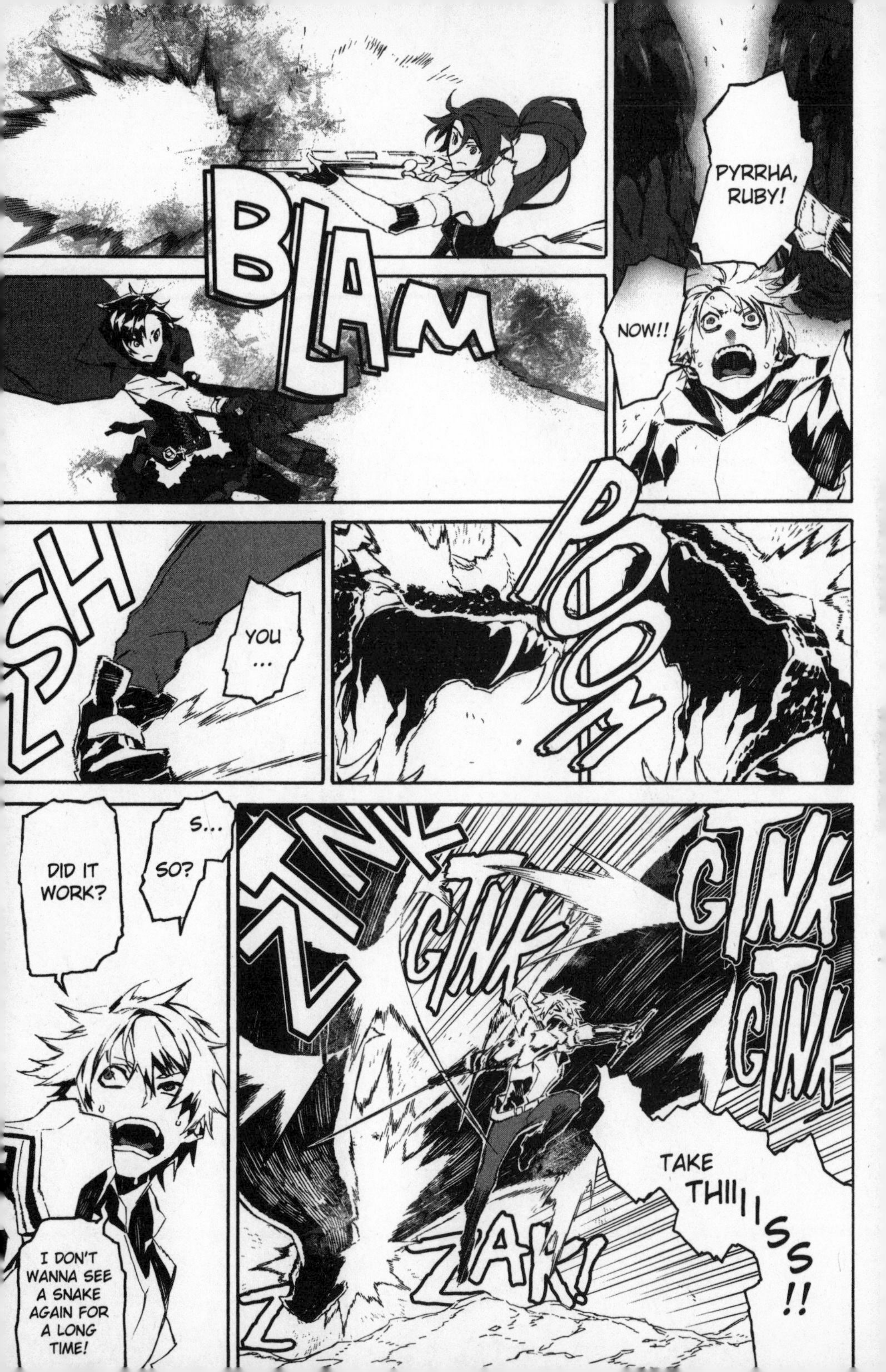
PYRRHA, RUBY!
NOW!!
BLAM
POOM
ZSH
YOU ...
CTNK
CTNK
CTNK
ZTINK
CTNK
TAKE THIIIISS!!
ZAK!
S... SO?
DID IT WORK?
I DON'T WANNA SEE A SNAKE AGAIN FOR A LONG TIME!

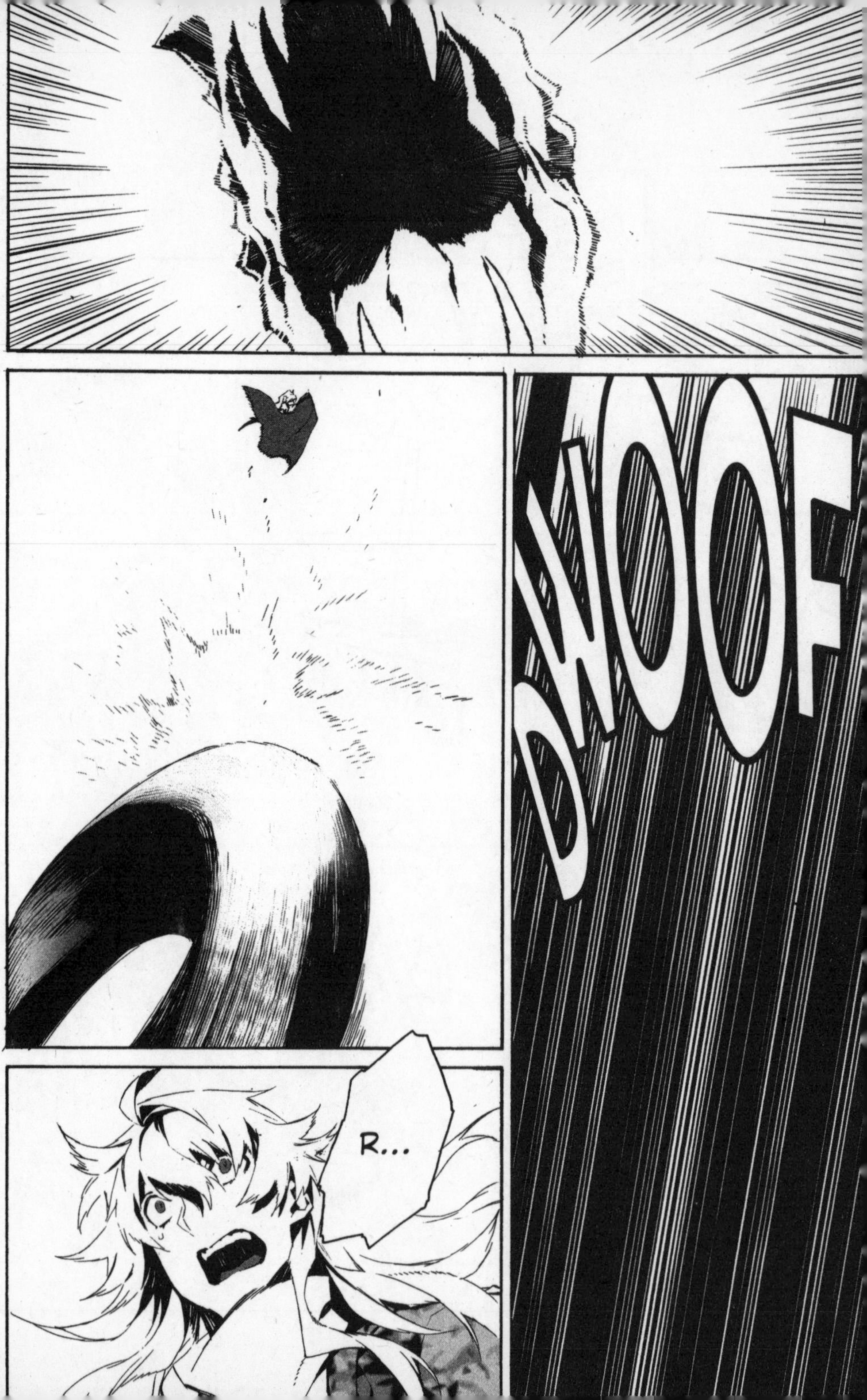
DWOOF
R...

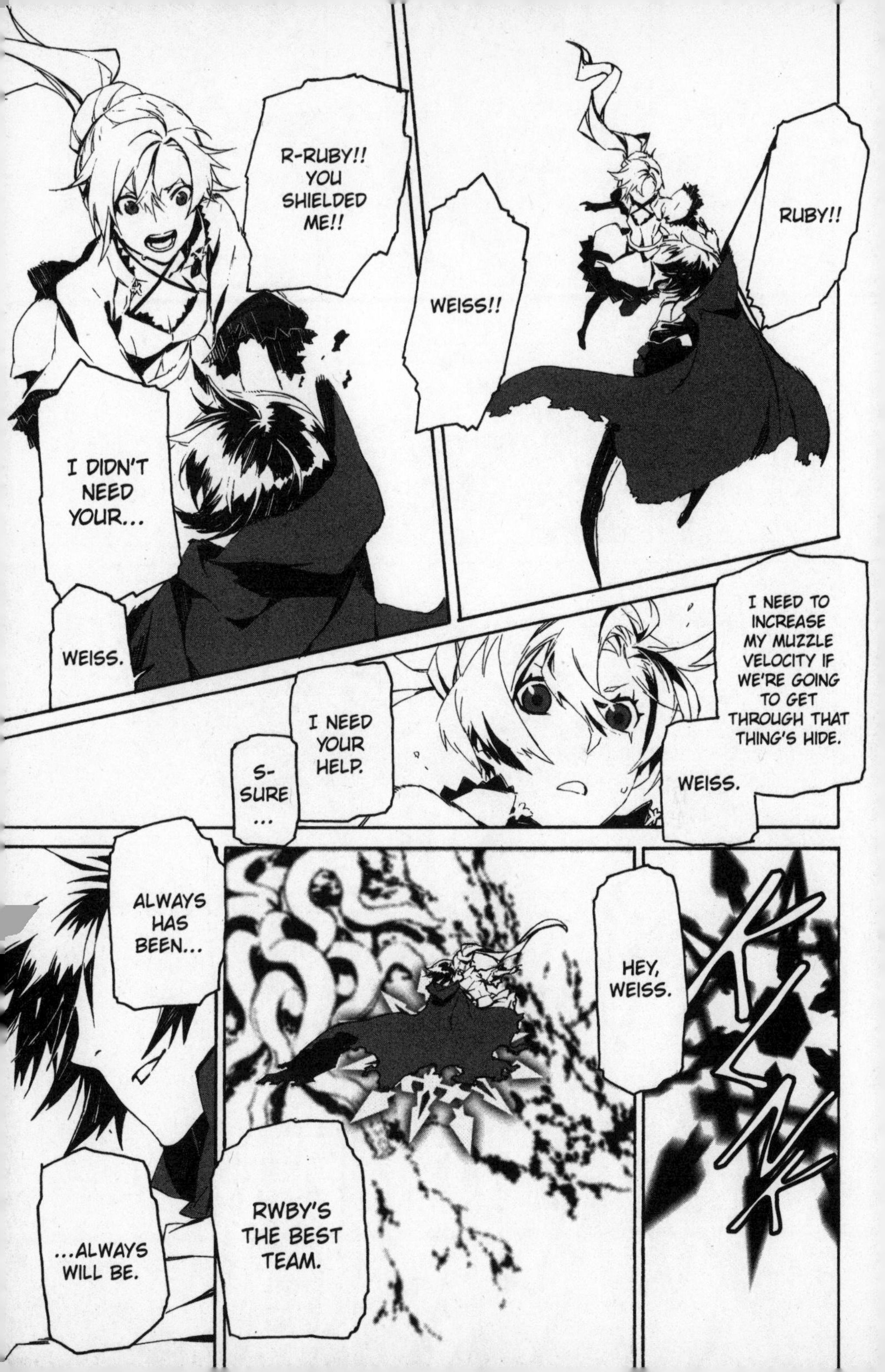
RUBY!!
WEISS!!
R-RUBY!! YOU SHIELDED ME!!
I DIDN'T NEED YOUR...
WEISS.
I NEED TO INCREASE MY MUZZLE VELOCITY IF WE'RE GOING TO GET THROUGH THAT THING'S HIDE.
WEISS.
I NEED YOUR HELP.
S-SURE...
KLNK
HEY, WEISS.
RWBY'S THE BEST TEAM.
ALWAYS HAS BEEN...
...ALWAYS WILL BE.

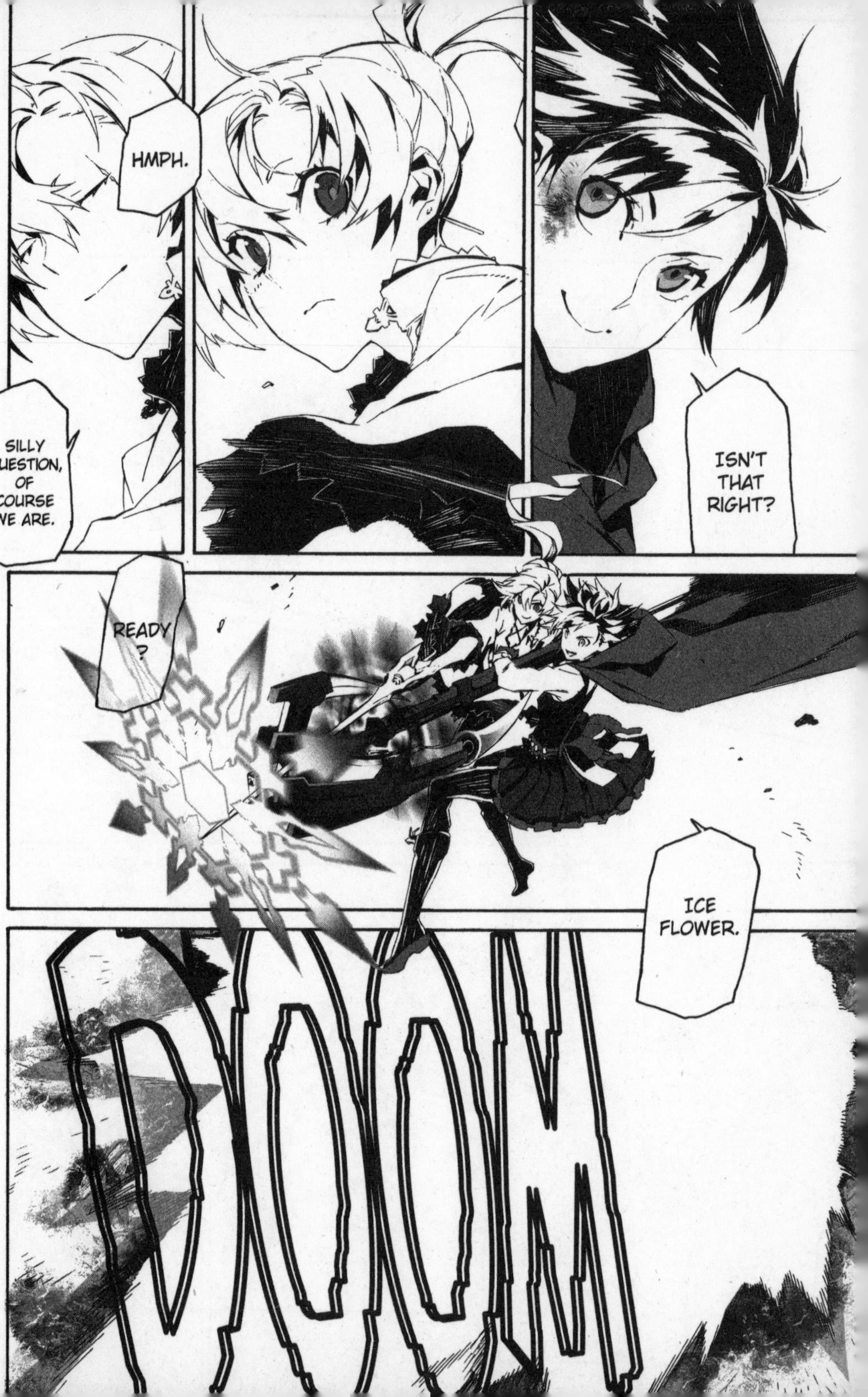
ISN'T THAT RIGHT?
HMPH.
SILLY QUESTION, OF COURSE WE ARE.
READY?
ICE FLOWER.
DOOOM

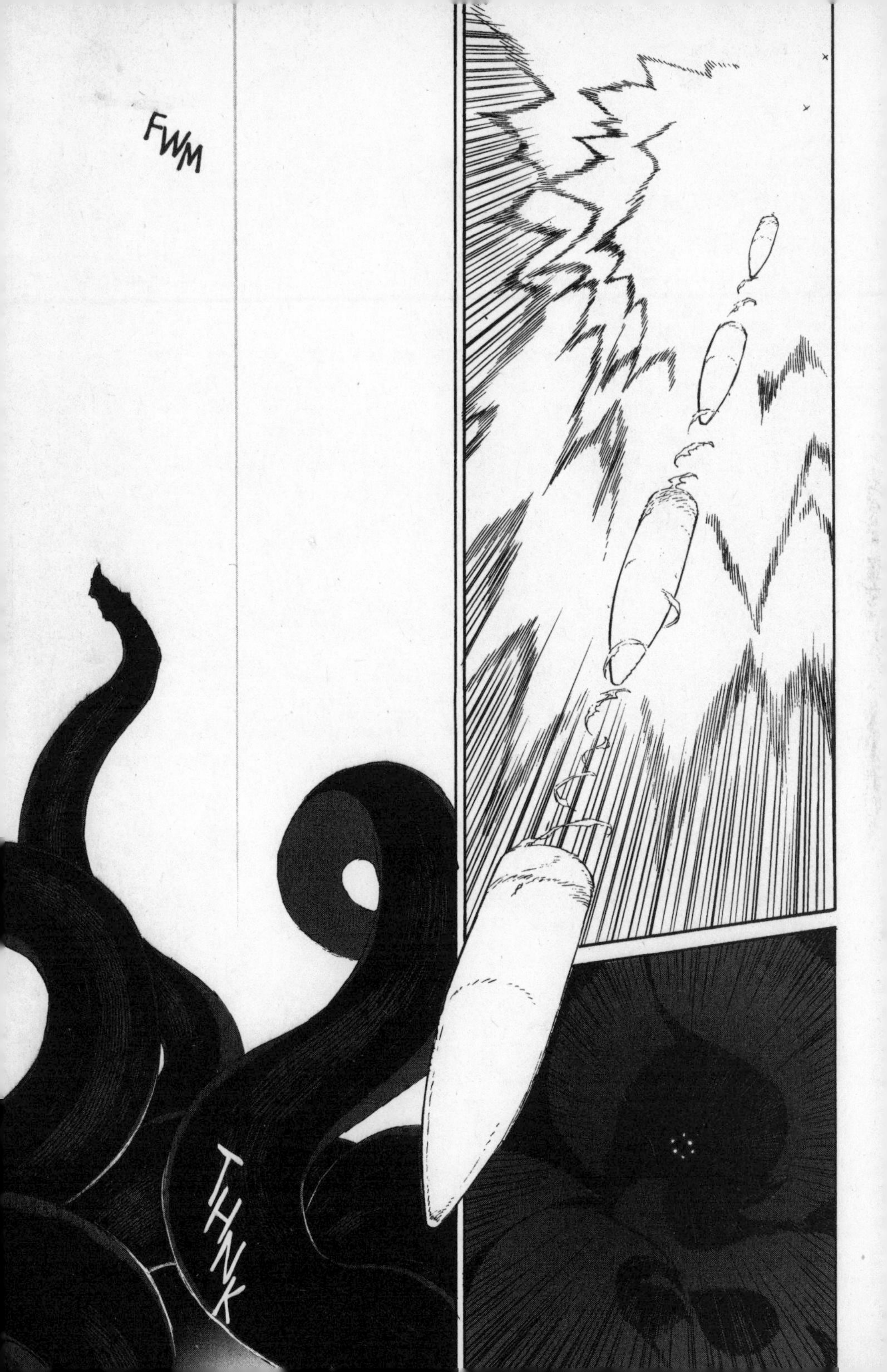
FWM
THNK

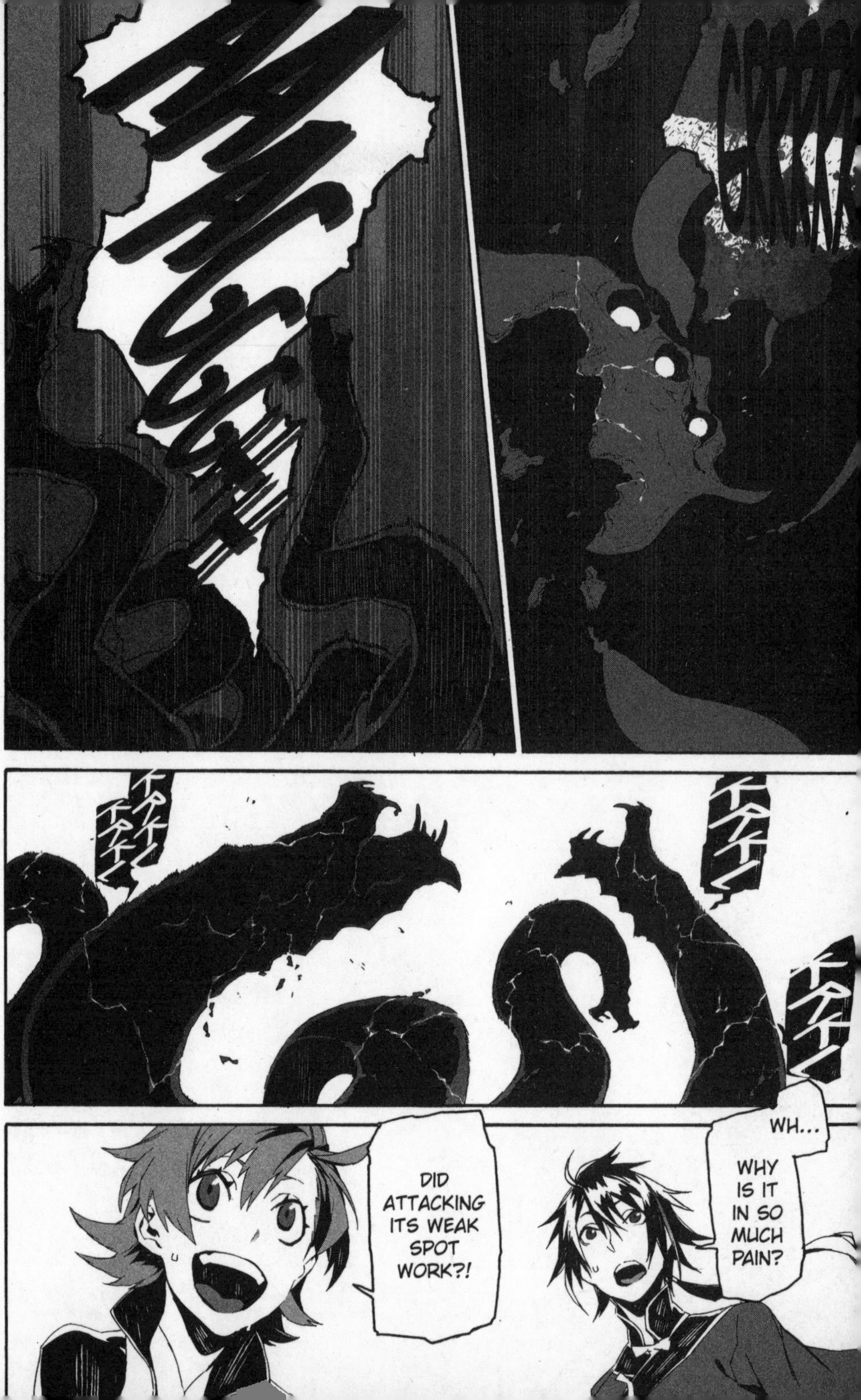
GRRRR
AAAGGGH
KRKL
KRKL
KRKL KRKL
WH...
WHY IS IT IN SO MUCH PAIN?
DID ATTACKING ITS WEAK SPOT WORK?!

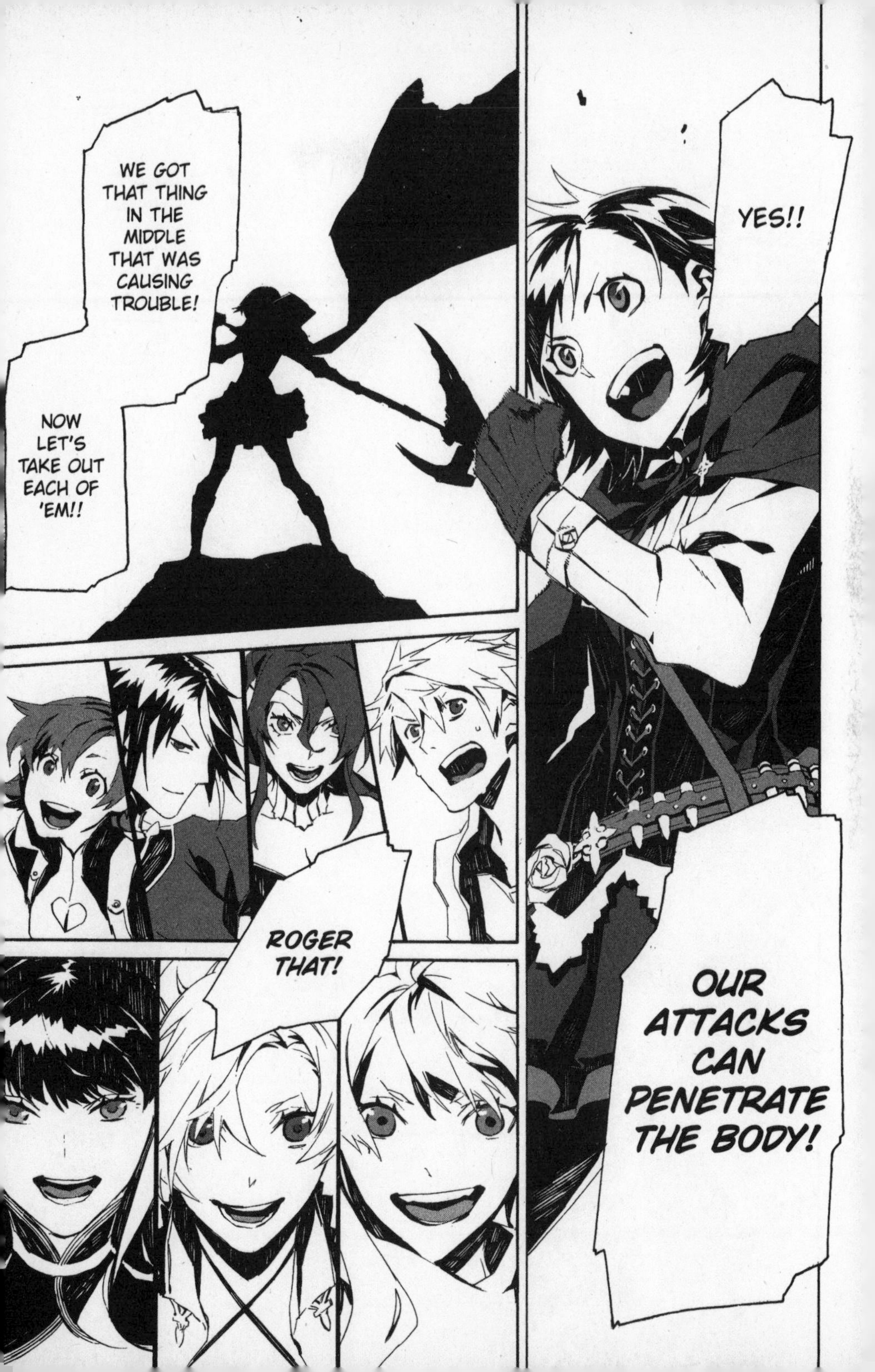
YES!!
OUR ATTACKS CAN PENETRATE THE BODY!
WE GOT THAT THING IN THE MIDDLE THAT WAS CAUSING TROUBLE!
NOW LET'S TAKE OUT EACH OF 'EM!!
ROGER THAT!

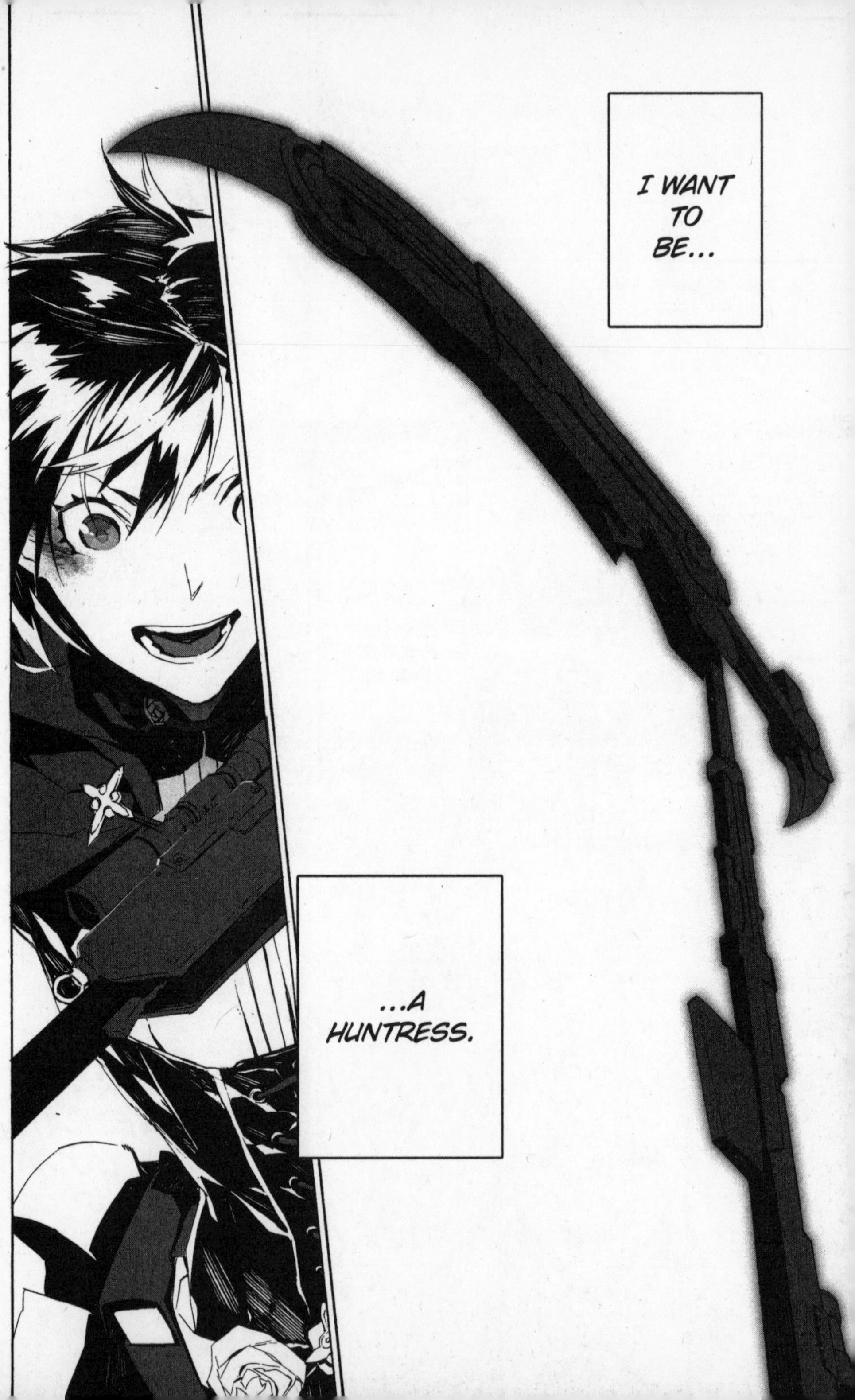
I WANT TO BE...
...A HUNTRESS.

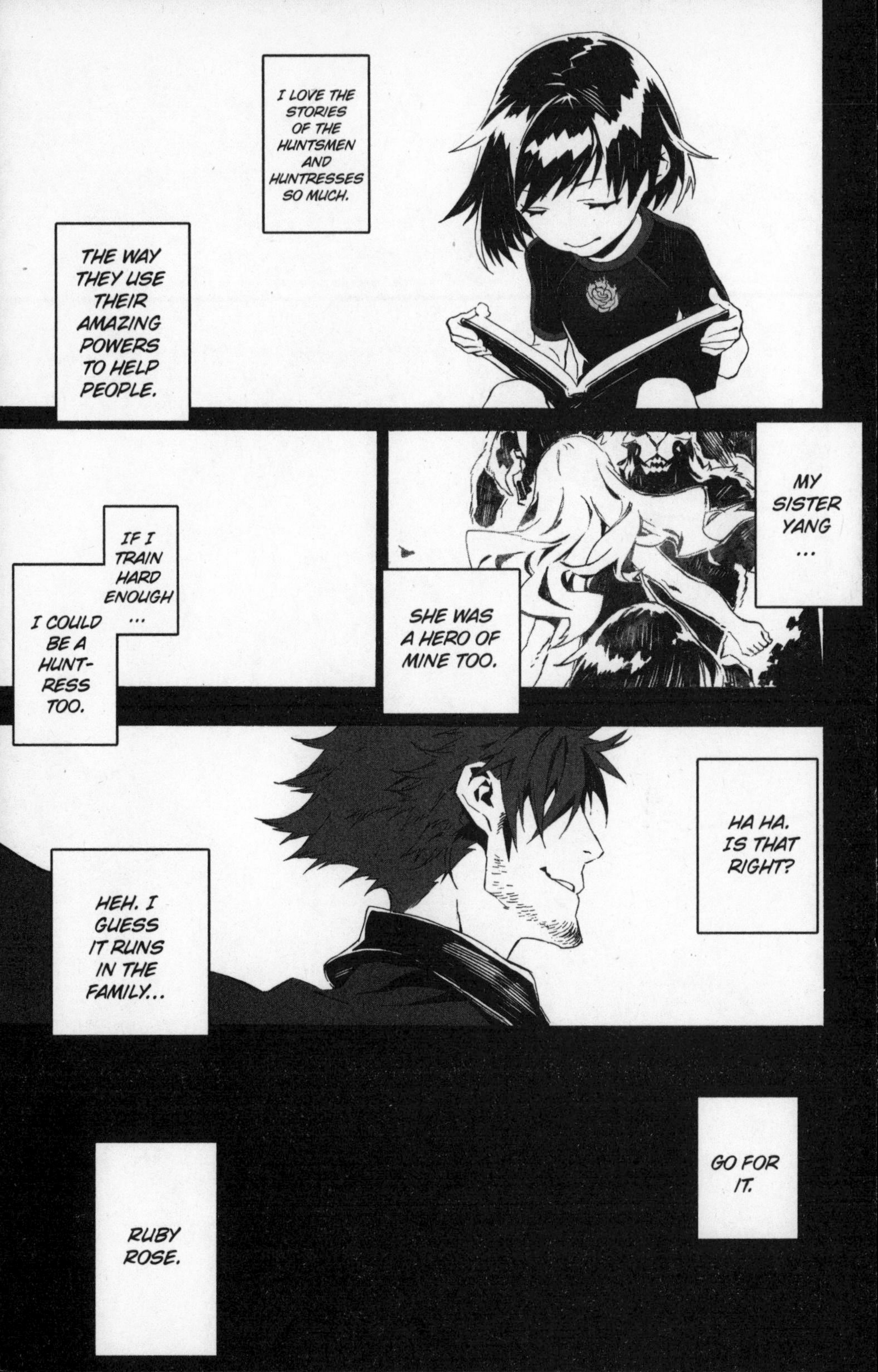
I LOVE THE STORIES OF THE HUNTSMEN AND HUNTRESSES SO MUCH.
THE WAY THEY USE THEIR AMAZING POWERS TO HELP PEOPLE.
MY SISTER YANG ...
SHE WAS A HERO OF MINE TOO.
IF I TRAIN HARD ENOUGH ...
I COULD BE A HUNT-RESS TOO.
HA HA. IS THAT RIGHT?
HEH. I GUESS IT RUNS IN THE FAMILY...
GO FOR IT.
RUBY ROSE.

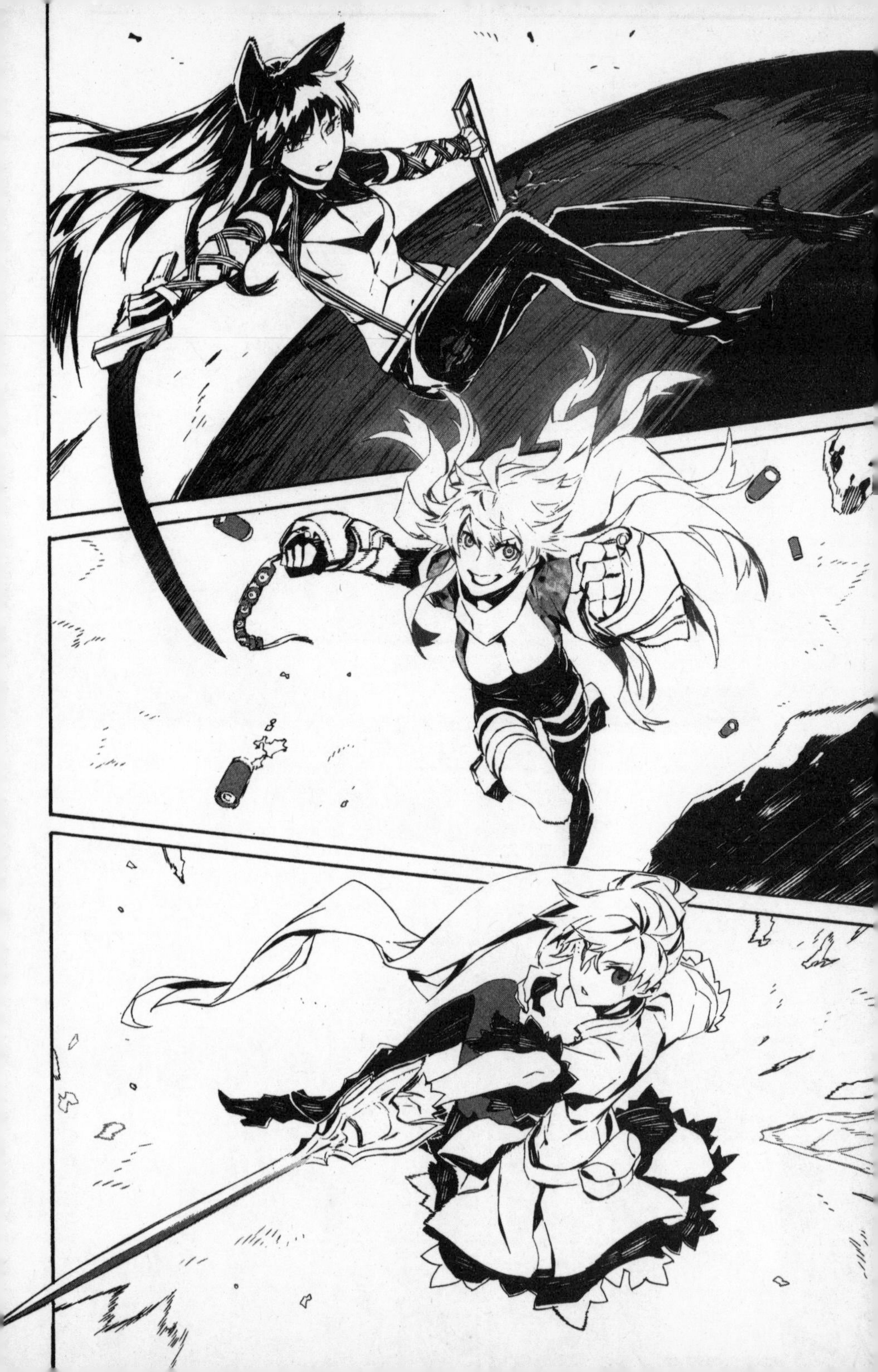

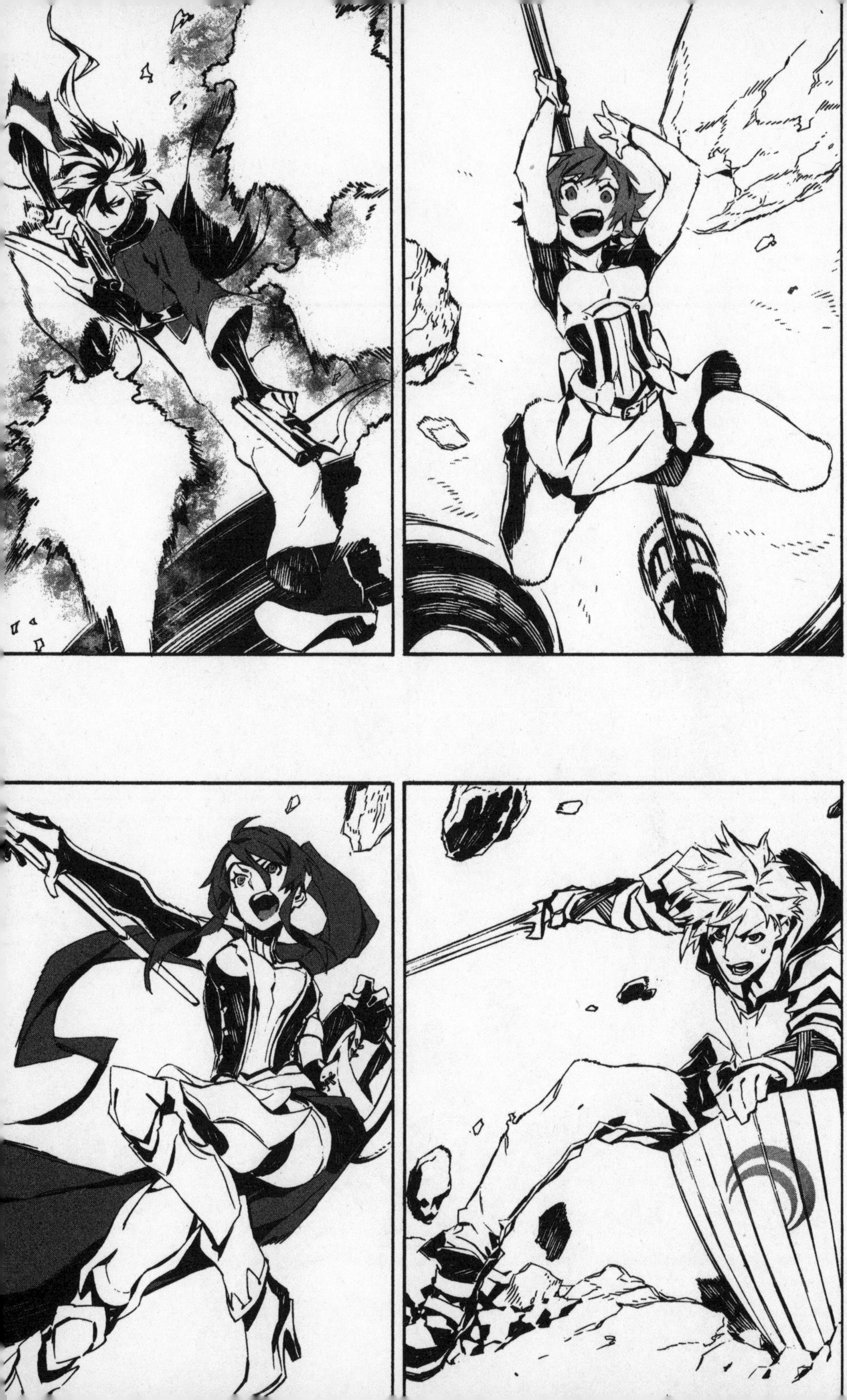

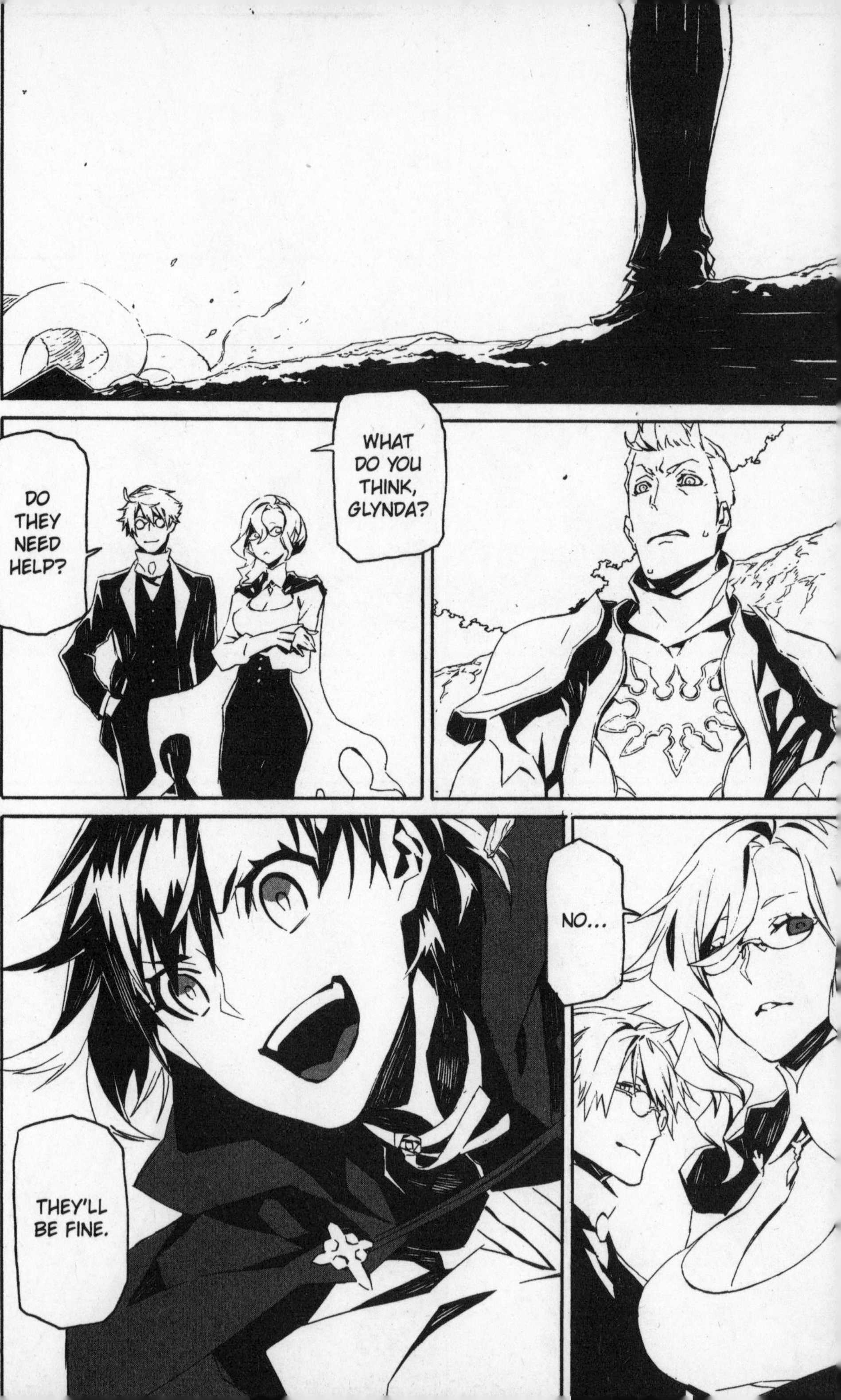
WHAT DO YOU THINK, GLYNDA?
DO THEY NEED HELP?
NO...
THEY'LL BE FINE.

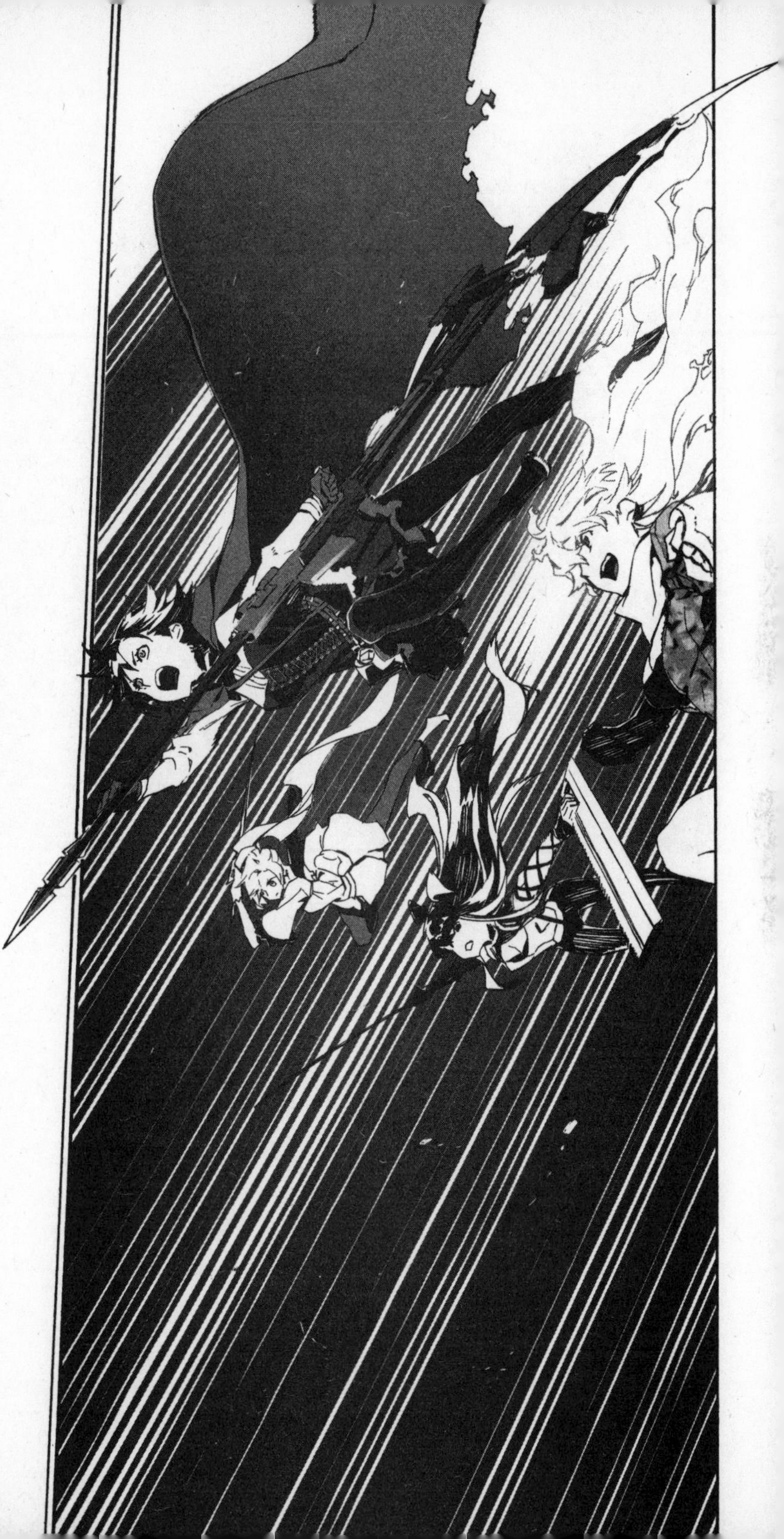

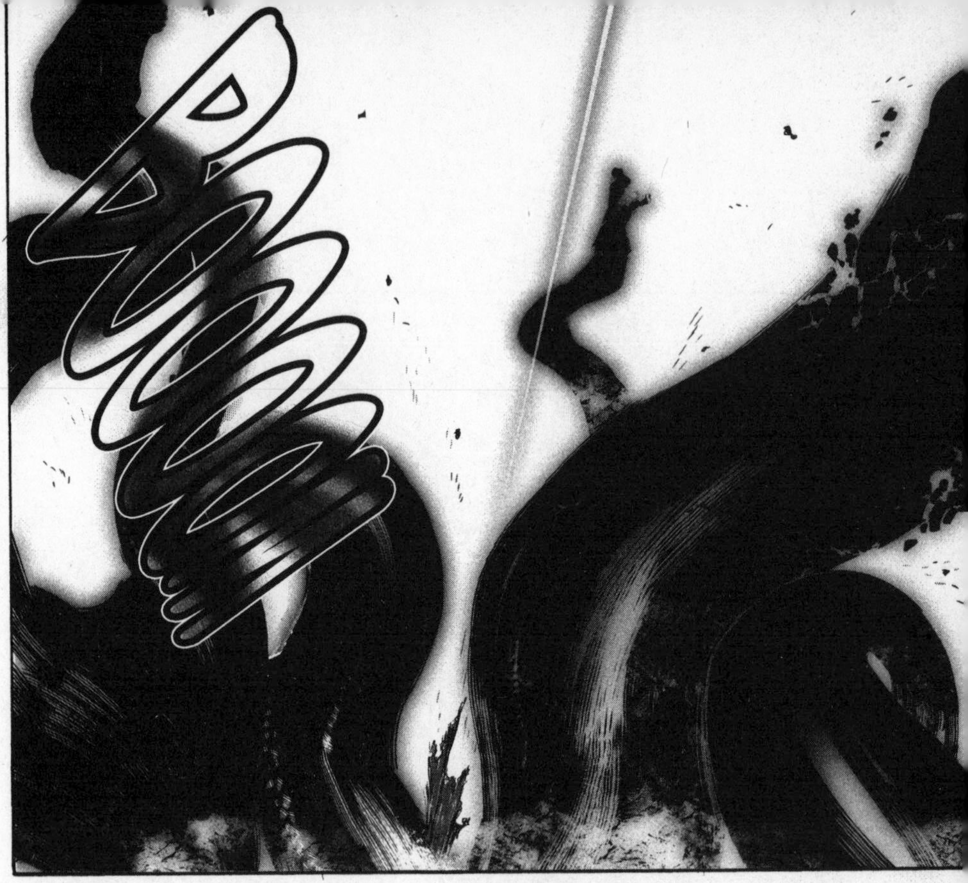
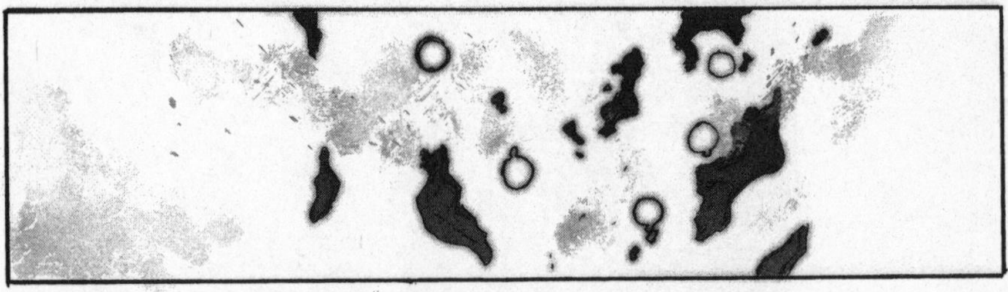
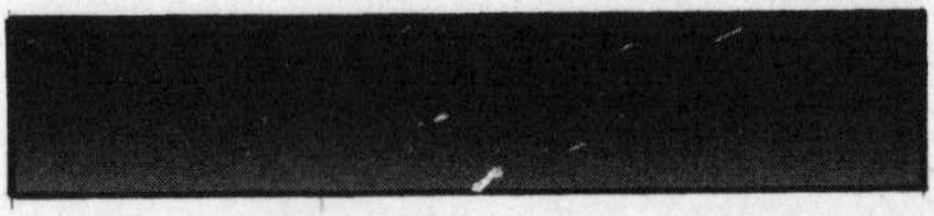

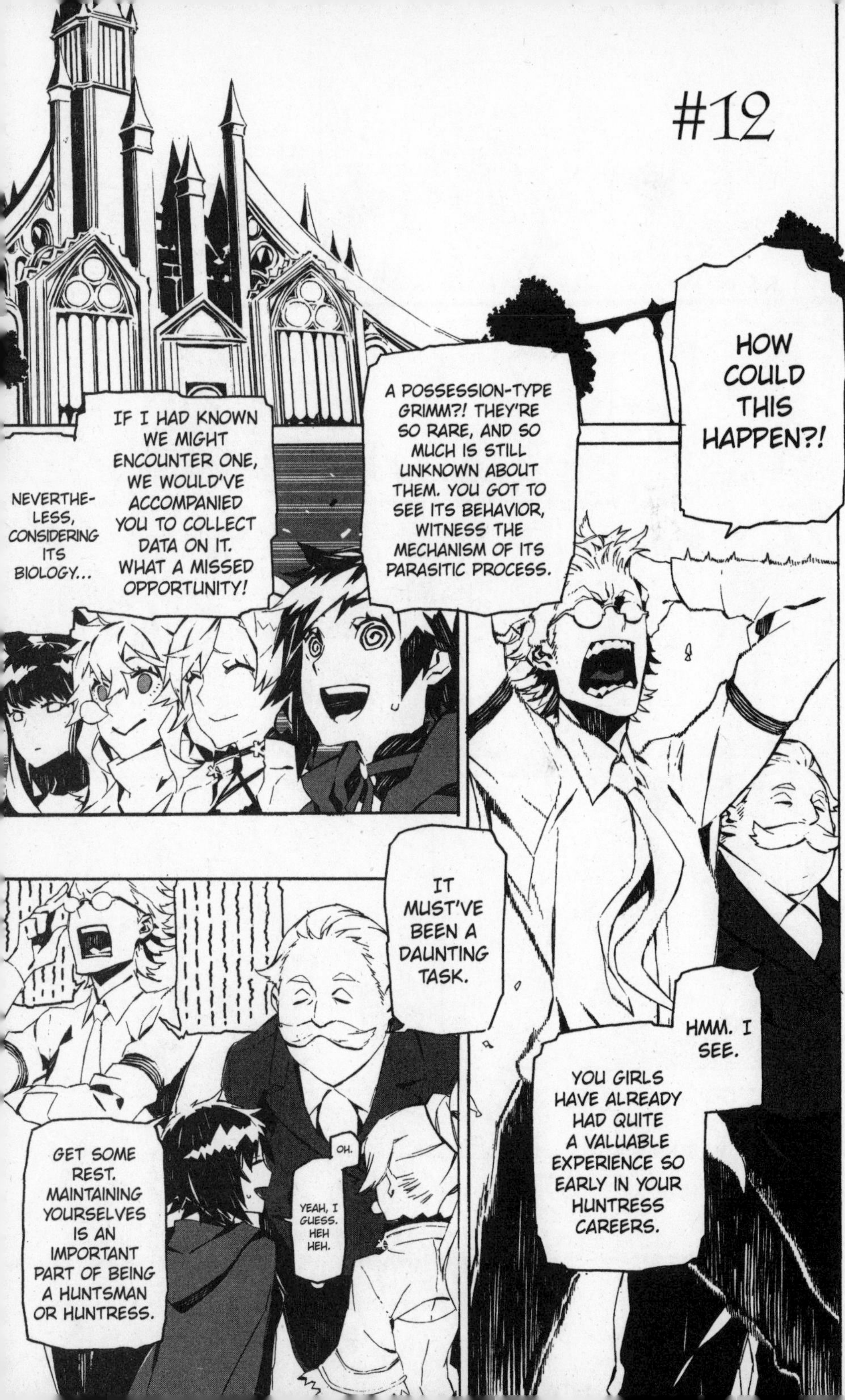
#12
HOW COULD THIS HAPPEN?!
A POSSESSION-TYPE GRIMM?! THEY'RE SO RARE, AND SO MUCH IS STILL UNKNOWN ABOUT THEM. YOU GOT TO SEE ITS BEHAVIOR, WITNESS THE MECHANISM OF ITS PARASITIC PROCESS.
IF I HAD KNOWN WE MIGHT ENCOUNTER ONE, WE WOULD'VE ACCOMPANIED YOU TO COLLECT DATA ON IT. WHAT A MISSED OPPORTUNITY!
NEVERTHE-LESS, CONSIDERING ITS BIOLOGY...
HMM. I SEE.
IT MUST'VE BEEN A DAUNTING TASK.
YOU GIRLS HAVE ALREADY HAD QUITE A VALUABLE EXPERIENCE SO EARLY IN YOUR HUNTRESS CAREERS.
OH.
YEAH, I GUESS. HEH HEH.
GET SOME REST. MAINTAINING YOURSELVES IS AN IMPORTANT PART OF BEING A HUNTSMAN OR HUNTRESS.

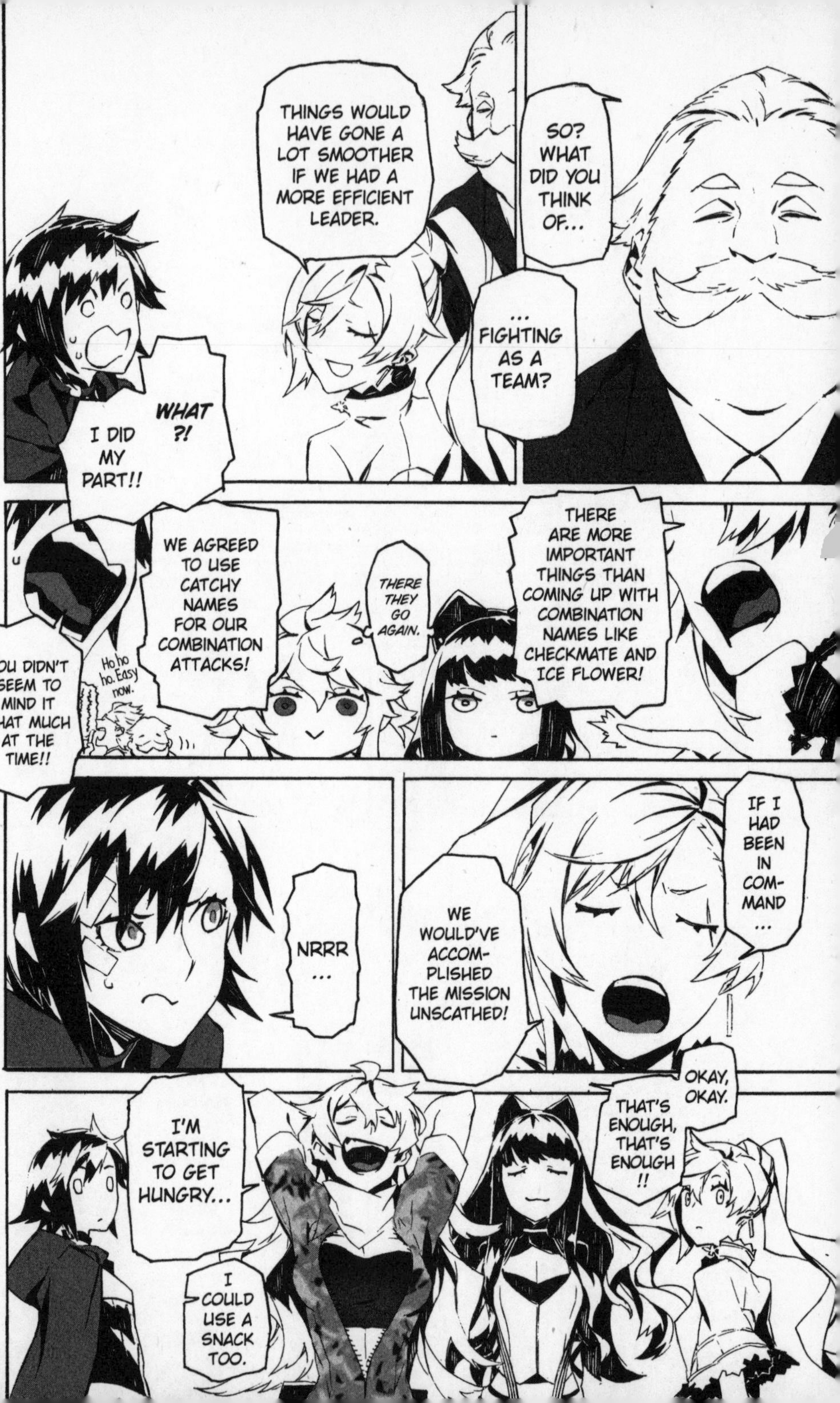
SO? WHAT DID YOU THINK OF...
... FIGHTING AS A TEAM?
THINGS WOULD HAVE GONE A LOT SMOOTHER IF WE HAD A MORE EFFICIENT LEADER.
WHAT?!
I DID MY PART!!
THERE ARE MORE IMPORTANT THINGS THAN COMING UP WITH COMBINATION NAMES LIKE CHECKMATE AND ICE FLOWER!
THERE THEY GO AGAIN.
WE AGREED TO USE CATCHY NAMES FOR OUR COMBINATION ATTACKS!
Ho ho ho. Easy now.
YOU DIDN'T SEEM TO MIND IT THAT MUCH AT THE TIME!!
IF I HAD BEEN IN COM-MAND...
WE WOULD'VE ACCOM-PLISHED THE MISSION UNSCATHED!
NRRR...
OKAY, OKAY.
THAT'S ENOUGH, THAT'S ENOUGH!!
I'M STARTING TO GET HUNGRY...
I COULD USE A SNACK TOO.

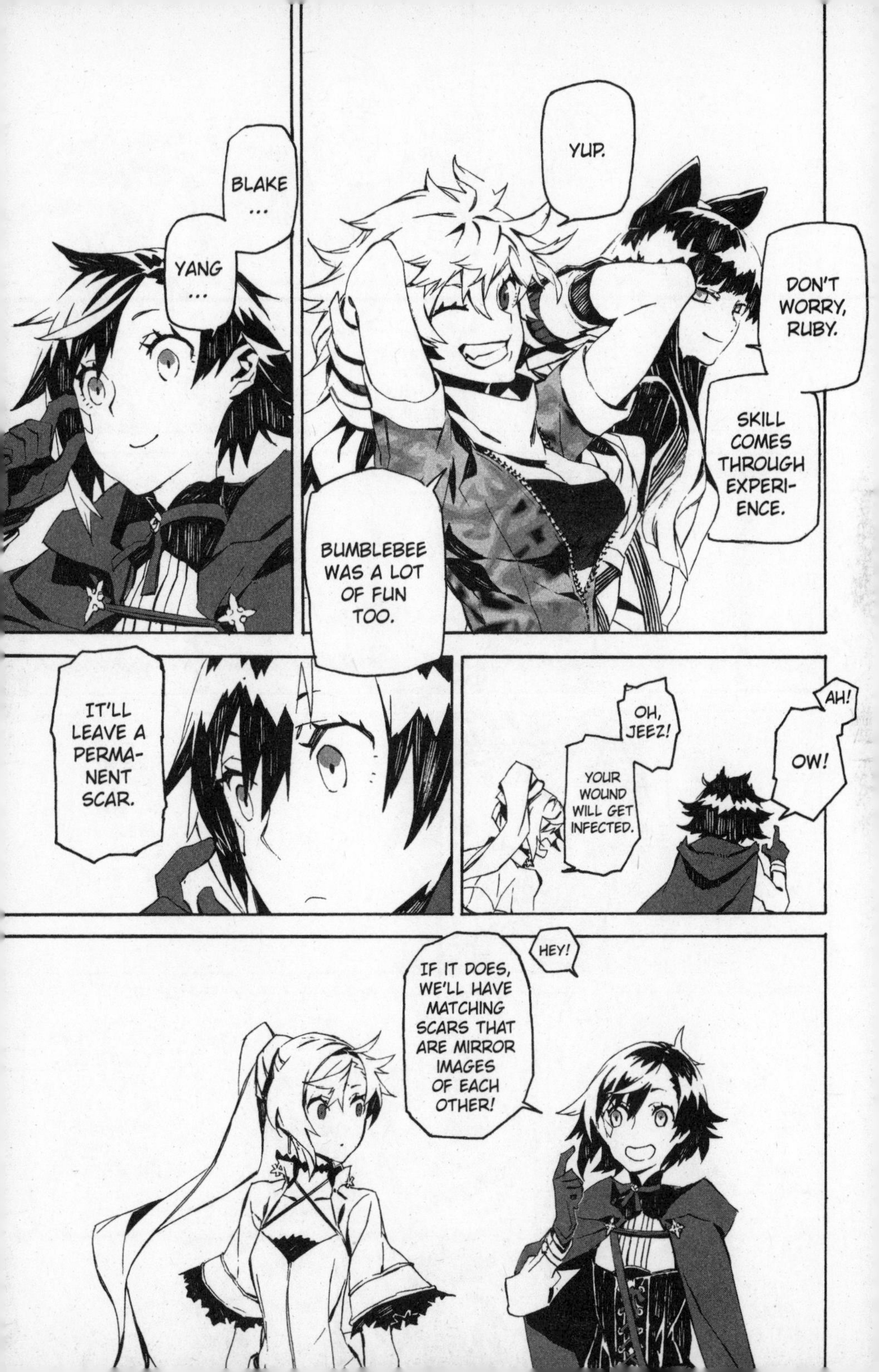
DON'T WORRY, RUBY.
SKILL COMES THROUGH EXPERIENCE.
YUP.
BUMBLEBEE WAS A LOT OF FUN TOO.
BLAKE ...
YANG ...
AH!
OW!
OH, JEEZ!
YOUR WOUND WILL GET INFECTED.
IT'LL LEAVE A PERMANENT SCAR.
HEY!
IF IT DOES, WE'LL HAVE MATCHING SCARS THAT ARE MIRROR IMAGES OF EACH OTHER!

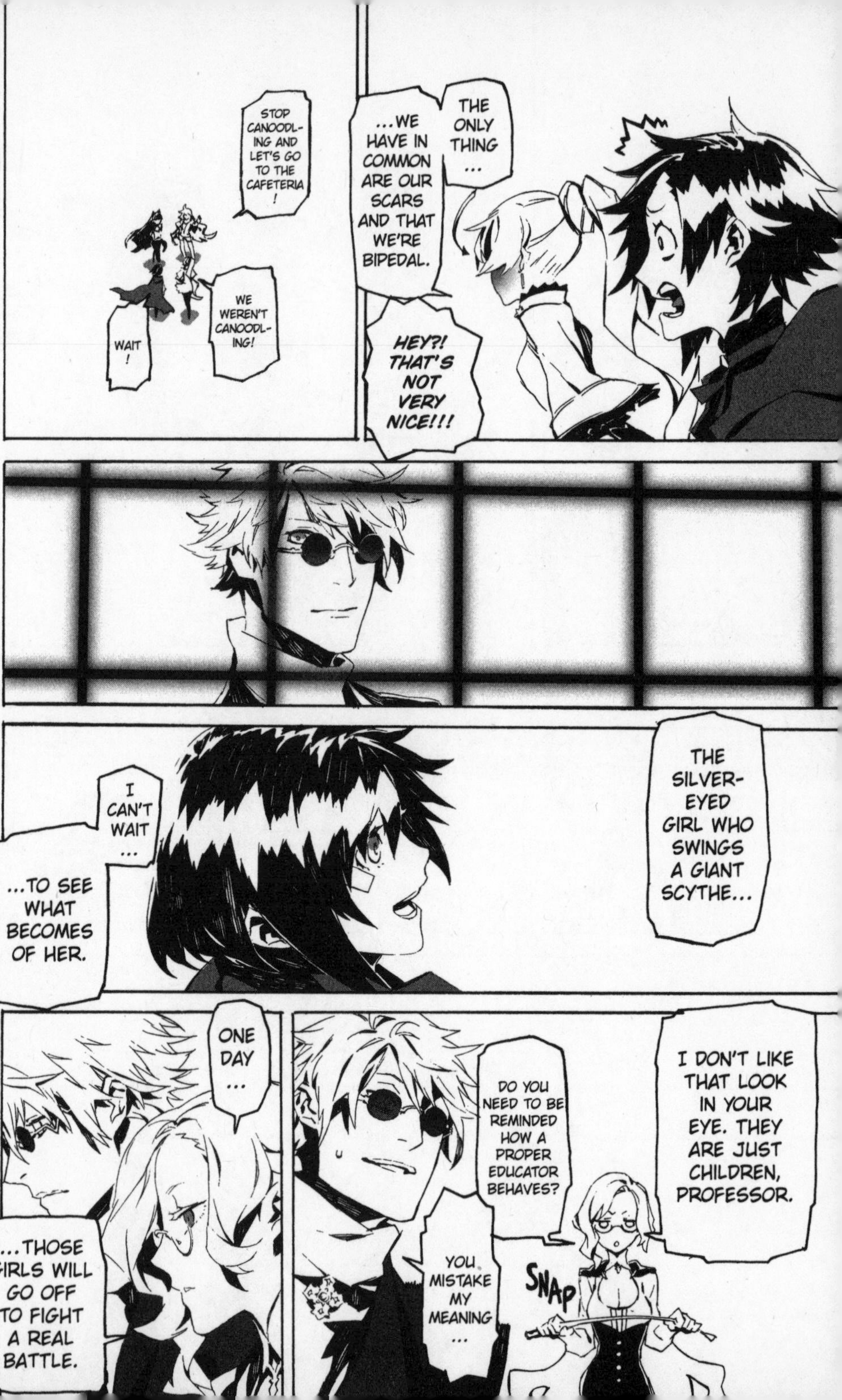
THE ONLY THING...
...WE HAVE IN COMMON ARE OUR SCARS AND THAT WE'RE BIPEDAL.
HEY?! THAT'S NOT VERY NICE!!!
STOP CANOODLING AND LET'S GO TO THE CAFETERIA!
WE WEREN'T CANOODLING!
WAIT!
THE SILVER-EYED GIRL WHO SWINGS A GIANT SCYTHE...
I CAN'T WAIT...
...TO SEE WHAT BECOMES OF HER.
I DON'T LIKE THAT LOOK IN YOUR EYE. THEY ARE JUST CHILDREN, PROFESSOR.
SNAP
DO YOU NEED TO BE REMINDED HOW A PROPER EDUCATOR BEHAVES?
YOU MISTAKE MY MEANING...
ONE DAY...
...THOSE GIRLS WILL GO OFF TO FIGHT A REAL BATTLE.

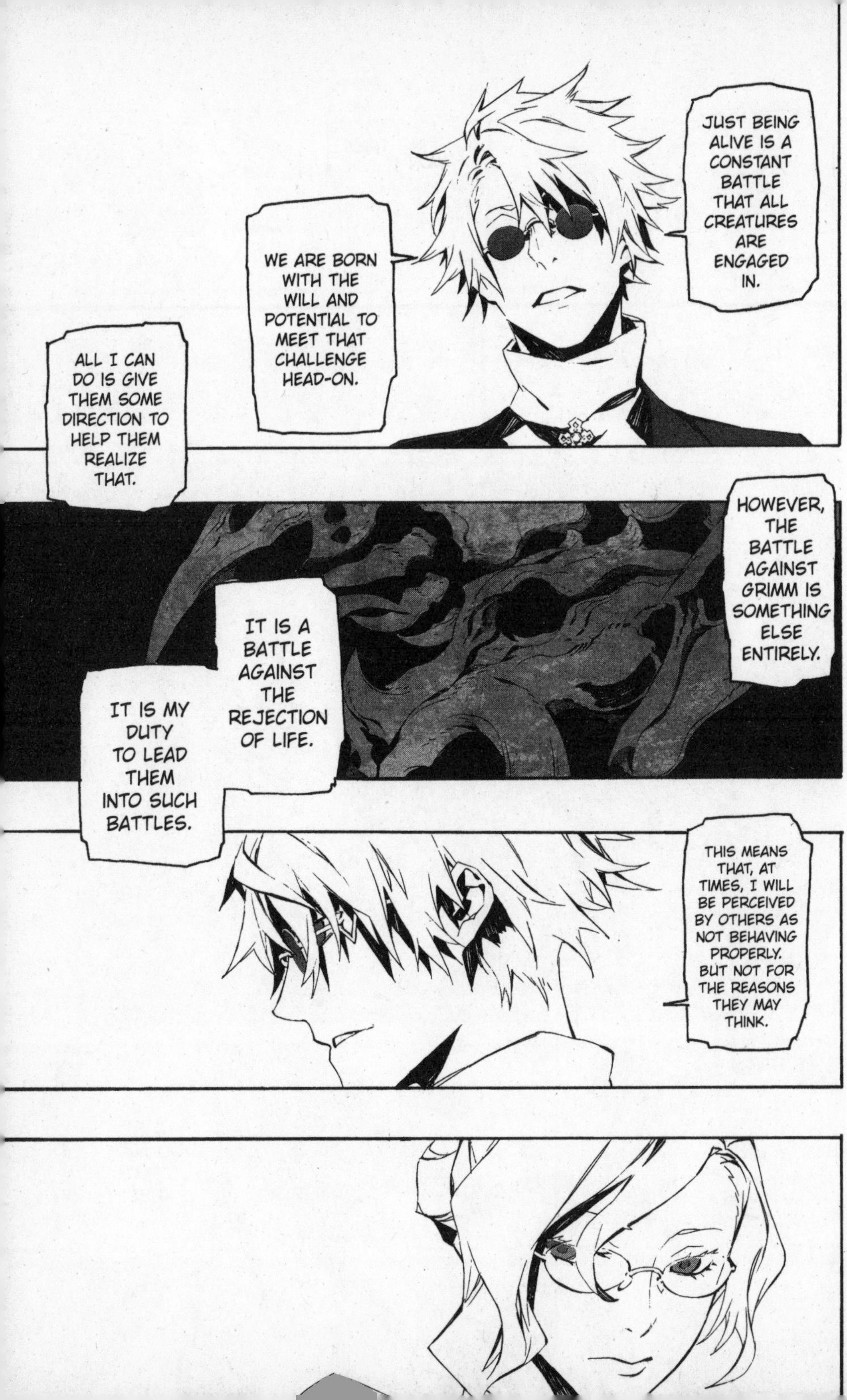
JUST BEING ALIVE IS A CONSTANT BATTLE THAT ALL CREATURES ARE ENGAGED IN.
WE ARE BORN WITH THE WILL AND POTENTIAL TO MEET THAT CHALLENGE HEAD-ON.
ALL I CAN DO IS GIVE THEM SOME DIRECTION TO HELP THEM REALIZE THAT.
HOWEVER, THE BATTLE AGAINST GRIMM IS SOMETHING ELSE ENTIRELY.
IT IS A BATTLE AGAINST THE REJECTION OF LIFE.
IT IS MY DUTY TO LEAD THEM INTO SUCH BATTLES.
THIS MEANS THAT, AT TIMES, I WILL BE PERCEIVED BY OTHERS AS NOT BEHAVING PROPERLY. BUT NOT FOR THE REASONS THEY MAY THINK.

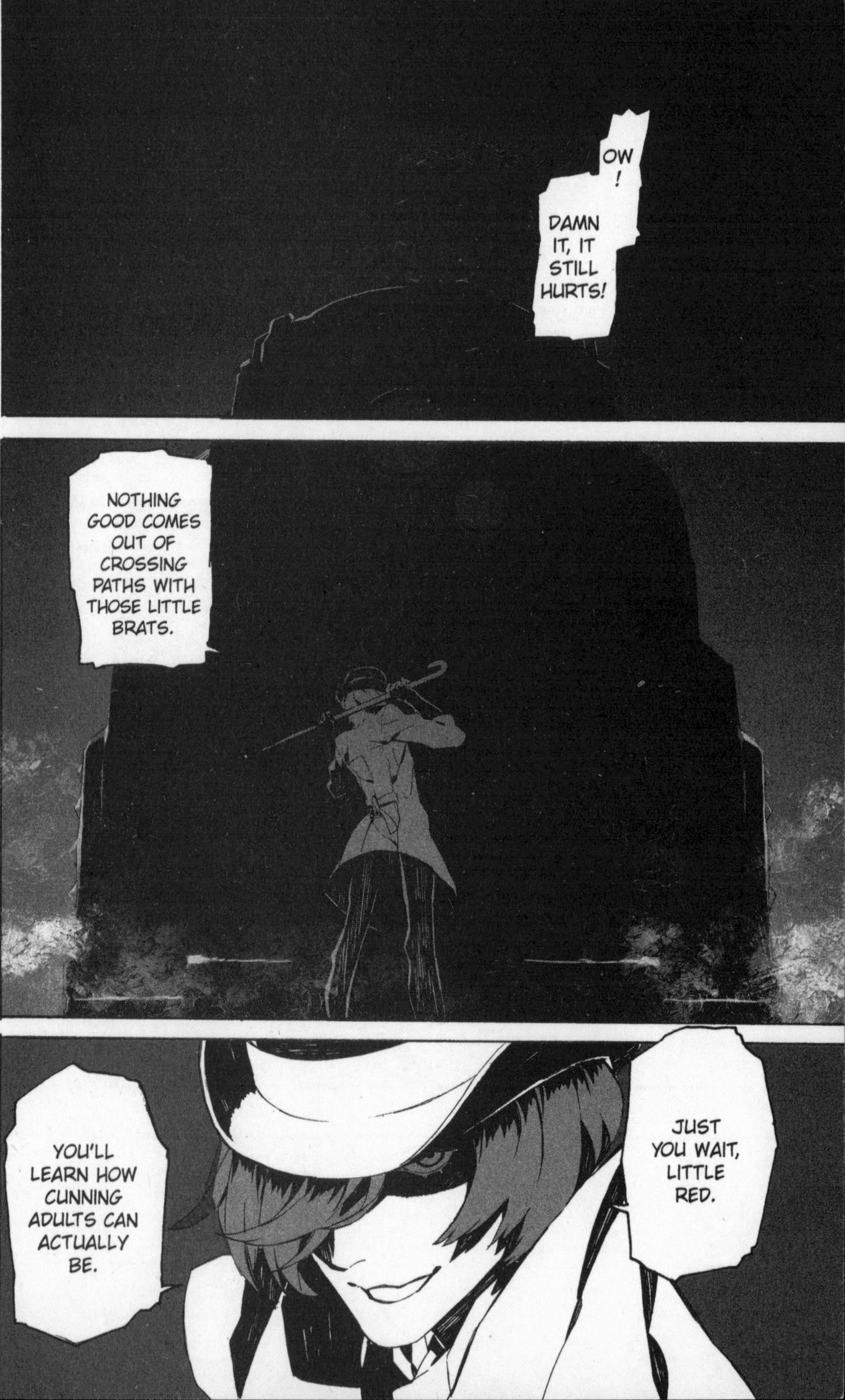
OW!
DAMN IT, IT STILL HURTS!
NOTHING GOOD COMES OUT OF CROSSING PATHS WITH THOSE LITTLE BRATS.
JUST YOU WAIT, LITTLE RED.
YOU'LL LEARN HOW CUNNING ADULTS CAN ACTUALLY BE.

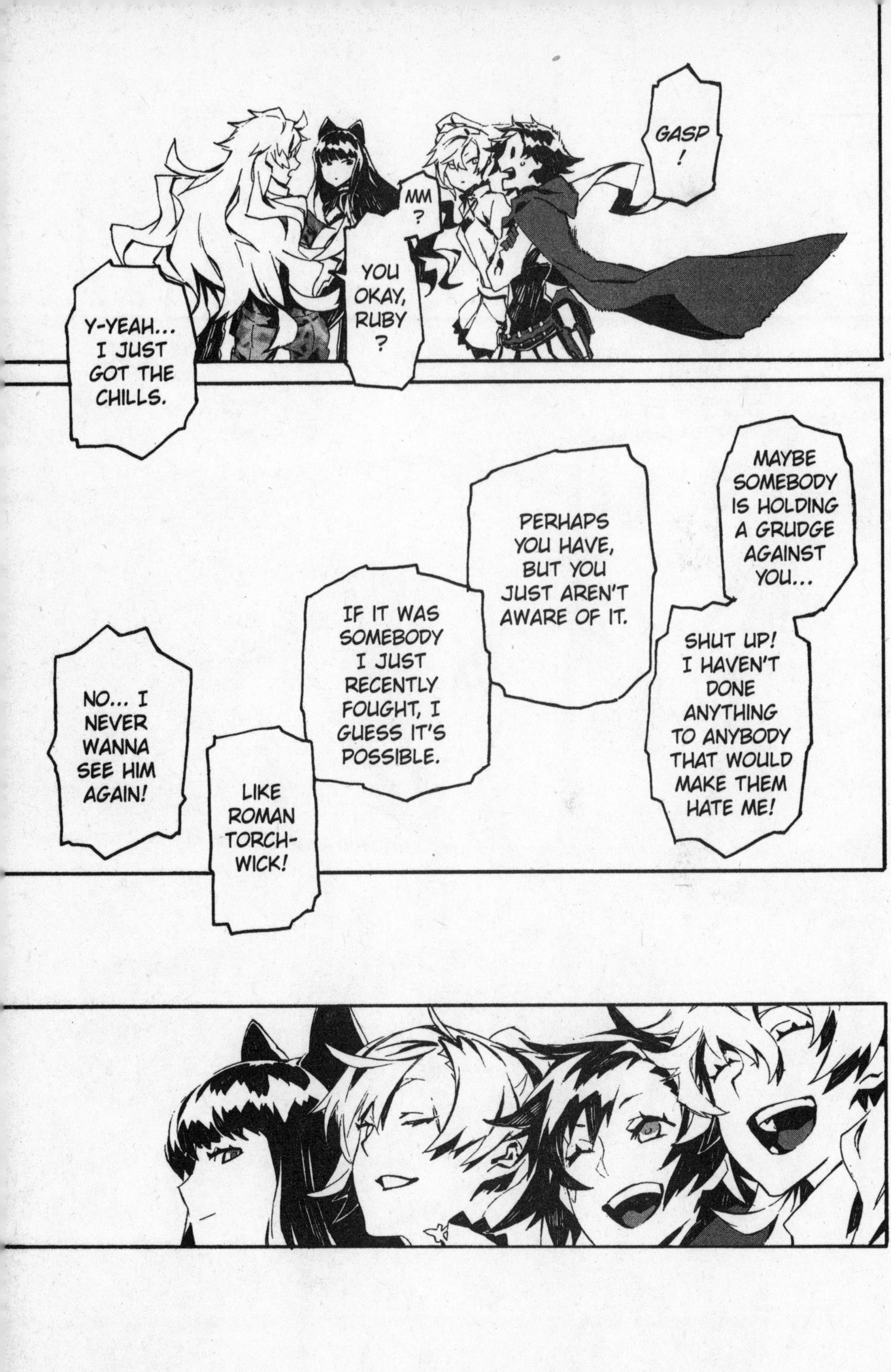
GASP!
MM?
YOU OKAY, RUBY?
Y-YEAH... I JUST GOT THE CHILLS.
MAYBE SOMEBODY IS HOLDING A GRUDGE AGAINST YOU...
SHUT UP! I HAVEN'T DONE ANYTHING TO ANYBODY THAT WOULD MAKE THEM HATE ME!
PERHAPS YOU HAVE, BUT YOU JUST AREN'T AWARE OF IT.
IF IT WAS SOMEBODY I JUST RECENTLY FOUGHT, I GUESS IT'S POSSIBLE.
LIKE ROMAN TORCH-WICK!
NO... I NEVER WANNA SEE HIM AGAIN!

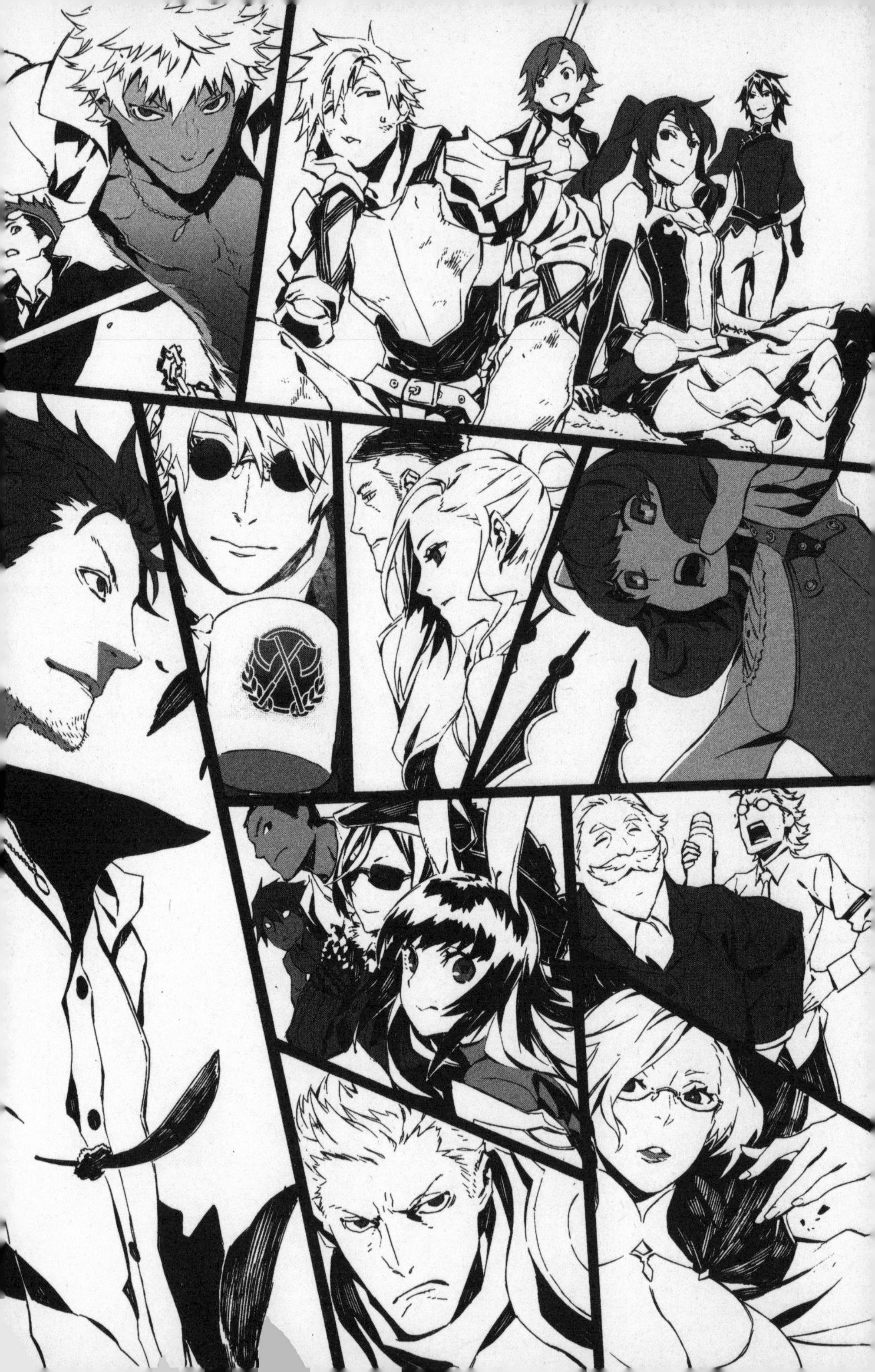

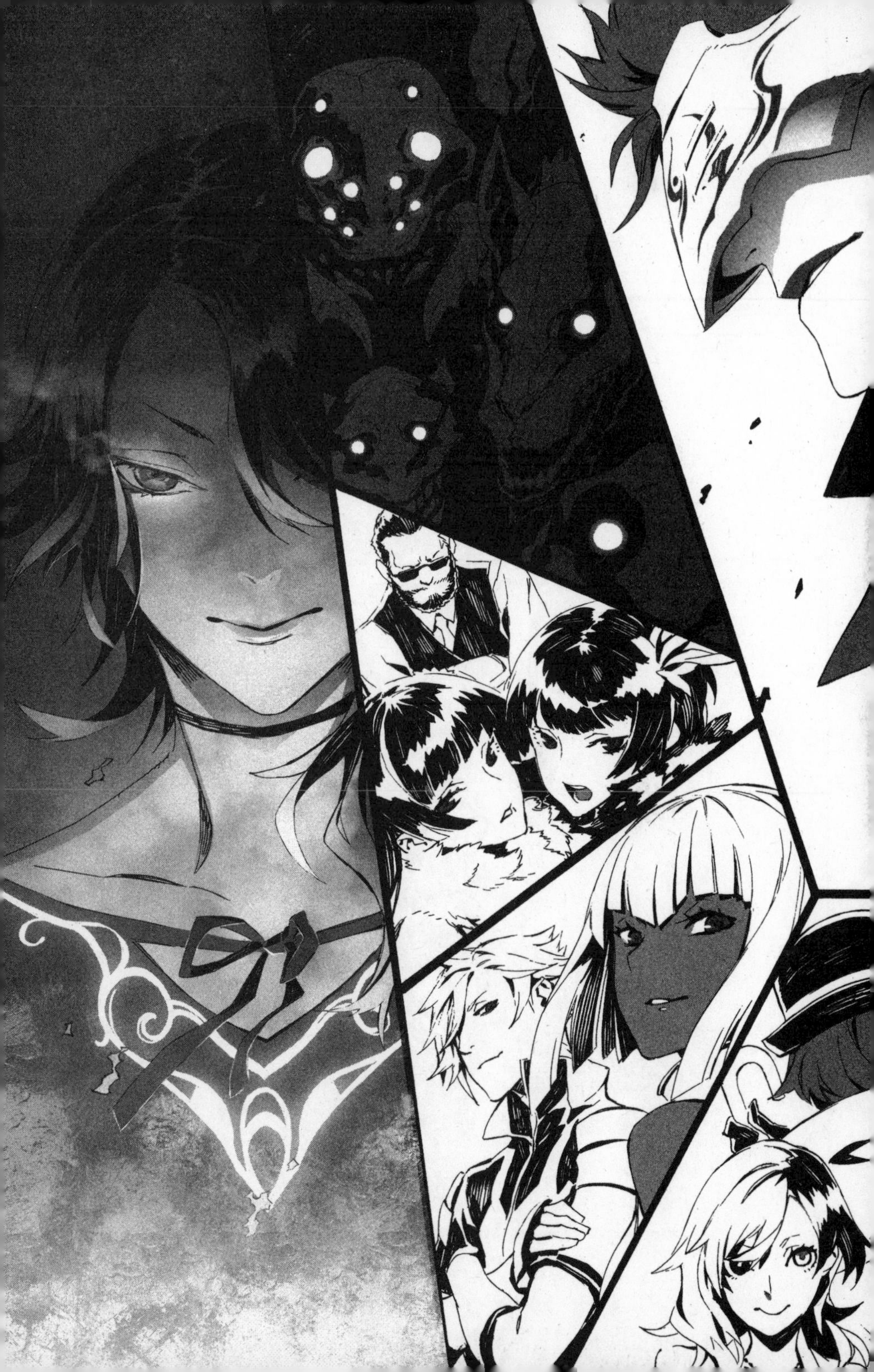

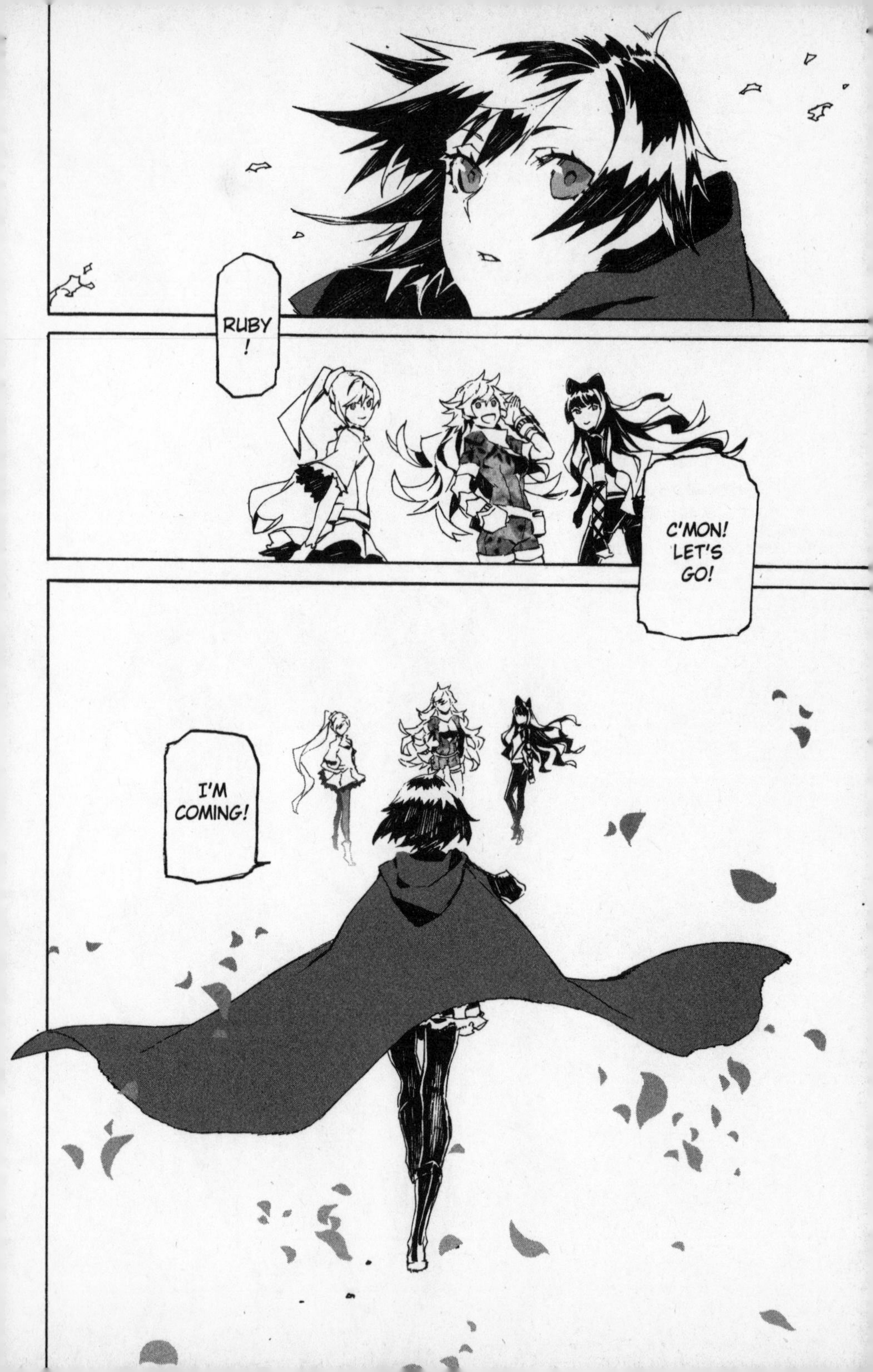
RUBY!
C'MON! LET'S GO!
I'M COMING!